The Politics of Public Opinion in the Novels of Anthony Trollope

The Politics of Public Opinion in the Novels of Anthony Trollope

A 'Tenth Muse'

Jan B. Gordon

ANTHEM PRESS

Anthem Press
An imprint of Wimbledon Publishing Company
www.anthempress.com

This edition first published in UK and USA 2025
by ANTHEM PRESS
75–76 Blackfriars Road, London SE1 8HA, UK
or PO Box 9779, London SW19 7ZG, UK
and
244 Madison Ave #116, New York, NY 10016, USA

First published in the UK and USA by Anthem Press in 2023

British Library Cataloguing-in-Publication Data
A catalogue record for this book is available from the British Library.

Library of Congress Control Number: 2024951182
A catalog record for this book has been requested.

ISBN-13: 978-1-83999-495-1 (Pbk)
ISBN-10: 1-83999-495-9 (Pbk)

Cover Credit: Photo of #77 of Goya's "Los Desastres de de la Guerra" from the 1st (Harris)
Edition (1863) owned by Jan Gordon

This title is also available as an e-book.

FRONTISPIECE

"I'll tell you what's the greatest power under heaven," said Felix, "and that is public opinion—the ruling belief in society about what is right and what is wrong, what is honourable and what is shameful. That is the steam that is to work the engines. How can political freedom make us better, any more than a religion we don't believe in?"

George Eliot, *Felix Holt XXX*, p. 401, ital. added

Opinions are to the vast apparatus of social existence what oil is to machines: one does not go up to a turbine and pour machine oil over it; one applies a little to hidden spindles and joints that one has to know.

Walter Benjamin, "One Way Street," *Selected Works* I,
1913–1926, ed. Marcus Bullock and Michael W. Jennings
(Cambridge: Harvard Univ. Press, 2004), p. 444

Just now a word
while eavesdropping on the absolute
is enthralled to a wise unsaid.

In gala pretense
it finds in hearsay
no memory of its own
but the ghost of relevance.

Aaron Rosen, "A Word in Play" from Daubs for
Needy Space: Selected Poems

CONTENTS

PREFACE: OVERTURE TO AN
INITIAL PUBLIC OFFERING

This volume conceptually began as a response to an exposure to public opinion formation: literary criticism. A reviewer of my *Gossip and Subversion in Nineteenth-Century British
Fiction: Echo's Economies* found, to my pleasant surprise, much to praise. But in the same
essay, the reviewer who, like much public opinion, should perhaps remain anonymous,
also queried a conspicuous absence: the lack of interest in victims, those *gossiped about*.
Her criticism, as the best criticism always does, initiated self-criticism. For, it was not the
first time that my lack of sympathy for the victimized had been queried.

Compassion for the unfamiliar is always difficult, but perhaps particularly so for the
critic who risks imaginary detachment (a fictional autonomy masking as objectivity)
from feelings that risk *senti*mentality. Given the expanding population of those who see
themselves as victims of some prejudice, sympathy is tempered by the universality of
the experience. Ours is an age marked by the proliferation of the presumably sincere
account of harm at the hands of unacknowledged institutional or personal aggression.

Although each of us is immersed in it and lives in our negotiated responses and
defenses to public opinion, it can be manipulated for temporary or permanent advantage. It seems a *medium* of existence as well as exchange that we cannot avoid insofar as
we have a place in a discursive society, enhanced now by speedier platforms and easier
access. In the novels of Anthony Trollope public opinion becomes a master narrative,
often displacing other narratives.

In discussing public opinion and how it is formed, *negotiated* and represented to those
who live in it (and are re-represented in their responses to it), we should admit at the outset that it resists easy address as a traditional subject. For public opinion lacks a proper
"self," more nearly resembling a "form," "structure" and movement of potentially infinite *referral (renvoi)*, as Jean-Luc Nancy once described the non-indexical and non-sign-
ficational modes of listening characteristic of musical performances.[1] When we address
public opinion formation in the *Barsetshire Novels* and the *Palliser Novels* (often referred to
as the *Parliamentary Novels*) of "our" Anthony Trollope, the Victorian novelist who continually probes how his characters both shape it and respond to its shaping of them, we
are really addressing a new kind of *philosophical subject* in the novel. Trollope engages us
for two obvious reasons: (1) his interests correspond to us current readers insofar as the
creation of public opinion now has so many heretofore unforeseeable entry points and
(2) authentic character development is devalued at the expense of a managed, calculated
reputation exemplified in Trollope's career. He was a respected civil servant, inventor
of a convenience (the pillar post box), popular novelist who self-consciously played an

opinion market for his "wares" and a less successful candidate for public office who retained enduring political interests.

Because public opinion seems to be listening to us as we listen to it (or are interpellated *by* or *in* it) and respond to it, our reputations exist in its addressivity. Yet, we simultaneously often have an unacknowledged share in its production through our participation in life and its institutions. We often *negotiate* (*negotiari*, Lat. "to clear an obstacle") its real or imagined presence. Even the absence or evasion of timely response, as many political leaders discover, remains a response nonetheless. Public opinion shares some characteristics of a genre: it often incorporates its potential negations.

Ironically, however, nothing appears less sonorous, more unmoved, than most models of transcendence in western culture. Yet, public opinion appears so intensely, even obsessively, *interested* and easily, albeit unpredictably moved, even at an irreproachable distance. Its voice is often imperfectly represented as diversity within unity: an occasionally singular, yet often undisciplined "rabble." It has a curiously punctuated temporality that may lend it an immanence that threatens other models of transcendence like those addressed from the church in the clerical *Barsetshire Chronicles* or its Establishment partner, the state and its representatives, in the six *Palliser Novels*. These ironies should not be lost on us. Public opinion simultaneously divides us into separable ideological interests even as it often unites us into a collective, a community. This community is a listening and reading public that anticipates some ultimate *resolution*, or, to borrow from the late Frank Kermode, the "sense of an ending" even as we are held in thrall.[2] Unlike novels, however, public opinion seems interminable and inescapable: imperfectly recognizable cultural background music.

One difference between public opinion formation and generally subversive gossip might revolve about the latter's dependency on the revelation of a secret for which a narrator often exacts a promise not to repeat a narrative. By exacting such a promise from a prospective listener, the consumer is endowed with a privilege, defined as a unique exception to the rule. The secret becomes inseparable from a set of accompanying operating instructions regulating the conditions of its disclosure. Public opinion formation appears to lack the instructional material for regulated dissemination and varies depending on the performative environment and the responses—or not—of an audience of often competing interests. It shares all of these features with the novel itself.

The very phrase "public opinion" has a curious history, suggested by consulting the chronologically arranged entries in the *Oxford English Dictionary*. As long as the public can be managed—*management* becoming, as we shall see, a key feature of public opinion in Trollope's developing parliamentary interests—in such a way as to maintain social civility and alliances, the concept is associated with harmonic values. The public constitutes an aggregate of individual parts working together each in its assigned place, yet nonetheless producing a consensually harmonic tone.

This admittedly orchestral model of public opinion formation would of course work to maintain social discipline for an effect. But as early as Temple's essay, "Popular Discontents" (1689–90), public opinion was imagined as both easily deceived ("cheated") and potentially deceptive ("commonly mistaken"). This would imply that what I (after Trollope) call the "Tenth Muse" of public opinion possesses a dual nature. In

representation, metaphors of implied consensual harmony were being implicitly challenged long before the rise of the bourgeois institutions to which Jürgen Habermas has
attributed an instrumental role in the creation of a deliberative, if not always potentially
antagonistic, public opinion that held out hope of the consensual.

The suspicion that public opinion, even at the outset, lacked a univocal tone informs
my discussion of Trollope's achievement in addressing its continual reformation. Even if
public opinion were to be accessible to the "fine tuning" from the pulpit, as J. H. Blunt
argued in 1868 vis-à-vis the role of the Church of England, there is a lingering suspicion
that society as a whole cannot be kept in tune with the Establishment as its conductor.
One of the most memorable, yet unelaborated, images in Trollope's fiction is that of the
Rev. Harding, in semiretirement as custodian of aged pensioners in *The Warden*, continuously playing an imaginary violoncello, a pantomime of a communal harmony lost
when his sinecure is legally challenged.

To address public opinion formation is to address a peculiar type of *agency*. It is a
discursive effect which may appear "out of position" insofar as the occasion of its emergence endows it with a kind of *jouissance*, an arbitrary playfulness, not unknown in the
behavior of the traditional nine mythical muses. It is perhaps best imagined not as a
neutral frame filled with attachments, or associates like society columns in newspapers
or gossip, but rather more akin to what Slavoj Žižek in another context has termed a
"strange attractor" which distorts every element of the totality even as it appears so
totalizing.[3] Public opinion could be both a composite and a fractional part of many narratives. His model is that of a blue light shining from an invisible source on a room. It
has no visible presence in the air, but a white curtain appears blue; a red one, purple; a
blue one, invisible. Form would no longer be *a formalism* with its implicit notion of some
neutral apparatus and frame, but is the space of an implicit partisanship which shapes
its function as a (prospectively) mutually responsive mechanism rather than a genuine
Enlightenment. Yet, public opinion often poses as a spirit of Enlightenment, disinterest-
edly illuminating dark secrets and institutional errancy.

Public opinion is provisional, even ghostly, yet exists as a quasi-Ur-narrative which
often displaces other third person narrators and even the Divine or its representatives
in Trollope's novels. It commands acknowledgment with a unique operational dynamic:

1) Because it operates through its effects on diverse lives in ways different from historical determination or symbolic identification, the occasions by which we become
   aware of its operations are inseparable from its operations.
2) Because it is constituted as an anonymous quasi-collective, the specific proportional
   individual contributions of various official organs of public opinion formation are
   difficult to identify.
3) Public opinion can be either repressive (to those unable or unwilling to escape its
   external or internalized judgments) or liberating (to those held in judgment by legal
   or theological institutions of state, church or historical antecedents).
4) It seems to demand an *investment* in some future outcome which is never articulated
   or defined, combining promise with the threat of exclusion. So fluid is it that public
   opinion can never be quite identified as a signification. In a culture privileging

landed or entitled measurements of social and economic value, the dialectical movement of public opinion formation nonetheless mimes alternative belief systems.

5) The volatility of public opinion formation invites a reciprocal counterplay as
   affected parties invest in its ups and downs—one definition of the political that
   depends on *timing* a market, indicating a possible operational analogy with other
   markets.

6) This market in public opinion often enables the real or illusory participation of people and ideas heretofore ideologically without representation or access and hence
   may mark the intersection of democracy, speculation and unrestricted inclusion.

***

Chapter one of *The Politics of Public Opinion in the Novels of Anthony Trollope*: The *"Tenth
Muse,"* "The 'Prosthetic Body' of Public Opinion in Barsetshire," elaborates the "figure" of various bodies (corporeal and ideological) "out of tune" and hence synchrony
with themselves. These disruptive voices are often internally and externally discontinuous insofar as they appear as under construction, incompletely developed or otherwise
socially excluded, combining sympathetic identification with a call for public assistance.
This plurality instantiating itself as a unitary or collective voice leaves gaps in comprehension, yet has a persistent *intentionality* which causes the reader to question ownership: "whose intentionality is this or what experience is speaking *through this*?" Like the
newly licensed, albeit suspect, locally independent press in nineteenth-century Great
Britain, unaffiliated with political parties, the voice of public opinion penetrates previously neglected spaces, even creating niche markets that are then exploited. This particular suspect body of public opinion cannot be either historically or in performance
consistently *read* because we never know how, where or even *if* it *stands*. It is simultaneously intrusive and heavily demanding, yet light enough and slippery enough to evoke
a polarization of public response such as that evoked by the Rev. Slope and Madame
Neroni in *Barchester Towers* and Rev. Harding in *The Warden*. Those who invest in an
attempt to influence public opinion face obstacles in recovering any undiluted, solitary
voice.

Chapter two, "Miming the Law," elaborates the ways in which public opinion formation imitates both the law and the power of noble families through a claim of antecedence which it in no way consistently possesses. As early as 1817, James Mill in the second
volume of *British India* was talking of the "great sanction" of public opinion—as if it had
the transcendent power of the sanctified—even as his fellow reformer, Jeremy Bentham,
was addressing the so-called tribunal and bar of public opinion in his "Introduction" to
Parliamentary Reform. Many of those who become involved in politics or organs of public
opinion have had some previous tangential relationship with the law or legal studies, as
did Trollope's own father. At times public opinion operates as a kind of appellate court
of an altogether different order (hence beyond the reach of the law), redefining *accountability*. Unlike the law, however, public opinion sets no historical or procedural limits on
access nor does it require court-appointed representatives to administer its procedures.

Leaving no one outside its potential jurisdiction, public opinion appears totalizing for a variety of reasons in Trollope's overlapping clerical and parliamentary worlds. Contemporaneously, John Stuart Mill in an infamous passage in *On Liberty* (1859) asserted that even in its absence, oppositional minority opinion must be "imagined" (and is thus borderless) in order to test the validity of an opinion endorsed by the parliamentary majority, giving the imagination a crucial role, if not a share, in the power it possesses. As we shall see, public opinion is on occasion a corrective and on others, allied with Wordsworth's repressed "still, small voices" of humanity. Hence it has both an internal and external existence, speaking in numerous voices even as it claims a consensuality resistant to further deliberation. Those who invest in this unanimity and thereby come to exist *in* it often experience an awakening and a loss of personal sovereignty, as in some religious experiences. As both an instrument of belief-formation and a repository or bank of raw informational material, public opinion increasingly appears as a perpetually absorptive, tirelessly efficient and largely unregulated machine that benefits some and grinds down others much as does the machinery in Dickens's fictional Coketown of *Hard Times*.

Chapter three, "'Playing' the Opinion Market," examines the operations of this machine in a society increasingly dependent on new information rather than legacy to assess social value. In both the *Barsetshire Chronicles* and the *Palliser Novels* public opinion formation comes to be imagined as operating analogously to a traditional market economy, an uncontrollable force under pressures of modulation, determining the current value of reputations that fluctuate over time. The metaphor of a self-adjusting market (over the long run) is challenged. Risk is arbitraged away by a variety of increasingly speculative strategies, many of which divert attention from the ideal of social harmony insofar as skill is necessary to enter what has become a public opinion market, replete with other "market opening" initiatives, including an aggressive press.

If public opinion is consistent with Cardinal Newman's allegation in *Difficulties of the Anglicans* (1894), notably that it makes every conclusion absurd except its own self-recognition, then public opinion exists largely in self-consciousness rather than possession. This would imply that it comes into being, as do most IPOs (including this one), only in a perpetually present and inconclusive self-advertisement that is a plea for the public investments known as faith and credit creation. If plagiarism is the studied avoidance of clear citation, of giving due credit to an antecedent *author*(ity), then the recognized plurality of public opinion would be the logical corollary of authorial dilution. Public opinion often takes speculative "credit" outside the traditional conventions of ownership, a unique *author*ity different from the traditional elision of *prop*erty, *prop*riety and doctrinal orthodoxy. Remounted necklaces, discounted notes, duplicate keys and two classes of stock certificate are instrumental in Trollope's plots.

Public opinion, along with speculative capital formation, shares an ahistorical periodicity for which there is neither consistent notation, nor text, nor assurances of permanent redemption in some incompletely defined future day of reckoning. Increasingly, the privileged Establishment in Trollope, with unsustainably high levels of personal consumption, put their trust in alternative credit markets in which they might place an increasingly leveraged trust in *Framley Parsonage* (1861), *The Small House at Allington* (1864) and *The Last Chronicle of Barset* (1867).

Chapter four attempts to address the complex relationship of a burgeoning state bureaucracy in both shaping and responding to public opinion formation. Though the bureaucracy is composed of the "people" it also mediates between the public and both its elected representatives and historically descendant noble families as well as the non-native children of empire. Among the pantheon of nineteenth-century British authors, Trollope was uniquely placed to understand the operational dynamics of this increasingly semiautonomous machine as a consequence of his 33-year employment at the post office. The civil service concerns itself, much as does public opinion, with a watchfulness endemic to systems dedicated to social distribution. Yet in *The Three Clerks* the bureaucracy exchanges security of employment for low wages that tempt bureaucrats into speculative adventures.

By means of various "conductors"—whips, cabinet members and first secretaries— a patina of fellowship is maintained while at the same time displacing internal and external rivalries. Any potentially subversive procedural or ideological innovation (the "new") is either totally absorbed and diluted so as to escape recognition or altogether denied through a variety of less than sufficiently transparent strategies. Like many other commodities, the members of the state bureaucracy as well as MPs are pretty interchangeable, even ideologically, as will be seen in *The Three Clerks* (1858), *Phineas Finn* (1869), *Phineas Redux* (1874), *The Prime Minister* (1876) and *The Duke's Children* (1880).

As with other market values, one's position and esteem on the bureaucratic career ladder within a party or service fluctuates over time, coming to depend on unstable use-value rather than ideological purity. The civil service as well as Parliament inculcates an artificial sense of "duty" to the realm among its members who, even in private are, like the clergy in Barsetshire, always on call. Like those enmeshed in public opinion, they feel the pull of vigilance, an openness to constant reevaluation, less consistently applied to the clergy ensconced in "The Close" at the beginning of each novel of the *Barsetshire Chronicles*.

Like the Barsetshire clergy, bureaucrats and politicians use variations of both horizontal (among disparate branches or organizational divisions) and vertical (an increasingly leveraged noble patriarchy) to create a new kind of politically expedient "state family" of a-*filiation* whose members are nonetheless vulnerable to being disowned or to inherit diminished "expectations." Less publicly visible than the clergy in its worldly ministrations and unlike scheduled visitations to parish worshippers or landlords at their ceremonial fetes or in their expensive social lives, those who come to live the life of civil administration have no identifiable product in Trollope except self-sustaining organizational practices. Anxiety regarding what this family of bureaucratic interests actually socially produces mimes the anxiety of the noble patriarchy over the deeds of their idle offspring. The activities of both families are often incompletely or unpredictably regulated.

Chapter five, "The Sugar," suggests that as the irresolution and strategic indecision of public opinion are dispersed or dissolved through the system, its collective contributions are obscured. As candidates and ethnic arrivistes strive for political or social acceptance, they cultivate a calculated resistance to a consistent reading which obscures (established) ideological and tribal identification.

The fragile and highly speculative "deal" displaces imperfectly embraced ideals, now dissolved, like sugar, as invisible presences within the system, in the process that Weber characterized as *rationalization*. The solution to ideological difference is often paradoxically an acknowledgment of the *fabrication* that placates a public as an alternative taste: a yielding of the sovereignty of singular authorship to the "sweet meats and sugar plums" of consumer preference. Political life is no different from selling any other commodity, be it a department store (*The Struggles of Brown, Jones, and Robinson*, 1862) or a fictitious railroad established on speculative credit (*The Way We Live Now*, 1875), in an open market. Once betrayed by the public opinion which it embraced or in flight from creditors, projects lose their substantive purpose or find themselves co-opted. Public opinion in his novels is both transparent (an empty signifier) and opaque, to which even Trollope himself confessed to having yielded. This lends public opinion a capacity for circulation as an illegible abstraction, both soluble transparency and easily precipitated, but disguised in combination with other carriers to whet a variety of appetites, opening us and it to *feelings*.

Notes

1 See the marvelous treatise on the different ways in which we differentiate "listening" from "hearing" and comprehension, in Jean-Luc Nancy, *Listening*, trans. Charlotte Mandell (New York: Fordham Univ. Press, 2002), especially pp. 6–9.
2 Frank Kermode, *The Sense of an Ending: Studies in the Theory of Fiction* (Oxford and New York: Oxford Univ. Press, 1967), addresses a quasi-critical complicity to impose structures of resolution and terminal reckoning upon literary genres.
3 Slavoj Žižek (ed.), *Revolution at the Gates: Žižek on Lenin, The 1917 Writings* (London and New York: Verso, 2002), p. 190.

Although this book bears a single author's name, it is, like public opinion, a plural achievement. Some investors-cum-auxiliary muses will never realize their investment, dissolved and made invisible within my critical opinions.

The late professor Herbert Grabes inserted himself vigorously into a preliminary talk at the triannual meeting of the International Association of University Professors of English in Lund, Sweden.

Ms. Jessica Mack, an acquisitions editor at Anthem, reminded me that Trollope anticipates our contemporary "cancel culture" by a de-monumentalization whose timed *marking* is inseparable from its meaning in circulation.

Dr. Hitomi Shoji, a former student, reminded me that the mobilizing precipitate of public opinion is frequently a self-styled cosmopolitan who becomes thereby a double agent, polarizing while universalizing public opinion.

Professors Simon James and Francis O'Donoghue, early intellectual investors, who, having read preliminary versions, told me I was "on to something hard to define."

Jan B. Gordon
Kyoto, Japan, Autumn 2022

Works Cited

BT Barchester Towers, Edited by Michael Sadleir and Frederick Page with an Introduction by James R. Kincaid (Oxford: Oxford Univ. Press, 1980).
W The Warden, Edited with an Introduction and notes by Robin Gilmour (Harmondsworth: Penguin, 1984).

CYFH Can You Forgive Her?, Introduced by Kate Flint, Edited by Andrew Swarbick with an Introduction by Norman St. John Stevas (Oxford: Oxford Univ. Press, 1982).

SHA The Small House at Allington, Edited with an Introduction and notes by Julian Thompson (Harmondsworth: Penguin, 1991).

FP Framley Parsonage, Introduction and notes by David Skilton and Peter Miles (Harmondsworth: Penguin, 1984).

DT Doctor Thorne, Introduction and notes by Ruth Rendell (Harmondsworth: Penguin, 1991).

PF Phineas Finn: The Irish Member, Edited with an Introduction by Jacque Berthoud (Oxford: Oxford Univ. Press, 1982).

PR Phineas Redux, Introduced by F.S.L. Lyons and Edited by John C. Whale (Oxford: Oxford Univ. Press, 1983).

PM The Prime Minister, Introduced by John McCormick and Edited by Jennifer Uglow (Oxford: Oxford Univ. Press, 1985).

DC The Duke's Children, Edited and with an Introduction by Hermione Lee (Oxford: Oxford Univ. Press,1983).

LCB The Last Chronicle of Barset, Edited by Peter Fairclough with an Introduction by Laurence Lerner (Harmondsworth: Penguin, 1986).

WWLN The Way We Live Now, Edited by John Sutherland (Oxford: Oxford Univ. Press, 1982).

ED The Eustace Diamonds (Harmondsworth: Penguin, 1993).

SBJR The Struggles of Brown, Jones, and Robinson, Edited by N. John Hall (Oxford: Oxford Univ. Press, 1992).

A An Autobiography (New York: Harper and Bros., 1883 facsimile rpt. Scholar Select).

RR Rachel Ray, John Sutherland (Annotations) (Harmondsworth: Penguin, 1996).

TTC The Three Clerks, Introduction by N. John Hall (London: The Trollope Society, 1992).

VB The Vicar of Bullhampton, Introduction by John Halperin (London: The Trollope Society, 1997).

Chapter One

THE "PROSTHETIC BODY" OF PUBLIC OPINION IN BARSETSHIRE

It would be a calumny on Mrs. Proudie to suggest that she was sitting in her bed-room with her ear at the keyhole during this interview. She had within her a spirit of decorum which prevented her from descending to such baseness. To put her ear to the keyhole or to listen to a chink, was a trick for a housemaid.

Mrs. Proudie knew this, and therefore she did not do it; but she stationed herself as near to the door as she could, that she might, if possible, get the advantage which the housemaid would have had, without descending to the housemaid's artifice.

(*BT* I 166–67)

If the path to heaven is as narrow as the proverbial "needle's eye," a doctrinal idea entirely consistent with the evangelical bent of both the Rev. Obadiah Slope and Mrs. Proudie of *Barchester Towers,* the traditional channels of gossip appear equally constricted. Because, at least conventionally, the lower classes democratically gossip about the behavior of the upper classes (so as to bring them down to the level where they might be trafficked) rather than the other way around, Bishop Proudie's wife would do a disservice to her pronominal station were she to physically *stoop* to keyholes or chinks. She remains in posture as well as morally, upright, even if it is a strain. In contradistinction from the eavesdropping posture of the lower-class gossip, Mrs. Proudie misses another communicative channel of political culture: "that friendly pressure," a little "extra squeeze of the hand" (*BT* I 167). Such is the inarticulated *pressure* conveying a bishop's consent to his chaplain's scheme for denying his wife's choice for an impending vacancy for the new warden of Hiram's Hospital. Although escaping the auditory register, it does not escape the omniscient narrator's awareness of a "force" having a formless *mediacy.*

Her social pride distances her from a lineage of gossips in nineteenth-century British fiction like Mrs. Bates (*Emma*) and Mrs. Norris (*Mansfield Park*); Nelly Dean (*Wuthering Heights*); Mrs. Cadwallader (*Middlemarch*); or later, the unforgettable Mrs. Bolton (*Lady Chatterley's Lover*). Not the unmarried singer of a community's hidden songs and secrets, typically beyond the age of marriage, an exemption which liberates them from participation in the marital market, Mrs. Proudie is the spouse of a bishop of the Church of England. A variant on the fictive sibling of the Divine (whose etymological root "godsib" grounds the word "gossip") by marrying its earthly representative, she rather acts to exert genuine political power by influencing decisions or rearranging preexistent associations into relationships of mutual benefit. The *vacancy* due to the resignation, under another kind of pressure, of Rev. Harding in the antecedent novel *The Warden*, is not a repressed secret, but a widely advertised opening *in* and *to* the political life of a relatively closed community. The initially unexplained *vacancy* in fact corresponds to a curious feature of the public reception of the two novels: only after the popularity of *Barchester Towers* did its prequel become widely known. Many of the clerics in both novels live in the perpetual adjacency termed "The Close" in the first two novels of the *Barsetshire Chronicles*. Mrs. Proudie is but the first among many women in Trollope who will come to participate in the political life of the community by shaping public opinion formation, responding to it and hence reframing social issues, and by using their variable affection and disaffection as levers by which more contested interests enter a community's discourse. Felt pressures resist easy representation and, often, easy empirical verification.

The scene in which Mrs. Proudie does not witness the inaudible "pressure" is immediately preceded by an admonition from her husband, the bishop, that "if Mr. Harding be not appointed, *public feeling* would be against us, and [...] the press might perhaps take it up" (*BT* I 161, ital. added). The press has a role now in "taking things up," circulating for public consumption what would otherwise remain at rest, confined to "The Close." The press is now another *press*ure, of public opinion formation *in situ*, defined as a vague, threatening *feeling*, fully competitive with that imposed in Sunday sermons or soft positions on spiritual issues by a clerical hierarchy and derivatively, the God who invests such representatives.

These various pressures, including the unforeseeable circulation of information as a consequence of leaks, cannot be quantified in advance. But for a church entrusted with the maintenance and management of public opinion on spiritual issues, someone must be dispatched to bear witness to public opinion. In demurring from his wife's scheme— the first of many spousal intrusions in Trollope—to appoint the Rev. Quiverful to assume Harding's vacant position (and its income), Bishop Proudie remarks, "Mr. Slope may be useful in finding out how the wind blows" (*BT* I 161). Initially then, a bishop's chaplain, Slope, is entrusted with an essentially instrumental function, an early instance of public opinion market research, a quasi-canvasser whose presence will become more deeply felt in the *Parliamentary Novels*. He thus competes with other pressures as a (measurable) force to detect the speed and direction of other forces shaping public opinion, a new role in Victorian fiction.

The postponement of resolution that enables a surrogate (whose findings might be disavowed later) as a symbolic wind sock entrusted to discover in what political direction things have been blown or "taken up" is compatible with a new vehicularity with which *Barsetshire Towers* commences. At the outset, the death of the old bishop, Dr. Grantly, is described as "long and lingering" (*BT* I 1), a man who dies much as he has lived, "without pain and without excitement" (*BT* I 2). Yet the extended time of the dying allows for the passive fermentation and consolidation of public opinion formation along a newly formed marginal line of divisive interests, initially represented as unified and harmonious ("without excitement"). Attenuated *grief* releases repressed *griev*ance, in an interregnum, during which "it became a matter of interest [...] whether the new appointment should be made by a conservative or a liberal government" (*BT* I 1). Will the outgoing or incoming government make the new appointment (a shared ad interim) in which the direction of public opinion is to be forecast? Heterogeneous to any identifying determination, public opinion potentially transforms all into speculative *readers*.

Perhaps it is worthwhile to digressively touch upon the extent to which this discontinuity in the titular control of social and political harmony seems a variation upon another symbolic representation of generational discontinuity, the familiar orphan figure of Victorian fiction. Lacking acceptable biological or historical antecedents, the Heathcliff's, Jane Eyre's and Pip's of nineteenth-century fiction are in some sense "taken up" by alternative families of often competitive interests. An inability to reproduce a timely succession or the reproduction of an unacknowledged successor creates a metaphysical absenteeism in historical lineage that has little to do with the *reality* of how that place is actually occupied.

In both clerical and civic life, a similar presence-in-absence and absence-in-presence occur. The largely absentee cleric, often with multiple "livings" upon which to (only pro forma) attend, finds its political counterpart in the MPs of so-called rotten boroughs, sparsely populated, of which he lacks even minimal local knowledge. Like the absentee landlords of expansive estates in the colonies, these are institutional "placeholders." In possession but deflected from full emotional investment, they share what might be termed a *rentier* presence. Similarly, public opinion in Trollope will come to have some of the dimensions of intermittent or passive custodial *attendance*. As orphan figures often generate action in the Victorian novel, so public opinion, a kind of orphaned discourse insofar as it is resistant to being *claimed* or otherwise fully possessed, becomes a quasi-character in Trollope, unpredictably *taken up*.

Whatever be the ironies, this temporal limbo during which the contest of opinions emerges is also marked by an emergence of political ambition, a new kind of hurry, later to be described in *The Way We Live Now*, as "the hurry of the world" (*WWLN* I 169) in both those choosing and the chosen. Previously unarticulated or repressed, Dr. Grantly's son, Archdeacon Grantly, though not avaricious through "love of lucre" (his father having left him a comfortable inheritance as compensation for a mandated reduction of income for bishops) is nonetheless ambitious for its material surrogate, political power:

> He did desire to sit in full lawn sleeves among the peers of the realm and he did desire, if the truth must out, to be called "My Lord" by his reverend Brethren.
>
> *(BT I 10)*

Political ambition as a member of the House of Lords is "outed" now as a competitor for the heretofore outwardly (because its materiality has been repressed) unworldly, quiet clerical life. It coincides, perhaps not coincidentally, with a weakening of material support for one party to the Establishment by another, revealing internal competition and partition within a former monopoly.

The announcement of the appointee of the vacated position is accurately foretold by the *Jupiter*, later confirmed by notice of formal appointment by the queen. No reasons are given as to why the popular press should have had more information earlier upon which to speculate than do *The Anglican Devotee* or *The Eastern Hemisphere*, "an evening newspaper *supposed to possess* much *official* knowledge" (*BT* I 8, ital. added). Hence, within the temporal interlude a "chink" in succession is simultaneously opened between the official or semiofficial clerical gazettes and a popular, more speculative press which has the scoop in advance. Trollope's *reader* is left to speculate as to why the *Jupiter* either has access to unacknowledged "inside" information or is rather an anonymous, unacknowledged partner, even passively, in the appointment process, much as we would today about the intrusions of a press with disguised ideological interests.

These temporal and proprietary interstices during which the mysteries of political opinion formation gestate in Trollope's Barsetshire are entirely different from the gossip's incessant intrusions and interruptions. The gossip's often "run-on" rhetoric invites a dialogic response (even if that response is tantamount to dismissal). Rather than the prolonged waiting during which public opinion emerges, is amended and often inconclusively reformed, the discourse of gossip pretends to an access (often merely derivative) to some imaginary truth, indistinguishable from news with which it is easily confused. Hence timeliness is crucial, gossip having a short shelf life. While the gossip's discourse is often breathlessly dramatic as the players are identified by their role in a plot, public opinion formation is more self-consciously deliberative or at least makes a pretense of deliberation. How it is gathered and then "taken up" (like, say, knitting pastimes) suggests a constructed discourse, *composed* not merely by access to what has been hidden, but to relationships with other parties. Any identification may be strategically obscured by the short-term interest of securing a longer-term mutual sharing of prospective ideas in addition to information, all of which take time to assemble. This ad hoc, albeit occasionally modular, construction could be described as an *assemblage*, not far removed from the form and function of parliamentary and social assemblages.

But, in the interest of an increasingly illusionary harmony, it must initially have a fugitive narrative to displace. In *Barchester Towers*, Madame Neroni, not unlike those affluent bachelors who suddenly intrude into Jane Austen's village life, prompting inflationary discursive speculation, already has both a past and a challenged social presence. Either estranged from or abandoned by an Italian husband, the relatively financially secure daughter of an absentee prebendary of the Church of England, she is as physically deformed, as bent, as the initially competing narratives which accompany her.

Her history is an assemblage of jerry-built tales, which circulate in an attempt to "fix" her as an object of reputational consumption. Rendered relatively immobile by a lame leg that, Trollope's narrator intimates, may or may not have been suffered at the hands of domestic violence by her husband, Madame Neroni resists an internally consistent reading of her physical disability. Is it the result of an occluded act of sexual violence or the result of some permanently incapacitating illness?[1] Her marital history being inseparable from a distorted physical embodiment in a community's narrative, she leaves herself open to re-narrations, but only after dismissing the potentially subversive gossip of her former servant prior to *re-entrée* into polite society. Although she and her child were initially accompanied into estrangement by a Roman servant, she arrives in England with a new Milanese maid:

It was clear that the lady had determined that there should be no witness to tell stories of her life in Rome.

(BT I 75)

Usually seated in a passively waiting posture on a divan, she leads a vicarious life at the edges of social gathering before negotiating full presence as a "special effect." Everyone feels a perhaps embarrassing need, given her exotic, though handicapped, appearance in Italian garb, to find an inclusive place for her. Unlike the gout-ridden male patriarchy, her handicap appears exotic,[2] mobilizing the interests of those in her company. Although no one can take her away or ignore her—given her physical handicap—people pay court to her, an attendance tantamount to temporal submission, as in fact so many men do in Trollope's novel. Given her disability, the interstices of both physical and narrative compositions, any potentially interested party can disguise a desire to consort as universal sympathy, dedicated to securing Madame Neroni's well-being and hence immune from romantic speculation. Immobility being another inconvenient interregnum, she becomes the locus of a public opinion which combines curiosity with moral critique.

The Signora is strategically restructuring her reputation, much as do Trollope's ne'er-do-well scions of nobility in the *Palliser Novels*, in the hopes of attracting interested investors like the Rev. Slope, willing to assume risks proportionate to their tentative passions. Madame Neroni's restructuring extends to an elegant quasi-brochure rather than a mere *carte de visite* which advertises a certain noblesse. Her card, framed by a deeply gilded border, contains over her name, a "bright gilt coronet," indicating a social rank to which she is in no way entitled, but nonetheless becomes the subject of narrative speculation:

> The gold coronet was equally *out of place*, and perhaps inserted with less excuse. Paulo Neroni had not the faintest title to call himself a scion of even Italian nobility. Had the pair met in England, Neroni would probably have been a count; but they had met in Italy, and any such pretense on his part would have been simply ridiculous.
>
> *(BT I 77, ital. added)*

Supplementing the pretension is Madame Neroni's curious appropriation of the name "Vesey" by which her father was christened, as her own Christian name. As with the Melmotte of *The Way We Live Now*, she is very adaptive, assuming new names and eliminating a past life in the interests of grounding a new narrative by which to attract and manipulate community interest, a composite of disharmonious narratives.

In other words, Madame Neroni seems to be curiously continuous with names and titles to which she has no rights at the same time that she is discontinuous from a legal (marital) contract regarded as binding in her estranged husband's native country. She is thus simultaneously ontologically present and absent, much as had been her absentee father or, for that matter, much as she is at Barsetshire's social occasions by virtue of her physical challenges. Both physically and historically, she seems "out of joint," given her indeterminate marital status throughout the novel, even as Rev. Slope attempts to test the waters of eligibility. Although she professes "to care nothing for what the world can say" (*BT* I 281), that would only be true for public opinion itself, which is defined as totalized (internal and external) *care* for the opinions of the world.

Madame Neroni resembles the force of public opinion formation in one more important way: she makes no secret of her extraordinary power to command submission, while remaining detached from assuming responsibility for any social effect:

> The signora was subdued by no passion. Her *time for love had gone*. [...] It was necessary for her to have some man at the feet. It was the one customary excitement of her life. She delighted in the exercise of power which this gave her; it was now the *only food* for her ambition; she would boast to her sister that she could make a fool of any man, and the sister [...] good naturedly thought it but fair that such amusement could be afforded to a poor invalid who was *debarred* from the ordinary pleasures of life.
>
> (BT *I 270–71, ital. added*)

Her power is not the antithesis of her weakness but dependent on it. Those in the Signora's power sympathetically seek to assist her because she seems debarred from ordinary life. Hers is the combination of the need for assistance (so that everyone becomes a symbolic accessory to her functioning), a ravenous appetite ("food for her ambition") and a flirtatious playfulness partially abetted by a voice that trails off into inconclusiveness—all in concert—which nonetheless seems to belong to a unitary subject. The three helpers needed to lift her respond to what Trollope describes as an invisible summons, a felt pressure to respond characteristic of those enmeshed in public opinion.

Madame Neroni surely shares features with a cultural icon of the mid-nineteenth-century popular and culturally dedicated press, earlier used decoratively in Tom Tower's editorial offices of the *Jupiter* in *The Warden*. Like the legendary PRB woman, the Signora is a femme fatale who has had a literally tortured flirtation with Catholicism, as has had the Rev. Arabin. She shares with that detached presence along the margins of social and verbal discourse, a curious catatonia that freezes her responses at the level of occluded intention, drawing sympathetic affection at the same time that she pushes it away in the interests of her independence. Hers is a divided consciousness, absorptive of attention, partially dependent on others, yet simultaneously quasi-autonomous insofar as she can partially regulate her attendees' responses.

The Rev. Slope, sent out to test the winds of public opinion by his superiors, will find that Madame Neroni *neé* Stanhope, both in her ontology and in her impact upon the culture of Barsetshire and its *structurations*, has an operational dynamic similar to that of the public opinion which he is entrusted to seek out. Not unexpectedly, their relationship provides the prophylaxis that renders her immune to it by virtue of a curious "mirror effect" that opens public opinion formation as a literary and philosophical subject.[3] She moves from existence as a potential subject (in some double sense) of gossip or merely another Victorian curiosity like those which populate Dickens's curiosity shops, to something of deeper philosophical interest which attracts Trollope's attention throughout his career. A new but estranged local presence becomes a repository for "rationalizing" political domination by rendering the clergy (a kind of quasi-state unto itself) accountable. She is the locus of a public square of expansive interests, which nonetheless, like Slope and Towers, seems self-assembling as it goes along. She unites diverse public interest by her mere presence.

Jürgen Habermas has always imagined public opinion as the discursive side of a public sphere, a site for the unrestricted discussion of important public issues.[4] Public discussion was to be open and accessible to all; exclusively private interests were inadmissible. Inequalities of status or achievement were to be tacitly suspended (even though both rhetoric and alliances might betray confidence in the suspension), so that the participants might regard themselves as peers. This suspension of private interests would presumably have enabled the best argument to prevail in an open market with few limitations, much as it would in John Stuart Mill's *On Liberty*. The procedure was co-terminal with the resulting product to whose formation everyone was encouraged to contribute. As the discursive domain would be communally shared, genuine public opinion formation would be identical to an achieved consensus "worked through" for the common good. Rhetorical questions nonetheless pose themselves. How can a collective dialogue suspend private interests, save in the liberal imagination? If it operated as autonomously as the private opinions that it collected, what advantages would accrue to public opinion formation in terms of the common weal? And, perhaps most importantly, what would prevent the incorporation or amalgamation of diverse opinions from exerting a monopoly effect on further entry to the marketplace?

Public trust is compromised when people feel that the common good does not exist or has been expropriated for private benefit. Because public opinion is both a public good—in so far as it illuminates diversions from itself—but is also open to claims of easy privatization, it seems at least presentationally self-contradictory. The Israeli philosopher, Moshe Halbertal, has argued that politics involves the sublimation of everything to the preservation of some form of power which threatens a certain *sacredness* with the sectorial. Attempts by Mill and Habermas to create a secular, public plaza would, for Halbertal, substitute a marketplace of the rough and tumble exchange of ideas for a different form of *listening* as understood by the French *attendre*, for example, *a dedicated listening*.[5] Rev. Harding prior to Bold's suit for recovery would be a marvelous example of this *attendance*. An increasingly self-politicizing activity, as opposed to a partner in an Establishment, is at the fulcrum generating the shared themes of Trollope's *Barchester Chronicles* and the later *Parliamentary Novels*.

For these (and doubtlessly other) reasons, Habermas's utopian potential has not been realized. Society is polarized by an easily disguised class struggle or fragmented into competing interest groups, some of which abjure any idea of a marketplace of ideas. Like Madame Neroni in *Barchester Towers*, public opinion can demand submission (as would God's word) while retaining an autonomy and arbitrariness typical of despotic rulers. Because some people and institutions claiming to represent public opinion are not chosen in the same way as its elected representatives (the Church of England of the Victorian era being a perfect example), there lingers the suspicion even in the last quarter of the nineteenth century, that the concept is an empty abstraction with a highly self-reflexive modus operandi, like the gathering whirlwind. Virtually anyone could claim to represent it or see himself as a victim of what is confusingly blown about.

Public opinion formation is imagined rather early on as the creation of those whom it will come to haunt, as a competitive authoritative "voice" stripped of all identification with those who have had a share in its production. For Leslie Stephen, the power of public opinion was like a cacophonous production machine—perhaps a forerunner of the mechanism that will bring about Michel Foucault's de-individualizing "Death of the Author," as a singular voice, within a plural, unaccountable reproductive process:

> The power exercised by the press finds no *external fulcrum* from which to move the earth. It is a *machinery* for methodizing and rendering articulate the confused utterances of what is *called public opinion*, but it does not dictate them. [...] The public whisper confused guesses and opinions into a kind of ingenious acoustic machine, and mistake the echo which comes back for the utterances of independent wisdom.[6]

A methodical machine (with productive laborers) and material inputs here supplants the wisdom of the singular lever or author. Trollope's contemporary shaper of public opinion ironically sees a structural relationship between the hermeneutic life cycle of public opinion formation and its highly mechanical operational efficiency as a converter of what would otherwise lack any authorization, "confused utterances." His public opinion, as with Longus's version of the myth of Echo, transforms a nymph's resistance into her dismemberment. A resistant, independent wisdom is diluted by the machinery of public reproduction which stamps it as somehow "already received."

Although limitations of space do not allow for an extended discussion, the anonymous, de-territorialized voice heard in the somnolent daydreams of the Barsetshire clergy has a long nineteenth-century history which informs Trollope's remarkable extended critique. In 1819, King George III distinguished between "public news" as a textual category—gazettes, shipping information, parliamentary proceedings—and so-called newly published news. The second category included all commentary and was accordingly taxed by a special stamp duty. The government exacted a payment for potential criticism, beyond official announcements. This had the effect of inhibiting the dissemination of a new, potentially intrusive category while reinforcing the monopoly held by five or six largely metropolitan newspapers. New news (not unrelated to gossip, surely) was regarded as potentially subversive of state interests.[7] Timeliness was an agent of its potential subversion—hence taxed.

The repeal of the stamp duty in 1855 obviously had the anticipated effect, insofar as a lively provincial press quickly evolved and with it, increased fears about the erosion of so-called national values, tilted toward metropolitan values. George Eliot's elder Brooke of *Middlemarch* betrays a whiff of the anachronistic (in a novel written in 1871 but set on the eve of the First Reform Bill) when he purchases a provincial newspaper in the hopes of assisting his political campaign. Similarly, the proliferation of provincial newspapers in Trollope's clerical and political novels is astounding. As we shall see, this expansion puts large parts of the privileged and governing classes into a kind of perpetual response mode. They are effectively placed in a new position, as a relatively new local medium.

The anxieties of the ruling classes were hypostasized in two seemingly oppositional figural representations: a light, airborne insubstantiality stemming from either the absence of corporeal substance or the artificially assembled body of an impostor with a lethal effect for which there was no resistance. Madame Neroni is intermittently speechless and yet necessitates the assistance of an excess of support while possessing an immunity that lends her a perpetual resistance to comfortable "settlement." Her very being seems borrowed from some indeterminate contributors, not unlike the imagined position of a newly emergent local press:

> These things called papers were bred to grow up and pester society, flitting about for a time with a borrowed brilliancy, encased like the beetle in the brittle armor of a grub capable of depositing a poison, insidious and fatal.[8]

The self-contradictory nature of the provincial press in public opinion formation after 1855 surely impacted the way in which this elusive body assumed an admittedly only partial, life of its own. On the one hand, the lack of weight, the speculative lightness and self-effacing, fleeting nature of commentary was seen as poisonous to British national consensus. Yet, simultaneously, the same lightness lent it power to penetrate all levels of society, even those characterized by relatively marginal literacy.

In this light, it is intriguing to think of Trollope's early work as a deputy surveyor and then surveyor of the post office assigned initially to Ireland, as resembling in purpose that of a press newly mandated to cover local markets. Having learned that isolated villages in Ireland could not expect regular mail delivery without either bribing the postman, or traveling long distances to collect their mail, Trollope dedicated himself to the establishment of an early form of rural home delivery, "the object [...] to create a postal network which should catch all recipients of letters" (A 80). The letter carrier had the duty to take letters to every house with Trollope forced to hedge the financial records, remarking that the "accounting was in our hands" (A 380). A penetrative democratic network catches all, suggesting an interest in the *public distribution of private enclosures.*

Eneas Sweetland Dallas, among others, characterized this new form of journalism as a fugitive or underground literature that, instead of being displayed and consumed in libraries by those who could afford to subscribe, was on offer in such unedifying enclaves as inns and street hawkers. This transformation of informational logistics must of course impact content. These epistolary and journalistic penetrations into new markets could be read as some attempt either to segment the market into "niches" or to respond to previously ignored "niches," like the chink to which Mrs. Proudie refuses to stoop in the early pages of *Barsetshire Towers*. Given the expansion of the market, the organs that penetrated it came to regard themselves as representing its newly discovered *base*, as our contemporary parlance might have it. Hence, as with Rupert Murdoch's tabloid empire, it comes not merely to mirror public opinion, but in some dialectic has a hand in creating it, a great force that reacts on the life it represents, half-creating what it professes only to reflect.[9]

Displacing the model of the mirror, public opinion would become an incompletely created body, an assemblage born by a double maneuver, rather than a body to be uncovered by the suspension of private beliefs in Habermas's idealized arena. Yet, the precise relationship between the private envelopes that constitute it and the potential political hegemony of the whirlwind that sweeps much before it (even inclusively) is left unclear. This structuration implicitly democratizes victimhood.

In the first half of the nineteenth century, the monopoly enjoyed by the urban press had insured some ideological alignment along either side of the axis that traditionally defined Whig and Tory interests. But by the 1860s, something like Herbert Spencer's law of the differentiation of organ function following in the wake of the rapid growth in the circulation numbers of the provincial press, guaranteed a redistribution of traditional ideological alignments. Special interests were again nurtured in the appeal to a new audience beneath the auditory field of what had been previously enunciated as a unified public opinion voiced as the exclusive preserve of a national press.

How was a unified public opinion to emerge from a newly democratized press that spoke in a variety of voices to a multitude of interests? By a spectacular sleight of hand, at least one prominent commentator evoked another kind of conversion apparatus, whereby the Babel of a buzzing, poisonous hum of speculation could be processed into a more consensual model of public opinion formation:

> The multiplication of newspapers will create a Babel of opinions which will neutralize each other. The more newspapers, the weaker each will be, the more harmless will be the aggregate result.[10]

Rather than social chaos, a "most startling unanimity" could come to prevail as the production of the acoustic machine becomes self-cancelling buzz. Not a restricted market where all were granted access conditioned upon the suspension of private interests as in Habermas's model, but an unrestricted free market where competitive voices drown each other out would be a form of operational censorship. What emerges, presumably, would be neither a reflective index, nor voices half-created by organs that represent them, but a "force" without the notation of force, rendered harmless by a secondary conversion. Genuine public opinion formation would be paralyzed by polarization.

Madame Neroni contains all of these contradictions within a body that in nomination as well as self-representation seems to undergo continual historical and figural reformation. She retains her position as the calculated object of a community's interest by virtue of being both physically and audibly difficult of access, with

> a way of whispering that was peculiarly her own, and was exactly the reverse of that which prevails among tragedians. The great tragedian hisses out a positive whisper, made with bated breath, and produced by inarticulated tongue-formed sounds, but he is audible through the whole house. The Signora, however used no hisses, and produced all her words in a clear silver tone, but they could only be heard by the ear into which they were poured.
>
> (BT *I 185*)

This would be possible only if her utterance were directly channeled or if, as with those who hear religious voices, the listener was predisposed to be receptive in advance, much as he might be if he thought he were addressed by a comparable passion, public opinion. This peculiar, affected intimacy is abetted by the posture in which the Signora always leans forward, as if on the verge of addressing her listener. Upon being called upon by

Slope, she informs him from her sofa that she was "caught" as it were, "in the act of writing to you" (*BT* I 172), *in flagrante inscripto*, the unfilled intention of some "plan[s] to communicate with him after tea" (*BT* I 180). She is the repository of an intention that can never be raised to the status of a completed, verifiable text that might be enclosed. One of the more elegant ways of combating the censorship imposed on her return to England as a consequence of public exposure would be the self-censorship, a reduction of a "stand" with which she might inform *intention*.

Public opinion, like the intermittently attentive Madame Neroni, would be a composite body, then, made up of contradictions that *in concert*, comes to be defined as an elusive embrace, often inseparable from an acknowledged dependency that limits full realization of potential in return for practical benefits.[11] Although it lays claims to a proportionate inclusion, it contains a residue of particularity which evokes a "collective social conscience" which is not universally audible. Hence, public opinion has difficulty fully embodying addressivity because the particularity, strategically handicapped subjectivity, wordlessly summons assistance.

This may explain the fear, widely held, among the ruling classes in the 1860s that, as A. J. Lee exclaims, a "host of nobodies," anonymous reporters as opposed to signing authors, would come to dominate the shaping of public opinion.[12] Such trepidation, tantamount to a denial of propriety and property, was simultaneously "there" and "not there," a curious existence which Jacques Derrida in a different context, has likened to "a silhouette of a phantom."[13] But public opinion might also be increasingly imagined as an alternative host in Barsetshire nomenclature, as we shall come to see. Slope's indiscreet letter to Eleanor Bold during her stay with relatives as a chaperoned widow during a prolonged mourning does prompt a community's gossip. The untimely *outreach* on the part of a man of the cloth (another attempt at seeing which way prospective marital winds might blow) must be forwarded, lending it some of the circulatory efficiencies needed to sustain gossip over time, the vulnerability to being "passed on," without which it dies. Public opinion formation is less dependent on the mobility of spreading a narrative for its survival, as it balances centrifugal and centripetal models of force in such a way that the whirlwind seems a lovely functional model.

Madame Neroni's *playfulness*, even while so handicapped in her reach as to draw our sympathy (or in the case of the Rev. Slope, an active courtship), is revealed as a game that she enjoys over the course of the novel. The enjoyment seems altogether different from the punishing revelation of truth provided by the charade game in Jane Austen's *Emma*, the truth of self-knowledge. Signora Neroni has that in abundance: the surplus that allows it to spill over as a performance, comparable to those of dramatic actors.

In *The Savage Mind* and elsewhere, Claude Lévi-Strauss addresses the historical evolution from rituals to myths to games. Rituals are essentially *conjunctive*: a shaman or priest-like figure who is in charge of a set of historically endorsed practices, exhortations, homilies and ceremonial gestures draws the uninitiated into a larger body of belief so that all are symbolically equalized. In the Church of England, baptism might be an appropriate example. Myths would involve the participation in an ancient ritual unrecoverable as a result of the passage of time, except in coded reproduction. It would be a symbolic reenactment of the ritual, like the annual celebration of say, Passover for

Jews, and is restorative. It has a particular date fixed on a lunar calendar in which the flight from Egypt is celebrated annually in the spirit of a renewal that conjoins a community to its history.[14]

Games, however (which Lévi-Strauss imagined, with perhaps too much exaggeration, as crucial to the *tristesse* of modernization), are seen as moving from equality of participation at the outset to a *disjunction*: the determination of winners and losers at the end of some contest with mutually accepted rules. Though the finalists at Wimbledon begin at 0–0 with the coin toss, one contestant emerges victorious at the end of the afternoon. Insofar as it divides the world into winners and losers within a specific time (until the next tournament), games belong to the world of pre-match analysis, speculation as to the outcome, measurement, evaluation and assessment. In individualizing games, one represents oneself or one's team, but can *play* with the historical protocols of the sport along the boundaries where rules are enforced, as electoral contests reveal. Although rituals, myths and games (as well as faith) are all subject to testing, perpetual testing actually *defines* the champion rather than being a mere adjunct to the practice. Public opinion, even in the nineteenth century, gave evidence of being open to statistical evaluation, perhaps testifying to an abstraction whose separable components could be individually analyzed.[15]

Public opinion is, after all, a body under continuous construction in which variously indeterminable agents come to have profound influence. Although open to certain kinds of quantifying metrics, it remains continuously elusive, while those accustomed to participate in ritual are more committed to performative, immediate enactment. But, as with Austin's comments vis-à-vis the phrase, "I pronounce you man and wife," the act of utterance is not descriptive or analytical, but inseparable from *enactment*, and hence belongs to the ritual/myth paradigm.[16] Whoever is entrusted with enunciation in a self-fulfilling prophecy, endorses and confirms, without any need of public opinion formation and the analysis and manipulation attendant upon it. Since utterances *perform*, there is no space in which traditional notions of representation or symbolic representation might be assessed. In this perhaps fortuitous example, clerical pronouncements might prompt participation. Yet, like biblical injunctions, these inclusive "speech acts" *squeeze* the possibilities of symbolization and hence representation. In eschewing the need for mediation, the enunciator is *already* transcendent, entrusted by the Divine.

In Trollope's analysis, an important step in the feeding of public opinion occurs when a relatively minor agent, or someone speaking for a superior, identifies his private interests with those of the larger institution or state in such a way that he cannot identify his specific share in the totalization. This would effectively narrow the gap that normally separates private from public domains, creating a curiously shared community defined only by its interests, but which achieves this presumptive sharing only by confusing material, ideological and personal interests, resulting in polarization. Rev. Slope is a mere bishop's chaplain who nonetheless identifies his calculated private ambition with the advancement of belief in general, in an amalgamation *cultivated* over time:

> *He had taught himself to think* that in doing much for the promotion of his own interests he was doing much also for the promotion of religion.
>
> *(BT I 136, ital. added)*

This attempt to convert the separable into an imaginary unity of interests, it must be remarked, is *learned*. He simultaneously individually *is* (by self-education) and *is not* (for that has been surrendered a priori as a condition of membership) part of a larger body, hopefully able to withdraw his material interest when necessary: a flexible *accommodation* which occurs frequently in the *Barsetshire Chronicles* as a subtext of its *proxemics*. Although initially resistant, Bishop Proudie is informed early on that his private, inner study and library is no longer sufficient, given the demands upon the church's *outreach*, forcing his consent to "receiving his clergy in the dining room should they arrive in too large a flock to be admitted to his inner sanctum" (*BT* I 88).

Later in *Barchester Towers*, Rev. Arabin accepts the living of St. Ewold's, a relatively impoverished suburban parish, but only after resolving a spatial dilemma. Unwilling and unable financially to extend the walls of a tiny parsonage, Arabin convinces his superiors to substitute a round table that diminishes differences in rank. The clergy is both excessive for the space provided (a condition of the bureaucracy in *Framley Parsonage* and later in the *Palliser Novels*) at the same time that some of its representatives, like the Stanhopes, are absentee clergymen. Like the public opinion formation of Trollope's continuing interest, the religious army seems already either excessively present as an unseated surplus in need of literal reform to be comfortable, or on occasion, absent. Institutional territoriality is under more permanent pressures of spontaneous revision or a less spontaneously rearranged environment by a succession of watchdog Ecclesiastical Commissions (*BT* I 9) which foreground Trollope's narrative of clerical life in Barsetshire: not unlike the public press, another self-appointed watchdog.

A bureaucratically bloated institution that has no room for itself on the one hand, or alternatively, an indifferent, yet placeholding *faux* political representative like the Phineas Finn chosen by party elders to represent the fictional Tankerville (perhaps a rotten borough clone of the historic Old Sarum constituency) in *Phineas Redux,* reveals the urgency of self-maintenance. Neither so-called representative has any knowledge of his supposed constituency, but is "placed" as a candidate because his party needs to fill the vacant seat as part of its defensive *thick solidarity* under constant re-figuration in the face of pressures. Between these extremes would be religious or political institutions whose faith, practices and dedicated public service prevailed because they advanced the most meritorious argument, garnering public support as a consequence of some contested superiority in an open public opinion market. Although such a meritocracy may well be a remedy for the endemic weakness of many administered institutions, the nuanced Trollope reveals, as he will more deeply in the *Palliser Novels*, how elusive that goal is.

The ideal discursive "level playing field" might resemble, as Levi-Strauss's game analogy might suggest, the sporting *fête champêtre at* the Ullathorne (*BT* II 82–104) estate wherein tenants compete with the family of the landlord in lawn games and contests. All participants begin as competitive equals in physical skills (ritually, on one day of the year), but not at all as bearers of social prestige. The tenants in fact allow their less physically adept social superiors to win some of the contests, suggesting a willingness to comply by confusing two competitive activities for pragmatic reasons, as part of an unspoken contract binding tenants and landlords. Slope similarly exploits the incipient defects of such a now contested (because compromised) regulated market when applied to ideology. In the contest for the changes in doctrine, he adopts the position, "let him be supreme who can" (*BT* I 30) early on. This competitive spirit has implications for public opinion formation, in a marketplace defined by a newly competitive press.

In a continuation of a plot line shared with *The Warden*, the omnipresent *Jupiter* in an attempt to convince its readers that the newspaper was merely reflecting public opinion rather than having a role in its creation opens its pages to readers' opinions. These are supposedly written comments regarding the vacancy at Hiram's Hospital created by the forced resignation of Rev. Harding, its titular Warden. These supposed "Letters to the Editor," one presumptive measure of public response, however, are never identified by the sender's name. For all the reader may know, the published letters may be *selected* from subscribers who share a particular view endorsed by the publication itself, making use of its platform:

> The wisdom of this scheme was testified by the number of letters which "Common Sense," "Veritas," and "One that loves fair play" sent to the *Jupiter*, all expressing admiration, and amplifying on the details given. It is singular enough that no adverse letter appeared at all, and therefore none of course was written.
>
> *(BT I 12)*

Trollope's cynicism is quite openly displayed: the editors are half-creating a public opinion that they are entrusted with only reporting or proportionately representing. This is achieved by stripping the letters of any authentic signature of the sender which are melted into anonymous euphuisms. As we shall see, letters stripped of the sender's signature, counterfeit drafts and forged signatures, names used without permission and forwarded letters continually reappear so that authenticity and intention always evoke the question, "whose intention?" Public opinion can be *directed* by seamlessly eliding editing and censorship to shape *contributing* responses. Given Trollope's familiarity with the postal service, one wonders if public opinion formation is being imagined as a kind of editorially written "dead letter" repository containing imaginary positions?

A supposed neutral instrument of public opinion formation is advancing its own interest under cover, as it were, as presumptively at one with the populist anti-intellec-tualism of the forgotten common people. Open access combined with confected ano-nymity enables the manipulation of public opinion by a locally penetrative press, the same features which encryption and the Internet utilize today in the creation of "fake news." Various institutions charged with maintaining a "level playing field" for discus-sion and debate so that the best ideas might prevail are in fact tilting the field so as to influence rather than measure outcomes in the interest of monetization. As with altering the shape of the conference room at St. Ewold's or altering the ideological map of the country by "inventing" an electorate body that does not exist or suppressing skills so that the landlords win a few physical contests at Ullathorne, a contested space defined by freedom of access is invariably compromised in very imaginative ways.

Oscar Negt and Alexander Kluge in *Public Spheres and Experience* have argued that this admittedly artificially *created* (in the sense of being territorially "marked off") discursive space is but a necessary preliminary stage in establishing "an illusory synthesis of the totality of society" as part of a self-consciously productive process that disappears in the act of articulating "use-values."[17] Such an organizational context enables the development from *possibilities* to something like *interests* that can be used to define exclusions. As is the case with other forms of production, a considered anti-intellectualism is part of this guise of a neutral toleration that creates an illusion of shared solidarity amid a well-defined, but often obscured, division of labor and ideas.

The newly anointed bishop Proudie gives every indication of rearranging the arenas of clerical deliberation so as to cooperate with the other shareholders in the Establishment in the spirit of a self-effacing toleration of difference. His role is that of a figurehead who lends his name (on and for credit) to generic causes in the same way that other people and letters come to have assumed names. The object is not to get too out in front of reforms, but to assume expediently comfortable positions:

> In the arrangement of those church reforms with which he was connected, the ideas and original conception of the work to be done was generally furnished by the liberal statesmen of the day; and the labor of the details was borne by officials of a lower rank. It was, however, thought expedient that the *name* of some clergyman should appear in such matters, and as Dr. Proudie had *become known* as a tolerating divine, great *use* of this sort was made of his *name*. If he did not do much active good, he never did any harm.
>
> (BT *I* 20, ital. added)

The pragmatic usefulness of a bishop's support is, from an alternative perspective, a hollowing out of special, local interests by a "tolerating divine" who allows his name to be affixed as a brand to lure purchase. As a consequence, his "name began to appear in newspapers" (*BT* I 19)—the same papers that will become players in the forum of public opinion—in association with a variety of ecumenical commissions and enquiries as far away as Ireland and the Presbyterian Synods of Scotland and Ulster. He believes that as a consequence of his reciprocal theological "internationalism" public credit would redound to the church's long-term advantage. The ecumenical values in which he invests opens the church to a wider discursive tent that might find its counterpart in today's so-called neoliberal advocates of interdependence, often purchased at the cost of perceived neglect of local issues and lurking resentments.

In one sense, this outreach is an extension of a practice of the Church of England following the Glorious Revolution of 1688. Brent Sirota argues that throughout the eighteenth century, the Anglican Church embarked on building a civil society not dependent upon law, ordination or election through the support of various alternative institutions that might engage the interests of the *public* at large.[18] The Society for the Diffusion of Public Knowledge was supported by the church in what would now be called the public interest: a better (secularly) educated society. Into the evacuated space of ritual (miming the gap in succession left by the death of Archbishop Grantly) moves a newly established local press and a low-level administrator (a bishop's chaplain) in an attempt to restore a more reactionary, ritually restorative function for those less amenable to alternative knowledge societies.

Hence, a tolerant theological internationalism may result in debit as well as credit, as the investigation into the Hiram's Hospital bequest in *The Warden* had revealed. Adaptability and the receptive toleration of adversarial views come to be internalized, even physiologically, in the bishop's chaplain. Rev. Slope's oily, ingratiating manner and his absorptive "spongy, porous appearance" enable him to appear as his superior's ideological alter ego, until he represses his mentor's mild, tolerant flexibility to create a separate, self-sustaining market that might appeal to those more conservative souls who feel left behind by liberalizing modernization.

Realizing early on that "public life would better suit the great man's taste" (*BT* I 27) the chaplain and his ally, Mrs. Proudie, move quickly to "master the small details" (*BT* I 27), the niche market of bureaucratic administrators. These niggling, local details of diocesan duty have been abandoned because public opinion formation, like ecumenism, must give the illusion of assuming a broad-based monopolizing universality, even while crippling itself locally. To embrace the local details and practices of daily life would "fix" public opinion in private, contingent practices and needs rather than elevating it to a more general, wider sympathy and toleration. Yet, belief in the significance of small acts and defining daily practices being one definition of faith, Slope places his private interests in the *cause* of use-values which come to include a reduction in train schedules on the Sabbath and the promotion of Sunday schools for the poor in Barsetshire.

A question arises as a consequence of this division of political labor: Does public opinion formation depend on broadening the base or consolidating local support for minor, albeit ideologically defining issues? The freewheeling discussion of highly partisan, local issues when ultimately resolved contributes to public opinion formation just as surely as does the more patrician dedication to establishing a consensual, non-divisive public life usually involving (as it did in Britain prior to 1850) some suppression of dissenting local presses. The Church of England is faced with the same choice as the larger community when it comes to belief-formation. Can narrow provincial interests and practices granted to belief-formation unify?

This public opinion market is impacted by nostalgia for lost populist causes, characterized by a persistent interest in strategically narrow and divisive rather than broad values: ones that can be used as motivational levers. These are shamelessly defined in terms of private, heretofore neglected, interests whose connection with larger issues is only associative. In his first sermon as a bishop's right-hand man, Slope uses the inaugural occasion to "explain how the word of truth should be divided" (*BT* I 50), adopting the doctrinal equivalent of a limited market just as does the emergent local press. His penchant for parsing of the Word is of a piece with a more significant embrace of adversarial divisions that he creates, having "conceived it to be his duty to know all the private doings" (*BT* I 31) of the flock entrusted to his care, affecting intimacy. In pursuit of this knowledge, the chaplain segments his potential consumers, much as would anyone else desiring a specialized knowledge of a market. With the male members of the congregation, he is often "at variance" (*BT* I 31), but with the female congregants he projects, self-consciously (as something thought through) an image, "as he conceives, all powerful" (*BT* I 32). He parses his audience as well as the word.

This parsing of Word and public opinion market in Barsetshire extends to a campaign against rituals that have the unification of attendants as a function, including the appeal represented by choral participation. He condemns the symbolically unitary *voice* as an unreasonable emotional expression, though Trollope makes clear that the specific practice of his calumny, intoning in parish churches, "as a practice was all but unknown in the diocese" (*BT* I 50). In other words, Slope resurrects an anachronistic practice, a calculated restorative nostalgia, so as to polarize public opinion. This precedes, as is common political practice in the *Palliser Novels* and even now, an ideological pivot back toward the center of public opinion in the hopes of expanding a conservative base.

Considered as an arena of theological and social practices, the Barsetshire clergy is collectively afflicted with self-doubts about both its position and how that position is to mesh with new, *competitive* community organs dedicated to the role of a guardian. This "post-ideological moment"—if it is that—it should be noted, has little to do with the challenges posed by the scientific discoveries of Chambers and Darwin, so common in the nineteenth-century discourse, but invisible in Trollope's narrative. Both *Barchester Towers* and *The Warden* seem to belong to a historical interval when the power of intellectual ideas to define a topography and range seems much diminished. The Rev. Arabin, while a student and tutor at Oxford, had wrestled long and hard with the attractions of the Puseyites and their insistence on the need for a more historically authoritarian, ritual-bound Church of England (*BT* I 204) with the hope that a strong titular head and defined apostolic succession would minimize internal and divisive doctrinal disputes. Such a faith would have left no room for public opinion formation. But, having accepted the living at St. Ewold's, Arabin concedes to Eleanor Bold that his conscientious search for spiritual truth has altogether ceased, giving birth to a vision of the church as amoeba, pulled this way and that as it responds to public opinion and the issues it defines:

> It is the bane of my life that on important subjects I acquire no fixed opinion. I think and think and go on thinking; and yet my thoughts are running in ever different directions.
>
> (BT *II 232*)

The equally (doctrinally) slippery Slope, whose very name suggests the need for similar balancing act which fails to sustain him on his ambitious climb up the ecclesiastical hill, eventually tries to be all things to all people. His later ideological indeterminacy evokes an apt comment from one of his perceptive adversaries: "it is not possible that his ideas should have changed so soon" (*BT* I 171) His ideological adaptability was part of his early clerical apprenticeship, sent out to test the winds of public opinion in the first pages of the novel. It would be very difficult at a time when the church elders have abandoned local details and practices in favor of an enhanced ecclesiastical sociality that may grant it enhanced monopoly power in belief-formation, to redefine itself by an appeal to traditional rituals.

These difficulties in self-definition suggest, as Alain Badiou has intimated, a profound difference between the truth that religion purports to advance and the communicative sociality that public opinion advances in the name of truth, often under cover.[19] The former, at least in elaboration, purports to be *for all* so that in some sense it can only be achieved against dominating opinion which, contrary to truth propositions, would be for the benefit of *some* rather than all. The proffer considered by opinion is always grasped by/in a constructible set, one comprehended under a rubric that must classify preliminary to evaluation. While from the perspective of a truth-process, the same proposition is enmeshed in a generic set (as truth or falsity).

Public opinion in this sense would be *beneath* the true and the false because it is only compatible in communication, never when questions of fidelity arise. Obviously, both Rev. Arabin and Slope work through their positions, perhaps with a more or less ulterior purpose, subject to change or accommodation. There is another group of people inhabiting Trollope's world who are alienated in various ways: they find the social order remote, incomprehensible or fraudulent and hence combine cynicism with an apathy that leaves them self-consciously nonparticipants, albeit often keen observers along the edges of public opinion formation. They remain "of" it, but not actually "in" its deliberations like Signora Neroni and Madame Goesler (of *Phineas Finn* and *Phineas Redux*), who both arrive on the scene, in fact as part of an alien presence in England. Both women seem, in Madame Neroni's case in some double sense, "subdued by no passion," though inducing it in others, like, say, Towers's editorials in the *Jupiter*.

Ideational wavering in Trollope's clerical community may reflect either an institution in doubt about recuperating its foundational moment (as the intermittent lure of Newman's Oxford Movement may indicate) or, conversely, an attempt to direct its energies away from the exploration of the doctrines and tenets of belief and toward the formation of other social alliances and institutional missions. What initially appears as a chronic inconstancy of the Church of England, an allegory of which might be Slope's relationship with Signora Neroni, may in fact reflect what Slavoj Žižek in another context has termed the sublime nature of the object of ideology, insofar as it provides a view, in a negative way, of the dimensions of what is un-representable. It hence could never be shared, save as a negation.[20]

The mediation of this very inability—the successful presentation by means of failure, of the inadequacy itself—is what distinguishes a modest comfort from a fanciful fanaticism. This residual negation is often, as in the example of a bishop who does little good but less evil, imagined as institutional inertia (the merger of laissez-faire with boredom), symptomatically not unlike Madame Neroni's somewhat exaggerated and hence partially manipulative, paralysis. We demand the comfort of our beliefs in *attendance*, and hence are biased toward the negations of negations endemic to it:

> We are not forced into church! No; but we desire more than that. We desire *not* to be forced to stay away. We desire, nay we are resolute, to enjoy the *comfort of public worship;* but we also desire that we may do so without an amount of tedium which ordinary human nature cannot endure.
>
> (BT *I* 52, ital. added)

Throughout the *Chronicles of Barsetshire*, the negation of a negation (the sacrifice of material desire) is often seen as *always-already* inscribed (as opposed to a mere lapse) *in* the structures and practices of clerical and political life. This knowledge surely foregrounds

Signora Neroni's question when told of Slope's desire to share her life: how much of his "fat life" he is willing to give up for her special needs. This unwillingness to give up material pleasures is exhibited by other members of the privileged classes. The behaviorally and narratively anonymous "Earl of—," upon receiving the telegram announcing Dr. Grantly's death, hastily tucks away a copy of Rabelais in a "secret drawer" (*W* 69), the hiding place of a sensuous life. But like the various absenteeism(s), these negations are often written into the rules as well as the practices of the church:

> There is a rule in our church which forbids the younger order of our clergymen to perform a certain portion of the service. The absolution must be read by a minister in priest's orders. If there be no such minister present, the congregation can have the benefit of no absolution but that which each may succeed in administering to himself.
>
> (BT *I 239*)

As with other bureaucracies, there would be a threat to the administered life by an unregulated individualism in which attendants self-reflexively absolve themselves, "standing in" for the absentee cleric. This would reinforce the role of the church, at least on those occasions, as an awaiting sanctuary produced by its mild regulations.

Trollope's narrator's imaginative exploration of the place of the negative would presume to define the Church of England and its ministers as neither an institution designed to overcome doctrinal differences in a blurring ecumenism nor an institution dedicated to reviving doctrinal differences used to separate those who were ideologically disloyal, but a third option: a refuge from the tedium of all things politically disagreeable. This non-adversarial sanctuary, ideally, would be a quietist version of Habermas's *public sphere* where private interests and the hurly-burly of life and private opinions are temporarily suspended. Obviously in Trollope the suspension of private interests is the pipe dream (negation) at the heart of any institutional framework dedicated procedurally or ideologically, to inclusiveness.

Such an idealized suspension of private interests is precisely the opposite of the unpredictable, destabilizing intrusions of gossip which, as we shall see, can and does impact public opinion formation, although qualitatively and functionally very different. Gossip's value is rather totally dependent on its timeliness, which gives it the trappings of the *new*, the consequence of an interruption in the flow of ordinary time. It is chronically then, in surplus. Suspension in the form of neglect or censorship (or its lack of immediate relevance because already realized) would be the death of any use-value that gossip possesses. As a time-dependent, fugitive discourse, it often strikes the consumer as something he should have realized and perhaps did, and hence may function as a reminder. Hence in its effects, *gos*sip and *gospel* share the éclaircissement of an awakening (news) rather than the subtle negations and attendant speculation that define the operational space of public opinion formation.

Undeterred in his materialistic courtship by either the gossip surrounding his inamorata's past or her own indisposition, Rev. Slope attempts to raise his own position. Appealing to the transcendence of public opinion over either the immanence of gossip or the irreconcilable antimonies and consistent backtracking of his own theological positions, he has learned from Bishop Proudie's "outreach" that the cultivation of public opinion through public institutions is beneficial to his own ambition to displace it:

> I can count upon assistance from the *public press*: my name is known, I may say, somewhat favorably known, to that portion of the press which is now most influential with the government, and I have friends also in the government.
>
> *(BT II 52, ital. added)*

In the midst of the important nineteenth-century British debate over the relative jurisdictional range of ecclesiastical and civil courts, the bishop's chaplain proposes a "third way," the tribunal of public opinion, trusting that it will absolve him of both his ideological inconsistencies and his heart's inconstancy. The public is now a player which of course, given the reciprocities of public opinion formation, can also be played. Among all the Victorian novelists, Trollope alone empowers public opinion as a kind of alternative consolidating church which also provides a refuge for the undecided or wavering. As we shall see, throughout the *Barsetshire Chronicles*, and especially in *The Last Chronicle of Barset*, this body provides a thematic bridge between the clerical novels and the political novels.

One way of thinking about this is to imagine the quasi-monopoly of the Church of England at mid-nineteenth century as being like that of electrical utilities in the UK and the United States in the late 1980s. Ecclesiastical courts, politically unrestricted appointments, unimpeded access to the press and the unregulated use of income from historically defined (and hence, unmarketable) assets were being questioned; the expansion of a relatively unregulated public sphere with increasingly deregulated organs came to have its own separable interests, often competitive with those of the church, a heretofore relatively unregulated distributor of influence. Hence, it is entirely understandable that reform might come to be represented in Trollope's text as the ever-present potential of a censoring, partially imaginary (in the sense of speculative) voice that threatens previously sacrosanct distributional authority. The alternative distributor of power can be "bought off" only if the sanctified distributor reforms itself, a gesture which would ironically guarantee an otherwise unverifiable, albeit antagonistic, identification where there might be perceived to be little to choose between them.

The periodical literature of the mid-nineteenth century is replete with metaphorical comparisons of public opinion and organized religion, culminating of course in the work of August Comte. W. J. Fox was perhaps the most diligent in identifying a historical trajectory that began with the priests and gradually included men of letters. His Public Opinion Succession traced a line of descent resulting in a withering away of what he termed a "reign of patronage."[21] The press came to exercise patriarchal duties of a slightly custodial nature, taking the place of a disciplined sponsorship. The now displaced patriarchy could metaphorically be compared to the absentee father of Victorian fiction, though he never goes so far as to see an emergent local press as discontinuous orphan.

Any appeal to the newly recognized power of public opinion, as with the judgments of church or state, frame its decisions in terms of rendering summary judgment with a schedule of punishments and rewards (for plaintiffs), represented along some *continuum* that sets limits. The political scientist, John Zaller, has suggested, however, that the evaluations and assessments by public opinion do not work in that way.[22] It rather exhibits considerable vacillation and indecision that is not to be attributed to some "response instability," but to real feelings. In the act of seeking redemption or at least an accommodative relationship, the legitimacy and sovereignty of public opinion is questioned because it lacks both a foundational moment and historical notation. The absence of which, in tandem, endows it with the qualities of abstractions.

All political systems and their judicial apparatus and mandates endorse their claims to legitimacy in an infinite variety of ways: the divine right of kings, the iron law of history or the eighteenth-century "rights," supposedly derived from nature. Because of the lack of empirical verification, the claims of democracy, anticipated by polls and pollsters, have appeared to have an advantage insofar as it is periodically (at election time) a self-validating legitimacy. Yet, what the history of politics suggests is that belief-formation quickly separates genuine ideological issues from a more idiosyncratic cluster of ideas and attitudes, like the revival of intoning in Barsetshire, which comes to have symbolic value even if previously it was never an issue, per se. Symbols matter for purposes of identification. Ideological capital is found in strange repositories of taste.

While he was a candidate as president of the United States, the most widely remembered fact about George H. W. Bush, according to polls, was his dislike of broccoli.[23] Might it be that the part of the electorate that responds to political debate and differing ideological positions is outweighed by a group that responds to something else? Even if our ideological and theological preferences are imbued by family history, economic situation or cosmetic values like voice and demeanor, our preferences may be profoundly dictated by other factors, including a locally penetrating press or hearsay, which is then, like strange hobbies, "taken up" as an amateur interest. If true, information (applicable or not) is slowly displacing blood, education, qualification and class membership in Trollope, as an alternative carrier of cultural capital.

The reduced appeal of the permanence of ideological stances or political platforms in transitional cultures in favor of an attention to public opinion has recently drawn the attention of political scientists concerned by the instability of predictive models. Some of them argue that the populace uses shortcuts—the term adopted not entirely accurately is heuristics—about not only those who represent opinion, but the issues themselves.[24] We might, so the argument goes, buy into opinions in the same way we buy other products, like broccoli. We ask our friends (who may have recently invested in the product) or perhaps cursorily listened to some promotional enunciation or otherwise tested a sample. In short, we engage in a kind of ad hoc shopping. More recently, accompanying the perceived unreliability of trusted national polls in the U.S. presidential elections of 2016 and 2020, several pollsters have begun to ask an additional question in their surveys: "How do you think your friends and neighbors will vote?"[25]

That question, a supplement to the usual queries about a respondent's private ideologies, income and past voting record, would suggest that the choices that we (freely) make remain perhaps remotely the will of the people (in aggregate), but it is a will partially shaped by *derivatives*: one's opinions of the opinions of others in the same social circuit.

The separation of public opinion from private choices is questionable if there is a heuristic feedback loop in which our opinions of the others' opinion can be quantified as an input. As René Girard's notion of "mimetic desire" makes abundantly clear, we often desire not an object of desire but the "desire of desire," that is, the desire of the Other,[26] with Madame Neroni as a perfect example.

Whether in affection or ideology, this desire (or belief-formation) of desire creates a secondary market and later, a market in derivatives. This may account for a new category and strategy, the attempt to identify some so-called underlying value. Even in today's market-driven evaluation models, there exists a residual conviction in some core value resistant to exchange value or speculation on futures. In Trollope, any reputation, like that of a product, is increasingly determined by how many people desire to invest in a choice (and why), having little to do with the product.

This represents a *pulling away* from what had formerly appeared as theological or ideological *content*. Once subjected to the marketplace of conflictual or similarly held opinions, value assumes another meaning. What we call reason, as Habermas's deliberative rationality, may well be but a confirmation of arbitrary and idiosyncratic choices, a hollow rationality tested, as progress in school is, by tests and polls after the fact. If so, then the symbiosis between deliberative rationality and the choice of representation may exist only as yet another negation. The presumption of representation may be but the representation of empty content.

Public opinion may not *necessarily* be advancing our own interests in our own political choices and advocacy any more than we would when we buy into other products. But we might feel the need to justify these often-intuitive decisions by appealing to a rationality that gives the appearance of quantification. Trollope's Barsetshire, with its privileged clerical communities, logically might be the perfect arena for exploring the operations of this market, a kind of heuristic of heuristics. One cannot explain one's attendance and dependence on public opinion except perhaps intuitively. But we may feel compelled to justify any devotion. The forms assumed by our justifications reshape the public opinion market.

***

In the *Chronicles of Barsetshire*, the church, like public opinion formation, is in the process of hollowing out doctrinal *content* by purging itself of encumbrances so as to become what Slope refers to as a "fulcrum" of public opinion with a presence beyond the walls. With consumers who are neither enthusiastic (as might be attendants of services at nonconformist churches and chapels), nor forced to stay away, the church's role becomes that of maintaining territorial and ideological equilibrium, which, like public opinion itself, has a curious absence-in-presence and presence-in-absence. But, as Philip Converse has suggested, public opinion is most volatile not among the most politically aware (who are slow to change their opinions over time, as Slope will discover) or the least politically aware (whose lack of interest or access immunizes them from appeals) but from those moderately aware.[27] This group is sufficiently attentive to belief-formation to be exposed to partisan influences, but not so sufficiently committed to their initial preferences as to be immune from persuasion to reevaluate their ideological portfolio. They are staked to nimbleness.

Hence, the Church of England at the time of Trollope's novels has developed a new kind of critical attendance for which there was previously no need, always ready to *weigh in* lightly at the boundaries, playing one constituency off against another so as to maintain pressure, a balancing pressure. This demands that the clergy, in a practice which will come to disgust Phineas Finn in the later novel that bears his name, speak in different voices to different interests, appealing to them where they "live," and hence anticipating social demand. Even as it projects the need, as does the Rev. Slope, to speak in "one voice" (*BT* II 58)—a metaphoric "intoning"—the church must address multiple and subtly different letters of appeal depending on whether the audience is a member of Parliament, the editor of the *Jupiter* or his clerical superiors.

Although ostensibly these letters are at least grammatically written as if the speaker is the church and nation, Slope is making a continuum of his own interests with those of the institutional persona that appears to be the speaking subject. To an influential peer of the realm, he instantly discounts the possibility that a mere epistle might be interpreted as an interruption (like gossip) by repetitioning a previous discursive context. Agents of public opinion formation, like those of the law, attempt to establish a continuity of *reference*:

> My dear Sir Nicholas,—I hope that the intercourse which has been between us will preclude you from regarding my present application as an intrusion.
>
> *(BT II 56)*

As a self-appointed manipulator of public opinion, Slope has developed, perhaps under the tutelage of Signora Neroni, the value of creating the illusion of a continuous, but unfinished order of communication in which a *presumptive consensual marker* ("as you know" or "it goes without saying") replenishes ellipses to reestablish an illusory continuity. In many ways the grammar performs the same semiotic function as Trollope's plot device at the beginning of each of the first two volumes of *Barchester Towers*. Someone in a high ecclesiastic position is hovering between life and death, surviving for a time the most pessimistic medical expectations, yet existing as (a mostly semi-comatose) silent intentionality, albeit ideologically an *empty weight*. Not unlike passive consumers of his faith, neither too engaged nor absolutely detached from the Church of England, its titular authority lies at the margins of relevance, going forward.

Though he invokes a different, less urgent tone to Towers, the editor of the *Jupiter*, Slope, uses a rhetoric calculated to evoke a pluralizing inclusion. He delocalizes the subject of the letter by omitting any allusion to "The Palace," the seat of the very bishop whose name or letterhead should be prominently affixed as part of the customary inside address on official correspondence. Public opinion formation, as often those who contribute to it, has no fixed residence and thus no place in his letter, a strategy that is mimed in recontextualization. The press is now being raised to a nominating status, a "position," equivalent to the twin legs of the Establishment:

> The time, in fact, has come in which no government can venture to *fill up* the high places of the Church in defiance of the public press. The age of honourable bishops and noble

deans has gone by, and any clergyman, however humble born can now hope for success, if his industry, talent, and character be sufficient to call forth the *manifest opinion of the public in his favour.*

(BT II 60, ital. added)

The Slope maligned for his hypocrisy is surely onto something: history is being displaced by appeals to merit, but only if it calls forth an incipient (manifest) opinion, subsidized by the press. The advocate of intoning now markets himself as creating a new order. But, because in the absence of tests (which Trollope addresses in both *The Three Clerks* and *Framley Parsonage*) to determine merit, it is not as easily quantifiable as what Bishop Proudie terms "honourable commissions" or age. It cannot easily call itself forth, needing other voices (like evaluators of verifiable qualifications) to speak and act in its behalf. Public opinion in this passage is made *manifest*, that is to say, currently *suppressed* in the same way that merit is on occasion. Public opinion can never speak in its own (real) name—again, giving it an uncanny resemblance to the "love interest," Signora Neroni, existing only in the manifest of intention.

The Rev. Slope has evolved from one with his "ear to the ground" of public opinion to a position as a self-appointed press officer for the church. Earlier in *Barchester Towers*, a doctrinal dispute over clerical authority had been carried on between the sexual and ideological rivals, Slope and Arabin, in the *Jupiter*. In foreclosing the continuation of their debate, the editor advises a persistent Slope who insists on replying to everything, as does public opinion, that any further letter from him would be treated by the editor as an advertisement to be paid for at regular commercial rates (*BT* I 128). To be seen to speak too vehemently for a predefined ideological cause is obviously to become a separable advocate, a partisan spokesman rather than one living closer to the margins. Such would define a *position* that runs counter to the vague presence-in-absence of public opinion that conditions it as always in situ, undefined save as a readiness to weigh in, tilting the scales of value. Once identified as a spokesman, Slope's influence on the public opinion market would be discounted as self-serving.

Gestures are designed to generate a response from which later one can claim to have been misunderstood. The code is strategically susceptible to false allegorizations. Tom Towers's characteristic evasions involve a willingness to be literally ir-*responsible* so as to have no voice independent of his organ. Those who confront these manipulators live in a situation of perpetual alertness ("How am I doing now?") in a competitive, volatile, *attention economy*. Strategic ambiguity is crucial to their empowerment as interlocutors who cannot be ideologically or physically pinned down.

Towers's threat to reframe the genre of the "letter to the editor" as a paid political advertisement does not alter the content or syntax of Slope's letter. What it would achieve, as Slope clearly understands, is a contextual repositioning of an inherently sincere opinion, one that putatively stands on principle, to an expression of the ambitious salesman. The letter becomes a self-advertisement within a public marketplace synchronizing his own private ambitions with those of the church now in a new "lodging" (*BT* I 129) or placement. This would imply that theological or political opinion would thereby become another product offered for choice in the pages of the *Jupiter*.

The daily paper would become a bazaar, an idea later exploited in the failing department store detailed in *The Struggles of Brown, Jones, and Robinson*, to which the Church of England contributes goods on offer. Opinion formation as advertisement also subjects the ideational to a different time cycle, one controlled by the periodicity of daily issue. The attempt to influence public opinion formation with an ulterior purpose is difficult in one self-entrusted with maintaining the *subject*. Once an opinion becomes another product on offer, it comes to have a shelf life.

   The (then) new media generates a surplus of information at the same time that it increases the production among its consumers. Both Slope and the *Jupiter* must be nimble as they continuously respond to the nineteenth-century version of today's "Breaking News." Long before cyberspace created a world where everyone had his own "Blog" or "Website," sustained attention becomes a very rare resource, as Michael Goldhaber noted over two decades ago.[28] One becomes attracted, even addicted to the crosscurrents of information, but in a curiously detached way, mirrored in Slope's compulsive, yet defensive, attraction to Madame Neroni, as he periodically checks in on her. This is perhaps replicated in Trollope's plots, from which readers become easily prey to *distraction*, a surfeit of digressions and minor (yet reappearing) characters lacking any identifying moral or immoral (or even memorably physical) traits. Enjoying community sympathy as the victim of an "international/ecumenical" marriage gone awry, she needs no "likes" on the "platform" which supports her public appearances, unlike the manipulative, Obadiah Slope. Does compassion, which needs no continuous flow of information to sustain it, represent an attempt to diminish the importance of informational currency?

   As it is subjected to the periodical circulation of the public press, opinion comes to belong to a time cycle of *news*, more like gossip or say, fashion in which timely originality is privileged. No wonder that Walter Benjamin charged in "One-Way Street" (an interest continued in the unfinished "Arcades Project") that advertising transformed every conversational inquiry and political dialogue into an attempted evaluation of any commodity that our discursive partner was wearing or had experienced.[29] It interrupted the free flow of information into a temporally spliced or confected space which forever occluded interactive dialogue in the interests of a niche, parsed market. The limitation of choices into acceptance (buying) or rejection (selling) amounts to parsing the consumers into those who are interested in the commodity and those who walk away, excluding the vulnerable to temptation on the borders. Meaning in advertising is similarly generated by juxtaposition, splicing and the nature of presentational values: location, packaging and what products are adjacently displayed. Just as inherited land is being "broken up" in the *Barsetshire Chronicles*, so antecedent repositories of belief or spiritual value are being converted to another object "for sale."

   The long process of ideology formation (production) is abbreviated within a new time, the time of *circulation*. Just as the Establishment is being given the wider circulation sought by Bishop Proudie when his "name began to appear in newspapers," his minion, the maligned Rev. Slope, is carrying out his initiative with his own scheme of *publicité*. He divides opinion only to attempt to then unite the differences with an appeal that eliminates nuance in favor of an imagined consensus of consumers, but as the paper's editor, Tom Towers, perceives, it is an exercise in public relations: "spin."

The manifest nature of public opinion formation is perfectly illustrated in Tom Towers's curious method of controlling all potential social encounters with visitors to the offices of the *Jupiter* by a curious absentee/presence miming that of the "long and lingering" (*BT* I 1) Archbishop Grantly or the handicapped Madame Neroni:

> He was lingering over his last cup of tea [...] when John Bold's card was brought in by his tiger. The tiger never knew that his master was at home, though often knew that he was not, and thus Tom Towers was never invaded but by his own consent.
>
> (W *123*)

Again, there is this characteristically curious waiting, more an existential loitering than a consequence of some physical handicap, at the heart of an institution instrumental to public opinion formation.[30] An editor's controlling negation seems crucial to its operational disclaimers, allowing the newspaper to easily incorporate the arguments of its (often invented) adversaries or even the absence of a counterargument (and hence adversarial silence) into its own investigative editorials. Unlike the law and its representatives or the Church of England and its ministers, the putative representatives of public opinion formation have no consistently occupied habitat nor habit (like robes) by which they can be visually recognized, displaced by a calculated, intermittently homeless anonymity or reluctant full presence, but always about to speak.

When a series of investigative editorials, critical of an aging Warden's disposition of the Hiram's Hospital Trust, begins to appear in its pages, the responsible clergy meet to synchronize their response, as if a collective or aggregative, and hence prosthetic body was needed to rebut the voice of the *Jupiter* imagined as a similar collective. The press has assumed the role of defender of the so-called commonweal as well as an investigative detective against a perceived maldistribution of financial assets. In the process, it exerts a perceived mastery of the word with an absorptive capacity of self-styled instruments of public opinion formation to foreclose any attempt by church elders to mount a fearful defense *against* or reply *to* public opinion: "you will leave out some word, and the cathedral clergy will be harped upon" (*W* 60). Any reply, including the absence of a reply or negation, becomes part of the pagan divinity, the public information factory, that speaks from on high, known as Towers's *Jupiter*. Public opinion has become so hegemonizing that it apparently leaves nothing outside itself, a very "broad" church indeed, that increasingly compels competitive attendance.

Just as with most faiths, public opinion demands that those who seek sanctuary therein make some self-sacrifice. This is imagined as a hope that its members might "abandon useless talking, idle thinking, profitless labor" (*W* 119) and other types of free-floating, deracinated speech which is part and parcel of provincial life in Trollope as among other nineteenth-century British novelists. In *Being and Time* Heidegger lumps "idle chatter" and gossip together into the category of *Gerede*, a deracinated speech that floats about modern culture in contradistinction to a work economy, wherein the individual wrestles with the object of understanding in order to make it in some sense, *one's own*.[31] An implicit confusion clearly constitutes the Being of public opinion: it is both a repository of idle speech or silence, a kind of warehouse where fragmentary thoughts, gossip and private opinions are collected and stored, but also a quasi-institutional, manufacturing presence that invisibly filters, edits and unifies them into an imaginary, potentially monopolizing, vox populi. Whoever touches it literally recognizes himself as/in public opinion to such an extent that he becomes inseparable from this massive repository of previously separable individuality.

Little wonder that Towers, editor of the *Jupiter,* seems such a secretive, yet simultaneously omnipresent character, even in nomination, challenging the local religious edifice and cathedral town that lends one of the novels its title, *Barchester Towers.* In other ways, too, the newspaper office combines the sybaritic lifestyle of at least the upper echelons of the church with a faux pantheon of inscriptive goddesses and their associated tools, which Trollope nominates as "Pica" and "Castalian" (inks). In this editorial office, Trollope observes the fearless leader of a new faith, tied to the law, but a law of his own making based on continuous enquiry, where there

> reigns a pope, *self-nominated, self-consecrated,*—ay, and much stronger too—self-believing!—a pope whom, if you cannot believe him I would advise you to disobey as silently as possible, a pope hitherto afraid of no Luther; a pope who manages his own inquisition.
>
> (*W 118, ital. added*)

In Trollope's hands even the *Jupiter* library, overseen by a reproduction of Charles Collins's Pre-Raphaelite-style painting, *Convent Thoughts,* seems ironically appropriate. Portraying a nun beside a pond of lilies, the familiar painting evokes an implicit comparison between newspapers, church and a highly stylized example of popular culture (soon to go out of fashion as quickly as it came in). Religious dedication is being reappropriated as pagan interior decoration, simultaneously thematically fitting (for the self-consecrated sanctuary of the press) and out of place. Although the retreat from the world emblemized in Towers's taste points to the various *closes* in which the clergy live in close proximity in both *The Warden* and *Barchester Towers,* public opinion formation seems inescapable as part *of the world.* If the Pre-Raphaelites were a short-lived aesthetic cul-de-sac of mid-century (with an au courant stylish appeal to an ascendant industrial class represented by its collectors like the Lever family), Collins's painting is appropriate to a faux sacred which public fashion might petition.

A residual anti-Establishment (if not pagan) stance implicit in belief-formation is enhanced by Trollope's further comic portrayal of the *Jupiter* offices as "Mount Olympus," the title of Chapter 14 of *The Warden,* with Towers as the cultivator of an imaginary "Tenth Muse" (*W* 122). Public opinion has become an imaginary supplement to the mythical nine, a group of (originally) undifferentiated muses in Homer that later came to be separated with separable attributes (e.g., Calliope of the beautiful voice) in both Hesiod and later sculpture. Trollope's metaphor is very rich: his "Tenth Muse" is a late addition to a group of inspirational spirits that comes down to us as simultaneously a collective reservoir, yet potentially separable figures in later literature. Of course, his muse of public opinion leaves less of a footprint in inspirational literature, more like that of say, Keats's Psyche, "too late for antique vows." But the *Jupiter* remains a new shrine furnished with trappings of allegorical frozen friezes, stylized.

In one sense, *Barchester Towers* is a thematic and chronological continuation of its antecedent novel, a similar supplement to *The Warden*, beginning where the previous novel ended, with similar thematic ellipses: a shared unanticipated vacancy in what had previously been seen as an established clerical sinecure (the Hiram Trust and the death of Bishop Grantly). The provisions of the Hiram Trust are being legally challenged in a suit advanced by a wealthy surgeon, acting, somewhat uniquely as public advocate, John Bold. In its "continuance," *Barchester Towers*, the Rev. Slope is both challenging and imitating the attempt to enlist public opinion on the side of a challenge to what had previously been held in ideological trust, the doctrines accruing to a defined succession. The law represents of course a certain kind of (ambitious) merit as does the relatively impecunious Rev. Slope's plans: self-interest is allied with real conviction as to the merits (of merit). Both attempt to engage public opinion through the agency of the press in an alliance. The law creates the challenge that will generate a vacancy, an abnegation of trust, in *The Warden*. Similarly, *Barchester Towers* commences with the exploitation of both internal dissent and lapses of succession, which jointly are both responses *to* and productive *of* vacancies in ideology and personnel. Septimus Harding in his position as warden/custodian in *The Warden* or Bishop Grantly as warden/custodian of clerical doctrine and opinion, both linger longer than they should. The press, however, is defined as a more strategic lingering—in the sense of a continuously maintained deliberation—over issues unrelated to succession, but adjusting more quickly than other institutions to any gaps in continuity.

The negation or protective self-censorship of the individual voices that contribute to public opinion formation is nowhere better illustrated than when the uncompensated representative for the plaintiffs, John Bold, request that Towers put a stop to the extended editorial commentary in the *Jupiter* that had pilloried his prospective father-in-law, Septimus Harding, even though it was Bold's comments to the editor that had initiated the investigation into abuses in the way the trust was administered. The editor-cum-censor, Towers, refuses to suspend a continuing series of investigative journalism (one of the very early examples of the genre in fiction). The refusal to embargo the series is couched in terms of the separation of voices. The editor, though he may write we are told, cannot *speak* for the *Jupiter*. He has transformed writing into a "collective," an oral register no longer responsive to individual utterance or amendment. This is achieved by a separation of *writing* from *speaking*, a strategic schism, not unrelated to the Rev. Slope's "parsing" of the Word or similar schisms which establish new faiths, historically. Towers as a singular voice cannot, so he claims, supplant a collective assemblage (achieved by his redactions), made almost a self-sustaining machine of public opinion formation. "Everybody" and "nobody" would be possible euphuisms for public opinion which Towers admits to having awakened, even as he acknowledges the possibility of their being in error. He picks and chooses when to endorse their knowledge:

"My dear fellow," said he, when Bold had quite done speaking. "I really cannot answer for the *Jupiter*."

"But if you saw that these articles were unjust, I think that you would endeavor to put a stop to them; of course, nobody doubts that you could, if you chose."

"Nobody and everybody are always very kind, but unfortunately are generally very wrong."

(W 133)

"Nobody" and "everybody" are components of the curiously hybrid "body" of public opinion, combining insufficiency and surplus, unanswerable negation and totalization.

Claiming that if "certain men [...] employed in writing for the public press" (<i>W</i> 114) were to either write or abstain from writing out of private motives, newspapers would lose their newly found independence from existence as party mouthpieces, Towers refuses to intercede. He imagines public opinion as so weighty as to be resistant to any fulcrum, "too <i>heavy</i> to be moved by private request" (<i>W</i> 134). Poor Bold abandons the climb, given that the paper and its editor are on "such high ground that there was no getting on it" (<i>W</i> 134). The metaphoric Mt. Olympus of the press, the home of muses that willfully intervene, yet are inaccessible to private individuals save at the prerogative of its residents, establishes editors as dedicated to another lord, hence ironically resembling both the state and church bureaucracies. As with the law, permission to take exception to public opinion is difficult to obtain, even though, like the law, public opinion is an aggregate of individual wills, which, over time, build it into an arbitrarily constructed and absorptively flexible, but on occasion, unmoved, body.

Bold, with an exceptional, educated familiarity with the law, is the concerned public advocate, a new figure in British fiction who wishes to withdraw his interest. After requesting that his letters (which opened the case in behalf of the plaintiffs) be returned to the sender, he is informed by Towers that they (as with many Letters to an Editor) carry no symbolic return addresses, constituting a "one-way street," to borrow again from Benjamin. Once deposited into the consuming mouth of public opinion, such missives can no more be retrieved by the writer than those letters deposited in the mouths of pillar post boxes which Trollope introduced as an innovation on the Channel Islands (before it was adopted throughout the country) during his work at the GPO at St. Martin's-le-Grand.

Along with his scheme of establishing postal districts for the Greater London metropolitan area, his day job reveals interest in the efficiencies of local market penetration which enabled faster collection and distribution.[32] One such efficiency, debated during Trollope's contentious time at the GPO, was the institution of the cancellation of affixed postage stamps with a marked date and time of deposition. The innovation gave circulation a timed entry so as to prevent reuse, while simultaneously severing the temporal sovereignty of authorship from the temporality of a circulation system: not the last time a "cancel culture" imparts a transactional meaning.[33]

The "Tenth Muse" of public opinion formation appears as a strange body, metaphorically combining an ear (held "to the ground" or testing the wind) or leaning forward as a listener, and a mouth that uses what is fed it, often against the interests of the provisioner. Though regarded as a collective and therefore indivisible, any resultant production is first digested, before coming to exist in a social context which can be owned and disowned at random, as would any other manufacturing process. Raw material submitted by individual informant is often transformed: original "input" can never be recovered *as is*, for it is already processed when the ideology of the recipient opposes that of the donor:

> I know he got his information from me. He was ready enough to take my word for gospel when it suited his own views, and to set Mr. Harding up as before the public as an impostor on no other testimony than my chance conversation; but when I offer him real evidence as opposed to his own views, he tells me that private motives are detrimental to public justice! Confound his arrogance! What is any public question but a conglomeration of private interests?
>
> *(W 134)*

Bold, believing that public opinion is a mere conglomeration of individual private queries, does not understand the ways public opinion is manufactured so that its "outputs" cannot be deduced from its "inputs." The machinery can work to either separate private from public opinion or incorporate them within in it, just as "spongy" Slope had argued in eliding his private clerical ambitions with the larger (or are they?) aim of the church he serves.

As the philosopher Raymond Geuss has done recently, citing it as one of the cornerstones of nineteenth-century political liberalism, Bold would narrow a traditional distinction between public and private interests.[34] He would achieve this in part by making public opinion the creation of individual investment, but one that could be withdrawn on demand. It is perhaps intriguing to recall that the limited liability corporation (newly protected by law in the 1850s)—a new economic body—liberated (by setting limits upon) the fiduciary responsibilities of "conglomerations," like Melmotte's South Central and Mexican Railway of *The Way We Live Now*, to its shareholder/contributors and customers.[35] Limited liability, like public opinion in operation, insures existence as a totality, defending officers and shareholders against individual responsibility.

Hence, in this confrontation between the law and the editor of the *Jupiter*, Tom Towers uses a hybrid oxymoron, if not entirely prosthetic, phrase "public gossip" (*W* 133) to describe his product. This suggests some conversion mechanism in which the editor cannot intercede in a process even if he so desired. Gossip could be stopped in a variety of ways, but "public gossip" would have a continuous life, in which the operator of the machinery is not an author, as Towers reminds, but a *consolidator* or *assembler* of previously dissimulated idle depositors' narratives from which he distances himself. It is an elusive *nobody* as testified to by all the preserved anonymity and pen names prefixed to Letters to the Editor or its unsigned editorials. Yet, this curiously detached/deformed body resembles that of other abstractions, however, with a crucial difference: it can be mapped as a curious location. The premises of the *Jupiter*, like the peripheral position of Madame Neroni in the life of Barsetshire, are "close to the densest throng of men, but partaking neither of the noise nor the crowd" (*W* 118).

John Bold might justifiably have another complaint in addition to the denial of his letter's return. His contribution has entered circulation without his authorization, like those solitary inventors who will see an innovation copied or licensed to a larger market. The publisher secures free raw material, adds tiny increments of value to it, repackages it in such a way as to appeal to a targeted consumer and then adjusts the product in response to reconfigured demand.

Throughout the *Barsetshire Chronicles*, public opinion formation comes to be associated with images of uninterruptible mechanization, even in grammatical constructs like "it has already gone forward" or the pronouncement from a supervising editor that he "cannot answer" for the *Jupiter*, endowing it with a voice which does not accommodate human query and hence resists the dialogic. It is as self-validating as the machine whose maintenance recommendations Walter Benjamin offered in the citation on the frontispiece of this essay.

If public opinion formation is analogous to other mechanically- reproductive processes, it both creates consumer desire, but a-typically perhaps, it also exists as an unaccountable repository to which Lawyer Bold, the Rev. Obadiah Slope, and an ecumenical bishop all deposit information or influence. It could be at least potentially an instrument of credit formation, but also of warehousing future consumption in terms of enhanced circulation and advertising revenue. Public opinion thus must appear as *liminal*, insofar as it presents the reader with a condition of the possibility of a structure that can in no way enclose it. Little wonder that the penetration of the local by Madame Neroni's physically handicapped (and visually assembled) body with which the novel commences seems an early synecdoche for the curious powers of engagement possessed by public opinion in both irregular assembly and impact.

If increasingly marginal differences in upgrading raw intelligence, consumer preferences or "framing" result in a proportionately greater competitive advantage for organs of public opinion formation, then it would be logical to expect market *timing* to loom large. Towers's work often consists of placing double quotation marks around single quotation marks so as to obscure whose utterance we are reading in the *Jupiter*. The characteristic rhetorical style of the paper—no less than the Signora's speaking style—forces the reader to *listen* to the production of voices in one case or a singular voice in the other, *once again*. This effect is identical to that of the pastor on Sunday morning upon an often-indifferent congregation. It is a market decidedly different from the marital "meet market" that attends upon, for example, Jane Austen's women in the autumn of their marital eligibility. In Trollope, neither consumers nor producers are singular, and the survival of one's self-respect does not depend on accumulated merit or acquired skills (like playing a musical instrument), beauty, financial resources, or social manners and grace, but upon manipulating fickle demand.

***

It might be instructive to compare the role of public opinion in Trollope's early work with that of the aforementioned gossip figure (Figure 1). The mediating figure of the detective, who will initiate a genre that transforms the evolution of the novel format, shares characteristics of both gossip and agents of public opinion formation. Both share a purposive revelation of some secret, the discovery of which propels the plot to resolution. The gossip or detective's insensitivity, even "cattiness," might be an example of a *singular* voice, posing as an indifferent—because indifference is a presumed condition of objectivity—unit of communication. Her solitude and relative social impotence demand an obliging listener. But as with the Inspector Bucket of *Bleak House*, any

FIGURE 1: COMPARATIVE OPERATIONAL DYNAMICS OF GOSSIP AND PUBLIC OPINION

Gossip	*Public Opinion*
1. Singular interruption to another narrative of events	1. Plurality of voices to be consolidated as an imaginary aggregate
2. Easily dated/consigned to history by new information	2. Maintains hegemony by remaining au courant and endlessly revisionary
3. Erases ownership of narrative by claiming that it is mere repetition of an Other	3. Erases ownership of narrative by obscuring individual contributions as an anonymous empty mouth: a vox populi
4. Uses direct address with restrictive operating instructions for reproduction	4. Uses indirect address or rhetorical omniscience by mediating "organs"
5. Often narrated by the socially excluded who hope thereby to gain inclusion in a privileged narrative	5. Democratic narrative committed to the (imagined) consensual interests of some Arbitrarily defined community
6. Physically embodied	6. A virtual or prosthetic body/ a phantom
7. Perceived by addressees as an irresistible claim upon attention	7. Perceived as a "representative" intention (a paradox) to be recuperated
8. Maintains a neutral narrative posture to enhance credibility-as-objectivity	8. Continually adjusts its narrative to accommodate new data
9. Stylistically impressionistic, often as an "aside" to enhance exclusivity	9. Stylistically, mimes the permanence (and force) of law in its continuance
10. Resembles traditional narratives in the interests of maintaining suspense (a plot)	10. Resembles literary criticism in its bias toward a community dedicated to establishing canonicity

exchange would be equivocal, for the auditor is not asked to take part, only turn toward the interruption as if "hailed" in an attempt to understand a demand or intrusion, like that which accompanies policing.[36] The gossip reinforces an identity as a "chatterbox" either in order to anticipate (and thereby acknowledge) the appraisal of her limited social significance or to identify herself with a speech that lacks identity. Like the editor of the *Jupiter*, she behaves as if she wanted to nullify a relation to others as a condition of making the relation. Any perspective interlocutor often confines his questions to questions of *access*. We want to learn the *productive conditions* of her narrative: how and when she learned. Hence the "I" of the gossip is already a fable for itself to such an extent that it must tell stories in an attempt to recover itself *in them*.

The detective is not a casual observer or listener (unlike the typical defense of the gossip as only an accidental presence), but is looking and listening *for something* of which, at the outset, he may be incompletely aware. In the beginning of narratives of detection, there is only a disruptive event in an environment of instruments, social practices, remains of one sort or another, a "scene" and some mutual relationship to a particular position or timeline, which have yet to acquire what qualifies as a *signification*. They will acquire *signification* only in relationship to other objects, events, practices, alternative chronologies and intention (often deduced after the fact) that can be characterized as *intention* (motive). To be sure, he does often have specialized equipment (like Bucket's bull's eye), prior experience in other cases and if not actual state sponsorship, public toleration, if not endorsement. But, as with authors, whatever *signification* attaches to his encounters with others is acquired only in the establishment of nontraditional relationships that the inspector or detective later aligns in such a way as to become part of a new syntagmatic order. The detective resembles the novelist, but working in reverse to ascertain what happened at an occluded beginning in such a way that it is inseparable from the ending. This suggests a new kind of "progressively realized" time that differs not in kind, but in degree from the ways in which we arbitrarily measure either narrative or chronological time. A precursor of Bergson's fin de siècle interests,[37] the time of public opinion formation is conceptually neither a unity nor a multiplicity and resistant to measurement as an aggregate, but exists as the continually provisional "trace" of *duration*, an emotion shared by those who read Trollope's massive output.

We can and often do, however, abandon gossip, turning away with a variety of justifications for the rejection of its narrative: (1) the information is already in circulation and is hence irrelevant; (2) we have other, presumably higher interests that renders it trivial or irrelevant and (3) the narrator has an ulterior interest, a past relationship to the events, that is not reflected in her narration and renders it untrustworthy.[38] Abandoning public opinion, however, as both Bold and Rev. Slope discover, is not possible because we are *always-already* in it and in fact, constitute it. Neither religion nor the law, nor their respective agents, having once worked to influence and alter public opinion for their own benefit, can ever recover their investment *in* its structure, but merely reveal the operational dynamics *of* the structures and its human and strategic weaknesses.

Nevertheless, crucial questions remain. Does public opinion erase autonomy altogether or rather absorb, by preempting, an as yet *unrealized* autonomy, which would lend it some of the hybrid characteristics of markets? As we have seen, public opinion must sustain the claim that it is monopolizing, in much the same way that the Church of England does: by means of an implied "we," which, like that of the encyclical or the royal "we," is an indivisible transcendence. Yet, it cannot quite sustain that claim as long as it remains *continuously under revision* in ways that cannot be anticipated with certainty—an immanent force. One could, for example, imagine that radical individualism could be so successfully adopted in practice or as an idea as to eliminate the concept of a *public* or *society*.[39] Or one could imagine what constitutes a *public* as changing due to adjustments in access to the franchise, immigration or new organs of informational distribution. Were public opinion a genuine totality, nothing could ever challenge it, as does the obstinate Rev. Crowley of *The Last Chronicle of Barset*.

The one invariable characteristic of public opinion formation is its temporal variability, as statistical (as opposed to historical) information. It recontextualizes without totally eliminating historical markers and values attached to its subjects, to enable future projections that may or may not be accurate or even applicable. It adjusts quickly (and may excessively adjust) to contemporary events or temporary reevaluations of reputation. *Stat*istics is both linguistically and institutionally bound to an emergent *state* under whose sponsorship the discipline enjoyed incremental growth from about 1860 onward. Initially, statistics was a form of social "mapping" (or for some historians, Foucault's state of surveillance). Later, it was used to relate previously disparate connections (the rate of marriage to the price of corn). But eventually, it evolved into a tool for prediction.

The logical trajectory of this evolution was the application of statistical analysis so as
to place wagers on futures, be it on beast (horses) or future politicians—evolving into
instruments to cover risk with "handicapping" and deniability.

This prosthetic body of public opinion is therefore always potentially in a *false position*, insofar as it uses imperfect knowledge to anticipate possible projects, "stances" or
evaluations, selectively reproduced in those who *attend* upon it. All of these features
make it open to speculative investment, to finding our *place* in its vanishing markers. An
example might be reflected in the way in which Trollope's narrative addresses the various anachronisms embodied in the practices of the Church of England, now subjected
to a repurposing which he opens to a new temporality. His omniscient narrator is *com-
plicitous* with the inflationary speculation of the *Jupiter* in fueling more material speculators in property, even as (out of the other side of its mouth) it would seem to defend the
disappearing values of traditional spaces as they make way for the masses and massive
structures and thoroughfares:

> Old St Dunstan, with its bell-smiting bludgeoners, has been removed; the ancient shops
> with their faces full of pleasant history are passing away one by one; the bar itself is to
> go—its doom has been pronounced in the pages of the *Jupiter*; *rumour* tells us of some huge
> building that is to appear in these latitudes dedicated to law, subversive of the courts of
> Westminster, and antagonistic to the Roll's and Lincoln's Inn; but nothing *yet* threatens the
> silent beauty of the Temple.
>
> (W 121, ital. added)

Nothing is with certainty exempt from revisionary inputs. Anthony Trollope miraculously
includes an organ of supposedly neutral information as a source for the prophetic imagination that will inform the speculative side of public opinion formation. Still a dim rumor
in 1852, the information does initiate a speculative narrative that wagers on the future.
And if one is obedient to one of the so-called laws of investment—"buy on the rumor; sell
on the news"—so as to maximize value, the reader of Trollope should have bought. There
was in fact a rumor regarding the planned demolition of a gate that historically separated
the Strand (a public channel) from Fleet Street (the traditional home of the press) that was
finally realized in 1878. Instruments of public opinion formation were getting closer to the
public they presumed to inform and represent by a demolition of barriers between them.

There is, therefore, something self-reflexive in public opinion formation: it behaves
like a universal (hence delocalizing) in the same gesture by which it concentrates a highly
local, yet provisional knowledge. It is, even formally, uncannily self-maintaining, both
separable *from* and contained *within* Trollope's narrative—like an absentee landlord.
This homeostatic presence gives it a resemblance to financial markets that enabled the
construction of a number of other "public channels" in the last quarter of nineteenth-
century England. This continuous recontextualization of the local lends public opinion
formation and its agents an elusively restless, emergent quality. A close analogy might
be the work of Trollope's contemporary, the French engraver, Charles Meryon, who
engraved Paris city-scapes that inseparably mixed historically factual with speculative
renderings of a Paris under reconstruction during the Second Empire.

Matthew Beaumont in *On Finding and Losing Yourself in the Modern City*, however, reminds us that the trajectory is a two-way street.[40] A formerly collective (public) space can be colonized, reinvented or repurposed as a constellation of private spaces often limiting access by enhanced image or upscale prices. Vavasor's proposal for a repurposed Embankment Project as a shopping mall in *Can You Forgive Her?* resembles public sports arenas renamed by corporate sponsors. The distinction between a public plaza and private speculation/sponsorship may be obscured by *marketing*.

This *praxis* enables public opinion to be both an agent of perpetual reform while *in itself* under revision and reform, as it absorbs, dilutes, adulterates and repurposes antecedent opinion, social space and performance. This curious historical position lends it a resemblance, as the *Jupiter's* location adjacent to Lincoln's Inn might suggest, to the domiciles of legal practice. Public opinion does indeed become "a law unto itself," as Archdeacon Grantly complains in *The Warden*, but only after it comes to strategically differentiate itself, even as it mimes canon law, in the disguised operations of Trollope's "Tenth Muse."

Notes

1 The resistance to a coherent, self-consistent reading posed by the advent of the handicapped body is the subject of David T. Mitchell and Sharon L. Snyder in their introductory essay, "Disability Studies and the Double-Bind of Representation," in *The Body and Physical Difference: Discoveries of Disability*, ed. Mitchell and Snyder (Ann Arbor and London: Univ. of Michigan Press, 1997), pp. 1–31.

2 See my essay, "'The Key to Dedlock's Gait': Gout as Resistance," in *Literature and Sickness*, ed. David Bevan (Atlanta and Amsterdam: Rodopi, 1993), pp. 25–52.

3 David Wills, *Prosthesis* (Stanford, CA: Stanford Univ. Press, 1995), sees the thematic alignment of disability with fears of humanity as highlighting a conflict that pervades language itself. Because language is always burdened with the task of narrating an artificial representation as if it were natural, the act of speaking or writing is characterized by the substitution of the artificial for the natural. In language dedicated to public opinion formation, the response of the dialogic partner(s) is deposited for later reconfiguration to be "realized" (or not) later.

4 Jürgen Habermas, *The Structural Transformation of the Public Sphere: An Inquiry into a Category of Bourgeois Society*, trans. Thomas Burger and Frederick Lawrence (Cambridge, MA: MIT Press, 1991).

5 Moshe Halbertal and Stephen Holmes, *The Beginning of Politics: Power in the Biblical Book of Samuel* (Princeton and London: Princeton Univ. Press, 2017), argue that both David and Saul upon achieving sovereign political power are progressively corrupted by it to such an extent that God becomes a mere passive onlooker rather than a sovereign protector in guiding attendance.

6 Leslie Stephen, "Anonymous Journalism," *St. Paul's Magazine* 63 (May, 1868), pp. 212–220, ital. added.

7 Andrew Pettegree, *The Invention of the News: How the World Came to Know About Itself* (New Haven and London: Yale Univ. Press, 2014), pp. 310–317, argues that many "correspondents" in the late eighteenth century were in fact workers from the city, law courts, and shipping companies. With the exception of Brice's *Weekly Journal* from Exeter, there was no preferential ordering of news determined by content or importance. Priority was determined by the time of receipt of the story.

8 Anonymous, "The Newspaper Press Reviewed by a Quarterly Reviewer," *Quarterly Review* (1857), pp. 5–8.

9 Eneas Sweetland Dallas, "Popular Literature—the Periodical Press," *Blackwood's Edinburgh Magazine* (January, 1859), p. 97.

10 Anonymous, "Popular Literature—the Periodical Press," *Blackwood's Edinburgh Magazine* (February 1859), pp. 192–194.

11 Ai Weiwei, "How Censorship Works," *International New York Times* (May 9, 2017). The Chinese dissident artist addresses the ways in which in totalitarian regimes, dependency is embraced by all parties in return for practical benefits. These may include government contracts or subsidy in return for thematic restrictions. The repressions of censorship thereby become a (collusive) exchange system: hence a market designed to mitigate risk for artists and government.

12 A.J. Lee, *The Origins of the Popular Press in England* (1855–1914), cited in Aled Jones, *Powers of the Press: Newspapers, Power, and the Public in Nineteenth-Century England* (Aldershot: Ashgate Press, 1996), p. 91.

13 Jacques Derrida, "La Démocratie ajournée," in *L'Autre cap* (Paris: Minuit, 1991), p. 103.

14 Claude Lévi-Strauss, "The Structural Study of Myth," *The Journal of American Folklore* 68, no. 270 (October–December, 1955), pp. 428–444. Although developed in other better-known works, it is in this essay where Lévi-Strauss first discussed myth as an elaborate translation mechanism wherein elements of ritual are preserved according to the formula, *traduttore, traditore*.

15 Although social scientists and political historians regard the oral interviews conducted by Henry Mayhew for *London Labour and London Poor* (1851) as crucial to public opinion formation, it may have had an antecedent. John Stuart Mill's *System of Logic* (1843) in a diversion from his subject very briefly discusses the logic of crowd response to "news."

16 J.L. Austen, *How to Do Things With Words*, ed. J.D. Urmson and Marina Shisa, 2nd edition (Cambridge and London: Harvard Univ. Press, 1997). A performative utterance is neither true nor false, since its performative function is effective only conditionally: it is believed by a listener or the listener acts *as if* he believed it.

17 Oscar Negt and Alexander Kluge, *Public Sphere and Experience*, trans. Peter Labani, Jamie Owen Daniel, and Assanka Ohsiloff (Minneapolis: Univ. of Minnesota Press, 1993), pp. 56–57.

18 Brent S. Sirota, *The Christian Monitors: The Church of England and the Age of Benevolence* (New Haven, CT: Yale Univ. Press, 2014), sees the Anglican Church as influenced by works as diverse as Robert Nelson's *An Address to Persons of Quality and Estate* and those of Mandeville.

19 Alain Badiou, *L'être et l'événément* (Paris: Minuit, 1988), p. 86ff.

20 Slavoj Žižek, *The Sublime Object of Ideology* (London: Verso, 1989), p. 25ff., examines the ways in which Kant's sublime (involving a pleasure possible only through the mediation in effect) is an object raised to the level of an (Impossible/Real) Thing, stripped of ordinary representation. Madame Neroni refers to the "ghostly, ghastly love" (*BT* I 176) that she brings to any suitor, a marvelous description of public opinion. Her physically challenged body functions as an effect, not a representation.

21 W.J. Fox, "On the Duties of the Press Towards the People," *Letters Addressed Chiefly to the Working Classes* IV in *The Spectator*, no. 868 (February 15, 1845). The progressive evacuation of the "reign of patronage" began with the clergy and then extended to "men of letters," leaving public opinion as a patron by default—a metaphoric stepfather.

22 John Zaller, *The Nature and Origin of Mass Opinion* (Cambridge: Cambridge Univ. Press, 1992), p. 43.

23 Louis Menand, "The Unpolitical Animal," *The New Yorker* (20 August 2004), p. 94.

24 Philip Converse, "The Nature of Belief Systems in Mass Politics," in *Ideology and Discontent*, ed. David Apter (New York: Free Press, 1964), pp. 206–261.

25 The Trafalgar Group, founded by Robert Cahaly in 2015, was a more accurate pollster in the 2016 U.S. presidential electoral cycle as well as (considering state by state tallies) the 2020 electoral cycle—closer to actual outcomes than Quinnipiac, Monmouth, Reuters, or Pew. Believing that people are more likely to lie or dissemble in an age of untruthful social media, Trafalgar transforms every respondent into a "pollster" by including their opinion of their neighbors' opinions and reasons for them as a parameter along with education, past voting experience and major issues. Public opinion formation thereby becomes another data point.

26 René Girard, *To Double Business Bound: Essays on Literature, Mimesis, and Anthropology* (Baltimore and London: Johns Hopkins Univ. Press, 1988), pp. 32–44.

27 Philip Converse, "Information Flow and the Stability of Partisan Attitudes," *Public Opinion Quarterly* 26 (1962), pp. 578–589.

28 Michel Goldhaber, "Attention Shoppers!", *Wired Magazine* 5, no. 12 (1997), *http://* www.wired .com/wired/archive/5.12/es. attention.html? pg-34 topic—

29 Walter Benjamin, "One-Way Street," in *Selected Writings*, Vol. I, ed. Marcus Bullock and Michael W. Jennings (Cambridge and London: Harvard Univ. Press, 1996), p. 453.

30 Ross Chambers, *Loiterature* (Lincoln: Univ. of Nebraska Press, 1999), addresses directional deviancy afflicting the assorted *flâneurs* of much modern literature. The loitering in which public opinion dwells, however, seems calculated to enhance a nuanced inconclusiveness: a similar difficulty in making up its mind.

31 Martin Heidegger, *Being and Time*, trans. John Macquarrie and Edwin Robinson (Oxford: Basil Blackwell, 1980), p. 222 ff. Heidegger differentiates the idleness of those who transact gossip with the "hard struggle" necessary to attain "authentic" knowledge. *Gerede* is a kind of deracinated speech which disqualifies it from the work ethic of genuine decision-making.

32 R.H. Super, *Trollope in the Post Office* (Ann Arbor and London: Univ. of Michigan Press, 1981), addresses these and other innovative ideas of Trollope, not always supported by his supervisors.

33 I am indebted to my Acquisitions Editor, Ms. Jessica Mack, who commented on the surplus regulatory role in the establishment of a "cancellation culture" in contemporary public opinion formation, both regulatory and potentially tyrannical. One of the early cancellation designs of the 1840's used on affixed stamps was a Maltese Cross.

34 Raymond Geuss, *Public Goods, Private Goods* (Princeton and London: Princeton Univ. Press, 1999), exposes the profound flaw in a liberalism that would assume a clear distinction between "public" and "private." Geuss's nuanced approach is especially critical of our common criteria for distinguishing a public from a private commodity. As a corollary, he criticizes the ease with which consensus can supposedly be reached by a renomination of private goods as public goods or vice versa.

35 The Limited Liability Act (1855) was a genuine innovation in company law. Previous to its enactment, all partners were individually liable for the whole of the debts of any concern. Prior to 1844, incorporation was possible only by royal charter or private act, and any litigation had to be carried out in the joint names of all the members. The notion of "Limited Liability" offered a version of immunity similar to that which Towers is advancing both personally and for the *Jupiter*. See R. Harris, *Industrializing English Law: Entrepreneurship and Business Organization 1720–1844* (Cambridge: Cambridge Univ. Press, 2000).

36 Louis Althusser, "Ideology and Ideological State Apparatuses," *Essays in Ideology* (London: Verso, 1984). A question left unanswered by Althusser, but crucial to any study of public opinion, would be how the operational automatism of the ISA would be internalized in the absence of the kind of interrogatory experience that Althusser describes. How would it produce nuanced effects on ideological belief in the absence of a real or imaginary injunction?

37 The "time" of public opinion formation (relative and open-ended) seems to differ from ordinary, chronological time insofar as it involves the difference in degree rather than kind that Bergson came to attach to the notion of "duration" at the end of the nineteenth century. Henri Bergson, *Time and Free Will: An Essay on the Immediate Data of Human Consciousness*, trans. F.L. Podgson (Montana: Kessinger, 1910), pp. 76–77, 142.

38 See my *Gossip and Subversion in Nineteenth-Century British Fiction: Echo's Economies* (Basingstoke and New York: Macmillan, 1996), pp. 151–152, regarding Lockwood's initial dismissal of Nelly Dean's narrative as "gossip," before understanding its oral relationship to an assortment of diaries and sacred texts.

39 An extreme example of the denial of "society" or the "public" as a concept might have been Prime Minister Margaret Thatcher's often cited assertion that "only individuals and families exist," not society, in an interview with Douglas Keay, *Women's Own* Magazine (October 31, 1987), p. 3.

40 Matthew Beaumont, *On Finding and Losing Yourself in the Modern City* (London: Verso, 2020), argues that uncertain directionality amid a surplus of unaffiliated markers lends a walk in the modern city some resemblance to unorganized information flows. The proliferation of official and unacknowledged public opinion networks serves as threats to my individual *position*.

Chapter Two

MIMING THE LAW

Public opinion has its Bar as well as the law courts.

(*WWLN* II, 117)

Jacobite pamphleteers, spies, citizens in eighteenth-century coffee houses and ideologues such as Cobbett, all in their separate ways, sought to influence public opinion formation long before the self-appointed instruments and individuals of Trollope's Barsetshire.[1] What is new, however, is a level of self-consciousness by "spokesmen" who claim to represent *and* influence public opinion, rather than merely criticize or subvert a preexisting order. As a wealthy surgeon, John Bold has no identifiable material self-interest or ideological commitment to the causes he champions early in *The Warden*, only attempting to recover excessive tolls on a turnpike which he seldom uses. His is an ideologically disinterested pro bono advocacy, with only marginal interest in an issue of abstract injustice to which he calls public attention: a crucial distinction.

The infirm pensioners at Hiram's Hospital, socially invisible in their dotage, until awakened to an abstraction by an advocate who lacks even the unanimous support of his plaintiffs. They remain divided about endorsing his effort:

> "We wants what John Hiram left us," said Handy: "we wants what's ourn by *law*; it don't matter what we expected; what's ourn by *law* should be ourn."
>
> "*Law*!" said Bunce, with all the scorn he knew how to command—"*law*! Did ye ever know a poor man yet was the better for *law*, or for a lawyer?"

> *(W 34, ital. added)*

For some impoverished pensioners, apparently, going to law is a rich man's game; for others, possession is already established by historical deed as an inalienable gift.

The intriguing legal case advanced in *The Warden* hinges on a material revaluation—and hence possible redistribution—of the proceeds from a charitable bequest. The annual return now far exceeds the initial principal of the gift, willed four centuries previously by John Hiram: a bequest now in surplus. At issue is who should benefit from an unforeseeable *surplus*—an as-yet unrealized inflation in the value of rents. Should it be part of the "living" of the relatively impecunious and aging Warden Harding or to be used to increase the daily welfare allowance of the truly impoverished men in his custodial care? Although the bequest stems from a death contract (Hiram's will), the donor's original intention is no more recoverable than is Madame Neroni's marital status or familial entitlement. The contractual has lost all but historical relevance.

What challenges the jointure of an Establishment comprised of church and state (the duopoly reflected in Trollope's successive *Barsetshire* and *Parliamentary novels*) is the jointure of civic law and its appellate division, public opinion formation. Seams develop, not merely in the conflictual jurisdictions of ecclesiastical and civil law elaborated in the case of the poor Hogglestock curate in *The Last Chronicle of Barset*, accused of theft, but in the increasing vulnerability to public judgment, lacking an established tradition and implicit procedural or institutional guarantees and protections.

The first indication of such a widening seam may well have been anticipated in the third and fourth chapters of Coleridge's *On the Constitution of Church and State*. Coleridge was concerned by an anomaly within the Church of England. The ordained clergy celebrated feast days, administered the sacrament and provided pastoral care while also in possession of vast quantities of inherited terrestrial property. The Anglican Church was simultaneously emergent, party to an ever-originating social contract, yet vested with a materiality. Ministering to the faithful (a person) and maintaining property would risk confusing means with ends. In a maneuver similar to that deployed by so-called deconstructionist critics in dividing the singular into implicit plurality, Coleridge generates something altogether different from the conflict of church and state. In these chapters of *On the Constitution of Church and State* he establishes a reserve which he calls the "Nation" or "Nationality," but which is in fact more nearly akin to the fiction of an alternative sovereignty, tying both to a continuous, symbolic self-determination, the "Third Estate" known as the *clerisy*,[2] which attends without possession.

It is both excess and safety net as opposed to the proprietary (property) as institutionally held: a mediating adjunct, yet also a supplement to the traditional Establishment. Conservators of tradition as well as interpreters of logic and ethics, the *clerisy* adds value by continually redefining the *prima Scientia*, Coleridge's "ground knowledge" which is both immanent and transcendent.[3] He borrows (with acknowledgment) from the Tribe of Levi the outlying 12th tribe of Israel in the Old Testament—prohibited from owning land, but custodians of the faith insofar as they were arbiters of the public weal, charged with sifting claims. For Coleridge similarly, the *clerisy* was a permanent class and fountainhead of the humanities entrusted with the cultivation, enlargement and distribution of knowledge throughout the country. They were (perhaps impossibly) both a guardian of cultural stores and, simultaneously, entrusted with making improvements and adding value to what was to be collectively shared as a kind of *intellectual commons*. The German critic, Klaus Stierstorfer, has gone so far as to suggest that Coleridge's *clerisy*, nonproprietary guardians of cultural assets, is an embryonic version of a National Trust.[4] Although not a National Trust in the sense of a commonly shared material heritage, public opinion becomes a publicly shared facsimile warden or custodian. Bold's suit for redistribution of the enhanced proceeds recasts a bequest as a contested space between church, law and public opinion.

If, as Nietzsche's Zarathustra believed, society is really not a question of contracts, but rather a long search (with its attendant waiting), then this searching is in some sense opposite the contractual. The various eighteenth-century social contracts were in effect extensions of covenant: certain rights were guaranteed if the parties agreed to defined responsibilities and loyalties, much as were last wills and codicils. The assumption of obligations, even those obligations we would now describe as noblesse oblige, created a community into which one was born or which appeared to demand accession as a price for guarantees of security. But once the contractual is compromised—by time (in the case of the Hiram bequest) or violence done to a party to a contract (Madame Neroni's physical challenges due to a marital partner's violence)—there is a fundamental shift *away from a priori* duties and obligations and into other forms of *settlement* and *distributive judgment.*

In its eighteenth-century manifestations, the notion of individual rights was estab-lished a priori, insofar as they had a tangential relationship with the laws of nature. These rights were independent of any power that would be the original share of each human being in the random distribution of natural forces or society's influence. Jean-Jacque Rousseau's pedagogic manual, *Émile, or On Education*, could be read as an extended diatribe against the child's immersion *in* and obedience *to* public opinion which pre-tended to operate by laws. For Rousseau, public opinion represented an unnatural force, removing the adolescent from direct knowledge of the natural world and the invariable laws of nature. In place of natural law, public opinion mimed (as a false representa-tion) man-made law while maintaining the unpredictable variability of natural law. As eunuchs were condemned by nature to a sedentary life,[5] so obedience to opinion condemned man to a sedentary life of subjection to tyrannical laws of social judgment. Rousseau rather urged the acquisition of a trade in Chapter 3, an important defense, by which the child "give[s] nothing to opinion" and thereby "nothing to authority":

> Lower yourself to the artisan's station in order to be above your own. In order to subject fortune and things to yourself, begin by making yourself independent of them. To *reign by opinion, begin by reigning over it.*[6]

Opinion is a false authority in competition with nature and natural rights in Rousseau.

These so-called natural rights were also independent of any acquired merits or vir-tues, as Towers will remind John Bold, then seeking to recover some extra-referential understanding of a relationship previously regarded as contractual. Because these rights were also prior to entitlement, tradition, inherited or acquired privilege, even jurisdic-tion itself in so-called natural rights, they need not be conferred. What is important in the ontology of such rights is an independence from the *referential*, tantamount to a unity before some *sign*. Man would need no other persons, institutions or even social practice as enabling agents, a new *naturality* replacing inheritance.

This a priori character of the rights of man, insofar as they are independent of what is conferred, endowed, developed or earned over time, is tantamount to an investment in the singularity of each individual. Such radical independence is profoundly antisocial insofar as the child would possess them without reference to any *alterity*, the absence of which is precisely what makes these rights irrevocable and inalienable and may account for Rousseau's emphasis upon an artisanal trade. Because no Establishment could either confer or revoke such rights, they obviously represent the potential for excess, an unde-fined extraterritoriality.

This may account for the radical loneliness experienced by Rousseau's Émile (one recalls the foregrounding provided by Defoe's *Robinson Crusoe* in Chapter 3 as well as

among Trollope's clergy). Rev. Harding resigns his sinecure as warden of an eleemosynary institution under the pressure of public opinion, so that the suit might be "finally
adjudicated upon in a court of conscience, a judgment without power of appeal duly
registered" (*W* 163). Like Rousseau's laws of nature, radically internalized individual
conscience cannot be appealed, thereby in an uncanny way, resembling public opinion.
Harding's abject resignation to the privacy of *conscience* (an internalized court of appeal)
is opposite the response of Lily Dale, after her broken engagement to Adolphus Crosbie
in *The Small House at Allington* upon learning that public opinion has silenced her now dis-
possessed voice with its overwhelming *excess*: "I can never again have anything of *my own*
to talk about" (*SHA* 460, ital. added). Does public opinion represent the revenge of the
collective voice (disguised as a singularity) against the radical singularity of conscience?

Although both find it difficult to respond to public opinion for different reasons, both
Bold and the custodial Rev. Harding experience a similar radical solitude, albeit different in both kind and degree from that which ensues upon other forms of abandonment:
Miss Havisham of *Great Expectations* or religious *condamnées*, Catherine and Heathcliff
of *Wuthering Heights*. Phineas Finn, charged in a court of law in *Phineas Redux*, begins
his appeal by addressing public opinion (through the patronage of Madame Goesler)
which recontextualizes the narrative of his crime as narrated by the law. Yet, on occasion, as when Septimus Harding seeks refuge in the radical solitude of conscience—as a
limit of self-possession—no secondary judgments are admissible: "I cannot boast of my
conscience when it required the violence of a public newspaper to awaken it" (*W* 154).
Public opinion has the power to induce "woke-ness" [*sic*], overpowering resistance, the
price of felt aggression.

The metaphor of public opinion as an external wake-up call intrigues. It is as if
"the world" associated with, but on occasion detachable from, the law or history, *sings*.
Conscience can be a law unto itself, not unlike public opinion, held (initially) silently,
albeit tyrannically self-authorizing—which enables them to differentially mime each
other. The effect of the call of public opinion, however, would not be so different from
those touched by the *call* of faith which public opinion operationally often mimes.

An initially unacknowledged *excessive subject* would seem to be crucial to the emergent trajectory of public opinion formation in Barsetshire.[7] In *The Warden* it is surely
represented in Bold's decision to work for those who have no voice, by colluding in the
assimilation/accumulation of a *public voice* which speaks in behalf of someone else. A
genuine political act always involves the *risk* of producing some *excess* or surplus. In *The
Warden* the surplus might be a genuine sympathetic identification by an aging Warden
to his infirm, aging flock. In *Barsetshire Towers*, the surplus had been represented in an
overextended outreach to other previously antagonistic beliefs and practices, not traditionally included within the interests of the Church of England. This theological internationalism opens the way for the intrusion of narrower, local interests, vulnerable to
privatization for a specific agenda. We never know (save retrospectively) whether an
act is an irrational self-destructive gesture, an expression of a conviction, a temporary
negotiating position or an entrée to democratic deliberation. In addition to the surplus
in historically accumulated income from bequests long forgotten, these excesses would
suggest that no genuine political act can ever be entirely *disinterested*. The *extraterritorial*

surplus generates a new field in what had been a largely contractual or semi-contractual relationship with limited exposure to public opinion.

An individual's surroundings are no longer defined *by* or constituted *in* axiological intention, which already has a noetic structure. Neither the individual nor his sponsors may have previously recognized the plurality embodied in the very notion of a public for a number of reasons. In the case of Rev. Harding, it may have been clouded by regarding the men in his custodial care as objects of pity and compassion rather than legal assertion, with (admittedly divided) wills of their own. In the cases of Alice Vavasor of *Can You Forgive Her?*, Lily Dale of *The Small House at Allington* or the prematurely aging Lady Mabel (Grex) of *The Duke's Children*, the marital promissory note of a long engagement or assumed familial dedication to an advantageous prenuptial contract, effectively removes women from one definition of public opinion: the exposure to social circulation and speculation that characterize all free markets, including marital prospects and the gossip about them. Even the resort to litigation, as John Bold soon understands, would offer no escape from public opinion, since current and hence circumstantial, opinions might trump historically embodied legal opinion encoded in supposed contract law.

This is a "Being-with" which is both more and less than a relation or bond that is conditioned by the preexistence of the terms and conditions of its existence. This awakened sociality is nothing less than the recognition of a contemporaneity, surely one reason why the enlistment of the local media is so important: the "with" denotes the sharing of time–space that Jean-Luc Nancy has addressed in his *Being Singular Plural*.[8] This sharing clearly involves some reduction, a diminution of the radically individuated self, defined only as a locus or locale of obligation and contract or conscience, a radical contract with oneself. The contractual, because it is activated either by a foundational moment or some joint pledge (a promissory bond to be redeemed later) is context specific insofar as it is exclusionary, binding only parties and their sponsors. Public opinion is a guided interest that threatens to banish the autonomous (rather sleepy, in the case of the paternal Harding) self. But no identifiable organs possess it; as with the *Jupiter*, they only "take credit" after evoking it from some noncontractual institutional neutrality. As with other developments like railroads in mid-nineteenth-century Britain, a social field that obscures individual entry points is being assembled. The Rev. Slope is no longer a mere granter and receiver of messages (the Lord's word) from afar as the bishop's chaplain in *Barchester Towers*, but a node in a social nexus of inconsistently aligned ideological positions.

As soon as the issues at stake in the Hiram's Hospital Trust affair are made known, the *praxis* of the law in *The Warden* lends it a superficial resemblance to the supporting cast of Chancery in Dickens's *Bleak House*. The distribution of the procedural *copy* is antecedent to the distribution of the proceeds of a bequest and suggests an alliance between law-making and bureaucracy with attendant delays:

> Sir Abraham Haphazard had been consulted, but *his opinion* was not yet received; copies of Hiram's will, copies of wardens' journals, copies of leases, copies of accounts, copies of everything that could be copied, and some that could not, had been sent to him; and the case was assuming *creditable* dimensions.
>
> *(W 59, ital. added)*

The law is an accumulation (of antecedent references) to which one can over time grant a qualified belief, if aligned as part of a logically consistent narrative. As with the rejoinders and affidavits meticulously copied in *Jarndyce v. Jarndyce* in Dickens's *Bleak House*, the law in Trollope initially operates by repetitioning *reference* and derivatively, antecedence, even when the relevance of the antecedence is questionable due to surplus. The need for ever more referencing produces the characteristic waiting "to see justice done" (*W* 29), part of the procedural complexity and administrative delay of the law, but held within it. One of the delays involves discovery as to whether or not one of the aged pensioner-plaintiffs is or is not *non compos mentis* (W 29, original emphasis), of unsound mind. Whether he is or is not a qualified plaintiff can only be legally determined, so that the qualification to participate in the law's recoveries and discoveries is legally determined in a heuristic that abets delay. A procedural self-referentiality assumes an importance equivalent to the conditions of the initial historical contract.

The recourse to civil law in *The Warden*, as it will in *The Last Chronicle of Barset*, occurs only after a pro forma attempt to enlist a reluctant clergy: "to address a petition to the bishop as a visitor, paying his lordship to see justice done" (*W* 29). Yet, all along, Trollope's narrator makes clear that the appeal to religious authority is already regarded as only a polite formality. Early on, John Bold realizes that the clergy were unlikely to render judgment against one of their own, Septimus Harding, but he must retain strategic courtesy. Beset by procedural delays in the administration of civil law and institutional bias in the court of ecclesiastical law, Bold sends copies of a petition addressed to the bishop to "all the leading London papers [...] thereby to obtain notoriety for the subject" (*W* 29). The issue ceases to be entirely sub judice (of church or state) but has entered the extraterritorial surplus of *publicité*.

The errant *copy* of a petition has been *leaked*, further circulated extralegally and hence made excessive.[9] It addresses neither recuperation of precedent nor further testimony, but wider knowledge of the case under the assumption that there is an unawakened general interest to be "taken up" from an initially limited application. Bold and his attorney, Finney, set the groundwork for an appeal to the public, a detour around the law that must nonetheless resemble it, if it is to engage public interest:

> This it was thought would pave the way for *ulterior* legal proceedings. It would have been a great thing to have had the signatures and marks of all the twelve injured legatees, but this was impossible. Bruce would have cut off his hand sooner than sign it.
>
> *(W 29, ital. added)*

The press is enlisted as a unifying political channel for divided plaintiffs, mediating between a reluctant clergy and some "ulterior legal proceedings" where Bold and his tentative plaintiffs would hope the case is adjudicated. Its status as a class action suit could only be legally determined, hence furthering strategic delay. The defendant, with his love of quiet, has an increasing "horror of being made the subject of *public talk*" (*W* 46, ital. added). The absence of genuine unity or determined jurisdictional boundaries is filled by the *Jupiter* insinuating itself as amicus curiae. J. Hillis Miller is surely on to something, in suggesting that Trollope's obsessive writing of novels "was an attempt to write a novel which would assuage his need for a written ascertained moral law."[10] This book argues that a "Tenth Muse" of public opinion, resistant to inscription by definition, becomes a facsimile of that fictive moral law, equally prey to misreading.

The press offers for public consumption what had previously been a minor contract dispute by parties to a will long forgotten by history in the same way that intoning or train schedules on the Sabbath have been forgotten in *Barchester Towers*. The law calls attention to what has been allegedly suppressed, but newly brought to light, once distributed by organs of public opinion which enlarge the heretofore (provisionally) shared field of interests in its own interest. Temporal delay is monetized as income:

> As to Finney, the attorney, he was beside himself. What? To be engaged in the same cause and on the same side with the *Jupiter*, to have had the views he recommended seconded, and furthered, and battled for by the *Jupiter*. Perhaps to have his own name mentioned as that of the learned gentlemen whose efforts had been successful on behalf of the poor of Barchester! He might be examined before committees of the House of Commons, with heavens knows how much a day for his personal expenses—he might be engaged for years on such a suit!
>
> (W 61)

Organs of public opinion (the *Jupiter*) and the law have a working relationship. Advocacy in behalf of the downtrodden that had initially emboldened a pro bono gesture has its material compensations for the attorney selected by Bold as he would select any other commodity. An enhanced public reputation denoted by the concept of a career, unnecessary for members of the Establishment whose careers are determined for them by ordination or inheritance. The procedural waiting for the resolution of a minor civil contract dispute, once deposited in the larger plaza of public opinion formation, is incorporated into the trajectory of a professional life. If legally affirmed, historical possession (beneficiaries of a deed) by those without possessions, threatens to become a *universal* acceptance, miming public opinion.

Universal recognition by the House of Commons with a more than ample per diem maintenance allowance and the possibility of a temporal extension in the resolution of the suit are projected as long-term investments by Attorney Finney—all as a consequence of an alliance with the *Jupiter*. His life is imagined as *incrementally* spaced stepping stones represented in the accumulations of the curriculum vitae. Public opinion is a similar jerry-built "body" created in alliance with the incremental daily press which maintains interest day by day. Attorney Finney wants nothing less than what the new bishop Proudie desired in *Barchester Towers*: a political life that will leave the parsing and discipline of doctrinal or legal *sentence*—to borrow a medieval notion—to underlings who must carry on. There is an extramural *publicité* that afflicts the dedication to institutional practices that, as we shall see, thematically links the *Barsetshire Chronicles* to the *Palliser Novels*.

***

Trollope never fails to evoke a peculiar kind of emptiness, a powerlessness of the particularities that previously represented the life of the disadvantaged, which is partially a consequence of this wider sphere of interest in quasi-universals. In his reflective volume, *Emancipation(s)*, Ernesto Laclau conceives of this quest for universals by a dedicated professional class not as the pursuit of a substantive element with positive qualities, but rather pursuit of a placeholder lacking content:

> It is because the universal has no necessary body and no necessary content; differential groups, instead, compete between themselves to *temporarily* give to their particularities a function of universal representation. Society generates a whole vocabulary of empty signifiers whose *temporary* signifieds are the result of a political competition.[11]

This occurs most obviously when in *Phineas Redux* a number of his women admirers attempt to gain the support of the powerful Duke of Omnium to find a new place in a new government for the handsome Irishman, Phineas Finn, whose liberal views they endorse. Finn's succession of parliamentary seats—one of them, a so-called pocket borough—will be ultimately abandoned in the wake of the debate over the Second Reform Bill. But appeals by admirers fall on deaf ears of the power broker, the Duke of Omnium, who demurs with the comment: "I never interfere" (*PR* I, 336). As the aged patriarch of the Liberals, he is invariably consulted and often offers advice in the *Palliser Novels*, but demurs from direct intercession because his aristocratic status already constitutes a silent interference. The knowledgeable Lady Glencora, wife of the future prime minister, rejoins in an aside, "Who does interfere? *Everybody* says the same. *Somebody* interferes, I suppose" (*PR* I, 338, ital. added), before requesting of her husband, Plantagenet Palliser, that he accept no position unless he can bring along "one or two friends with you" (*PR* I 338). A conditional economy of political exchange has been initiated so that an anonymous *somebody* is separated only with difficulty from *everybody*. Ideology enters a quid pro quo exchange market.

This intensifying competition for influence determines the signifieds at any *given time*, effectively making a fickle public opinion, subsidized by the contemporaneity of the daily press, a crucial player in Habermas's *contested arena*. Public opinion in Laclau's model would be neither a potentially harmonious symphony with a strong conductor nor a self-cancelling acoustic machine with the intense, conflictual particularities that produce cacophony, but an *Ur*-emptiness, posing as a community narrative: the perpetually incomplete fullness of excess. It is *everywhere*, but we cannot locate it.

As society changes over time, an historically determined identification is opened to new particularities, each of which rushes in to fill a gap. Different projects and unpredictable interventions then try to hegemonize the empty signifiers, resulting in a competitive *field* among interests. They must, however, incorporate some of the emptiness into a new *body* that retains the empty signifier, existing largely as an abstract effect.[12] We inhabit the effects of an anonymous operation.

In one sense, Tom Towers, editor of the *Jupiter*, has made the characteristic career move in the public opinion game as will Phineas Finn (of the *Palliser* novel that bears his name). Finn, a native of Ireland, has been sponsored by his father to study the law as an apprentice to Attorney Low under the assumption that he will return to Ireland to practice law. Although he is an intelligent, albeit indifferent and restless student, Finn abandons the study of law, upon being recruited to stand as a candidate for the Loughshane constituency by the Liberals, as if substituting (even occupationally) the electoral verdict of public opinion over the law. His law tutor, Low, reminds him that he has his career trajectory backward: he should first complete a law degree (enabling the income needed for a life of service) before standing for Parliament, a course which by the end of the novel, Low himself fulfills by becoming an MP.

His recalcitrant student, however, simply sees the abandonment of his study of the law as a temporary change of educational programs. Learning how to practice law is really no different from learning how to learn procedural public opinion formation, but the latter involves no textbooks, only guidance from those who are in its *work*:

> Why, the *thing is a study in itself.* As for learning it in a year, that is out of the question. But I am convinced that if a man intends to be a useful member of Parliament, he should make a study of it.
>
> *(PF I 44, ital. added)*

The law is abandoned as a subject in favor of the study of how to court public opinion. Low, who will become an MP at about the time Finn is contemplating departure, reminds the new MP for Loughshane that absent a qualification as a lawyer as a career insurance policy, Phineas Finn will be a tool of public opinion. Indebtedness to the indeterminacy of devotion to the ministers who maintain the church of public opinion, "you will be the creature of some minister, not his colleague" (*PF* I, 46). If the interests of the law are in part an interest in the procedural, then Low, unlike his former apprentice, understands the interface between law, the institutional politics of Parliament and public opinion as a law unto itself that often rivals codified law.

Against the advice of his tutor to whom he has apprenticed himself, Finn takes up private residence with the Bunce family as a novice MP from Ireland in material debt due to the social demands of London life. Public opinion demands investment in the social life of political clubs and entertainment shared with wealthier MPs. In need of financial support, Finn imagines Lady Standish as an (impossible) marital partner even as we read of bills in arrears for six months. Finn is attracted to women *already spoken for* and hence out of circulation, albeit held *in durance* by the Victorian long engagement to a partner *always-already* spoken for.

In Parliament at the foot of his mentors in the formation and deformation of electoral public opinion, Mildmay and Monk, the dust of the academic discipline sticks to Phineas as it does to Tom Towers, in the form of his landlord's occupation and syndicalist politics. Would-be reformers must "moonlight"—holding down a plurality of occupations to support their political apprenticeship—a practice unknown to those born to political life:

> Mr. Bunce was a *copying* journeyman, who spent ten hours a day in Carey Street with a pen between his fingers, and after that he would spend two or three hours of the night with a pen between his fingers in Marlborough Street.
>
> *(PF I 67, ital. added)*

A lodger rather than a tenant—and hence disenfranchised until the passage of the Second Reform Bill now being debated in Trollope's pages—the struggling copyist, Bunce, is caught up in a mob demonstration—one representation of the ad hoc informality of public opinion—by fellow radical supporters of Turnbull, and arrested. Unable to gain access to his incarcerated landlord, like Trollope habitually dedicated to inscription, the fledgling MP, Phineas Finn, is denied access. When it crosses police lines, uncontrolled public opinion becomes a rival of the law, just as the application of law is reshaped by public opinion in a symbiotic relationship in Trollope:

> When they think that they have *public opinion* on their side, there is nothing in the way of *excess* which is too great for them.
>
> *(PF I 259, ital. added)*

Hoping to reduce the advantageous surplus on the "law and order" side of public opinion, the novice MP from Loughshane accepts the card of Quintus Slide, a recruiter of talent for "one of those excellent penny papers" (*PF* I 241), as Trollope's narrator ironically remarks, now penetrating the local information market. Although Slide initially presents himself as editor of the sheet, on later visits Finn meets the real editor who enables the later deniability of Slide, a trait shared with Tom Towers's curious recusals when imposed upon. There is always a phantom presence behind whomever seems in charge of shaping public opinion that offers cover against being held responsible as a hand in its production. *The People's Banner* would hope to keep Bunce's cause—a circumstantial cause given the accidental conditions under which he was seized by the law at an unruly political demonstration—alive by becoming a writer for the radical paper, initially in his spare time. Not yet a paid cabinet member, Finn needs both a voice and the money that may result from the literal care and feeding of a public, as a part-time journalist/politician/lapsed law student. In the words of Slide whose name, like that of the Rev. Slope, may suggest the inconsistently held opinions of both men:

> You'll find, Mr. Finn, that in *public life* there's nothing like having a horgan [*sic*] to back you. What is the most you can do in the 'Ouse? Nothing, if you're not reported. You're speaking to the country;—ain't you? And you can't do that without a horgan [*sic*], Mr. Finn.
>
> *(PF I 241–42, ital. added)*

The "horgan" [organ] of public opinion formation, a speculative vox populi, is a metaphoric open mouth. It is periodically fed in reciprocity with its own reciprocal periodic interventions initiated by a promissory deposit, upon which it offers to return a sustaining "interest." Again, competition, in this case energy of circulation vs. the boring, official parliamentary gazettes, defines the rather empty body of public opinion formation as promoted by Slide: "forty, fifty, sixty, a hundred thousand *copies* coursing through the arteries and veins of the *public body*" (*PF* I 238, ital. added). Master copyists of papers in circulation supplant the legal copy as part of the lifeblood of public opinion. This seems to fulfill a belief implanted by the Liberal whip, Barrington Erle, who has instructed his student, Phineas Finn, early on that parliamentary debate is useful only for creating public opinion among those "on the outside" or "creating some future House of

Commons," but not important at all for any deliberations of "great questions" (*PF* I 15). External orality (public opinion) is more important than soporific, because often mired in the procedural, bartered parliamentary trade-offs.

This would establish an exchange market with banked interests on which both parties—popular press and a novice MP with no other source of income—might draw upon request. The demands of public opinion seem to emerge when the traditional values (or individuals unable to find their place within them) are held *in durance*: existentially, in terms of career choices, the claims of the law upon them or negotiations by rival interests involving historical succession within institutions.[13] The cynical Madame Goesler, a wealthy European émigré accepted in London high society, warns a politically ambitious Phineas Finn living beyond his means about the gaps created in a fickle parliamentary democracy, defined by periodic interruptions represented in lost votes of confidence. To the Phineas Finn who fears he has been compromised by his first defection from his party's ideology, Madame Goesler sees periodic interruption by public opinion as a determinant of law-making in Parliament:

> Of course, I do not understand,—but it was only the other day when Mr. Mildmay was there, and only the day before that when Lord de Terrier was there, and then only the day before when Lord Brock was there.
>
> *(PF II 256)*

Political turnover and hedging are so frequent that the continental-born Madame Goesler has difficulty understanding its importance to the participants. Candidates are both standing *for* and held *by* an imminent surrender to an electoral process. Public opinion then mimes the irresolvable status of interrupted continuity which, as we shall see, characterizes certain aspects of the history of the law in nineteenth-century England.

Rather than being abandoned *to* the law as are Dickens's drifting orphans, Tom Towers and Phineas Finn abandon the law to which they had been initially bound as apprentices prior to devoting themselves to a "similar abstraction without a cause" (*W* 123), public opinion, as the oxygen of political life. As Phineas Finn is drawn into taking rooms in the dwelling of a copyist of legal documents, so Towers had moved from merely copying the court record to creative editorials for a relatively new medium, duplicating the institutional movement of nineteenth-century journalism from the papers that merely publicized government announcements ("gazettes") to creatively making (through editorial commentary) in some productive and less trustworthy sense, the news. Although Towers "wore no ermine" (*W* 124), as do judges, he regards himself as charged with "inward importance" (*W* 124), a disguised power resembling that of judges.

Absent full qualifications to practice law, like Phineas Finn, Towers moves easily between an abandoned practice, an occasional reporter for a number of papers and public opinion formation, not only geographically given the proximity of institutions dedicated to their activities, but intellectually as well. After abandoning his fledgling law career, Towers claims to have fallen in love with shaping public opinion through the *Jupiter* to such an extent that, even if offered "a judge's seat, he would hardly have left his present career" (W 124). Public opinion is so miming and displacing of the law as to become a quasi "law unto itself," attracting circulating petitions to papers. Read as an allegory of the complex relationship between law and public opinion formation (as opposed to a fortuitous career opportunity), Trollope's Barsetshire becomes the site of a continuous contest of the "forces" between law and public opinion. It has its most elegant historical articulation in A. V. Dicey's *Lectures on the Relation Between Law and Public Opinion in England During the Nineteenth Century* (1914).

Trollope's clergy find themselves gradually coming under civil legal jurisdiction as opposed to that of presumably more sympathetic ecclesiastical courts, perhaps an unexpected side effect of the ecumenical attempt to enlarge the field of their interests. This double-sided "opening" to litigation subjects the church to an unexpected, altogether different, watchful *presence*. Harmony is now recoverable only as the gestural pantomime on the imaginary violoncello mimefully played continuously as a mere gesture in idle moments by Septimus Harding.[14] In a world so filled with plural, cacophonous plaintiffs and antagonistic defendants there is little spare time to practice social harmony:

> "Very sorry to keep you waiting, Mr. Warden," said Sir Abraham, shaking hands with him, "and sorry, too, to name so disagreeable an hour, but your notice was short, and as you said today, I named the very earliest hour that was not disposed of."
>
> *(W 150)*

Like the physically challenged Madame Neroni, the barrister, Sir Abraham Haphazard, is slightly deformed at the waist as a consequence of "his constant habit of leaning forward" (W 150) in the act of addressing an intended audience of judges or attending upon their judgments, just as those leaning forward to attend upon assertion and gossip. As John Bold discovered early on when he had tried to engage Towers in a reasonable dialogue, Haphazard "never had time to talk, he was so taken up with speaking" (W 151), creating a distinction between formalities of address. This is surely one symptom of public opinion's commitment to continuous address—keeping it going (as/with the law)—rather than genuine engagement with a prospective interlocutor. It is a distinction not dissimilar from that between *hearing*, *listening* and *understanding* enunciated by Nancy.[15] In one sense, the *voice* of public opinion might represent an interruption in the potential of the dialogic, insofar as it resists easy singular engagement, either because of an anonymity in its representative or a surplus akin to a mob.

Those either in pursuit *of* or "caught up" (one way or another) *in* public opinion, initiated by those who attend upon the law, are or imagine themselves to be largely self-made or, like Madame Neroni, self-constructed, inventing themselves as they go along. Even Abraham Haphazard, the attorney entitled to a "Sir" prefixed to his name, entrusted to counsel Rev. Harding, *imagines* himself to be part of a meritocracy on an earned career slope to be negotiated as he climbs, without the benefit of wealth or connections:

> No one had thrust him forward; no powerful friends had pushed him along on the road to power. No, he was attorney-general, and would, in all human probability be Lord

Chancellor by sheer dint of his own industry and talent. [...] Why should he respect any
but himself?

(W *151*)

Attorneys initially appear as self-made and narcissistic. If the law as a profession creates a name for itself, even *haphazardly*, so the field of practice gives the impression
of being built up over time, as a function of reputation, just as are the new breed of
clergymen, editors and lawyers in the *Barsetshire Chronicles*. When the warden, Rev.
Harding, confesses to his attorney his fears that he may have unwillingly violated the
will of Hiram's Hospital's founder, Sir Abraham reminds him that "the altered circumstances in which we live do not admit" (*W* 152) in every instance the determination or recuperation of intentionality. There is no evidence he had even read Hiram's
will. Motives deduced after the fact open a space outside the operation of the law for
public opinion to suggest (even in the imagination) a will or motive, even when not
recoverable.

At the conclusion of *The Warden*, Rev. Harding resigns his sinecure in the face of
the opposition of public opinion, generated and maintained by the *Jupiter*. The kindly
old-fashioned councilor to the infirm retreats inwardly to another "close," in Trollope's
words, the "court of conscience" (*W* 163). This is by no means a completely successful retreat, for at the outset there remains some excess, the materiality exacted by the
procedural operation of the law, which looms over the court of conscience. Although
Archdeacon Grantly muses that "as the action was abandoned, the costs would not be
heavy" (*W* 161), there is some residual (excess cost) to be paid by the church nonetheless.
*The law is selectively abandoned both as a career path and by those seeking its determinations in favor
of an (externally financed) flirtation with public opinion.*

Public opinion in *The Warden*, like the law, seems simultaneously of great impact and
yet mysteriously on occasion, abandoned and abandoning, procedurally both "open"
and "closed," a presence simultaneously deferred, yet always potentially imminent. At
certain unpredictable moments it suddenly dissembles what had seemed its internal
concerts. The meaning of the world must be found, apparently, both *within* and *without*,
a strange faith that enacts a curious inadequacy to itself.[16] If the law resembles faith in
its attempted recovery of a legal equivalent to an antecedent, apostolic succession of
opinions and judgments and their interpretation, so public opinion has a resemblance
to both faith and the law. It is *there* and not *there*, obscured from direct access by intermediaries whose contributions and self-interests are often disguised.

Having wrestled with his conscience during a dark night of the sleepless soul in
London (a tradition common to a crisis of faith), the gentle Harding awakens to a prospect across the churchyard of St. Paul's to the London offices of his defense team, Cox
and Cummins, Barristers at Law. Shopkeepers go about their early preparations (*W*
162–63). The law must be paid when due and is hence *transactional* rather than transcendent or determining. Attorneys are no different from the shopkeepers whose mercantile interests are part of the same view. Other than awakening the attorney-general
for an *opinion*, the law's work is largely that of bureaucratic facilitation, a subject to which
Trollope, once a bureaucrat, will frequently return.

Though perhaps a "stretch" (public opinion tending to exaggeration), Harding's unanticipated exposure to public opinion surely has a resonance in more contemporary philosophical discourse. For Martin Heidegger, the disconnectedness attendant upon *ex*-posure (being placed outside oneself) opens the true foundation of each Dasein. An uncontrolled public trafficking allows no appeal to transcendence in this "thrownness":

> When in falling, we flee into the "at-home" of publicness, we flee *into the face of* the "not-at-home," that is, we flee in the face of the uncanniness which lies in Dasein—in Dasein as thrown-Being-in-the-world, which has been delivered over to itself in its being.[17]

There is a feeling of some deliverance attendant upon the radical homelessness experienced by a guardian spirit, entrusted with watchfulness over his infirm wards. This "thrownness" is narrated as an enlightening (awakening?) displacing sleeplessness. As we shall see below, the nature of the house (Hiram's Hospital) is transformed into a rationalized space of intermittent attendance rather than a family home.

Yet one difference between the operations of the law and law-making and those of public opinion emerges. The law has specific hours and does sleep just as do the soporific clergy (save for Harding's restless night) and in attendant members of Parliament in Trollope's rather snoozy novels, to borrow from an admiring reader, former cabinet minister, Roy Hattersley.[18] The shocked Phineas Finn who discovers that law-makers retire quite early as if in mere perfunctory attendance:

> At half-past seven so many members had deserted their seats that Phineas began to think that he might be saved all further pains by a "count-out." He reckoned the members present and found out that they were below the mystic forty.
>
> *(PF I 181)*

Surrounded by gentlemen's clubs, often sponsored by different political parties, Parliament appears to share some of the same contours: members nod off or absent themselves in other ways as does Phineas Finn, mentally. On a committee dedicated to bureaucratic trivialities like awarding the contract for potted peas used by the armed forces, Phineas interrupts the increasingly boring bureaucratic work of Westminster: "Twice he had gone to the potted peas inquiry, but he had gone to *The People's Banner* more often than that" (*PF* I 259). To abandon the law is apparently a stepping stone to the abandonment of law-making, in favor of courting public opinion in an innovative, but distrustful, press, which gives the illusion of speaking directly *to*, rather than always being previously *spoken for*, by interests. The law, politics and the clergy are strategically vulnerable to interruption and absenteeism, so prevalent as to be incorporated into their structural and operational efficiencies. But public opinion formation and the agents and organs who attend upon its care and feeding, by contrast, have a kind of eternal wakefulness in Trollope as they do in those who "tweet" at irregular hours, in perpetual response mode.

***

The prosthetic nature of the law that enables its structural evolution to be compared with public opinion formation in mid-nineteenth-century Britain is noteworthy. With its joint (and therefore divided) origins in courts of common law and courts of equity, until incompletely combined by the Judicature Act of 1857, there was created a curious opening in what constitutes a codified (and hence referentially accessible) body of the law. Lacking a written constitution, British courts of common law had recourse only to the application of (presumably commonly shared) custom, so that the law was in fact "in the breast of the judge."[19] Because Equity Law was developed to offset law determined by precedent and custom (as opposed to those based on laws established by legislation), it marked a new dispensation, now obscured in British legal history. *Equitable* relief could be obtained when there was no "adequate remedy at law" which frequently occurred when monetary damages were inapplicable. Like the censorship of public opinion, the Law of Equity was often applied as an injunction or restraining order against a continuing practice for which monetary compensation was either inapplicable or indeterminable. Public opinion can both enable and restrain.

Dicey was to intimate that public opinion had a more privileged role in the legal history of his country, than codified law intimated, bringing life to its moribund body:

> The amount of such judge-made law is in England far more extensive than a student easily recognizes. Nine-tenths, at least, of the law of contract, and the whole of the law of torts are not to be discovered in any of the statutes. Many Acts of Parliament [...] are little less than the reproduction in a statuary shape of rules originally established by the Courts. Judge-made law has in such cases passed into statute law.[20]

A large portion of contract law is already an aggregate of individual and often arbitrary voices—one definition of public opinion—perhaps fleeting, but having a permanent presence. In Dicey's lectures, Equity Law is a "voice of the judge" outside history, insofar as it initially leaves no historical record in the statues, though later codified to become virtually undistinguishable from common law.

Earlier, in Lecture II, "Characteristics of Law-Making Opinion," the slightly revisionist utilitarian legal scholar described the powerful role necessarily played by public opinion in the evolution of a British legal tradition. Dicey compared it to the same breezy force to whose direction the ideological wind sock, Rev. Slope, had been charged with determining in the early chapters of *Barchester Towers*:

> A cross-current of opinion may be described in any body of belief or sentiment which, while strong enough to affect legislation is, yet in a measure *independent of,* though perhaps not directly opposed to, the dominant legislative creed of a particular era.[21]

Public opinion is a powerful effect, yet somehow independent of what is regarded as the law even as it informs the law. How could it establish independence while not being on occasion opposed to the law, unless it possessed incredibly amorphous qualities, easily afflicted by informational crosscurrents? Public opinion is, for Dicey, never entirely separable from the law, both informing each other, but with different temporalities. The implications of such a view are more profound: *law* would thereby become less an object of truth and more a matter of understanding how to feed public opinion and (over time) learning how to digest and equitably metabolize what it offers.

For Dicey further adds that these crosscurrents, as also "public opinion of a given time," on close examination may be found to be "due to some general or common cause."[22] But, if the cause were indeed common (as in the commonness of common law), one wonders how it could possibly at the same time be "in a measure independent?" Is public opinion for Dicey a constituent part of the law at the same time that the law is clearly embodied in public opinion and vice versa in a symbiotic relationship? These admittedly rhetorical questions would arise only if public opinion (1) could inform the law and law-making, (2) detach itself from the law so as to be an object of extralegal appeal or (3) serve as an agent in the successful application of the law in the interests of garnering public support. Some might argue that the two facets of the law are distinct and that the impact of public opinion on the findings of courts as to guilt or innocence in specific trials is very different from the impact of public opinion on elections to Parliament which enact laws, occasionally in response to public demand.

As did Dicey, the late theologian-philosopher Emmanuel Levinas would find the same "crosscurrents" affecting both. For Levinas, ethics describes the encounter with other human beings not merely as that of acknowledging the Other, but of being called to responsibility *for* the Other. In ethics, a singular subject substitutes itself for the "face" of the Other—that which cannot be grasped by concepts or represented by the memory or other historical programs or even felt by the emotions—a relationship beyond essence. Politics, on the other hand, is an ontological praxis of mediation among three or more members (Levinas's infamous "Le Tiers"). What emerges is a calculation of what is due to each of them, unrelated to autonomy. Questions are raised about duties, rights and what is owed to each other.[23] The "I" is placed in a relationship with a human totality, but not a totality of a unity. The search for justice could never be terminated in Levinas's scheme, but is a continuous search for apportioning shares of responsibility in the fairest way possible, after positing possible thematizations of events and outcomes.

In *The Three Clerks* an ambitious civil servant with experience of dabbling in shares, made highly volatile by rumor, becomes trustee of a ward's fortune. Involved in a scheme of misappropriation at the urging of her relative who wishes to entice the funds for an investment, Alaric Tudor is charged with criminal breach of trust. He stands trial at the Old Bailey, defended by the same wily Chaffanbrass employed by Phineas Finn in a later novel. A jury is initially divided on the degree of Tudor's responsibility as he had made an honest attempt to restore the paper loss by urging his coconspirator to sell his shares at a profit. The pugnacious attorney admits that he is fighting a rearguard action "of washing a blackamoor" (*TTC* 480) by impugning the role of a peer of the Scottish realm, the civil servant's unindicted coconspirator, Undecimus Scott. The jury indeed apportions shares of responsibility, finding the accused guilty of one count and not guilty of the other four charged in the indictment. An initial narrative that had held the defendant entirely responsible, attempts to assign proportional blame "to palliate his guilt" (*TTC* 477), at the same time as British political life gropes its way through a concept of enhanced proportional representation. More than determining guilt or innocence, justice must consider the distribution of responsibility.

This is achieved when a legal advocate shifts the narrative of a crime so that a jury (as opposed to a summary judgment from the bench, more common in the villages) reaches a consensus on a shared narrative of transgression. As per Levinas, justice is an endless search through law, like politics, to overcome the violence of indifference. Chaffanbrass must become an imaginative writer of "high art" (*TTC* 461), to affect a believable scenario, much as politicians search for an engaging platform and writers, a plot sufficiently believable for audience investment.

This intimate, but on occasion detachable, relationship between law and public opinion results in an entirely different outcome in *The Vicar of Bullhampton* where marked class distinctions empower men like Harry Gilmore, "country gentleman, the county magistrate, the man of acres" (*VB* 209), hence part of the squirearchy, to stand in biased judgment as a magistrate in local criminal cases. The substance, framework and social objectives of law (as a contract) become uncertain, a contested arena of potentially conflictual, rather than an alliance of shared, interests in Trollope's novel. Although multi-plotted, the novel centers on the transgressions of two children of an impoverished, aging miller, Carry and Sam Brattle. The daughter has been banished by her strict father and the ravages of public opinion as a "fallen" woman, deserted by an unknown partner and in popular opinion now a "woman of the evening." Sam, equally itinerant in his periodic, unexplained absences from the mill, is indicted for the murder of Farmer Turnbull. Although the evidence against the youth is entirely circumstantial—his having been seen previously in the presence of two known petty criminals nearby—Brattle is initially even denied bail, despite the intercessions of the mild Vicar of Bullhampton, Francis Fenwick, a fishing companion during Brattle's childhood. The vicar has a mysteriously intimate knowledge of the character of his parishioners, a rare accessibility, even when they jump bail. A man of ecumenical flexibility, he gives the benefit of doubt, unlike local magistrates, as a necessary first stage of redemption.

Previously known to filch the odd apple from neighborhood orchards, the itinerant Sam Brattle is condemned by landholding squires and especially the dependent farmers who hold leases from the powerful, rich Marquis of Trowbridge, owner of two-thirds of the acreage in the county. In a village community any past, trivial transgression upon landed interests trumps the absence of evidence in a capital case, where legal opinion is initially controlled by privilege and those attached to it. Because the Marquis' numerous tenants are in his pocket politically, public opinion has such unanimity as to function like a feudalistic contract, a jury unto itself, leaving no room for slow deliberations. What had been the fulcrum of an Establishment—landed interests and church—becomes a wedge so large that the bishop himself is petitioned to mediate the growing enmity between the Marquis of Trowbridge and Rev. Fenwick over the youth's guilt.

The Marquis is so opposed to the release of Sam Brattle (for whom the vicar stands bail) as to personalize the dispute. The county's prime landlord is opposed by one serving a different Lord. The division in influencing public opinion widens to such an extent that in a pique of revenge, Trowbridge donates land for a dissenting Methodist chapel, that nearly encroaches upon Fenwick's vicarage, partially supported by tithes.

The new chapel with its prosthetic, jerry-built façade, open at all hours to chanting voices of dissenters heard through open windows, is virtually an "open Church" (*VB* 238). Because the chapel "spreads dissent at the cost of the [Established] Church" (*VB* 281), it would resemble Habermas's model of open, deliberative plazas—the space of public opinion, standing amid a Queen's Way and a vicarage of the church on land donated by the privileged. The encroachment of unregulated voices, a synecdoche for public opinion, leaves it open to judicial challenge, but ultimately to tolerance. It is grudgingly allowed to stand by the Vicar of Bullhampton, even though legally exempted. On those occasions when it surrenders self-interest, religious faith can use its unique knowledge to reconfigure the relationship between public opinion and the law.

The heretofore privileged voices of those who make the law and their subsidized, dissenting cohort are challenged by another narrative which slowly comes to change the trajectory of public opinion, as it questions whose justice is sought:

> Yes, justice's justice! We know all about that. Put an old man in a prison for a week because he looks into his 'ayfield on a Sunday; or send a young boy to the treadmill for two months because he knocks over an 'are! All them cases ought to be tried in the towns, and there should be beaks paid as there is in London. I don't see the good of a county gentleman. Buying and selling—that is what the world has to go by.
>
> *(VB 194)*

The speaker is Mr. Cockey, a commercial traveler, who makes his living through an intimate knowledge of his customers' lives and their au courant preferences, rather than holding land or traditional belief, in words spoken to the strict constructionist magistrate (and jilted suitor), Harry Gilmore. Traveling salesmen and circuit-riding vicars share extended local contacts, private sources of information on the whereabouts of those abandoned to a ban by their remoteness or the condemnatory law of public opinion which initially seems to mime law in its arbitrary application. The vicar's informants extend from London slums to the pot houses of ill repute in Salisbury: the repository of denizen-ship. Initially as unbending as the law written to protect the privileged, public opinion with new information can detach itself from legal narratives to construct new narratives that recontextualize the prejudicial representations of the fallen and their persecutors.

As it turns out, the Marquis' *donated* land for a Methodist chapel was not his to donate. Mr. Cockey's interrogation of "whose law" extends to the question of "whose land." The London lawyer, Mr. Quickenham, Q.C., discovers that the land was historically glebe land (held by the vicarage in freehold), now illegally enclosed by the wealthiest man in the county for weaponization against his political enemies as another "open Church." One cannot be such a strict constructionist because "good law is not defined very clearly *here* in England" (*VB* 283, ital. added). Law is no more a singularity than is public opinion, but can be locally variably read and enforced, while pretending to unanimity it does not possess. Legal discovery on occasion limits the monopoly power of both the advantaged and their attempt to control public opinion.

Public opinion calls ownership—of information, material accessories like land or diamonds, a consistent narrative of the circumstantial (gleaned by those who *circulate*)— *into question*, because *questioning* is its being, including the continuous questioning of its own judgments. In *The Vicar of Bullhampton* so much of the *contractual* is revealed as provisional or obscured—assumed marital engagements, deeds of land title, obligations to be present at judicial hearings and religious loyalties. Public opinion literally occupies a space formerly occupied by other bonds: *"public opinion* in that part of Salisbury was averse to Sam. *Public opinion* was averse, also, to poor Carry" (*VB* 235, ital. added). Both public opinion and law can be errant.

Even as it establishes itself as an appellate division of the law, public opinion can multiply its misapplications, miming the monopolistic strategies of the law to insinuate itself as more representatively democratic voice(s). The relationship of law to public opinion resembles that of partners in some modern ballets, alternately miming, subverting, complementing and establishing a separate identity, but continually reshaping their incompletely shared spaces. Rhetorical questions almost call attention to themselves. In an increasingly, but reluctantly, open society, is there a spectral shadowing of public opinion and the law, like that which earlier, came to exist between Ecclesiastical Courts and Courts of Assize in nineteenth-century England? Is there a division within applications of any law, including the laws of public opinion?[24]

***

Although the Liberal MP and recurrent prime minster, Plantagenet Palliser, feigns an indifference to his aristocratic lineage, that legacy is defended when his son and heir, the Earl of Silverbridge, seeks permission to marry a middle-class American rather than Lady Mabel, the patriarchal choice. When, in the face of his father's initial rejection of Ms. Boncassen, the son, Lord Silverbridge, threatens to "go to law" to assert his choice of a wife over a father's opposition, Palliser suggests that the law itself is a questionable resource. To regard the law as either a guide to life or a remedy to conflict resolution is to abandon *contractually obligated* (by class) *duty* and *dutifulness*:

> Do you recognize no duty but what the *laws* impose upon you? Should you be disposed to eat and drink because the *laws* would not hinder you? Should you lie and sleep all day, the *law* would say nothing? Should you neglect every duty which your position imposes upon you, the *law* could not interfere. To such a one as you the *law* can be no guide. You should so live as not to come near the *law*,—or to have the *law* come near you.
>
> (DC *485, ital. added*)

For the noble family, law is an electrified fence, warning of the approach of a general public (the feared masses) now needed to awaken the conscience of the nobility.

To be touched by the law is to confront a schedule of *negations* or *prohibitions*, never a guide to life and its duties and obligations and redistributions which exist as part of an unwritten law wherein the (oral) word of the gentlemen is his bond. Public knowledge that one has gone to law to resolve a dispute (conveniently at hand given an active press) would partially subject the privileged classes to an alliance of the law and public opinion. The nobility is spatially both above the law, inhabiting a rival inherited field of conduct (that in some sense competes with it, enforcing an alternative set of values), and yet is entrusted with *making* the law and in mid-nineteenth-century Britain, *informing* the institutions which apply it. Operationally, public opinion makes no claim to transcendence, nor is it embodied in some aggregative historical custom or code nor can we anticipate in advance the identity of interested parties which are increasingly variable over time, alternately drawn to it and avoiding it.

An uneasy, provisional alliance of law with public opinion in practice opens what had previously been enclaves of probity to the threat of nonnative intermediaries who open the metaphoric "close" to unpredictable outcomes which mime legal reasoning but often no reason-ableness. Hence, going to law would represent a failure of compromise. Furthermore, the privileged would necessarily be forced to deputize a specialized legal authority which might compromise, ironically, a sense of legacy authority. This would constitute a distraction from the self-serving illusion of historically benevolent governance. And, so the logic of the argument goes, the irrational can never be delegated to adversarial models for determining rationality, but is nonetheless residual:

> No one can *depute an authority*. It comes too much from personal accident and too little from reason or law to be handed over to others.
>
> *(DC 522, ital. added)*

If one definition of public opinion is a continuously anonymously self-deputizing authority, it would be a challenge to authority accumulated as property or proprietary estate to be maintained and judiciously improved over time. Authority, as defined by the privileged, is *accidentally endowed* (stemming from birth or inheritance) and singular, whereas *reason*—allied here with the law—can be deputized, to others who intercede as questionably trustworthy, legal representatives for discursive determinations.

In this interpretation, law might, like public opinion, have its basis in operational *secondment*, a dilution into the secondary even in subsidiary or alternate jurisdictions. This potentially delegated authority of the law would already contain other historical voices some of which belong to a plural public whose debates contributed to its codification and acceptance. The *law*, as a composite of winds from different directions, is not so easily distinguished from the plural (mass) of public opinion, which nonetheless represents itself as a faux singular authority. If legal determinations are defined as appeals "handed over to others," then the law must ipso facto represent some liquidation of authority. Duty and social obligation, in contrast, is a space carved out separately from reason and law, yet sharing certain features of the transcendence accorded the law. Law and public opinion can be supplemented under unique circumstances, like Equity, in the absence of codified remedy.

If public opinion has a body at all—even one not fully under self-control and hence deficient in full sovereignty—it would seem to be defined largely in terms of its *relationship* as a voice. That massive voice has an absorptive capacity that maintains a *suspensfulness* like that which accompanies legal judgments. In the eagerly anticipated sermon which kicks off his ambitious campaign to become dean of Barchester Cathedral, the Rev. Slope adopts the rhetoric of the courtroom in order to maintain full *attendance*. Like the public opinion he will later manipulate, the ambitious Slope's sermon deploys a Manichaean judgmental model common to the concentrated rhetoric of another discipline in order to maintain the attention of a largely passive, obligatory flock:

> Let a barrister attempt to talk without talking well and he will talk but seldom. A judge's charge need be listened to per force by none but the jury, prisoner, and gaoler.
>
> *(BT I 52)*

Slope divides his audience by using different registers in addressing men and women, part of a polarizing strategy directed toward people rather than parsing the Word.

Rev. Harding, having discovered that his minimally audible internal voice of conscience has been awakened by the "clarion voice of public opinion" (*W* 154) and surprised at learning from his attorney that the suit instigated by the pensioners has been abandoned without explanation, is uncomprehending. Initially brought as a legal case, nurtured and informed by public opinion, the case is then withdrawn under pressure from public opinion. Public opinion appears especially fickle, awakening then abandoning to a radical subjectivity. It clearly leaves a diminished, polarized community, but not one abandoned to a ban. The *domus* has become rationalized:

> Mr. Harding did *not desert them*; from him they had much consolation as a dying man may receive from his Christian pastor, but it was the *occasional* kindness of a *stranger* which ministered to them, and not the *constant presence* of a master, a neighbor, and a friend.
>
> *(W 182, ital. added)*

Harding becomes an occasional, intermittent presence in lives,[25] rather than adhering to the dutiful benevolence of pastoral care demanded by the office of warden. Escaping condemnation by the law, but awakened, the former intimate becomes a stranger, merely an attendant, somewhat indifferent, administrator: in short, a clerical bureaucrat, serving virtually at the behest of an intrusive public.[26] One possible interpretation of this *alienated kindness* might be the endemic qualities it shares with other British historical compromises: the Anglican Church, the practice of foxhunting (both tolerated and restricted depending on area) and today's Lib-Dems in Parliament. This is surely part of the Eeyorish, "muddling through" philosophy—often interpreted as an urge to split the difference separating fabricated polarizations.

This attendant, yet merely formally custodial presence, like other "long lingering" intervals (Archbishop Grantly) or being held "in durance" (the Rev. Crawley of Hogglestock) is not a resolution. To be held in a restless indecisiveness different from physical or intellectual confinement—given the theological context—mimes some representations of purgatory, a notoriously ambivalent condition for Anglican divines.[27] The perpetual intermediacy of "neither here nor there"—like public opinion—derives part of its hegemonistic potential from a suspension of terminal judgment, keeping its targets wondering and spiritually wandering, attempting to read themselves *in it*.

Although Harding and Bold are well meaning, the fact that public opinion forces them to continually reaffirm good intentions suggests a fragility of traditional appraisal of goodwill.

The *Jupiter* in its coverage adopts the rhetoric of the allegedly inclusive, editorial "we," previously utilized by royalty or messengers of the Divine. A self-assumed monopoly of public opinion leaves no space outside itself for the resistance of conscience:

> *We* do not wish to take praise to ourselves whether praise be due to us or not. But the consequence of our remark was, that the warden did look into the matter, and finding on so doing that he himself could come to no other opinion than that expressed by *us*, he very creditably threw up the appointment.
>
> *(BT II 183–84, ital. added)*

Here, the *Jupiter* inserts itself as a subject allied with "we" (as in "we the people"), on this occasion, to which another "they" (a provisional "people") must decide how much credit to grant to itself! The editorial establishes its own consequentiality. Editor Towers cannot separate his editorial acumen from the "opinion [...] expressed by us." The social media of the day, perhaps like Silicon Valley high-tech CEOs now, is really not in need of a free press since it has imagined itself as already controlling the distribution of shared "likes" (the plural made singular).

Trollope's narrator had recognized in the earlier, *The Warden*, that the division of material interests that initiated the original lawsuit remains present in the culture at large, even after the legal/public opinion intercessions were supposedly socially unifying. In fact, however, it has only socially reproduced existing divisions:

> Opinion was much *divided* as to Mr. Harding's conduct. The mercantile part of the community, the mayor and the corporation, and council, also most of the ladies, were loud in his praise. But the gentry were of a different way of thinking—especially the lawyers and the clergymen. They said such conduct was weak and undignified.
>
> *(W 175, ital. added)*

To be found at fault by public opinion is to have lost authority among the gentry and professional classes, but not those who must face the undignified public and its demands. The position of warden remains vacant, until Slope attempts to manipulate public opinion in the determination of how the vacancy is to be filled in *Barchester Towers*. Chastened by the intermittent alliance of the law and public opinion, the avuncular warden of Hiram's Hospital, though acquitted of any malfeasance, is imagined as weak by half the people.

Occasionally the individual particularity feels called to a singular *duty* whose origins are equally obscure. When in *Framley Parsonage* Whig politicians at Gatherum Castle initiate a plan to abandon their own party position (as Phineas Finn will do) in favor of ideological independence, Trollope narrates it as a transcendent *calling*:

> When a man gets it into his head and idea that the *public voice calls* for him, it is astonishing how great becomes his trust in the wisdom of the public. *Vox populi, vox Dei.*
>
> *(FP 118, ital. added)*

The voice of the public in the proper setting approaches transcendence, miming both man-made law and God's law, an extraordinary flexibility: an alternative conscience, like that awakened in Mr. Harding's dark night of the soul in *The Warden*. But on occasion, as with the ingratiating Rev. Slope, "the mouthpiece of the Bishop" (*BT* I 58), it is difficult to directly access it, given deniability and intermittence, consequent upon the bishop's (and the church's) frequent *absentee presence*. But for Trollope, the existence of the "mouthpiece" entrusted with public opinion formation endows an alternative *calling*, as those called to bar or ministry, but in this case, a self-anointed representative.

There are times, to be sure, when public opinion, like the law, seems protective of a persecuted, albeit privileged, minority interest, as occurs after the lonely Sir Roger Scatcherd is elevated to an honorary knighthood, though born to the working class. Although he wants to impose harsh discipline on his wastrel son and heir, to do so would render a newly noble father ignoble in the eyes of a public who make rather liberal provisions for any heir of the privileged who might exhibit antisocial behavior. The same is true of "Honorable John" Courcy, the ne'er-do-well third Courcy son, who escapes both the law and his father's law because public opinion expects nothing else, given his skill "to measure his father and in accurate balance" (*SHA* 175). Even more noteworthy and infamous is Plantagenet Palliser's second son, sent down from Oxford in *The Duke's Children*. Public opinion seems to set territorial parameters by moving the posts (with wider boundaries) for the misbehavior of the scions of the well-heeled, accorded some forbearance: "though they may possibly go astray, they have a fair chance given to them of running within the posts" (*DT* 285). Like the law in carving out exemptions, public opinion selectively demarcates an expanded field of play. It has a role as social referee of a contest, acting in loco parentis (with an abundance of probationary yellow cards) mediating between permissive and overbearing fathers and the idle sons of the rich.

If not the fulcrum by which to move belief to which the Rev. Slope had aspired, public opinion, when not miming the law in its hegemony, is informed by some logic of redistribution. In the opening chapters of *Framley Parsonage*, Lady Lufton is established as the insurer-cum-protector of "country values" (foxhunting), imperial adventures in the Crimea (as long as France is not allowed to share the victory) and the ability to influence political appointments and marital choices dedicated to maintain those values. The consent of her tenants and assorted "protégées" (*FP* 39) to "pastors and master" (*FP* 47) in return for dry, clean houses is part of the unspoken social contract. It includes a very young Vicar Mark Robarts who has obtained life, wife and a clerical living due to her ministrations. This is yet another social contract, made vulnerable not by the neglect of the local and its penetration by a newly empowered media, but by a ne'er-do-well son who seeks a more liquid form of patronage after running up gaming debts.

As it turns out, Lord Lufton's gambling habit involves the threat of *publicité* in the form of exposure to city moneylenders—the "scores of hands" (*FP* 244) through which the note will pass before redemption—as opposed to the confidentiality of banks or sales of assets to related family members, previously insuring a measure of discretion. The family fortunes are opened to both oral and financial speculation, in a fiduciary ecumenism that includes anonymous "city" moneylenders, some of Jewish persuasion, hence implicating further exposure to public speculation. But as with the Rev. Slope of *Barchester Towers* or the infirm pensioners in *The Warden*, Parson Robarts's role as guarantor, by cosigning a promissory note to his investor/sponsor's wastrel son, suggests confusion between reciprocal obligation and worldliness. Church representatives now indirectly invest in the sponsorship of the flesh (even horseflesh on gaming tracks), symbolic of a contract between "the upper classes at prayer" (one traditional definition of the Church of England) and its sponsorship of a lifestyle. The church, to borrow from current financial nomenclature, is "leveraged," gambling with borrowed assets.

The abandonment of Mark Robarts to the law, contemporaneous here with his abandonment to public opinion formation, is represented in two different, but analogous ways in *Framley Parsonage*. In the first instance, the private drawing room of the parsonage is invaded by the law's agents who parse/sully the household effects to be auctioned off to the public by cataloging them with an assortment of dirty hands:

> O ladies, who have drawing-rooms in which things are pretty, good, and dear to you, think of what it would be to have the bailiffs rummaging among them with pen and inkhorn, making a catalogue preparatory to a sheriff's auction; and all without fault or extravagance of your own.
>
> *(FP 515)*

Robarts's "living" (and cultivated reputation) is possessed by the people's representatives who would otherwise have little hope of gaining invasive and liquidating possession of church property, open to oral public speculation. Public opinion and auctions share the same invasive space, subject to narratives that tend to inflate value by exaggerating information or *provenance*, of which the public is made aware. Ironically, in a characteristic legal redundancy, it is *already* being held for the people, but the liquidation before the eyes of congregants is tantamount to repossession at the hands of another public institution *manqué*, public opinion. Gambling shares with public opinion the tendency to speculate, to play, with what one does not completely possess in the hopes of adding value.

Trollope deploys the same thematic maneuver in *Phineas Finn* when the moneylender's agent, Clarkson, physically enters the halls of Westminster to seek out the freshman MP for payment of a note Finn has guaranteed. Even though the "privilege of the house prevented him from arrest" (*PF* I 197), Phineas Finn wonders if he signed the bill, thereby assuming responsibility for the wastrel, Lord Fitzgibbons's debts, believing that "he was so protected" (*PF* I 197) by the law. His logic prompts the fear that the collector, like public opinion, "could harass every hour of his life" (*PF* I 197), having previously boasted of a distinguished clientele, with both a prime minister and a lord chancellor's name "in his portfolio" (*PF* I 194) of underperforming debt instruments.

His fellow parliamentarians do take notice of this intimidating intrusion of private mercantile demands into the heretofore protected space where law is made and studied, effecting Finn's reputation even before he has made his first speech. But, an increased access to what had previously been a private enclave, given that the debt is now described as "that bill which Laurence Fitzgibbons had sent *afloat*" (*PF* I 191, ital. added), is part of the spatial logistics and proxemics of public opinion formation, dependent on the vehicularity of floating speculation. As we shall see, politically tactical debts and redemptions of obligations have constituted the business of life at Westminster.

What had previously been the *protected* space of law-making, Westminster, is being progressively opened, making it vulnerable to access by those who previously could never intrude upon inner sanctums that defined the private deliberations of the privileged. But for some, the secrecy of the ballot, supported by radicals, might produce unexpected consequences: the repression of oral, open *expression*. The advent of the secret ballot, an amendment to the Second Reform Bill, the support of which divides Phineas Finn's opinion from that of his prime minister, could be seen as an attempt to reprivatize opinion so that it might be expressed secretly by each individual voter, immunizing him against Dicey's "crosswinds" of public opinion. The advent of a private ballot would return all deliberations to the individual, privatized conscience, hence a retreat to a realm untouchable by *community* in the interests of the myth of autonomy.

Prime Minister Mildmay (a paragon of compromise) opposes the private ballot on the grounds that the measure would impede, not enhance, public opinion formation given the control of the ruling class in mid-nineteenth-century British politics to dictate how tenants vote. He believes, counterintuitively, in the *expressive* as opposed to the *inscripted* register, that

> everyman possessed of the franchise should dare to have and to *express* a *political opinion of his own*; that otherwise the franchise is not worth having. [...] As the ballot would make any courage of that kind unnecessary, I dislike the ballot.
>
> *(PF I 182, ital. added)*

Public opinion formation, for the politically nuanced Mildmay, demands an oral openness disguised by the so-called privacy of a secret ballot, where choices were often dictated by landlords. This "secrecy" would be as (literally) *ir-responsible* as certain features of public opinion formation, under cover.[28] For Mildmay, as for the cynics of ancient Athens, democracy should be suspicious of the secret (written) ballot, the provision for which became law in 1870. For him, genuine democracy requires hard-won habits of the freedom of *speech*, persuasion and collective decision-making in some consensual oral arena. Mildmay's suspicion of the dictatorial potential of the *written* word is perhaps of a piece with the historical reluctance for a binding written constitution in Great Britain.

Prime Minister Mildmay, in practice as well as ideologically, wants an enlarged table where private interest is suspended for thoughtful, open oral deliberation in the manner recommended by Habermas, as opposed to the tyrannies of anonymously dictated "texting." As with the enlarged table of the Rev. Arabin at St. Ewolds', more individual opinions are literally "at (an oral) table." Similarly, Prime Minister Mildmay in *Phineas Finn* temporarily staves off his expected resignation by enhancing the seating arrangements for cabinet meetings so that he could "see his colleagues' faces clearly" (*PF* I 269) and hear their independent voices. Those initially committed to enlarging the "plazas" dedicated to rational, consensual deliberation are paradoxically the first to become sensitive to the risks pursuant upon public exposure by an intrusive press that is

often less than transparent. Trollope's narrator is conscious of life during a transitional
period before penetrations at the hands of a local press:

> As there was no reporter present—that plan of turning private meetings at gentlemen's
> houses into public assemblies not having been as yet adopted—there could be no need for
> energy.
>
> *(PF I 153)*

A consensually deliberative *slowness* would ideally resist, for Mildmay, as for John Stuart
Mill, both the hegemonistic monopolies of historical or class determination and the
energies of a monopolizing voice of public opinion that would swamp the various plazas with another form of dictatorship. This energy is always possessed of *urgency* (hence
allied with ambition in Trollope) that is opposite consensual deliberation. This is exemplified by Reporter Slide, "an *energetic* but not a thoughtful man," yet one who becomes
a "people's friend" *(PF* I 242, ital. added). Those who "go public" possess a strategic
energy on the one hand coupled with the deniability illustrated in Towers's demurrals
and strategic absences. Those who speak to and for an imaginary public opinion, like
Slide or the radical Turnbull, whose speeches are modeled on the rhetorical skills of
Bright, are denominated by Trollope as surges of empty energy.

Turnbull speaks neither to the question on the floor nor to individual MPs, but to an
incipient, latent populist audience despite his independent income. Speaking on behalf
of a public's opinions, its putative representative adopts the forces that endow it with
random, albeit not specifically addressed, *propulsion*. Turnbull's speeches on the floor of
Parliament are seldom addressed directly to the House, as he turns aside from eye contact (always associated with thoughtfulness in Trollope). Having captured the ear with a
phrase, the real object of his rhetoric is enhanced circulation and distribution:

> He had obtained the ear of the House and the favour of the reporters, and opened his voice
> at no public dinner, on no public platform without a conviction that the words spoken by
> him would be read by thousands.
>
> *(PF I 161–62)*

Organs of public opinion amplify his *charisma* to the written word, giving it weight to
hold in one's hand and hence an *afterlife*, like that of sacred texts.

Every occasion and appearance for Turnbull displays for the Whig MP Monk an
"ignorance that there is, or should be, a difference between public and private life" *(PF*
I 166). For Turnbull, all politics is ultimately, public life, as he leans forward or tilts his
head upward while speaking to an imaginary audience, even when close to colleagues:
the "Twitter" enunciation of his day. Above all it is the stickiness, the *endurance*, of those
who cultivate public opinion, be they the *Jupiter's* Towers, the reporter Slide or the radical Turnbull "so intent on his monopolizing speech that it may be doubted whether he
heard this interruption" *(PF* I 165). Like the public opinion to which Turnbull caters, he
resists interruption in order to maintain monopolizing circulation.

Perhaps it is appropriate to make a necessary distinction between the literal or metaphoric
meaning attached to Turnbull's parliamentary speeches and what might be termed a kind

of *messaging*. As opposed to systematically truth-directed methods in the interest of advancing an argument, persuading an adversary, or forming a consensus, the radical attempts to directly evoke an absent, "silent majority." *Messaging*, as its name implies, is often coded, sent in a kind of shorthand, which uses code words rather than content to evoke sympathy. Indeed, Trollope narrates little of the content of Turnbull's orations, limiting description largely to its performative effects: inciting a disturbance outside the Houses of Parliament which comes to involve Phineas Finn and other journalists. A more obvious instance of the technique might be the obligatory public apology which compels acceptance, the offense forgotten, or conversely, comes to be regarded as insincere, a kind of advertising.

By the end of the novel, Quintus Slide, the reporter from the *People's Banner*, will, like Clarkson—the moneylender's agent, indirectly penetrate the precincts of Parliament with these contagious energies and real or imaginary demands of public opinion to pay up. Financial debts resemble political arrears, insofar as there exists a "call" date for both obligations. He attempts to convert his incendiary journalism (to which Phineas Finn is initially a partner), "feeding the 'horgan,'" to a political competition with Finn for the fictional "rotten borough" constituency of Loughton.

Slide is surely a harbinger of twenty-first-century politics in moving between journalism (representing public opinion) and candidacy for a seat which represents no one at all save his own ambition, enabled by a successful journalistic assault on Finn. This chameleon's changes of ideological color ultimately result in the withering away (by consolidation) of the rotten borough which Finn only nominally represents anyway. There could be no better symbol of the representation of a contested emptiness than standing for a seat from a rotten borough from a previous position as an editor (disguised as a mere reporter) of a polemical journal.

***

Personal assets and confidential information are sent similarly *afloat* by centrifugal energies of *dispersal*. Personal debts of the gentry, personal effects and private information are passing into the hands of *negociants* and assorted agents as previously illiquid assets come to be contaminated under the threat of imminent liquidation at diverse hands: one synecdoche of public opinion. And surely herein resides a crucial difference between public opinion and the law: whereas the latter makes a pretense of distributing justice equally (but only under the law), public opinion, as astutely analyzed by the Slope of *Barchester Towers*, is "the great arranger and distributor of all *future* British terrestrial affairs" (*BT* II 182, ital. added). In place of the arranged, historically mandated loyalties of custom and class, public opinion looks *ahead*, its possible (new) dispensations accessible to speculative wager—much as is faith. Such is a foreshadowing of the IPO, of "going public" by soliciting investment-as-belief. It would remain both above and beneath the law. At one point the indebted Lord Lufton of *Framley Parsonage* openly refuses to repay the loan guaranteed by Robarts's endorsement "unless the whole matter should be exposed openly in court" (*FP* 243).

To charge the matter in a civil proceeding, however, would literally *ex-pose* the plaintiff (by placing him outside the carefully cultivated accoutrements and boundaries of civility in Trollope, always threatened by continuously amended indictment at the hands of public opinion. Open to etymological scrutiny, *ex-posure* denotes the sudden revelation common to both religious and intellectual enlightenment (on occasion in conflict). To find oneself suddenly in a false position often exacts the price of a feared diminishment of a perhaps fictional sovereignty and the trappings of self-possession. Even if justice under law is obtained, some taint of a legal proceeding might impact reputation as an oxymoron: the *permanent sentence*. The precise relationship between traditional belief, belief in the verdicts of law and the belief that forms the curious body of public opinion and the spaces they, respectively, *occupy* is very complex, though it provides a continuous thread from the clerical novels of Barsetshire to the more obviously political *Palliser Novels*. The territoriality of public opinion is engaged, a new distributive dispensation, when a question arises as to jurisdiction. After the perpetual curate of Hogglestock in *The Last Chronicle of Barset*, the Rev. Crawley is accused of misappropriating a check, "*opinion* in Silverbridge, at Barchester, and throughout the country, was very much *divided* as to the guilt or innocence of Mr. Crawley" (*LCB* 65, ital. added).

But the disequilibrium in public opinion seems initially a derivative of the *divisions* (parsing) of legal jurisdictions, as if there was a simultaneously dependent yet differential relationship between the law and public opinion. Although arraigned in Assize Court, Bishop Proudie, at the urging of his wife, quickly moves to vacate Crawley's living, sending another curate pending the outcome of a civil trial. Crawley refuses to step down, even temporarily, as he questions what "temporality" would not allow him to remain innocent until proven guilty. Does the temporality of the Church of England differ from the *sentence* of the law and from the dispositions of public opinion?

One answer might be the unique temporality advanced by and in public opinion. Does hostile public opinion to a proceeding render one unfit for office *in anticipation of* or *in lieu of* a pending legal judgment? If so, the church, responding to public opinion, would shape legal interpretation rather than merely replicating it. Crawley could not be tried in the ecclesiastical Court of Arches, say, without prejudicing any ensuing civil proceeding. Yet, conversely, in the event of a verdict of "not guilty," the church could in no way find in a separate trial that Crawley was unfit to minister to his flock of largely impoverished masons. Were he to be found guilty of theft and sentenced to the year customarily meted out to first offenders, an ecclesiastical court that removed him would be enabling "a double prosecution for the same offenses" (*LCB* 565). Though technically not double jeopardy, "the feelings of the country" (*LCB* 565)—a lovely euphemism for uncodifiable public opinion—would nonetheless be offended.

Trollope's irony has escaped critical commentary: the dilemma for the Church of England resembles that faced by the accused curate, its representative. There could be no better representation of how the partisan, divisions in which it *lives*, is publicly acknowledged. Its practices had formerly been continuous with those of civic authority, the Crown and the church being part of the same body from the time of Hooker.[29] This shared, curious body is revealed when the right bishop consults his legal counsel, whose physical proximity affirms an intimacy. John Chadwick, the bishop's counsel, summoned to advise the church on its legal posture, straddles the line between law and faith, as

one of those gentlemen, two or three of whom are to be seen in *connexion* with every see—
who seem to be *hybrids*—half lay, half-cleric. [...] They live, or at least have their offices,
half in the Close, and half out of it—dwelling as it were just on the borders of holy orders.

(LCB 347, ital. added)

Legal counsel dwells "half-in/half-out" of the church, as if continuous.

Just as Tom Towers had maintained a tangential geographic proximity with the
law and incorporated religious iconography in his office's interior decoration, so the
law had, once upon a time, enjoyed an intimacy with religion that Trollope now renders as an anachronism, given the displacing role of public opinion. When summoned,
Attorney Chadwick appears in Bishop Proudie's inner sanctum dressed as an old-
fashioned undertaker, as Trollope describes him. John Bold's sudden, speechless death,
like many deaths in Trollope, occurs in an interim between *The Warden* and its sequel,
Barchester Towers. Maintaining the gap between the jurisdictional prerogatives of church
and state, the recourse to law renders them competitive, differentially denominated
particularities, capable of appropriation or abandonment.

Throughout the *Chronicles of Barsetshire*, public opinion exploits rifts when territorial
control or some occlusion in established communicational channels erupts. Precisely
why this appearance of compensation—whereby a collective, allegedly consensual voice
displaces a repressed, private utterance—is less obvious. But it seems to gain strength
and self-authorizing audibility when patriarchal voices of the nobility die out or appear
incapable of speaking to everyone—neither internally unified nor any longer capable
of unifying others. The esteemed Duke of Omnium, even at a social occasion which
he ostensibly hosts, only "spoke one or two words in a very low voice to gentlemen
who stood nearest to him" *(DT 229)*. Gathered guests are told that "this was the duke's
practice on all such occasions" *(DT 229)*, the posture of demurral. The nobility has a
voiceless, non-engaging presence, as if traditional power had no need to speak out in
competition with the enhanced amplitude of public opinion.

Similarly, in *Doctor Thorne*, the humble-born Sir Roger Scatcherd has become an
industrial magnate, constructing the bridges and ports crucial to a commercial empire.
Yet he exists in a dialogic purgatory. He can neither talk to his workmen in their own
lingo (for they demur to an honorary peer of the realm) nor can he talk with the gentry (because of his lack of education and social etiquette). Afflicted by the catatonia
of in-betweenness, a captain of industry slowly drinks himself to death. Though his
achievement is publicly recognized, he can never enter the public realm that Habermas
defined, after all, as part of a communicational order. But public opinion rushes in to fill
his silence with the sublating summary of the newspaper obituary, impossibly celebrat-
ing him "as one who had lived and died happy" *(DT 192)*. In other words, public opinion
speaks *for* or *in place of* his lost voice, with a *fabricated*, pre-mortem summary of a sad life.

A man is nobody unless his biography is *kept* so *far posted up* that it may be readied for the
national breakfast-table on the morning after his demise.

(DT 292, ital. added)

The obituary in the popular press, then and now, is constructed in advance of death and kept on file so that it may be applied *au courant*, when the need arises, not as mere report- age, but to shape public reputation. Like the law, it must be made to seem relevant even when it is dated and not entirely applicable or even contradictory to all that we know of a sad alcoholic. The relatives of the deceased can no more recapture his autonomy that John Bold could request the *Jupiter* to return the information instigating a lawsuit in *The Warden*. Even the obituary, too, is *messaging*. In an age when anybody can become somebody, public opinion is shaped and packaged, an instrumentality in endowing life with an acceptable, consistently coherent narrative, even if false.

As Finney, the lawyer engaged by Bold in the Hiram's Hospital case, merely wants an early start on his resumé, and to keep it up, so the work of obituary writers suggests the composed, prosthetic nature of public opinion, "posted up," speedily assembled, not unlike the bridges and railways of nineteenth-century England, as a public opinion network.[30] This infrastructure too is "kept [...] up" (*DT* 292), maintained, long after everyone has gone home, or even died. The practice subsidizes a temporally monopo- lizing wakefulness, even if irrelevant, of public opinion and the organs which inform it.

This problematic dwelling in *temporality* (as opposed to espousing historically tested values and traditions), demanded of public opinion if it is to hold an audience, comes to affect those exposed to its vagaries. In *The Last Chronicle of Barset*, Trollope goes to great lengths to show that the Rev. Crawley, despite a very strong will, adopts rather than purely resists, the opinions of others because he too dwells in a temporality:

> *At that time*, people believed him to be innocent, and he so believed of himself. *Now*, people believed him to be guilty, and it could not be right that a man held in such slight esteem should exercise the function of a parish priest, let his own *opinion* of himself be what it might.
> (LCB *651, ital. added*)

Given its fickle nature and the equally changeable confidence we place in its judgments over time (often accepting them passively as a way of avoiding harsher judgments), Trollope would doubtlessly agree with Stanley Fish that anything one *believes* about a particular matter is logically independent of any account one might give of how his beliefs emerge, or what underlies them, or what calls them into question.[31] Every fact or presupposition cited in support of one's belief could itself be *in a position* of requiring support in an incredibly circular process. Public opinion could be the default position of the infinite regress of *accounting* and similar expressions of *rationalization* over time.

Because evidence is revealed or not in the light of some first premise that cannot in itself be put to a test (because any regime of testing w-ould have to be already estab- lished or consistent with its assumptions), evidence is never as independent as it initially seems, as the experience of both Rev. Crawley and the Phineas Finn, charged with the murder of Bonteen in *Phineas Redux*, reveals. Public opinion shifts, depending on what the community is willing to regard as evidence or the confirmation of evidence, which changes depending on what others regard as evidence. Among the beliefs internal to any social structure are the conditions necessary to revise that belief. Perhaps for this very reason, John Heil in his "dictionary" entry on "belief" in *A Companion to Epistemology* lends belief-formation the aura of the involuntary: acquiring belief is like catching a cold.[32] When "the matter has become so common in men's mouths at Barchester and Silverbridge" (*LCB* 32), public exposure is inevitable. This may be one reason for the fear and denigration in which public opinion is held by commentators like Negt and Kluge: a *common* nuisance, not worthy of genuine rational examination.[33]

This nature of this *ex-posure* is, however, somewhat confused, being both a general complaint and a specific inheritance which are incongruous. Grace, the Rev. Crawley's daughter, employed as a lowly assistant at Miss Prettyman's Academy, once apprised of the criminal charges against her father, can neither remain at the school (because of the ravages of gossip), nor return home (which would be tantamount to an admission of guilt), nor seek the sympathy of her fiancé, the well-bred Major Grantly, to whom she writes of her fear that "she was doing injury" (*LCB* 175), by continuing their engagement. The fear that one is highly contagious is a further symptom consistent with the affliction of public exposure: both homeless, in the sense of not being able to be comfortable anywhere, and self-quarantined. She is a waiting presence, not unlike other imaginable "confinements" in nineteenth-century England.

Her condition is analogous to that of her father upon being released on bail, furnished by his more affluent friends, while awaiting the resolution of his fate.[34] Intriguingly, the submission to public opinion is compared with exposure to the elements, a contributing factor to illness: "he was sitting saturated with rain—saturated also with thinking" (*LCB* 651), but a thinking no longer privatized. He exists at some territorial limit in which even private thought constitutes inclement weather from which there is no shelter from the *outside*.

Not yet proven guilty by a jury nor enjoying the unconditional freedom of the acquitted, the perpetual curate claims that he is being "kept in durance," his reputation "made to hang for a while on the trust which some friends or neighbors may have in it" (*LCB* 200). For so many Trollope characters enmeshed in public opinion, from clerics to politicians, life becomes an administered trust fund, producing a "thickness" which makes him silently responsible. Crawley's investor/friends abandon the strategy of having him admit to temporary insanity—entirely consistent with other features of his difficult character and past—on the grounds that it would appear as an exculpatory narrative designed *post facto* to supply heretofore absent unity of belief. As per Lacan's notion that Marx was "the inventor of the symptom,"[35] Crawley's advisers who urge the symptom upon him, would denote a point of breakdown *heterogeneous* to a given ideological field and at the same time *necessary* for that field to achieve its closure.

Public opinion comes to perform, like the chorus of Greek drama does for Nietzsche in *The Birth of Tragedy*, as a collective-speaking-as-one, in opposition to the arbitrary over-determination of the Apollonian forces of established (though equally fickle) law. Sir Peter Hall has interrogated whether the chorus in Greek tragedy was an archetypal individual or a representation of different types of individuals within a general, formal ensemble. For even if choral speaking is well drilled so that every syllable is precisely in unison (as often seems to be the case in public opinion), the very efficiency produces an equally dehumanizing effect—as is the case with the "swaying" of the masses. Uniform speech, like uniform movement, is so abstract that it could not provoke genuine *feeling*.[36]

In a crucial chapter dealing with the deliberations of the Clerical Commission entrusted with determining Rev. Crawley's fate, there is to be sure recognition of the possibility of a "double prosecution" as a consequence of overlapping jurisdictions (*LCB* 565), but the conflict in jurisdictions merely reflects a larger redundancy between ecclesiastical and criminal law on one side and the "feelings and traditions of the country" (*LCB* 565) on the other. The "feelings and traditions" of the country, like the jurisdictions of equity and common law, seem to be *absorbed* within public opinion which makes of it a kind of appellate division of the law or conversely, an injunctive mechanism that keeps one away from the law. Justice delayed may well be justice denied, but it can provide space for public opinion formation. Perhaps this is one reason why attorneys for those accused of particularly heinous crimes often seek a postponement of the trial in order to allow the crosscurrents of public opinion to abate, concentrating decision-making upon law rather than an au courant public opinion whose advantage over the law exists in its timeliness rather than the deliberative search for applicational relevance.

In *The Small House at Allington*, the fifth, chronologically, of the *Chronicles of Barsetshire*, the socially privileged Adolphus Crosbie is accosted and physically assaulted, adjacent to a rail station, "on a public platform" by Johnny Eames, offended by Crosbie's cavalier abandonment of his beloved, Lily Dale, in favor of a more aristocratic bride. Although "the first burst of public sympathy" (*SHA* 400) lies with the victim of the assault, Crosbie, the potential plaintiff, wisely realizes that to seek redress against Eames, a less privileged rival, in a court of law would subject him to the *equality* of the law, which carries risks to his social status. He also recognizes that the initial public sympathy with a socially prominent victim of gratuitous violence before others, brought to a legal determination, exposes him to the possibility that his cavalier treatments of women in the past might become known. Any redress might be revised or even reversed over time by public opinion, as Crosbie's history with women comes to be known, impacting his reputation. The law in its arbitrariness occasions not the resolution of a complaint, but evokes public sympathy for the defendant, as it raises the possibility of a law beyond the law for Eames:

> A man becomes an *outlaw* when he plays such a *game* as he has played. Anybody's hand may be raised against him with impunity. He can't show his face, you know. He can't come forward and answer questions as to what he has done. There are offenses which the law can't touch, but which *outrage public feeling* so strongly that anyone may take upon himself the duty of punishing them.
>
> *(SHA 400, ital. added)*

Here, public opinion operates as a supplement to the law, but its judgments are antithetical to those expected of the law, since "anyone," not merely a qualified judge, may dutifully speak in its name. Though this is surely a kind of vigilante justice, from another perspective it compensates for the immunity of the privileged, like Crosbie who, typically, had close relationships with local magistrates with whom they frequently shared the same interests.[37] This would not be different from the situation of ecclesiastical courts charged with judging their own. Public opinion is hence still *responsive*, albeit not to a public but rather to identifiable social networks. Law cannot independently and irrevocably judge, because the privilege of judging has shifted and public opinion is remarkably untouchable even as it touches all.

To "outrage public feeling" sounds like a legal offense, as in the charge, "to outrage a woman's modesty," still on legal schedules in former British colonies, albeit now often applied to improper touching of the female body on public transport. What intrigues is how public opinion formation has adopted not merely the strategies or procedural practices of the law, as Tom Towers illustrates, but its actual nomenclature. This is indeed the internalization of miming. Judith Butler has suggested that when this occurs, the same vocabulary is being used to subvert dominance, by suggesting the possibility of reappropriation by a subaltern class. This would imply some dialogic response as a form of "taking back what is [originally] ours." It raises the whole question of cultural reappropriation as a form of resistance to the dominance of Austin's "speech acts" as en*acting* judgments, immune to any revision.[38]

Urged by his friends "to pass over such a thing without speaking of it," Crosbie discovers to his dismay that people nonetheless "go on talking about it" (*SHA* 385), even after he hoped to put the incident to rest by foregoing any legal redress. There being no closure to public opinion formation as there would be for other legal judgments, his silence leaves extralegal discourse an open field for speculative play. In this particular case, the law is handicapped in dealing with the circumstances in which the assault is historically imbedded. Public opinion does not so easily separate law, fact and circumstances, thus appearing more contextually inclusive, as mass judgment usually is. Although they seem to arrive at antithetical sentences, law and public opinion actually function similarly with one notable exception: the law *claims to distribute justice equally*, whereas public opinion, because anyone can equally speak in its name, would make no such claim. Crosbie is in the *double bind* of condemnations, no matter which jurisdiction he chooses. Those with an excess of resources and contacts, like Adolphus Crosbie, and those entirely lacking them like Rev. Crawley, would both conform to Grace Crawley's description of her father's situation: "papa is under such a terrible ban" (*LCB* 423).

Characters in Trollope's work increasingly perceive of themselves as being tried by public opinion, as a space opens between the *sovereignty* of the law, under which theoretically all would be equal, and the *force* of public opinion which never advances such claims. Jean-Luc Nancy uses this opening to advance the idea that the effect of a certain kind of exposure to the law is in fact analogous to abandonment. But it is an abandonment that is *confined*, therefore remaining *inside* the *force* of the law, while nonetheless managing to escape its specific summons, like the *force* of public opinion:

> The destitution of abandoned Being is measured by the limitless severity of the law to which it finds itself exposed. Abandonment does not constitute a subpoena to present oneself before this or that court of the law. It is a compulsion to appear absolutely under the law, under the law as such and it its totality. In the same way—it is the same thing—to be *banished* amounts not to coming under a provision of the law, but rather coming under the entirety of the law. Turned over to the absolute of the law, the abandoned one is abandoned *completely outside its jurisdiction.*[39]

To be abandoned *to* the law is therefore in some sense to be abandoned to a ban, a curious exclusion. Public opinion initially seems to mime the law, even as it separates itself from its procedures and conventions to initiate a larger totality with inputs that would be banned under the law as irrelevant, or in surplus.

Speculative ventures, with which Trollope fills his characters' lives, challenge the relationship between law and public opinion, because the weakness of the law, as Chaffanbrass reminds us in *Phineas Redux*, is that it can never be speculative, only determining. Public opinion can be both. The law itself becomes subject to a form of speculation, symbolized by Madame Goesler's intercession to free Phineas Finn from an indictment for murder. The facts of a case with which law deals is a narrative of events, and when the events change the law is like a key (or a coat) that may not fit or has a duplicate solution.

***

The attorney most cynically aware of this *aporia* in legal discourse is Mr. Chaffanbrass, defending Phineas Finn against the charges of murdering Mr. Bonteen after an altercation in *Phineas Redux*. A veteran of legal battles, including the defense of Alaric Tudor for criminal breach of trust in *The Three Clerks*, the diminutive Chaffanbrass is relatively uninterested in Phineas Finn's narrative of the events preceding the alleged crime, rather dedicating himself to facts, with a profound distrust of the procedural operations of the law. Chaffanbrass believes wholeheartedly that juries do whatever judges tell them: "Jurymen are afraid of having their own opinion and almost always shirk a verdict when they can" (*PR* II 175), resulting in what he calls "mealy-mouthed" and "mealy-hearted" verdicts (*PR* II 175). Hence, law is a willful abandonment of opinion, a lost vacancy to which a legally dedicated voice creates, after the verdict, a larger field on which public opinion might play. Public opinion may then become a virtual "appellate division" created by default: an abdication of the opinion of one's peers in court. Chaffanbrass could care less, as he informs Phineas Finn in his cell, one way or another regarding the verdict of public opinion, but only wants to fight to keep his client alive. If he remains alive, his client "might fight better for it [his reputation] living than any friend could for him after his death" (*PF* II 183), where all would be hearsay.[40] He could reshape public opinion in life and as a continuous life only if he survives the death-dealing of the law.

Moreover, Finn's astute defense lawyer has constructed his own explanatory myth of this collapse of responsibility on the part of judge and jury. "When forgery ceased to be [a] capital [offense]" (*PR* II 176), dishonesty was no longer feared by men. Intriguingly, given the dependency on the copy and affidavit in the evolution of law in nineteenth-century Britain, Trollope's Chaffanbrass finds the toleration of forgery (a form of supplication) under the law, as the triumph of public opinion. Although never applied, capital punishment was previously on the books, creating a deterrent fear of the law rather than the tolerance of caveat emptor in everyday life. This tolerance shifted the burden to the consumer, making all law in effect, consumer law, held *jointly*. The law no longer speaks in its own voice, but carves out exceptions:

> What with the *joint-stock working* of companies, and the confusion between directors who know nothing and managers who know everything, and the dislike of juries to tread upon people's corns, you can't punish dishonest trading.
>
> <div align="right">(PR <i>I 176, ital. added</i>)</div>

One definition of public opinion might be "a market in the potentially dishonest trading of information." As no one can really trust anyone else, Chaffanbrass adopts the motto, "caveat lex" (*PR* II 176) as a punning extension of caveat emptor: the law is but another marketplace, even metaphorically. One man putting his name to the property of another without fear of long incarceration created a tolerance for joint ownership, counterfeit authorizations and the potential of extraordinary limits upon liability for damages. This fuels its collateral development. A singular-in-plural "collective," speaking as an imaginary unity known as public opinion, emerges contemporaneously with the systemic dispersal and dilution of singular legal responsibility onto a collective voice:

> But the *Jupiter* took all the credit for itself, and the *Jupiter* was not far wrong. All the credit was due to the *Jupiter*—in that, as in everything else.
>
> (*FP 119*)

This attempted totalization might be, somewhat paradoxically, initiated by a division between *formal authority*—which can be seized, interrupted or suffer the interregnums of clerical or political succession—and a*moral authority* which must be earned every day and for which the daily *Jupiter* claims undue credit. This is from one perspective a form assumed by plagiarism, like the wealthy enclosing land that is not theirs to enclose.

Neither Trollope's irony regarding the *Jupiter*'s assumption of easy credit nor the identification of the practices of public opinion with those whom it would put on trial masks the ease with which easy credit comes to be demanded and assumed in Barsetshire. In order to realize market value, however, a provisional public narrative, like its private counterpart, demands the pretense of universal acceptance, a shared medium of discursive exchange. But in practice, such a universality is elusive, betrayed by inflationary demands for credit (trust), the desire to preserve one's own private *account* of events, loyalties to one's own friends that constitute one manifestation of *protectionism* or even sudden changes as a consequence of inconsistent rates of informational exchange.

In taking credit for what does not, either historically or *prop*erly belong to it, public opinion operates no differently from those it would censure, like the Rev. Crawley accused, as regards a misplaced check, of having "picked it up about the house and thought it was his own" (*LCB* 123). The Rev. Crawley's alleged crime—the appropriation of a previously circulating check drawn on another's account—is replete with irony. His resistance to dominant public opinion serves to maintain the trajectory of the alleged transgression by miming it. The plot of *The Last Chronicle of Barset* is resolved when the check, believed to have been misappropriated by a clergyman with both a financial motive and a difficult personality, is traced to an altogether different criminal act by another party. But the difficulty of tracing the succession of hands through which the promissory note has passed and potentially altered is compounded by the sheer number of agents and intermediaries, commencing with a courier from the financially struggling inn, "The Dragon of Wantly," from which the payment originated.

Speculative credit is re-sold in *secondary* markets to such an extent that one is never quite sure who holds promissory notes or other claims and when or if they are vulnerable to redemption, nor who guarantees the note. Like public opinion with which it is compared on numerous occasions in Trollope, speculative money is endowed with a newfound velocity that appears as a threat to the lives of "stakeholders," literally those whose unmovable assets are marked with singular boundaries which can be measured. The proliferation of agents and intermediaries (Chaffanbrass's knowledgeable managers) as well as a proliferation of attorneys all come to have their own agendas, an internal, yet potentially fugitive presence. Public opinion, if not identical to this excess, this *secondariness*, surely is its intangible placeholder and enabler. And yet at times this very *excess* seems to function like an alternative identity.

Bruce Robbins is among the most astute critics of public opinion formation when he writes that politicians and philosophers must cease to posit spaces of freedom which "inevitably mask someone's servitude," when they address the liberating potential of public opinion.[41] The Rev. Crawley, who had vigorously opposed his bishop when faced with the demand that he vacate a living, nonetheless submits to his reinstatement to the position, even though he is not required to do so. Even after he is freed from accusations of theft, he continues to formally *submit* himself to an order, as if he were still saturated by some provisional law—an *as if*—indistinguishable from public opinion.

An emptiness that functions with the full force of the law and is often confused with it or serves as a secondary law to which appeals from legal judgments may be made, combined with difficulty in tracing inscripted authorization, lends public opinion a resemblance to the law. But it is free in Trollope's novels to disassociate itself from its twin or to bind itself to the law in the public interest. At these unpredictable times, public opinion points to the vulnerabilities of the law in nineteenth-century England both in its historical development and in application. Even when we abandon the law, which would apply historical precedent or customary utterance in order to determine its legal acceptability, we cannot escape another kind of judgment, that of public opinion which is no less arbitrary even though it lacks the thick burden of accumulated, codified precedent.

All thought or action, or even its negations, becomes *evidence* (of what?). And even if this evidence is inconsistent, merely circumstantial or identical with the construction of reputation, people come to invest in it, as an object of belief. There are no longer any "judgment-free" judgments. Although as often divided against itself despite pretensions of speaking in a universal voice (as does the church), no position has the power of an Establishment or God (nor any bestowed endowment) on its side. For public opinion to have any endowment, to become a self-sustaining Establishment, it must secure individual investment in its promises which on occasion it might manipulate.

Public opinion strategically disguises its *excess*, by coming to exist as a provisional *acceptance*. This characteristic lends public opinion a resemblance to certain material objects (like personal checks) which exist in a relationship with some *double*. A will that may not be authentic (*The Warden*); a chaplain who claims that he is the "mouthpiece" of a bishop as a cover for severing himself ideologically (*Barchester Towers*); a purloined check that may have been duplicated (*The Last Chronicle of Barset*); the existence of two coats and two identical keys that finally acquit Phineas Finn of charges of murder (*Phineas Redux*); a counterfeit deed, the existence of which convicts Melmotte (*The Way We Live Now*); and most notoriously, the question of whether a fake necklace has been substituted for real diamonds in *The Eustace Diamonds*, all qualify as objects and ideologies vulnerable to easy (because deceptive) exchange. Such an exchange is dependent on a resemblance, a potential copy, which can be accepted, even if misread, and then redistributed.

The specter (or reality) of the inauthentic duplicate describes a severed relationship to an antecedent body or value. Public opinion and the law often resemble each other to such an extent as to become at least operational duplicates. They have an equivalential status which enables mutual displacements, like the duplicate keys crucial to the acquittal of Phineas Finn; Melmotte's counterfeit deeds; or the possibility of fake diamonds in Lady Eustace's necklace. Alternately displacing and miming each other, law and public opinion are the alternating current armatures that drive plot energies. Public opinion stands in a curious relationship with the law, insofar as it both informs it, and on occasion, deconstructs its aporias, or may amend it.

In his *Reflections on Judging*, the noted American jurist, Richard Posner, has argued that the "internal complexity" of legal technique is a poor substitute for coming to terms with the "external complexity" of real-world issues.[42] Not merely the law, or its original *intention* (which Posner equates with formalism that is a mere cover for conservative, status quo judgments), but also the effect of the judgment in the real world should be considered in judgments, which would bring it closer to public opinion. The danger of course would be a blurring of the lines between judging and legislating. Social policy should be deployed not merely to break deadlocks—which abound in Trollope's political deliberations in the *Palliser Novels*—but rather as a kind of *field* which gives weight to precedent and antecedent judgments, but also to future social *impact* that might be dangerously speculative. This would involve finding a way through a maze of conflicting opinions so as to respect the limits of the power of each to affect the *field*. Formalism (or originalism) would be thereby converted from mere obedience to become partially *speculative* in nature: how it will impact a community going forward.[43] This would give the law some of the features of public opinion formation which Dicey noted; judicial realism, like investor pragmatism, would emphasize a community "bottom line."

If public opinion mimes the law both procedurally and as an adjunct enabling appeals from its judgments, the law can also be used as a tool against public opinion, if it poses a perceived threat to one's good name. The extension of *defamation* to include *libel* in Great Britain and some (but not all) of its colonies offers the possibility of relief from public opinion, without the necessity of proving malice in certain instances.[44] Phineas Finn successfully seeks suppression (a preliminary injunction) from Vice Chancellor Pickering, through the representation of his former housemate, and now attorney, MP Low, upon hearing that *The People's Banner* is about to publish a letter from the estranged husband of a friend and confidante, Lady Laura (Standish) Kennedy.

The private "Letter to the Editor" accuses Finn of alienating the affections of Lady Laura Kennedy, thereby corrupting "public morals." The crime against public morals, like say, a crime against public opinion, recognizes the mass of people as if it were a unitary body. The "peculiar" (*PR* I 233) request for the suppression of the "Letter to the Editor" prior to publication is granted, even though Trollope's narrator admits that were the defendants in Finn's affidavit other than a corporate body, *The People's Banner*, perhaps the restraining order would not have been granted:

Had the facts concerned the families of Mr. Joseph Smith and his son-in-law, Mr. John Jones instead of the Earl of Brentford and the Right Honourable Robert Kennedy, some readers will perhaps doubt, and may doubt also whether an application coming from a newly-fledged barrister would have been received as graciously as that made by Mr. Low, Q.C. and M.P.

(PR I 233)

The law is no more objectively value-neutral than the public opinion which seeks to supplement it. But, under certain conditions, the law offers protection against the extreme ravages of public opinion by invoking ad hoc bans. In the meantime, a competing paper, *The Evening Pulpit*, is carrying a story of the altercation between Phineas Finn and the estranged husband, consequent upon a meeting arranged by none other than Septimus Slide, now the editor of *The People's Banner*. Increased competition within the tabloid market does more than merely drive the story. As Slide had arranged a meeting between Kennedy, the author of the "Letter to the Editor" and the Phineas Finn, accused of a relationship with Kennedy's estranged wife, during which occasion shots were fired by the aggrieved husband, the papers are now not merely reporting on an event, but a third-party participant that instantiates the occasion on which it reports. Weighing the financial cost to the paper of violating a legal injunction embargoing publication, against the revenue from increased circulation, Slide feels that his paper suffers a painful sense of "diminished consequence" (*PR* I 240). Given its importance in public life (rivaling the traditional Three Estates), Trollope's narrator comes to see the organs of public opinion as having a quasi-endowment, effectively constituting a "Fourth Estate" (*PR* I 241).

Similarly, the prime minister is confronted with a damaging report in the same paper that the election expenses of the abandoned candidacy of Lopez for the Silverbridge seat were paid out of Palliser's own pocket. He asks the advice of his parliamentary secretary whether or not he should seek redress. Such a personal contribution violates no law and is a mere admission of responsibility for his wife's unwise encouragement of the Lopez candidacy. The support is not illegal, but the journalistic optics of the "donation" creates public suspicion. Advised to take no action and allow the accusation to go unanswered in order to protect the honor of the office, Plantagenet Palliser is shocked to see that the story has been repeated almost verbatim by *The Evening Pulpit*, in an enhanced competitive public opinion market place. If one has enough reserves of good will and honor, it might pay to allow public opinion to run its volatile course. Both of these incidents—the charge against Phineas Finn and the one against a prime minister—evoke judgment calls from the defendants on when to use the law to seek relief from public opinion and its organs and when to use public opinion to seek relief from the law.

When Slope had ventured to explain the politics of clerical appointments (as opposed to direct appointment by virtue of seniority) to Eleanor Bold in *Barchester Towers*, he cuts the explanation short with a metaphor of meshing: "wheels within wheels, all of which I could explain to you, only I fear that there is no time" (*BT* I 150). On occasion public opinion meshes with the law, but just as often not. It appears to the novice as if there was an extant rivalry for *timely* impact in oiling intermittently synchronized, yet potentially autonomous socio-informational machinery.

Admitting that as a writer, he often erred in describing the wrong season during which a flower bloomed, Trollope felt the most severe risk to the fiction writer arose when describing "those terrible *meshes* of the Law" (*PF* I 251, ital. added) from which a "benevolent pilot" (*PF* I 251), presumably knowledgeable of Dicey's "crosscurrents" of public opinion, must keep the writer clear. Trollope thus conceded a relative lack of any knowledge of the law, law-making and its relationship with public opinion formation. A mesh net, like "wheels within wheels," provides a metaphoric model of continuance with escapements, openings. The prey is held in *durance* by a carefully woven network only felt when he tries to escape. The net simultaneously *holds* and offers a (speculative) *opening*, much as does public opinion or the technical *loopholes* of the law.

Explaining his well-known, repetitively mechanical work habits as an author—arising early and completing a set number of pages each week ranging from 20 to 112 and then making up any deficit on ensuing days after consulting his diary—Trollope links his disciplined industriousness to that of a legal clerk. Conceding that more imaginative talents might find the discipline abhorrent, he subscribes to obedience to a self-imposed law described as a *force*, like "the force of the water-drop that hollows the stone" (*A* 109). This discipline is embodied in "those who sit themselves at their desks *copying* day by day, as though they were *lawyer's* clerks" (*A* 310, ital. added), held to seats by cobbler's wax.

The author as a self-described mechanical copyist within a distribution system (analogous to the post office) is an intriguing metaphor to those of us interested in the unauthorized redistribution of historical assets and allegiances in Trollope's work. Among nineteenth-century British novelists, he had a profound sensitivity to the negotiations which are inseparable from these continuous redistributions. In *An Autobiography*, he confessed to having plagiarized the plots of one of his early novels. Although acknowledging the appropriation, Trollope does note that Shakespeare and Ben Jonson *copied* a number of plots and that the objections raised against the practice are obviously historically conditioned, if not determined.[45]

Trollope's metaphor by which the law becomes a holed, mesh net—a force allowing spaces for escape—has a resonance in the Italian *plagi*, relevant to all the legal copyists and kidnappers of ideas. This was the net utilized by poachers (hence *plagiarists*) encroaching onto heretofore private territory, for unauthorized redistribution. Mrs. Proudie at the keyhole while a pressure escapes her ear is illustrative. The complex relationship of public opinion to the law in the *Barsetshire* and *Parliamentary Novels* is directed toward the leveraging of individual accountability under de-individualizing (and often imaginary) pressures. These pressures condition a speculative market in public opinion designed to protect reputation (assets) or prevent premature or uncontrolled exposure to market volatilities impacting reputation.

Notes

1 The majority of debate on public opinion formation has been confined to the work of eighteenth-century historians who attempt to align it with the hegemony of rationality, making both the products of an Enlightenment frame of mind. Daniel Mornet, *Les Origines intellectuelles de la Revolution francaise* (Paris: Minuit, 1967); Peter Gay, *The Enlightenment: An Interpretation*,

2 vols. (New York: Norton, 1966 and 1969) and Robert Darnton, *The Literary Underground of the Old Regime* (Cambridge, MA; Harvard Univ. Press, 1982), all imagine an amorphous public opinion as limiting the hard, rational despotism of the Old Regime. Hence, public opinion becomes invariably the utterance of reason against despotism. Public opinion, given its inclusivity, may straddle both "rabble" and corrective "reason," or mediate between them.

2 Samuel T. Coleridge, *On the Constitution of Church and State* (London: Hurst, Chance, and Co., 1830, facsimile rpt.) pp. 7–8.

3 Ibid., p. 48.

4 Klaus Stierstorfer, "Who Owns Britain? S.T. Coleridge and the National Trust," *Polemos, Rivista Semestrale de diritto, politica e cultura* 5, no. 1 (2011), pp. 173–185.

5 Jean-Jacques Rousseau, *Émile or On Education*, introduction, translation and notes by Allan Bloom (New York: Basic Books, 1979), p. 199. Protecting the child from opinion gives Rousseau's pedagogy its bias toward direct observation and deduction.

6 Ibid., p.196.

7 Molly Anne Rothenberg, *The Excessive Subject: A New Theory of Social Change* (New York and London: Polity Press, 2015), especially pp. 6–28, argues that it is difficult to distinguish excess, from insufficiency, or mere schadenfreude in our definition of the subject.

8 Jean-Luc Nancy, *Being Singular Plural* (Stanford, CA: Stanford Univ. Press, 1997), pp. 55–99.

9 David Pozen, "The Leaky Leviathan," *Harvard Law Review* (1913), argued early on that incremental "leaking" of information by public officials is thereby made to seem random insofar as the narrative is delayed. This variable timing gives it some of the qualities of news (on occasion prerecorded). It would create growing relevance from establishing an imaginary urgency to stimulate appetite.

10 J. Hillis Miller, *The Ethics of Reading: Kant, de Man, Eliot, Trollope, James, and Benjamin* (New York: Columbia Univ. Press, 1987), p. 98.

11 Ernesto Laclau, *Emancipation(s)* (London and New York: Verso, 2004), p. 35, ital. added.

12 Paul de Man, in "The Rhetoric of Temporality," in *Blindness and Insight: Essays in the Rhetoric of Contemporary Criticism*, 2nd edition (Minneapolis: Univ. of Minnesota Press, 1983), argues that allegory, insofar as it is committed to maintaining the illusions of temporal continuity, creates an incompatibility between history and irony. His discussion, however, omits the possibility raised by Trollope: history itself could be ironic, depending on how it is consumed, as with the The Collins' PRB-style painting as decorative accessory in the *Jupiter's* office.

13 R.D. McMaster, *Trollope and the Law* (Basingstoke: Macmillan, 1986), pp. 13–15, would add another gap in continuity, arguing that the laws of primogeniture—and hence the maintenance of one kind of antecedence—are made increasingly fragile in Trollope's work. He argues that Trollope foregoes embracing the custom of "strict settlements" (by which the father would grant the son an immediate share in the patrimony thus collaborating to bar the entail in return for a settlement) that would tie up the land for another generation.

14 Sherman Hawkins, "Mr. Harding's Church Music," *English Literary History*, XXIX (1962), pp. 202–223.

15 Nancy critiques a mode of listening by drawing a distinction between the French *entendre* which (even etymologically) relates listening to intentionality and hence to the intentional object whose sense is grounded on the closed reference back to the listening subject, and *écouter* which opens a space of reciprocity between sense and reference. Écouter does not entail listening *for something*, but rather a limitless sending and resending by which resonance becomes the structure of subject and sense. One might wonder if, additionally in public opinion formation, there might be an aggregative listening which simultaneously leaves a space for both individual and communal participation. See Jean-Luc Nancy, *Listening*, trans. Charlotte Mendell (New York: Fordham Univ. Press, 2007), p. 14, 61ff.

16 Jean-Luc Nancy has argued (by emphasizing the *Epistle of St. James* as opposed to those of St. Paul) that Christian doctrine early on was a religion "that provided the exit from religion" insofar as *Parousia* was no longer the *presence* of the Messiah, but rather what is near to us, yet often ineffably in retreat. His interpretation would lend credence to a shared operational dynamic with public opinion. See Jean-Luc Nancy, *Dis-Enclosure: The De-Construction of Christianity*, trans. Charlotte Mendell (New York: Fordham Univ. Press, 2008).

17 Martin Heidegger, *Being and Time*, trans. by J. McQuarrie and E. Robinson (Oxford: Basil Blackwell, 1962), p.234.

18 Former British Labor MP Roy Hattersley has expressed his admiration of the "sleepy" tone of his favorite among Trollope's novels, *Phineas Finn*, in an interview in *The Guardian*, April 11, 2015. He believes, however, that most debates are in reality policy driven and sincere, as opposed to distracting appeals to public opinion.

19 On the distinctions which, until 1857, gave Britain a two-track legal system that distinguished between written precedent and courts of equity that modulated legal history so that it came to exist in the "breast" of the individual judge, see Sir William Blackstone, *Commentaries on the Laws of England*, especially Vol. I, ed. William C. Jones (San Francisco: Bancroft Whitney, 1915), pp. 33–76.

20 A.V. Dicey, *Lectures on the Relation Between Law and Public Opinion in England During the Nineteenth Century*, with a new introduction by Richard A. Cosgrove (New Brunswick and London: Transaction, 1981), p. 362.

21 Ibid., pp. 40–41.

22 Ibid., p. 40, Footnote 2.

23 Emmanuel Levinas, *Otherwise than Being, or Beyond Essence*, trans. Alfonso Lingis (Pittsburgh: Duquesne Univ. Press, 1999), especially p. 157.

24 Not in his more familiar work, but just prior to his death Michel Foucault had become interested in a "field" created by the competing claims of freedom and governability as they are activated by alternating valences, on occasion antagonistic but at other times, miming each other. See Michel Foucault, *The Government of Self and Others: Lectures at the College de France*, 1982–1983, ed. Arnold I. Davidson and trans. Graham Burchell (New York: Palgrave Macmillan, 2010).

25 Recently, a number of sociologists have suggested that the widespread use of social media, designed to provide wider and faster access to information in local markets, results in ennui, a loss of focused attention in favor, as in Trollope, of responding to "currency," rather than subject. See Jim Rutenberg, "It's Not Quite Like Watergate," *The New York Times International Edition* (June 14, 2017), p. 9.

26 The terminal estrangement from his charges by Warden Harding seems a next of kin to the notion of "rationalization"—a disenchantment from the world such that the most sublime values have withdrawn from the public sphere in favor of formal efficiencies and rational calculations—articulated in the work of Max Weber. Whereas Weber attributes "rationalization" to the advent of capitalism and its divisions of labor, Trollope sees the withdrawal as sheltering from the criticism of public opinion.

27 Because the existence of a physical purgatory might imply that the sacrifice of Jesus was insufficient, the actual "state" has often remained problematic for Anglicans. Hence the "purification" aspect of the waiting for final judgment (the "Sheol") emphasized process over place. Harding is in the suspension of rationalization.

28 Among those who would agree with Mildmay in his critique of the secret ballot (and oppose Finn in his support of the Liberal cause) would be Jean-Paul Sartre, "A Trap for Fools," in *Life/Situations: Essays Written and Spoken*, trans. Paul Auster and Lydia Davis (New York: Pantheon, 1977). Sartre presciently argued that (privately cast) votes would become a serialized integer to be tabulated rather than becoming the "expression" of a sovereign group. Popular opinion for Sarte is "expressive" rather than "calculable."

29 See R. Hooker, *Of the Laws of Ecclesiastical Polity*, Book VIII, ed. P.G. Stanwood in the Folger Library. Edition (Cambridge, MA: Harvard Univ. Press, 1981), 319. The seamless unity of church and civil society in Hooker, a belief that is part of the clerical agenda in *The Warden*, in part rests upon the conviction that the original power to make "church law" resides in the "whole body" of the very church for which they are made. Hence, in the interpretation of the law there could be no disunity, because all conflicts would return to the condition of being the "property" of that alone which has the power of making law—that is, the commonwealth. As there would be no difference between *giving* and *interpreting* the law, the question of some "force" of the law would never arise.

30 Because price reductions and improvements in literacy rates coincided with the growth of Britain's transportation infrastructure, instruments crucial to the delivery of public opinion formation began to share with railroads, canals and wharves, notions of "mechanical invention," cheap convenience and rapid conveyance. Public opinion could be "manufactured" and hence it came to be associated metaphorically with jerry-built, fashionable and

occasionally error-prone structures in a network. See Gibbons Merle, "Journalism," a review of H. Carnot and P. Leroux, "Du Journalisme" (Paris 1832) *Westminster Review*, January 1833, p. 204.

31 Stanley Fish, "Belief About Belief," in *The Trouble with Principle* (Cambridge and London: Harvard Univ. Press, 1999), pp. 279–284.

32 John Heil, "Belief," in *A Companion to Epistemology*, ed. Jonathan Dancy and Ernest Sosa (Basingstoke: Macmillan, 1994).

33 Negt and Kluge, see especially pp. 73–77, wherein the illusory nature of the public sphere is seen to be differentially experienced by the bourgeois and proletarian segments of society. If so, the myth of "totalization" is counterintuitively instrumental in dividing what had previously been imagined as a common interest, just as it is with the universality of social media in the twenty-first century.

34 The entry for "bail" in the *Oxford English Dictionary* gives it as a derivative of the Fr. "bailler." Hence, the English word would have a resonance in the notion of "being leased out," simultaneously free, but under some other's restraint. This curious status is of course one definition of the dynamics of a *rentier* culture and society. In Australia, the word even today is used to describe a yoke by which cattle are loosely tethered.

35 In "R.S.I.," *Ornicar* 4, Paris, 104, Lacan argued that one must look for the birth of the symptom not in Hippocrates, but in Marx who was "first to capture [it] as coming into existence between capitalism [...] and what we call feudal times," when the worker came to recognize that he could "sell" himself (my translation). One wonders if Trollope's work might mark the occasion when the relatively privileged discovered that they could "bank" their ideas and defenses of actions for later political redemption or "cure" at the ministrations of a strong public opinion that supplants more traditional final judgments, that is, appraisal of reputation by other hands.

36 Sir Peter Hall, *Exposed by the Mask* (London: Oberon Books, 2000), p. 31. As if in response to this radical notion, the *Theatre About Glasgow* in a production of Sarah Wood's version of Sophocles' *Antigone* (September 2000), the chorus was cast as a single representative figure (played by William Elliott). It becomes a common man facing his own acquiescence to a growing totalitarianism that is partially a consequence of his own emergent singularity. The chorus hence becomes a tragedy of the creation of community, one way of reading the insufferable Rev. Crawley's tragedy in Trollope.

37 Recently, the power given the general public in public opinion formation has been criticized on the grounds that even high courts respond less to mass public opinion or to legislative initiative than to the comparatively elite social networks of a distant judicial community of peers. One result is a second-order division between social elites and the "public," evident especially in the United States with its highly politicized and polarizing judicial appointments. See Neil Devins and Lawrence Baum, *The Company They Keep: How Partisan Divisions Came to the Supreme Court* (Oxford and New York: Oxford Univ. Press, 2019).

38 Judith Butler, *Bodies That Matter: On the Discursive Limits of "Sex"* (New York and London: Routledge, 1993), pp. 206–207. Butler's examples are lovely: when the so-called N word is used by whites, it is a form of aggression, but reappropriated by African Americans for use among themselves, it opens the possibilities of continuous resistance by revision to what oppresses.

39 Jean-Luc Nancy, *The Birth of Presence*, trans. Brian Holmes (Stanford, CA: Stanford Univ. Press, 1993), pp. 149–150.

40 Uncorroborated "hearsay" (expressible) evidence continues to be admissible in British courts, unlike American courts where such evidence would be embargoed. This may stem from a British tolerance for custom (which would include oral opinion from beyond the bench) rather than the privileging of written "case" law and "precedence" in American jurisprudence. See my essay on the admissibility of such hearsay testimony under British law in "Hearsay Booked: Fugitive Talk Brought to Justice," in *Talk, Talk, Talk*, ed. S.I. Salamensky (London: Routledge, 2000), pp. 203–218.

41 Bruce Robbins, *Secular Vocations* (London: Verso, 1993), p. 10.

42 Richard A. Posner, *Reflections on Judging* (Cambridge, MA and London: Harvard Univ. Press, 2013), p. 81 ff.

43 The recent use of "victim impact" or "community impact" testimony prior to sentencing could well reflect the increasing admissibility-cum-inclusion of public opinion in the formation of legal judgments that admit community suffering as part of the crime. It would thereby potentially be continuous, raising obvious criticism from legal scholars fearing extralegal commentary as a distraction from the law.

44 British law is much more tolerant of libel suits—often advanced to protect private reputation. One's good name has some defense against public exposure (value in reproduction) that might be deleterious. Libel suits historically commenced as *defamation* suits, interestingly enough, as an alternative to assaults upon honor when dueling was banned, as a substitute action to protect honor, potentially applicable (albeit indirectly), to the dramatization of the duel in *Can You Forgive Her*. Section 2 of the *Libel Act of 1842* and its successor, the *Libel Act of 1845* authorized an apology and a payment to the court for newspaper libel. Gradually over time, newspapers were allowed more freedom when the issue entered public discussion. Known as the "critic's defense," the rights of the press to state matters of public interest such as government activity were gradually established. The case brought by Phineas Finn obviously straddles a thin line between a legitimate public interest and a personal slur, articulated later in *Thomas v. Bradbury, Agnew & Co.* (1906) which found for the plaintiff in defense of his "honor," compromised by a publication that had made a personal slur, confused with a matter of "public interest." How to separate "a matter of public interest" from a private slur when one or both are public figures might suggest that public opinion has *always-already* been brought into *play*, albeit unacknowledged.

45 *A* 104–5. Trollope admitted that his brother had provided the outline for the plot of *Doctor Thorne*. Subsequently, he came to feel that an author should demand "to be credited with no more of the work than he himself has produced." The Copyright Act of course interceded between the offense and the revision of Trollope's attitude. How and when to acknowledge the "share" of others, and how the derivative is deployed, is a feature of authors, commercial enterprises and public opinion, as shall be seen in *The Struggles of Brown, Jones, and Robinson*.

Chapter Three

"PLAYING" THE OPINION MARKET

She had so far played her game well and won her stakes.

(ED 7)

To address a specific kind of *play* in Trollope's *Barsetshire Chronicles* and the *Palliser Novels* is to encounter serious risks, not unlike those characters who commit to "gaming the system" in such radically different ways. If public opinion functions like traditional characters in a novel (as an imaginary, assembled body constructed by author, other characters, critics and readers), then we might logically expect development through time in the model of the *Bildungsroman*. A shared ideological body would mature into self-awareness, finding a secure place in the culture from which it initially seemed exiled. If public opinion, however, functions only as negation of the conventional body or part of some imaginary public sphere purged of individual interest, then its operations upon a system—its role in generating the consequential—would be of primary importance. It is, in a number of ramifications, "everybody" and "nobody" as we have seen. As part of an imaginary body, it would be defined in part by an account of inward investments of faith that enact it: Who came to believe in it and under what conditions? Who would hope to realize a return, be it professional, financial, comfort or public esteem, that might pay dividends in the future? To what extent are those who invest in public opinion really speculating on it, as opposed to pursuing or purchasing it, so as to be sufficiently nimble to vacate a position? The literary critic enjoys no exemption.

As a concept, *play* carries a considerable surplus of cultural baggage and literary history. We might, for example, commence with Huizinga's work and move through that of Roger Caillois to the various accounts of the performative "knights of misrule" in the Renaissance theater.[1] Although all of these may "come into play," Trollope rather uses the concept differently. It becomes synonymous with *insincerity* or the shirking of hard work and responsibility, hence duplicating the idleness of the privileged as they play social and conversational games that seem opposite to *work*. It is neither chance nor simulation, as Caillois suggested, nor is it invariably competitive. Not needing to work, a sophisticated amateurism ("giving it a go"), reaffirms social status as a qualified disinterest that may merely fill time (with play) rather than spending it. Implicit in this notion is a willed diminution or softened seriousness, as when a sports team manager (or foxhunt master) urges his players to remember that "it is only a game, after all," by which community is built. Metaphorically, it might also provide a defense against the possible seriousness of loss. Or, as in the case of "our" Signora Neroni, the *play* may be an assertion of independence by a very dependent person, who subordinates any expectation of sincerity in the world at large to a devout skepticism:

> It is needless to say that the signora was not very sincere on such subjects. She was never sincere on such subjects. She never expected others to be so, nor did she expect others to think herself so. Such matters were her *playthings*, her billiard table, her hounds and hunters, her waltzes and polkas, her picnics and summer day excursions.
>
> (BT *II 125, ital. added*)

Many social activities common to the life of the gentry in Victorian England are aggregated under the rubric of discursive playthings. Because of her severe physical and social handicap and the accompanying speculative narratives of abuse by a foreign husband, the possibility arises that her strategic play with the affections of the Rev. Slope is some compensation for her limited access to other, more traditional games which define the culture. Unlike the speculating Lopez or Melmotte in *The Way We Live Now*, Madame Neroni is an *arriviste manqué*, returning to her native country after a long absence. Hence, she knows how to present herself according to rules which, as Slope will eventually discover, limits his access to her heart while appearing to encourage him, as does his off-and-on dalliance with Towers's editorials. We might read her temptations as revenge, but there are other possible ways of understanding her pull/push behavior. We often put up for *play* (gaming) from a sense of both insufficiency and excess, as if we were speculating while hedging our bets.

Signora Neroni's metaphoric sports combine individual contests (billiards), socially regulated and therefore potentially unifying pursuits (hounds and hunters) and socially inclusive recreation (polkas and waltzes). Her highly inclusive canon of play would blur the distinction between conjunctive and disjunctive sport, a critique of Levi-Strauss's model. It would be more nearly akin to the antics of those deities who resided upon the inaccessible, "modern Mt. Olympus" (*W* 117) with which Towers's *Jupiter* is compared. They play with those of us beneath for their own sport. This playful turn in the plots of the *Barsetshire Chronicles* gives the "Tenth Muse" some of the qualities of Albert Brook's 1999 comedy, "The Muse," in which Sharon Stone plays a mercurial muse-for-hire, servicing politicians in return for trinkets from Tiffany's, a goddess of exchange.

Both pagan Gods (historically) and powerful men (on occasion) *play*, strategically, alternating distantiation from pragmatic collaboration with those adversaries who can be converted to a belief in mutually shared interests, even temporarily. Although the *Jupiter* originally supported the plaintiffs in Hiram's Hospital while at the same time disclaiming knowledge or responsibility for the events surrounding the case, it nonetheless takes credit for the efforts at "salutary reform" of an institution. The vox populi seems to speak out of both sides of its mouth, weighing in as fulcrum to whomever seems to have the upper hand at the time. This suggests that public opinion is both an object of speculation (to those who wish to invest in it), but also a subject insofar as it takes risks on its own initiative. Early on in *An Autobiography*, Trollope excuses his delay in commencing a career as a novelist until his sojourn in Ireland, not to any intellectual insufficiency, but rather to something else: "What I did doubt was my own industry and the *chances of the market*" (*A* 63, ital. added). A notorious haggler over contracts and advances with a variety of publishers throughout his career, *An Autobiography* reveals a relative lack of embarrassment at being perceived by Edward Chapman of Chapman and Hall as if he were "a highway robber" (*A* 106), a confession of participation in a "chancey" market, subject to being caught short.

Having previously threatened to reject a letter to the editor from Slope on the grounds that it was really an advertisement, Towers later writes to the bishop's chaplain that he will "help [...] if I can" (*BT* II 182) in editorial support of Slope's ambition to become dean of Barchester Cathedral. Opposition becomes strategic collaboration, as the result of a perceived shared interest in a market for public opinion formation in which the press (long before *Fox News*) became an interested participant. So many of Trollope's characters—Rev. Slope, Tom Towers, Phineas Finn and Plantagenet Palliser—share an interest with their creator in how public opinion is *made* and practiced over time.

> Mr. Slope had from his youth upwards been a firm believer in the *public press*. He had *dabbled* in it himself ever since he had taken his degree. [...] He had delighted in the idea of wresting power from the country's magistrates, and placing it in a *custody* which was at any rate nearer to his own reach. Sixty thousand broadsheets, dispersing themselves daily among his reading fellow citizens, formed in his eyes a better *depot* for supremacy than a throne at Windsor, a cabinet at Downing Street, or even an assembly at Westminster. And on this subject we must not quarrel with Mr. Slope, for the feeling is too general to be met with disrespect.
>
> (BT *II 182–83, ital. added*)

The word "dabble" intimates the playful, participation in a contested field from which the self-designated amateur could withdraw as if it were a hobby or pastime: more a secondary "taking up" than committed vocation. The space and time occupied by "dabbling" might mark out a recreational space or field of play in which ideology or belief is subservient to strategy.[2] There is an implicit determinism (rules) to be manipulated. Slope reflects "that he had made his first *move* well, as well as the pieces on the *board* would allow" (*BT* I 206, ital. added) so as to gain public credit, with the aid of Towers at the *Jupiter*. Successive moves would presumably determine success or failure.

Allied with personal ambition, the courtship of public opinion (like his "dabbling" with Madame Neroni) can be stockpiled or banked as a deposit or preliminary investment over which one might claim custody for future deployment or even supplementary speculation, not unlike what is termed political capital. Because never quite fully possessed, it has a continuity. If our concerns are essentially with private interests, then politics is of genuine concern only when it interferes with those interests.

Whatever had previously been defined as political comes to be merged with those interests, partially accounting for the confusion of Slope's ideological positions: alternately a reformist (in desiring to rid the Church of England of aging, redundant clerics) and traditional (in desiring the return to long-abandoned ceremonial practices). In another context, Sheldon Wolin believes this inconsistency to characterize an "illiberal proto-liberal."[3] That description is applicable to Trollope's own allegiance to the anachronistically ceremonial (the hunt; dedicated, old geezer wardens; benevolent dukes) as a necessary restraint upon reforms that must be negotiated in the future.

In his marvelous study of the development of liberalism in Great Britain, Alan Ryan has suggested that in liberal thought, individuals have an essential private interest in the maintenance of public goods (such as defense and law and order). Hence there is a tendency to reduce the common good to a product of negotiations between what are essentially *bargaining* interests. Traditional Republicans, for Ryan, tend to make participation in a shared enterprise the highest good, relying on citizen virtue to recognize what the highest good is.[4] As a later Liberal candidate for Parliament, Trollope would understandably seem to align himself with those who reduce the common good to negotiated compromises between competing interests, which may account for the excessive role of political haggling in a metaphoric market in his novels.

Yet, individual self-determination privileges knowledge of an ally or opponent's modus operandi, incorporated into tactical responses which resemble one aspect of what later came to be known as *game theory*.[5] Although each individual has choices, the payoff for each choice depends on the choices made by others. In what is termed "the prisoner's dilemma" game, players weigh the benefits of cooperation against betrayal partially by anticipating public response to each. Obviously, this may produce less than optimum conditions for the determination of public good while still engaging public participation. Slope's responses are predicated upon some familiarity with the rhetorical and temporal periodicities of the newspaper which shapes his participation:

> He was sufficiently conversant with the *tactics* of the *Jupiter* to know that the *pith* of the article would be in the last paragraph. The place of honour was given to him, and it was indeed as honourable as even he could have wished.
>
> (BT *II 186, ital. added*)

Whereas the clerical scholar encountered in the *Barsetshire Chronicles* is trained in sacred texts and accompanying commentary or elaborating the same texts for sermons, those who attempt to become a contestant in the public opinion market must read themselves in the discourse of the Other. Slope is sufficiently familiar with Towers's editorial style to know that the operative content (presumably after rhetorical to and fro-ing) is invariably contained in the last paragraph as ideological fruit to be separated from chaff. He has learned to read in a particularly reductive, some might say, allegorical way, but synchronous with that of another contemporaneous thinker from another discipline, W. S. Jevons's *A General Mathematical Theory of Political Economy* (1862). Like others who enter markets, he embraces a notion of marginal utility: the idea that the additional satisfaction a consumer is willing to pay from consuming one more, final unit of a good or service is a determinant of price. As the last drop of water for the man wandering in the desert is more valuable and expensive than water is for those of us who have it on tap, so the last paragraph of the *Jupiter* editorial is what those hoping to stimulate public opinion formation read *for*. This is surely a coded messaging board.

He learns, upon entering the market, of its heuristic dimension. Once noted, his entry has an effect on the entry of other potential investors in early polling:

During the entire first week Barchester was ignorant who was to be its new dean on Sunday morning. Mr. Slope was decidedly the favourite; but he did not show himself in the cathedral, and then he *sank a point or two in the betting.* On Monday he got a scolding from the Bishop in the hearing of the servants and down he went till nobody would have him at any price; but on Tuesday he received a letter, in an office, marked private, by which he fully recovered his place in public favour.

(BT II 217, ital. added)

Putative new information, even if false, is an accelerant to changing public opinion. As Slope enlarges his base of support with the assistance of an organ of public opinion formation, his future is increasingly a subject of speculation by supporters and detractors alike. To remain outside public view for a period is to fall a few points among the political punters in Barsetshire, but to be known to receive a letter marked "private" is to gain investors in his future. All behavior, even its formal negations, is put into speculative *play* by public opinion regulated by what will come to be a news cycle.

His conservative stance is unbelievably embraced by the *Jupiter* as a reform candidate who will drain the swamp of excess, redundant clergy, even as he pays court to the daughter of a redundant clergyman. Slope's is a candidacy, in the *Jupiter* endorsement, who "will not afford easy couches to worn-out clerical voluptuaries" (*BT* II 186). He is simultaneously a reformer of clerical personnel, yet a would-be restorer of antiquated ceremonial practices. The self-appointed instruments of public opinion formation are just as fickle as those who have learned how to *play* the press, because they attempt to weaponize the instability of public opinion to alter it.

In a culture where *strategy* has become *retail politics* (the last opinion/ price being determinative), the *Jupiter* proclaims itself a winner, on the side of a virtual renaissance in the fortunes of Hiram's Hospital as opposed to the "decadence" (*BT* II 184) which allegedly occasioned its initial, presumably meliorative intervention. The paper goes so far out on its editorial limb that it proposes—assuming an interest of Slope—a charity school for the children of the village poor to be attached to the institution, sweetening the pot with a populist proposal to expand the base. It assumes this *position* only in the interest of advancing the Slope whom it had previously condemned even while now conceding that such a proposal could only be decided "at the discretion of the new warden" (*BT* II 184). The press attempts to shape policy even where it lacks power, merely in order to maintain influence by a preemptive, anticipatory investment in a universally sympathetic, presumptively populist, issue.

Once having committed themselves to the game, all players are reproduced in it, albeit self-protectively as a form of *play*. Anyone can claim to be a *reform* candidate if the object is to secure public endorsement against some constructed opposition: populism sells because it is so apparently totalizing. Who could be against more charity for the poor child even if condemning it for aged parishioners? Clearly both the *Jupiter* and Slope are, in their newfound alliance, "hedging" risk in rather similar ways by appealing to public subscription against a soft and dated church hierarchy with diminished attendance. In supplementing their proposal to include charity for the young, Slope and his editorial partner are enlarging the charitable market: a "new" and "improved."

This may explain in the later *Palliser Novels* the draw of games, gaming tables, horse-racing tracks and even politics as an intrusion of unpredictable speculation into highly predetermined lives or career paths (as with the physically predetermined limits set upon Madame Neroni), upon which the people wager or stake other claims. The privileged often commence *play* with borrowed assets or appropriated positions, and then raise the stakes by staking others to it. Because there are risks of potential loss in all such speculative investments, a variety of strategies are devised to minimize losses through hedging. When one courts public opinion, there is always a danger of finding oneself in the *court* of public opinion: hence the need for risk management, as John Bold discovers too late in *The Warden*.

As we have seen, money and public opinion share a newfound vehicularity to such an extent that both are vulnerable to being either "snapped up" or "caught up": bought into or open to forfeiture in unexpected ways. Miss Prettyman, at whose academy Grace Crawley has been marginally employed, merely repeats what she has heard as part of a community's speculative opinion regarding the fate of her father, the Rev. Crawley in *The Last Chronicle of Barset*. But even the repetition creates unanticipated discursive risk not dissimilar from that of the theft of free-floating checks of which her father has been accused: "surely I may be allowed to repeat what I hear without being snapped up" (*LCB* 749). So free has the market in information become, that pressures toward control are emerging: repeated public speculation resembles purloined checks.

***

In Benoit Mandelbrot's Efficient Market Hypothesis (EMH), proposed in *Fractals and Scaling in Finance: Discontinuity, Concentration, Risk*, the speed of informational dissemination is a crucial factor in the definition of efficient markets. A truly competitive market (for securities or bonds or gossip all held in provisional trust) occurs when every price *already* reflects all the information that is available at that time.[6] The arrival of new information imparts imperfections, but the market operates under the questionable assumption that new data can be arbitraged away. If public valuations reflect all information at all times, price changes are unpredictable, because they can only be caused by new information and new information is always arriving. Revaluations are thus ongoing, but exogamous rather than endogamous. Hence the tardy, sleepiness of leaders and their representatives of the Church of England in Trollope's Barsetshire represents a respect for tradition which defines their role as a continued resistance to the currency of new information, despite gestures toward ecumenism and enhanced participation in civic life. If public opinion functions as a general plaza, central market exchange or depository anticipating future returns, then the so-called private individual, like any dependent investor, including the Church of England, lives life both troubled by it and engaged with it, even if not always willfully.[7]

More than mere matter, once deposited into an imaginary "bank" of public opinion, the heretofore private individual is endowed with an *excess*—a difference that renders information active, self-creative and unpredictable. Public opinion comes to be seen as both a quasi-materiality (that invokes immanent modes of self-transformation) and an elusive ideality. It is imaginable as possessing its own mode of self-transformation, self-organization (in the domain of unintended effects), and yet is assumed to directly speak. Unlike other materialism(s), public opinion, despite its susceptibility to mathematical measurement, is resistant to the determinism that Marx attributed to materialism, where the meaning of a commodity *is* its price. Public opinion, by contrast, is continually both determining and adjusting to the responses of those who feel themselves determined by its intrusions.[8] Similarly, once exposed *by* or *to* public opinion, there arises a need for nimbleness at odds with institutional inertia: an *awakening* from sleepiness into how things—like reputation—are made and cyclically, but unpredictably, vulnerable to unmaking.

Like the subtleties of commodity pricing, how public opinion appraises reputation can never quite be foreseen, be it in the course of production or later, when it enters the market. This endows both with some of the characteristics of what we might term an allegorical existence, perhaps appropriate to the clerical setting of the *Barsetshire Chronicles*. For those committed to an allegorical reading of texts or life, there is no guarantee that the profound insights will lead to one meaning rather than another. Though it once may have acquired such an historically or theologically foregrounded meaning, the modes of determining meaning can be modified or withdrawn. This allegorical mode of reading emerges when, in times of crisis, people think their *reading* of one idea in an editorial supports all their values.[9]

Speculation on what one does *not* have commences early in the life of Lizzie Greystock, the future Lady Eustace of Trollope's *The Eustace Diamonds*, the third of the *Palliser Novels*. She is the sole daughter of a retired admiral who loved whist and the good life (and hence a model of playing for money), who uses money borrowed against pawned jewelry to support the incidental expenses of his daughter's initially modest lifestyle. The Greystock family, as a nominative deformation of "bluestockings" might imply, lives on the faded outer fringes of polite society, in terms of lifestyle and demeanor, but never being part of it, given financial insecurity. They live on credit:

> They lived on the good things of the world, and mixed with wealthy people. But they never had any money.
>
> *(ED 23)*

As with Tom Towers, Phineas Finn and institutions like the *Jupiter*, they must maintain themselves speculatively by becoming the entrepreneurs of their own ambitions, dependently living *on* their wits rather than dependently living *upon* family resources. This necessarily includes speculative borrowing against future prospects.

Lying about her age (and hence the legal right to make financial decisions) barely eight months after her father's death, Lizzie (later Lady Elizabeth Eustace) visits Messrs. Harter and Benjamin to make herself responsible for her father's debt, but through a secondary loan by which she would "take the [family] jewels out of pawn" *(ED 2)*, a lovely metaphor. Responsibility is not antithetical to a "new issue" for further speculation. Announcing that she is the object of the attentions of Sir Florian Eustace who, upon marriage, would assume all responsibilities for Lizzie's debts—one cannot help but notice how debt is being passed on to third parties—she succeeds in gaining a speculative partner in the jewelers, not unlike that of Slope and the *Jupiter*'s Towers. Marriages of convenience breed investors for mutual benefit; Harter and Benjamin are investing in futures: a marital partner. Although the pawnbroker has some doubts that the wedding will come off, he is willing to speculate on available information and accordingly invest in it by means of a loan, given the fact that Sir Florian, "as *all the world knew*" (*ED* 2, ital. added), had an unembarrassed fortune. Although his reputation and wealth are known to "all the world," there are always limits to accessible information or misinformation masked as genuine. We ignore excess leverage to do the best we can with the insufficient information available to us:

> *From such information as Mr. Benjamin could acquire,* he thought that there would be a marriage, and that the *speculation* was on the whole in his favour. Lizzie recovered her jewels and Mr. Benjamin was in possession of a promissory note purporting to have been executed by a person who was no longer a minor.
>
> *(ED 3, ital. added)*

The evaluation of the ultimate guarantor is both partially determining and held within that valuation, much as would be the debt rating of a corporation with good prospects going forward. Lizzie's own jewelry, in hock, becomes an asset against which one might borrow to form a larger estate which will multiply to include the famous Eustace Diamonds, a necklace known to the world, and Portray Castle in Scotland. Although her methods may be open to criticism, Trollope comments with some irony in the double entendre, that Lizzie "had earned for herself" a "brilliant future" (*ED* 16), diamonds being synonymous with "brilliants."[10]

The relative ease with which an initially hesitant, if not skeptical, participant enters into a speculative alliance with future marital, financial or political partnerships is a theme common to both the *Barsetshire Chronicles* and the *Parliamentary Novels*. John Bold and Tom Towers in *The Warden*, Slope and Towers in *Barchester Towers*, Lizzie Eustache and Harter and Benjamin Jewelers in *The Eustace Diamonds*, Phineas Finn and Madame Goesler in both *Phineas Finn and Phineas Redux*, Lady Glencora and Lopez as well as Lopez and Sexty Parker in *The Prime Minister*, Melmotte and Paul Montague in *The Way We Live Now* and the Earl of Silverbridge and Major Tifto in *The Duke's Children* with their shared investments (as sponsorship and agent) in horses would all qualify as risk-laden partnerships from the outset. A shortage of ready money, the lack of access to credit on favorable terms or perhaps some sympathy with the social isolation of the outsider may provide a partial explanation for these associations across class lines. These are in effect unacknowledged mutual funds, an attempt to identify shared interests, perhaps instrumental to a certain kind of sociality, not unrelated to the hunt or dinner parties among the privileged classes.

The struggle among survivors over the whereabouts, possession, legitimate ownership and ultimate disposition of the diamond necklace and the struggle between the law and public opinion to determine its status and value at any given time are, writ large, the plot of *The Eustace Diamonds*. But it is important to remember that at the outset, the diamond necklace was a historical asset acquired on speculation that a marriage would occur. One can invest in objects but also in future *alliances*, on occasion indistinguishable from each other.

As with Towers of the *Jupiter*, Septimus Slide of the *People's Banner* or, as we shall see, with purchasers of shares in Melmotte's mythical rail project of *The Way We Live Now*, once an item or information is deposited through some speculative arrangement, to be redeemed later, the market becomes highly illiquid when recovery is demanded prior to maturity or consummation(s), including marriage. In the case of the Eustace Diamonds, the *status* of the necklace itself depends on the narrative conditions and location which accompanied its *presentation*, totally detached from its price, but impacted by potential alienation from its temporarily indeterminable, real owner.

Like the public and legal opinions which come to be attached to the necklace, value is largely determined by the conditions under which it will *circulate*. For the necklace could be defined as either (1) a wedding *gift* to a new bride or (2) a family heirloom to be ultimately bestowed upon an heir born to Lizzie following the untimely death of her new, young husband and hence inalienable (it could never have been given, being already *there* in possession of descendants). If a gift to the now young widow, Lady Elizabeth Eustace, it is hers to dispose of as she will, including a provisional dowry, bait with which to attract a new husband. The jewels, like the public opinion which accompanies speculation about their status, exist in two registers. Once defined as a gift (and hence alienable) the jewels which lend the novel its name have a value determinable by "use-value." The status of the necklace as an alienable object (a ready asset) open to market fluctuations over time is not unlike those attending upon a young, rich and attractive widow. To live in public opinion (fluctuating eligibility) is to live (at least potentially) in perpetual alienation from one's *proper* estate for all claimants, in Trollope's lovely symmetry.

There could be no better representation of the gap between old and new (in the sense of speculatively wagered) money. Hence, shortly after the premature death of her husband, Sir Florian, the family attorney, Camperdown, whose law firm had represented every Eustace in living memory, and hence shares in its history, initiates a claim for the obligatory return of the Eustace Diamonds to the (historic) family estate from its alleged temporary custodian, Lady Eustace. She deliberates moving them about as unprotected, ahistorical (and hence personal) assets, raising the whole question of when privatization becomes theft, a theme crucial to *The Way We Live Now* and in corporate culture now.

Yet, there is some hesitation in equating a gift with a disposable or fixed asset, which may be due, for some commentators, to the privileging of the notion of charity in Christian literature.[11] All *economies* function as in some sense a *legal* apparatus (a *nomos*) which designates what is owed to whom, thereby establishing obligations in order to partition them for subsequent distribution, a function common to wills, the general economy and political rewards. It includes home, property, hearth, but not genuine gifts. While bearing some relation to the economy, as Jacques Derrida has reminded us, genuine gifts are in another sense aneconomic.[12] If it is a genuine gift freely given—as opposed to, say, governed by the rather rigid code that prescribes the amount to be reciprocated when one receives a gift in Japan—the genuine gift interrupts the economy. What defines it as a gift is that it cannot be returned or reclaimed *as an obligation*. It is bestowed without reason or logic, which explains why we are often puzzled by a gift when it occurs outside the occasion which may have determined it.

Lady Eustace, when confronted with the value of the necklace and quasi-legal claims for its return to the Eustace family as an heirloom, is justifiably unmoved, regarding it as a "free gift." The distinction that she makes, given her youth, surely rivals that of Derrida; what defines a genuine gift is an intentional *caritas*:

> If I give you a present and then die, people can't come and take it away afterwards because I didn't put it into my will.
>
> *(ED 47)*

She concedes that a fixed asset—a house, a farm or a wood—can never be given away, but "a *thing* that he can carry about with him" (*ED* 47, ital. added), like a portable diamond necklace, can indeed be given away for any purpose, including speculation in circulation, by the recipient. Moveable assets, like volatile opinion which mimes it, circulate and can be monetized. Her decision to keep the necklace (and play both with it and use it as a portable plaything/accessory to draw a prospective future husband's interest) is based, like that of public opinion, upon its vehicularity. It cannot be tied down as a fixed asset any more than the *Jupiter*'s opinions of Slope or Slope's changeable beliefs. The logic of mobility threatens historical repositories of value with the status of a novel (and potentially perpetual) renewability or liquidation.

Fluid markets in whatever commodity induce the feeling, if not the fact, of adventure and the adventuress. Continuity is disregarded as we come to live in a kind of perpetual *present-ness* where life processes are raised to a point where both past and future are irrelevant.[13] This creates a kind of *continuous* watchfulness—one ramification of being held in *durance*—over the possibilities of devaluation or theft, as opposed to the historical (long-term) *continuity* of the immobile asset, presumably exempt from liquidation and hence, considered as stable, rather than a *plaything*.

At issue is the difference between a gift (whose *meaning* is separable from its economic value) and an heirloom (whose meaning in part is historically determined), held in trust by an estate inseparable from a state interest, given the landed—in the sense of fixed—interests of the governing classes. If merely pronouncing an object an heirloom makes it one, then the status is not created by the history of ownership, but by some "speech act" like "antique." To further complicate matters, in *The Eustace Diamonds*, a third term, the gift as the interest on a joint investment partnership with the pawnbrokers to secure the late Sir Florian's initial attentions, blurs the boundary between gift, heirloom and the returns on an antecedent investment partnership. Trollope is raising a profound question as to when a gift is individually owned and subject to free speculation and unrestricted *play* and when it is the possession of a family through time and hence forever inalienable, to be held on deposit for future generations in familial trust. The value of the asset in exchange is largely determined by its existential status, to which provenance (both narrative and historical) contributes a significant share.

A gap between the maintenance of historical succession (as an heirloom or as an already compromised apostolic succession) and an antagonistic maintenance of negotiable assets for potential future realization (and hence speculation on the open market) occurs with great frequency in Trollope. In *The Warden*, the law attempts to bridge a discontinuity when the will of the donor, like the Eustace Diamonds, is not immediately recoverable, but exists only in excess accumulation. But even the law, as is public opinion—its occasional appellate division—is divided on how and where the diamond necklace was given to her: at the Portray Estate, in London, or on the wedding trip to Italy, which would be instrumental in distinguishing between a gift "outright," part of an estate or something with no domicile (an international object), preferred in transit. The time and location of the acquisition is thus commodified in the gift, and as is true of the occasion of gossip, partially constitutes its value. Although Lady Eustace has been given a life interest in the Portray Estate in Scotland by virtue of her husband's will, the property provides only lifetime income for a very good maintenance. It is restricted as to both future disposition and speculation, by which she might entice a future husband, as she begins to feel the whole *weight* of the law, a kind of heaviness, pertaining to inheritance. Traditional family law firms have the respectable solidity of the Bank of England, whereas retail jewelers who advance money, though they deal in "rocks," are speculators in market futures, including the marriage market:

> Messrs. Mowbray and Mopus and Mr. Benjamin were the allies to whom she looked for guidance; but she was wise enough to know that Mowbray and Mopus, and Harter and Benjamin were not trustworthy, whereas Camperdown and Son and the Messrs. Garnett were all as firm as rock, and as respectable as the Bank of England.
>
> *(ED 35)*

In attempting to mediate the dispute over the ownership status of the diamond necklace, Camperdown consults the esteemed veteran legal councilor, Thomas Dove. Although Lizzie Eustace's claim to the jewels is seen in his determination as amounting to nothing, and as the jewels are not listed in any will, she, however, could, in Dove's informed judgment, lay claim to them as "paraphernalia" (*ED* 187) with use limited only to occasions when fully and formally dressed, a qualified possession, yet a potential self-advertisement of availability for the speculation of future suitors. The learned legal authority gives more weight to "custom" (and hence equity) than he does to common law, while admitting of some conflict between the two traditions. What would qualify the diamond necklace as an "heirloom" is precisely that it cannot be bequeathed (after death no less) nor can something become an heirloom merely by being so nominated, which would make of it a "speech act." Not mentioned in the will (along with other "chattel" of the estate to which Lizzie has drawn credit prior to the marriage), the necklace which lends the novel its name occupies a curious legal interstice which evokes public opinion. But Dove's final opinion is that "it couldn't have been an heirloom" (*ED* 187) to the disappointment of Attorney Camperdown, retained by the family to recover an illegally appropriated, heirloom.

In a later meeting in Dove's chambers, pressed by Camperdown to consider the necklace as falling under the legal protections normally accorded all forms of personal property and hence a qualified heirloom, the learned counselor demurs, by suggesting that genuine heirlooms belong to the *discourse* of "chivalry," not that of "simple dirty questions of money" (*ED* 213) and markets. A genuine heirloom is uniquely cleansed by a traceable provenance but contaminated by exogamous (unsettling) material sale:

> Whatever the *value of the thing* so settled may be,—but that the son or grandson or descendant may enjoy the satisfaction which is derived from *saying*, my father, or my grandfather or my ancestor sat in that chair, or looked as he now looks in that picture.
>
> (ED *212, ital. added)*

A large diamond necklace "is not only alterable, but constantly altered, and cannot easily be traced" (*ED* 212) materially, whereas the genuine heirloom is indelibly historically registered, presumably rendering it more resistant to easy partition. Speculative narratives can use historical legacy (narrative provenance) to add value that would encompass the discourse of future generations, as well as the cumulative narrative inventories of family property. Given the speculation as to the whereabouts and possible breakup of the necklace and piecemeal sale at the conclusion of Trollope's novel, the distinction seems more than prescient. Once it enters material circulation, like Lizzie's devalued reputation at the hands of public opinion, it belongs to "simple, dirty" questioning (*ED* 213). The interrogation of provenance, like the rhetorical questions posed by public opinion, is a metaphoric smudging that attaches to objects of speculation.

The necklace, like the reputation of Rev. Crawley and Mr. Harding in the *Barchester Chronicles*, is held in legal *durance* as to ownership and disposition which affect value, a crucial temporal dimension in many of Trollope's novels, as can be seen below. The omniscient narrator values the diamonds at anywhere from worthless to 24,000 pounds, depending on who is discussing the *thing* and under what market conditions during the course of the novel. Lord Fawn, a potential suitor for the widow's affections, no longer in mourning garb, suddenly experiences a cooling of his ardor: the *market* for Lizzie being inseparable from the status of an object that may or not be an asset. Although attracted simultaneously by the necklace and the neck of its wearer, Lord Fawn is reluctant to commit to a beautiful woman if in fact she is a mere thief, holding onto an item to which she is literally not entitled, despite her title. The most desirable asset would be simultaneously the most potentially destructive of reputation, if the demanded return of the necklace to the Eustace estate were made under court order. Public opinion, too, is a variable appraiser of value.

Lady Eustace, however, boldly and perhaps inadvisably, decides "to appear [in public] with the much-talked-of-ornament upon her person" (*ED* 129) at which time it occasions the division in public opinion familiar to Trollope's readers for whom the worn jewels are a synecdoche. She is condemned by some and praised by Lady Glencora, the wife of a future duke and prime minister, for her audacity in the face of hostility. The jewelry is *already* "broken up" by and in public opinion. People both admire its beauty and condemn the presentation, a judgment similar to that which Trollope's narrator holds of the wearer. The diamond necklace thus becomes indistinguishable from public opinion and its variable and inconsistent revaluations rendered over time in a community's narratives. Lord Faun postpones a visit during which she had expected a proposal, partially in response to the indiscretion of her going public with a problematic possession, the IPO on the marital market a bit premature. In a chapter entitled "The Diamonds Become Troublesome," Lady Eustace, fearing theft were the necklace to remain in rental lodging in London during her seasonal visit to Portray Castle or sequestered by Camperdown under court order, realizes that, like dwelling in public opinion, the Eustace Diamonds *are* henceforth, an inseparable part of her lived life in both a community's narrative and in her provisional custody of the actual necklace. Ownership is inextricably bound to "owning up" to its status.

The jewels, like the community narrative of public opinion, must accompany her wherever she travels, in a protective, heavy iron box or similar container, likely to draw attention of the press or thieves, while seeming to guard privacy. Even if the necklace did not, the conflicted public and legal opinions which narratively accessorize either her wearing of it in public or her attempt to secure it under lock and key changes her relationship to it. The necklace must now accompany her wherever she goes, that combination of excess and insufficiency that defines public opinion in Trollope's work. One ramification of this change is that she now *feels* it as an affect, rather than merely wearing it or storing it: a neutral occupier (a thing) felt, but hidden without marketability, like some narrative of public opinion, its accessory:

> In her sobbing, she felt the *thing* under her feet, and knew that she could not get rid of it. She hated the box and yet she must cling to it now. She was thoroughly ashamed of the box, and yet she must seem to take pride in it. She was horribly afraid of the box, and yet she must keep it in her own bedroom.
>
> *(ED 153, ital. added)*

Attorney Dove's legal opinion had tentatively concluded with an addendum that any genuine heirloom (by custom, a status he denies the diamonds) invariably has an element of a bygone age of chivalry about it. That element of course is an accompanying historical narrative. Although denying its status as an heirloom in favor of maintaining possession of the necklace as a private gift, Lizzie Eustace ironically endows it with the rhetoric of chivalry, *after the fact*:

> "I do feel like some naughty person in the 'Arabian Knights,'" she said "who, has got some great treasure that always brings him into trouble; but he can't get rid of it because *some spirit has given it to him.* At last, some morning it turns into slate stones, and then he has to be a water-carrier, and is happy ever afterwards, and marries a king's daughter."
>
> *(ED 236, ital. added)*

A gift over which one has neither control nor power of possession, like Bold's letter to the *Jupiter*, has a curious nonphysical status, like that of public opinion. One can escape from it, here lightly rendered as a spirit—and live a life free of its burdens—only through an inverse fairy tale of *demonetization.* In her myth the diamonds would magically revert to (*Grey*stock?) slate stones which would hold neither public nor monetary interest. Even if the jewelry could be magically rendered worthless in some riches-to-rags conversion, that narrative too would become part of the continuing life of the Eustace Diamonds. The variable relationship between the (oral) reputation of its guardian, speculation as to location and the physical integrity of the heirloom (?) and the impact upon interests drives the speculation of a supposedly omniscient narrator. That omniscient narrator's saturation of subjunctive mood and conditional clauses renders it not unreliable, but of a piece with the inconclusive voices of public opinion.

***

Public opinion formation would seem to have taken a material turn in Trollope, even in his descriptions where narratives and characters are increasingly defined in terms of their "creditable dimensions" (*W* 59). How much trust we place in their utterances determines how we invest and for how long. Signora Neroni, after initially professing "to care nothing for what the world can say" (*BT* I 280), almost immediately confesses to the need to "husband her *resources* better" (*BT* I 281, ital. added), so as to defend against a community's equally materialistic speculation. The initial near-universal sympathy toward Madame Neroni's condition risks being squandered by her insincerity. Her would-be suitor, Rev. Slope, who "tacks radical" as a populist believer in church reform in order to secure an endorsement from the *Jupiter* for his silent campaign to become dean of Barchester Cathedral, learns the cost of changing positions. As he speculates by liquidating old ideological positions and tentatively investing in new ones, so public opinion reproduces his characteristic wavering in their appraisal of his future chances at becoming dean of Barsetshire Cathedral. Intriguingly, the public speculation assumes the dimensions of fluctuating betting odds. To be graced by public opinion is to occupy a place:

> During the entire next week, Barsetshire was ignorant who was to be its new dean on Sunday morning. Mr. Slope was decidedly the favorite; but he did not show himself in the cathedral, and then he sank a point or two in the *betting*. On Monday he got a scolding from the Bishop in the hearing of the servants and down he went till nobody would have him at any price; but on Tuesday he received a letter, in an office marked private, by which he fully recovered his *place* in the *public favour*.
>
> *(BT II 217, ital. added)*

During a relatively short period of public opinion trading, his reputational standing fluctuates among both supporters and critics, just as they might in the results of political polling today. Every aspect of his behavior and his behavioral relationship to his colleagues (including disappearance from public view, like that of presidential or ministerial spokesmen in today's news cycle) is taken as neutral information with which to inform a community's investment decisions. Absence is "priced in" just as Lady Eustace's presence, festooned with the contested necklace at a social gathering, is used to evaluate her future marital prospects. Dependent on a plurality of believers and electoral appraisers and influenced by a host of relevant or irrelevant external circumstances and potential players, managing risk in an unstable market is difficult.

What is perhaps most remarkable is the way in which Trollope narrates the symbiosis between short-term volatility in the appraisal of public opinion and how the volatility invariably is symbolically denominated in a social plaza. At a lavish reception for the visiting emperor of China in *The Way We Live Now*, hosted by a Melmotte with political ambitions, the tickets fluctuate in market value. Initially, the reasons for the fluctuation in the price of the tickets seem rather normal, given that most attendees would have bought earlier at higher prices to be assured of a reserved place at a very large, ceremonial venue in high demand. But the prices drop precipitously as the privileged classes hear of the possible future indictment of the esteemed Melmotte for forging a title to property he does not own. The price of sociality is a derivative of other fluctuating values. The rumors are unsubstantiated at this stage, circulated by hairdressers, among others, preparing matrons for the evening's lavish entertainment. What ensues is a sudden devaluation either in anticipation *of* or a reflection *of* (this is not established with certainty in the narrative) impending social and legal condemnation that is tantamount to a panic. Tickets, diamonds and the promotion to *dean of Barchester Cathedral* for Slope—all come to function as indexes or benchmarks for speculation. If anyone can represent himself as speaking on behalf of the public, opinion can be indexed in a variety of commodities that, on the surface, have no necessary relation to it:

> Gradually, the prices fell;—not at first from any doubt in Melmotte, but through that customary reaction which may be expected on such occasions. But at eight or nine o'clock on the evening of the party, the tickets were worth nothing.
>
> *(WWLN II 97)*

Anthony Trollope, perhaps uniquely among nineteenth-century British novelists, invested in this volatility of the public opinion market, by assuming *calculated risk* when he offered a publisher a new manuscript. Whereas the tradition among nineteenth-century British novelists drawing up contractual relationships with publishers was to sign in return for an advance to be paid against future royalties, Trollope took exception to this form of risk-sharing in light of his enhanced popularity. He requested from Longman a negotiated contract for each novel, on the grounds that the publisher was assuming progressively less risk, because of his past sales and future anticipated sales. Each new novel therefore became a point on a cumulative, speculative field, a "tracker" of fiction which had become *heirlooms*. Their value would be determined partially by the cumulative history of previous public opinion/reception. In effect, he became what would now be termed in the world of professional sports a free agent, interested, as he asserts, in his good name only "at the bottom of a cheque."[14] This reached a culmination of sorts when Trollope agreed to terms with Chapman, with whom he had become a virtual partner, for a two-volume book on Australia and New Zealand, while simultaneously arranging to supply the *Daily Telegraph* with a very similar series of essays on the antipodean colonies.[15] Hedging was crucial to both Trollope's political ideology and his negotiation with publishers, but not so far away from using the facsimile reproductions to add value.

Although public opinion fluctuates in terms of its attentions and evaluations and may run counter to traditional repositories of value, it can on occasion assume the economic solidity of unmoveable assets. It can be arbitrarily hyperresponsive to a market or totally unmoved, as is Tom Towers's *Jupiter*, a characteristic of models of transcendence. The highly materialistic Miss Demolines of *The Last Chronicle of Barset* seeks a suitor with an estate because "land can't run away" (*LCB* 271), cannot absent itself, as presumably might lovers or in Lizzie Eustace's sticky hands, a diamond necklace, or public opinion subsidized by Towers's *Jupiter*. Public opinion has the quality of belonging to many different material registers simultaneously. It can be a fixed and inescapable environment, like incarceration, that holds one so firmly that a fulcrum is needed to move it. At other times, it is either fleeting or unresponsive, like an intermittently feared lurking presence. Or, like Grace Crawley's experience after her father's difficulty over a lost check, public opinion can seem to split the difference: a contagious illness that may afflict any one remotely exposed to anyone touched by it, a free-floating, yet irresistible pathogen.

When Melmotte of *The Way We Live Now* attempts to convince a recalcitrant Paul Montague into endorsing a totally bogus report of a compliant Board of Directors (supposedly serving as a watchdog over the condition of *The South Central and Pacific Mexican Railway*), he accompanies it with a lecture on the gossamer nature of credit to an innocent and uncomprehending phantom partner:

> Gentlemen who don't know the nature of credit, how strong it is,—as the air,—to buoy you up; how slight it is as a mere vapour,—when roughly touched, can do an amount of mischief of which they themselves don't in the least understand the extent!
>
> *(WWLN I 379–80)*

Like Iago's purloined handkerchief in *Othello*, credit is simultaneously thin and transparent (and hence impalpable and invisible), yet so heavy (and signifying) as to become symbolic of virginity. Montague's scrip, awarded to him in his capacity as a member of the board, has value in exchange only as long as it gains and holds the belief of future believers in the future good faith and credit of Melmotte's fictional railroad. He is at the pinnacle of the pyramid now known as a Ponzi scheme: the return on investment is entirely dependent on how many new investors can be secured, from which his returns will be drawn, rather than profit from a nonexistent railroad.

In both *The Eustace Diamonds* and *The Way We Live Now*, Trollope is tying credit to a circulatory system. To borrow from Ben Bernanke, the former chairman of the U.S. Federal Reserve during the world financial crisis of 2008–10, when credit markets froze after the so-called Lehman shock, credit is the "life blood" of the banking system. In a public lecture in 2012, Bernanke cited the influence of Walter Bagehot's *Lombard Street: A Description of the Money Market* (1873). Bagehot was writing in response to a contemporaneous panic with which Trollope was certainly familiar—that of 1857. The Bank of England's Banking Department exhausted its reserves despite lending rates as high as 10 percent, after transferring two million pounds of Bank of England banknotes (illegally because in excess of the legal ceiling) at a time when Britain had no statutory central bank but the Bank of England. Having promoted payment by check outside London, the use of Bank of England notes had fallen precipitously during a run on the banks. For Bagehot, as for Bernanke, the first task was to end the panic, marvelously described by Bagehot as those occasions when the metaphoric "life blood" turns to "sugar water."[16] The same can occur with public opinion.

Economists now recognize that panics often occur following periods during which new financial securities and instruments have been introduced, reducing the barriers separating capital from credit. Such instruments tend to increase *asymmetric information* between investors and purveyors, resulting in the underpricing of risk. Modern central banks in *fiat* money regimes do not face the constraints that concerned Bagehot, having the right to issue high-velocity money in various transfusions. It is surely one remedy for high-velocity, asymmetric distribution of information. Volatility in public opinion is less easily controlled, as can be seen from today's proliferation of high-velocity fake news "trolls," less trustworthy than so-called qualitative easing.

Hence, in Trollope's work, as in Marx's *Grundrisse*, this vulnerability to perpetual nomination and denomination endows public opinion with the recurrent instability (and lack of substance) of another gossamer, paper money. In Marx's analysis, it will be recalled, the value of any commodity is different from the commodity itself, because the specific commodity is a value (exchange value) *only* within a process of exchange which may be either real or imaginary. Value thus has a specific exchangeability that will have a characteristic metaphoric life that resembles that of the echo in acoustics: a double-life. Value has this dual nature because it is simultaneously an exponent of the relation in which the commodity is exchanged with other commodities, as well as the relationship in which it has been *historically* exchanged with other commodities.[17] The history of the relationship and the narratives which accompany it enter into the determination of values, as it surely does in *The Eustace Diamonds*. The historical *status* of the necklace, the narrative accompanying its presentation and the status of ownership are all composites of its value and shadow the conditions of exchange value, much as is the case with the narratives that inform public opinion.

If this admittedly economic metaphor also intimates a censoring or policing role for public opinion, such a role would also be vulnerable to manipulation by the shadowed. Public opinion would be thereby simultaneously *constituted* and *constituting*, just as is paper money,[18] simultaneously absorptive and denominating. In Trollope, public opinion is a unique solvent, on occasion both lifeblood and sugar water.

If the "double-life" of money is like the "double-life" (at least in material embodiment) of whatever may be the currency of public opinion, then we would expect to see professional opinion denominated materially. As with the newly established provincial newspapers that retail editorial and investigative opinion at a price for subscribers and would-be advertisers, so a slowly reforming medical profession in *Doctor Thorne* achieves the same end with innovative practices and professional journals dedicated to local penetration. The controversial provincial doctor, who lends the novel its title, experimentally provides his private opinion for a fee that nonetheless enhances his reputation with the public: "seven-and-sixpence a visit within a circuit of five miles with a proportionately increased charge at proportional distances" (*DT* 31). This change in the fee structure for opinion is significant on a number of counts, but how the time needed to render an opinion is incorporated into the price of the opinion (now a commodity) is of special interest, given a relatively free market in which other opinions are on offer. Carriage is priced in to medical opinion; it now has a material denomination, as part of a medical delivery *system* with an alternative potential for added value than what had previously been solidly valued and priced: purging, droughts, bleeding and lowering, all of dubious effectiveness.[19] A physician's *professional opinion* comes to have a materiality, comparable to that of capsules.

Fee-for-opinion (enabling opinion to be denominated in a marketplace) might well describe a paradigm shift toward valuing logistics that enables the growth of a professionally ambitious and innovative class, as with lawyers in Barsetshire, in the nineteenth century. Dr. Thorne's opinions come to have a "currency" in a relatively isolated geographic area as they are discussed in new organs of the profession—medical journals—further enhancing what was previously merely a local reputation. Dr. Thorne's competition, represented by the well-named Dr. Fillgrave, feels himself the victim of a public opinion now willingly bidding for service at fluctuating rates depending on access. The "gentleman doctor," the aged Fillgrave, had never condescended to charge for an opinion, perhaps believing that he is above mass opinion, collecting payment only for an excess: overprescribed material remedies with imaginary effects. No other British novelist of the nineteenth century explores the material ramifications of public opinion in so many different contexts and professions as does Trollope.

If public opinion is so divided as to be vulnerable to considerable volatility and alternative models of monetization, induced in part by those who *play* it for personal advantage in Trollope, then we might logically expect an increasing segmentation of the market (long term vs. short term) in other commodities like that which afflicts medical practice. That may explain why Slope is caught out, appealing first to reactionary practices and then through the *Jupiter*, to a progressive constituency interested in reform, ideologically tacking first one way, then another. Players can be caught, inconveniently "short" or "long," in an unpredictable market.

In *The Duke's Children*, this division comes to exist in the leisure market. In successive chapters entitled, respectively, "Crummie-Toddie" (XXXVIII) and "Killancodlem" (XXXIX), the narrator describes the amenities at two different hunting venues frequented by the gentry and their guests. Situated in the Scottish Highlands they have effectively segmented the market between those consumers whose sole interest is hunting game in season and those guests more interested in the life of a resort appealing to a public, for whom marketed social entertainment and amenities are a crucial draw, the perpetual *après chasse*, as opposed to après-ski, of its day. "Crummie-Toddie" is dedicated entirely to hunting, eschewing the mass tourist market and its social amenities in Perthshire. The few remaining inhabitants in the immediate area are "absorbed in game-preserving or cognate duties" (*DC* 301), deploring sociality, in the belief that "the congregations of men are detrimental to shooting" (*DC* 307). The Earl of Silverbridge is, to his credit, comfortable at both venues although his friends discover that there are few other activities and the food mediocre at best at "Crummie-Toddie." Its counterpart, however, though nominally a rustic hunting lodge where "on certain days a deer or two might be shot—and *much talked about afterwards*" (*DC* 307, ital. added)—is really dedicated to marketing a variety of auxiliary social activities: lawn tennis, billiards, dancing and shared opinions, where the guests can "play game after game" (*DC* 309) in the absence of dedication to hunting real game, a pastime Trollope embraced throughout his life.[20] And it is at this mixed environment venue combining dating, sports, fine dining and amateur hunting—like that of the modern international resort—where the future duke of Silverbridge realizes that he is in love with an American, Isabel Boncassen, and where the woman to whom he had previously pledged his love, realizes that she "had played her cards so badly that the *game* was now beyond her powers" (*DC* 318, ital. added). Killancodlem is a variant of the "hotel-of-the-world," catering to a cosmopolitanism which will include wider *access* to opinion from the world at large as well as easier access to Trollope's expanded postal service. For halfway between Killancodlem Castle and a new hotel where 120 people can sleep in luxury

> was the Killancodlem post-office. [...] At Crummie-Toddie they had to send nine miles for their letters and newspapers.
>
> *(DC 308)*

Later in the novel, access is enhanced when the hotel installs a direct telegraph wire to London, which, can be used to transmit the latest social gossip or, like the wire in *The Way We Live Now*, used privately to retrieve Marie Melmotte from elopement with an impecunious suitor not approved by her father. Logistics are crucial to the expansion of markets and their segmentation in the interests of adding value from passive clientele.

***

In Chapter **XXXII** of Thackeray's *Pendennis* (1848–50), one of many dealing with the role of journalism, the *Public* (capitalized as a proper noun in the text) had been described as a "great landlord" to whom the writer pays both allegiance and rent in return for security. But in Trollope, the public, if a landlord, has become a *negociant*, capable of liquidating positions on short notice. In one of the *Palliser Novels*, a landlord boasts that his tenants for the most part do not demand leases, so mutually trustworthy is the relationship, implying no distinction between long- and short-term contracts. But within less than a generation, what had been metaphorized as a landlord is detached from property as the basis of power, in favor of managers and investors in a less stable model of public opinion formation. The price of market entry no longer depends on the whim of a landlord, given alternative ways of financing this entrance into public life.

But they are invariably initiated when a presumptive protégé is either overlooked (escaping custodial care as does Slope) or finds himself out of favor. Becoming an MP displaces the landed wealth that was (pre-Reform Bills) a metaphoric if not a real, qualification. And, politics being an exchange system of favors, the public comes to ask an increased reward for their votes, resulting in a mutually speculative market in which donations are expected. In *Doctor Thorne* during a vacancy in the seat for Barsetshire, the two parties "had outdone each other in the loudness of their assertions that each on his side conducts the election in strict conformity to the law" (*DT* 186). They pledge to eschew bribery in any form as they address the public.

To address a *field* of public opinion in this way runs counter to both the tradition of internal reading, which considers works independently of the historical conditions of production, but also the tradition of external reading, associated with the economic and socially determining conditions of production. Public opinion formation rather involves the creation of a market for a class of practices that is often disavowed by those engaged in the practice.[21] Under such a rubric, we are addressing the formation of (1) temporal and (2) symbolic power. Temporal power is largely based on social status and the relationship of a party to certain kinds of financial, political or historical resources. Symbolic power largely resides in peer group recognition. But there is a third type of power which resides in presumptive access *to* and manipulation *of* knowledge about the other two. It would have a temporal relevance (like market-shaping information), but also symbolic insofar as it is never quite coincident with itself. Hence, it demands sufficient trust or destroys preexistent trust in order to create an investment community.

This activity is defined by a strategic refusal or repression of commercial interests and profits. In Bourdieu's work, it often accompanies progressive, reform or even avant-garde postures,[22] as occurs when populism dons the mantel of reform. The disavowal is not a real negation of economic interests, nor quite a dissimulation, but something systemic. Certain practices in public opinion formation come to resemble banking in which political debits and credits are accumulated over time, until a demand for some *settlement* of accounts, even though such occasions are either seldom acknowledged or read as *dis-grace*.[23] Where it might differ from Bourdieu's analogy with capital formation surely lies in the unforeseeably mixed denominations of informational inputs which make the balancing of narrative accounts so difficult.

Plantagenet Palliser, the eternal candidate of the *Parliamentary Novels*, warns his wife, Lady Glencora, against "the utter corruption which must come from mixing politics with trade" (*PM* II 15) following her aggressive support of a candidate (Lopez) as an investment in ideological *futures* of the Liberals. Yet Britain, among all European countries, was traditionally an advocate—at least internationally—of free trade, understandable given the empire as a supplier. Politics was always mixed with trade and trade-offs, as Phineas Finn recognizes during parliamentary debates on assistance to the (then) *Dominion* of Canada. Positions no more require a consistent ideology than commercial transactions require the physical possession of a commodity: "you scratch my back and I'll scratch yours." Politics is inseparable from a market in trade and trade-offs, even as trade presumably corrupts it for Palliser with his allegiance to privacy.

Like other forms of critical self-interest, the reflexivity of the commercial or political investor has immense potential for exaggerating both innovation and destruction. George Soros has recently advanced a controversial advocacy—since it may confuse systemic with cyclical disequilibrium—for a relationship between the "testing" that occurs in open markets and a similar "sifting" that defines public opinion formation in *open* political systems which grant full access to the deliberative process to its citizens.[24] There is of course no guarantee that the free market in either consumer goods or retail politics results in either the highest quality goods or the most dedicated political representation, an issue that Trollope raises in the last chapter of *The Struggles of Brown, Jones, and Robinson*. But the illusion of an open market does whet the gambling consumer's interest and the sense, if not the fact, of enhanced democratic/market participation. In this sense, it does not materially differ from what will become the so-called rational authority of the bureaucracy, an authority that is a supplement to both "traditional" and "charismatic" authority.

Both Mr. Moffat, standing for the Courcy-Gatherum interests, and Sir Roger Scatcherd, standing for the radicals, declare themselves proponents of reform, new economic stimuli for the region, and a shared dedication to the construction of social infrastructure, which Scatcherd has in fact earned his fortune developing. Superficially there seems to be little that would ideologically separate the two candidates, except for abstract family agricultural interests which Moffat presumes to represent, but for which he advances no program. Trollope goes to great lengths to equate their positions on issues, and preliminary canvassing shows the popular vote almost equally divided between them, despite each candidate's claims of unanimity, a recurrent pattern in the later *Palliser Novels*.[25] This is perhaps another suggestion of the narrowing differences in genuine (identifiable) belief among antagonists in Trollope, a splitting of differences.

What tips the electoral scales in Sir Roger's favor, as it turns out, temporarily (even election results being held in *durance* pending a petition for a *recall* by the public voice), is a belated appeal to the nominally undecided proprietor of the Brown Bear, owed an unpaid tap bill from a previous campaign celebration. He, as it turns out, holds both candidates in abeyance, thinking of his own immediate interest: an unpaid tab from a previous campaign. The landlord may have been reconstituted by public opinion and the tenants have some propensity to late payment, but the now undefined piper will be paid if market share is to be captured. Once the proprietor, Reddypalm, is crossed with payment for the overdue bill, he, along with his son, becomes materially, sufficiently politicized to reward the payee with a two-vote margin of victory. Politics is the business of recognizing indebtedness and unrealized dependences, masked as an "open market." This requires local knowledge and the timing necessary to know when to "call" obligations to achieve maximum political value.

Among the most imaginative forms of playing the electoral market in public opinion is that devised by Alice Vavasor in *Can You Forgive Her?* Fearing that her Byronic cousin (replete with facial scar) is more desirous of her inheritance held in trust than her love, she devises an investment plan that combines features of the long Victorian engagement with those of a joint stock company. Severing her body from her money, Alice Vavasor proposes a probationary 12-month engagement during which time she will loan George Vavasor all the money he needs to fulfill his political ambition for a seat in Parliament. She becomes a kind of "sugar momma," thanks to an unexpected inheritance from a grandfather that removes her from the dependencies of a certain kind of marriage market: the need to marry the respectably well-off, if uncharismatic, John Grey. The ne'er-do-well Vavasor has failed at a number of business enterprises. Alice Vavasor proposes to finance her cousin's "courting" of public opinion as both a distraction from his ardor for her and as a test for steadfast dedication to duty, defined as public office. Love marriages (as romantically undetermined by social obligations) apparently require a testing period, a willingness to submit oneself in durance. Alice's alternatives are the impoverished ambition of a romantic, but impecunious cousin or John Grey, with inherited financial resources, but no ambition and little affection.

In a prescient conversation with Alice Vavasor's father, Grey addresses the contemporary intellectual devaluation of political life in the hopes that John Vavasor will dissuade Alice from marrying a politically ambitious, yet economically and morally bankrupt, rival whose candidacy is financed by his daughter:

> There's another brand of public life for which I am quite unfitted. I'd as soon be called on to choose a Prime Minister for the country, as I would a cook for a club.
> "Of course you would," said Mr. Vavasor. "There may be as many as a dozen cooks about London to be looked up, but there are never more than two possible Prime Ministers about. [...] Moreover, now-a-day, people do their politics for themselves, but they expect to have their meals cooked for them."
>
> *(CYFH II 234–35)*

The dialogue comparing the selection of a cook for a club (a theme taken up again in *The Way We Live Now*) and a prime minister for a country can be variably read. John Grey is implying that important political choices are really no different from other kinds of consumer choices in a market, but also that the country itself is a club. His analogy hints at a somewhat traditional view of the public servant as just that, a hired servant. But Alice Vavasor's father, while appearing to concur, is actually suggesting that the market has changed, as people do politics and love for themselves (as opposed to being directed), without paternal guidance. Politics is becoming privatized; its autonomous investors and candidates do participatory ad hoc politics, unregulated by traditional parties and their allied organs, recommendations or historic familial allegiances.[26] We independently pick and choose, as in other open markets. These historically referential markers of party merit and social deference that insured perpetual electoral value are no longer adequate, enabling the intrusions of arrivistes like George Vavasor, Phineas Finn, Ferdinand Lopez or Melmotte of *The Way We Live Now*. An emergent *éconocratie* mediates to sponsor (as representative) those who previously would not have qualified in a closed system.

Alice Vavasor's campaign contribution is a curious credit instrument, a *loan* convertible to a marital *bond* upon successful, redemptive political marketing. The scheme involves measured risk: to live with the possibility of the loss of a solid income in place of the loss of her modesty to a historically impulsive lover. Rather than offering to save him with forms of Christian charity (as did Warden Harding his pensioners) or comparable historical models of feminine selflessness (Collins's "Convent Thoughts" painting adorning Towers's office at the *Jupiter* comes to mind), Alice Vavasor mortgages her innocence as members of the gentry in *Framley Parsonage* will mortgage their uncut forest land. If her political investment is successful, it offers the hope of marriage to a man whose acceptance (by public opinion) she would have in some sense *made* as an original, controlling investor. She speculatively launches his entry into the public opinion market.

Can You Forgive Her? dedicates perhaps too many chapters to the prolonged negotiations among Vavasor, his campaign manager, Scruby, and the cooperating Grimes,
the owner of the "Handsome Man" pub deputized with posting campaign flyers and
door-to-door canvassing, the media buy of the period. Electoral agents resort to the
blackmail of supporters who threaten to work for the opposition candidate unless he
is paid in advance. Belief is subsumed by speculation in an electoral contest which displaces ideas into merely strategic moves of a system that candidates, in their occasionally feigned devotion to party, forget. Scruby's memorable words suggest a division of
interests between manager and candidate never fully understood by those who regard
the *systemic parameters* of the game as mere incidental to electoral politics:

> It's the *game* I look to. If the *game* dies away, it'll never be got up again,—never. Who'll ever
> care about elections, then?
>
> *(CYFH I 126, ital. added)*

Although his candidacy succeeds once and fails twice, George Vavasor's failures are
largely attributable to being run out of ready money, needed to *maintain* the game.

Yet, even after his final electoral disappointment, and informed that he is in arrears
of his agents' bills, probably untruthfully, George Vavasor wonders if he can parley
his political contacts into a reputation as an entrepreneur without portfolio. If it takes
money (even borrowed money) from a cousin/fiancée to enter politics, then perhaps the
exchange system implies that the forcibly retired politician can use his experience as an
asset by which to both recover his losses and make more money from the residue:

> Then there were pickings in the way of a Member of Parliament of his calibre. Companies,—
> mercantile companies,—would be glad to have him as a director, paying him a guinea a
> day, or perhaps more, for an hour's attendance [...] and in the City he might turn that
> "M.P." which belonged to him to a good *account* in various ways.
>
> *(CYFH II 316, ital. added)*

Trollope is anticipating the much-maligned "revolving door," familiar to contemporary
political practice, by which a new political–commercial establishment replaces the more
historically enshrined Establishment. If "one must be going out when the other is coming in" (*CYFH* II 235) is repeated almost verbatim by Madame Goesler in *Phineas Finn* as
she struggles to understand an alien political system, then the excess without resources
must survive the interregnums. In this neo-Establishment, the candidate and his agents
share a speculative frame of mind, using one asset (political position) as a down payment
on a future (financial) investment or vice versa. The distinction between public and private realms is totally obscured by free movement in a shared market.

Endorsing and promoting candidates open to hire, such as Vavasor, electoral agents
are essentially freelance promoters. The political candidate, like the marital candidate
or the very productive novelist, must be *sold* to a potential consumer at negotiated prices
which are volatile. The consumer is subjected to short-term or long-term evaluation,
depending on different markets that can be played off against each other with the investor profiting from "the spread."

This requires replacing a candidate's sexual or economic history or re-branding it. Any political campaign attempts to impose a dominant definition of a candidate, thereby limiting the ability of another part of the population to impose an historical definition, hoping to make any "past" really past. Trollope is unique among nineteenth-century British novelists in his exploration of the dynamics involved in the buying, marketing and selling of candidates and the readjustments of both ideological and financial positions to alternately accommodate and shape consumers' choices, as would be the purveyors of any other product. The words of the aged, patriarchal duke of St. Bungay to his tutee, and now a reticent, weak prime minister are instructive. Politics is marketing salesmanship to a public consumer:

> Think about your business as the shoemaker thinks of his. Do your best and then let your customers judge for themselves. Caveat emptor.
>
> *(PM I 251)*

If public opinion formation shares some of the dynamics of *playing* a market, we might question the notion of some eventual equilibrium, advocated by those who believe in the EMH, for example, that reputation, like price, reflects all of the information available *at that time*. Does the arbitrarily fixed end determine equilibrium in the market or does equilibrium determine the end point? Obviously, the *speculative investors* in both political and market futures are drawn into the market when value drops and exits when it seems "frothy." It is in fact rather the perception of some imminent disequilibrium that induces participation;[27] if markets were never wrong, everything is already priced in. But like commercial life, entrance into politics demands some speculation—which may account for the easy transition from venture capitalism to venture politics with Melmotte and Lopez or the attractions of continental *gaming* tables and the fascination of Plantagenet Palliser's son, Earl of Silverbridge, a future MP, with gambling on race horses in the *Parliamentary Novels*. Risk is attracted to moments of perceived disequilibrium, as was true with Slope's intercessions in *Barchester Towers*.

Trollope's description of his vocation—the *"trade of authorship"* (*A* 69) combined with highly speculative agreements with competing publishers—would lend him the status of a commercial traveler. The electorate, what John Stuart Mill termed the "masses," has their opinions made for them by the press, "addressing them or *speaking in their name*, on the spur of the moment, through the newspapers," as if opinions were a counterfeit currency.[28] Anyone can speak in anyone's name, in a liquidation of individual autonomy that passes for democratic participation. Politics is a business and public opinion constitutes the goods in which it deals. Both parties have vulnerabilities: the subversion of having an anonymous someone speak (falsely represent) one's product.

In *Can You Forgive Her?* and elsewhere in the *Palliser Novels*, entry into electoral politics requires no firm ideology that might leave the candidate open to being "caught out." Hence, Scruby urges upon his charge, George Vavasor, an imaginary "placeholding" subject with which to address potential electors, wisely realizing that novice political candidates have the same difficulty as do so many of Trollope's clergymen on Sunday morning. Thus, Scruby's advice resembles the tactics of Rev. Slope in *Barchester Towers*:

invent a *local* subject, even if imaginary or archaic, in order to create a constituency which may be equally imaginary. The emphasis upon the *local* subject, as opposed to any internationalism, seems almost uncannily prescient, given recent electoral campaigns in the west:

> "You must have a *subject*," pleaded Mr. Scruby. "*No young Member* can do anything without a *subject*. And it should be *local*; that is to say if you have anything of a constituency."
>
> *(CYFH II 38, ital. added)*

Privileged senior members of Parliament (representing historical allegiance, values or property) need no electoral subject or party platform. Loyalty to them has been *accumulated*. But the political novice-as-drifter needs something on which to *base* his candidacy. Those who hold seniority, like Bishop Proudie in *Barchester Towers* or Plantagenet Palliser in *the Prime Minister* and *The Duke's Children*, have rather diluted subjects or vacillating stances on the issues of the day: a bishop by virtue of his outreach to other beliefs and the prime minister similarly, by the constant attempt to work on consensus-building, compromising bridges to Daubeny and the Conservatives.

Though a Liberal, Palliser does not favor redistribution to benefit the less well off, believing instead

> that the highest duty of those high in rank was to use their authority to elevate those beneath them [...] still to make them understand that their second duty required them to maintain their *position*.
>
> *(DC 519, ital. added)*

A concerned authority would elevate the less privileged, but defensively manage the elevation, so as to avoid equality. The word "liberal" did not historically refer to "equal rights" or individual liberty, later fearfully imported from France, but rather to religious tolerance in a state with an Establishment and noblesse oblige to those less privileged. Voluntary, charitable benevolence to the lower, un-propertied orders carried high obligatory moral connotations. This may well have restrained the advocacy of what would now be called individual rights.[29] The enshrinement of such rights in law would deprive the nobility of a (beneficent) charitable obligation that differentiates them.

The persistence of *positionality* to both themselves and others trumps all other values for those in power,[30] whereas the outsider must find an overlooked local issue which may be either repressed in mass consciousness or perpetually unrealizable. Trollope's narrator is surely aware of the irony: if everyone in the lower orders were socially elevated, the privileged would have no duty and no separable rank to stand upon. Politics would become a competitive free market lacking regulatory supervision.

To his allies and opposition alike, Palliser often appears, like Slope, to borrow from Phineas Finn's attorney, Chaffanbrass, "mealy-mouthed," far too willing to split the difference to build a coalition of the privileged. His position can be read as either intelligently nuanced, or hopelessly divided and vulnerable to easy compromise. Or, alternatively, this perpetual repositioning could be read as another form of cowardice, disguised as "playing one's cards close to this chest." As the maintenance of *social position* is equated with the maintenance of *political* position, he easily confuses the two, resulting in some wobble in maintaining both positions, as we shall see. The future prime minister's politics, not entirely condemnable, is untouched by any ideological or practical subject, only continuously revised and updated in a market of ideas.

By contrast, George Vavasor's prosthetic, makeshift and initially imaginary subject is ideationally a literal platform, ironically historically realized later on: embanking the Thames, prone to flooding, westward to Chelsea. He would propose to accompany local flood control with a large pedestrian mall, including shopping arcades (a new plaza for public opinion formation), between the Chelsea barracks and the river, partially financed by what he terms "city leeches,"[31] ignoring his own "leeching" of Alice Vavasor. His project is simultaneously imaginative, egalitarian and remarkably modern in improving the public good through private and presumably eventually profitable financing (through rentals in the mall) to create a space for public opinion to develop under shelter from the elements.[32] Although highly critical of other aspects of the democratic experience during his visit to North America, Trollope admired the presence of public spaces (village squares) in the country, with their potential for enhancing a spatial plaza of public opinion formation.[33] Sadly, Vavasor informs his manager Scruby (despite its later historical realization) that his promise is imaginary and cannot be fulfilled because there is no constituency for it.

Vavasor had been recruited to the Liberal cause, it must be recalled, despite his apparent lack of any ideology at the outset, by Palliser's secretary, the factotum Bott. Looking to the future, the party hack correctly sees the head of the exchequer as a future PM onto whose coattails any new MP should quickly mount so as to reap the rewards attendant upon the early investment of loyalty, as if loyalty too were a public good:

> If he came into power,—as come into power he must, according to Mr. Bott and many others,—then they who had acknowledged the new light before its brightness had been declared, might expect their reward.
>
> *(CYFH II 46)*

One can invest too early, or too late in the (then) Imaginary, putting a premium on timing market entry, a difficult endeavor here, even for party hacks.

***

John Stuart Mill's crucial chapter, "On the Liberty of Thought and Discussion" in *On Liberty*, is essentially concerned with finding a form of public rhetoric able to present different and conflicting political *content* that would not be based on pre-constituted or assumed ideological principles, but as the product of discursive exchange which puts a premium on Imaginative Projection. Knowledge becomes political knowledge only through an agonistic procedure in which plurality (as the acknowledgment of alterity) becomes a condition for the *circulation* of the political subject:

> [If] opponents of all important truths do not exist, it is indispensable to imagine them [...] else he will never really possess himself of the portion of the truth which meets and removes

that difficulty [...] their conclusion may be true, but *it might be false for anything they know*; they *have never thrown themselves into the mental position* of those who think differently from them.[34]

(ital. added)

For Mill, in the absence of material opposition, a party must *imagine* an *alterity-as-potential plurality*; otherwise, one does not know his own *position* in an assumed marketplace. The Imaginary thereby enters public opinion formation in the liberal consciousness, not as a material possession (like those of traditional landlords), nor the "Fancy" of the eighteenth century, but a free-floating, and entirely speculative, circulating *mental position* by which one invents some Other in its absence. Once public rhetoric comes to be mediated by an ambivalent faculty of the political imagination, a merely mimetic sense of belief-formation or value is permanently compromised. The Imaginary is by definition so singularly resistant to consensus, as to abjure participation in politics, save as a temporary placeholder for which, as George Vavasor discovers, there is no real constituency, except for those who share the Imaginary.

The direction of political change thus depends not only upon the state of the political system—the accumulation of possibilities that it offers—but on the balance of forces between those who have real interests in the different possibilities available to them and those who have stakes in an unresolved game. These "position-takings" on issues occupy a systemic field which is not at all the product of some shared intention or an objective consensus (even in the event of an assumed agreement on common principles), but is rather the site of a permanent conflict that Pierre Bourdieu has termed an *habitus*, a *sens pratique* (a sixth sense, perhaps receptive to the "Tenth Muse," as excess).[35] It inclines political players to act and react in specific situations that are neither invariably calculated in advance, nor a result of obedience to laws or rules, but is rather a set of dispositions generating social practices and attitudes that enrich the process through unpredictable *flows*, akin to the flows that mark sports contests.

Every *position* taken in the market is defined temporarily in relation to a range of possibilities, recognized as problematic by both producers and consumers of retail politics. As we shall see, the position-taking changes, occasionally abruptly, whenever there is a change in the field of options available to both producers and consumers of politics. Trollope's own political career, as we shall see, illustrates the fluidity of positions (partially narrated in *An Autobiography*) no less inconsistent than those of the Rev. Slope in *Barchester Towers*. When belief, however, assumes the status of a provisional offer (the proffer) by which to judge response to the position, it assumes the status of consumer goods on a shelf with a determined expiry date.

Having lost the financial position she had taken in her provisional fiancé's political future after his defeat and flight, Alice Vavasor discovers that her doubly bad investment—as a woman, unable to obtain a loan in her own name—and in a cousin's political future, is redeemed by his rival for her affections, John Grey. Unbeknown to Alice Vavasor, Grey had guaranteed her loan, as the silent, and therefore anonymous, co-signee/partner. In one sense, Grey buys her debts, much as were Lizzie Greystock's expectations, enabling a restructuring of bankrupt marital prospects.

Four of the bills she has endorsed in support of her cousin's candidacy have found their way into the money market, lending the title of one of Trollope chapters of *Can You Forgive Her*: "Alice Vavasor's Name Gets Into the Money Market" (*CYFH* II 201–11). The loss of money parallels both her loss of reputation and her cousin's loss of the election— *all being alternative ways of denominating public opinion* and playing the market. What had initially been a promissory equivalent of a bride payment becomes a political donation upon their estrangement. Finally, as if in anticipation of the legal challenges in *The Eustace Diamonds*, "she now well understood that it would be a *gift*" (*CYFH* II 205, ital. added), an economic transaction, to be "written off" as a bad political investment. Like the Eustace Diamonds, the status of Alice Vavasor's campaign donation is ambiguous: loan, gift, investment, payment for en*durance*, dowry and protection money against passion are all possible denominations.

Her discounted investment in the public opinion market is thus taken up in the derivatives market for love, public opinion and politics. Redemption being redemption, the covering of her loss on margin, leads to the altar. Marriage needs insurance, the variant of a prenuptial agreement, which instead of insuring a partner against material loss, in this case covers an a priori loss consequent upon political speculation. Subsequently, the previously politically disinterested Grey decides dutifully to stand for election, at the encouragement of his future wife. If one follows the money, Trollope's plot in *Can You Forgive Her*? can be read as a cautionary investor's guide to risk management amid the volatility of unresearched equity stakes in public opinion formation.

On occasion, those who buy in to a new public offering on the political market have insufficient information, an excuse not available to Alice Vavasor with her informed sponsorship of her cousin. Ferdinand Lopez of *The Prime Minister* is a genuine arriviste with no known past, even to the woman who does his laundry, "as though he had been created as self-sufficient, independent of mother's milk or father's money" (*PM* I 13). Multilingual, European-educated, cosmopolitan in tastes and appearance and apparently employed at a stockbroking company (hence in the line of professional speculation), Lopez comes and goes about London "not daily, like a man of business, but as chance might require, like a capitalist or a man of pleasure,—in his own brougham" (*PM* I 4), although already in debt to a partner, Sexty Parker, for 750 pounds. Lopez's rootless and unpredictable life of speculation is early on described as that of undisciplined, unsettled *circulation* in quest of silent partners.

Lopez speculates in the guano market, one of many nineteenth-century investment bubbles. Easily assimilable by society, he advantageously secures an occasional membership in the "Progress Club," a newish Liberal Party redoubt now fallen upon more difficult times as a result of the party's electoral failures and impending vacancies, hence more welcoming to new members. Befriending there Everett Wharton, a "man of nebulous lights begotten by other men's thinking" (*PM* I 14)—perhaps a prelude to Lopez' later dealing in derivatives or Trollope's confessed interest in plagiarism—Lopez parleys an accidental friendship with the whist-playing man to a meeting with Whartons's father and an eligible sister. The father, Abel Wharton, son of a baronet, is an illustrious Q.C. with an independent income and a fine legal reputation earned over the years. He is presented by the ingratiating Lopez with a proposal which combines an offer of marriage with promissory marriage settlement, not in goods or land, but a political investment in his provisional son-in-law's future candidacy for Parliament. Wharton, with more than a whiff of prejudice toward the swarthy Iberian, rumored to be Jewish, disapproves of the arrangement after queries as to the nature of Lopez' business:

> "I am engaged in foreign loans."
> "Very precarious I should think. A sort of *gambling* isn't it?"
> "It is the business by which many of the greatest mercantile houses in the city have been made."
> "I dare say;—I dare say;—and by which they have come to ruin."
>
> *(PM I 29, ital. added)*

Wharton, both a privileged wealthy MP and attorney, feels that political life is mere gambling and invests only in incremental, sparse dribs and drabs masked as a dowry. When the wily Lopez seeks a political donation to "serve my country" (*PM* I 273) as an MP, Wharton contradicts him to insist that politics is not a profession with an entry fee, but an *obligation* of the privileged to a public:

> Success in your profession I thought you said was your object. Of course you must do as you please. If you ask me for advice, I advise you not to try it. But certainly I will not help you with money.
>
> *(PM I 273)*

Lopez has no identifiable profession, but only a *practice*: speculation in a political market. Entrance to public opinion formation always requires seed money. Wharton's irresponsible son, Everett, has already dunned his father for support for another seat and been refused financial assistance. Politics is losing its value as an entrée into society, even for those with the scion's toe already dipped in it.

For the elder Wharton, politics is a public service donated (a gift) as a way of serving your country after years of residency—experience which the alien Lopez, in his early 30s, lacks. Everett Wharton's candidacy, like that of Phineas Finn, is imagined as a "parliamentary education" in preparation for "the life I have laid out for myself" (PM I 201). Parliamentary politics would more nearly resemble Phineas Finn's alternative university. Only Ferdinand Lopez defines it as a trade needing continuous financial investment as well as paid electoral agents to manage both public opinion formation and the risks attendant upon its unpredictable fluctuations. A question poses itself: Is the status of politics that of a profession requiring an investment or an education requiring tuition? Duty, by contrast, requires no training and no capital investment, for it presumably comes from a volunteered impulse of the heart—like other loves.

Lopez's speculations in commodities are confined to what are now known as speculative futures of a given commodity without ever contemplating physical possession of it, interested as he is only in incremental and often unpredictable reevaluations in the market. Hence, playing the market involves the player in a peripatetic life, on the lookout for real or imaginary opportunities which arise fortuitously. This is a kind of watchfulness, not unlike that which typifies organs and agents of public opinion formation like Towers's elusiveness at the *Jupiter*, so seldom to be found at home. Lopez's restless manner reflects unsettled markets in guano or copper, in contrast with the quietism of a privileged wife.

He logically regards politics as a commodity of variable value to which one is "staked"—an interesting metaphor given its derivation from markers of property—to a position which can be parleyed or evacuated depending on differentials along the margins of public opinion. One planned venture has him taking a share in the newly opened market in (then) British Central America. As a near bankrupt with the collapse of one bubble after another, he meets his end by either accidentally or intentionally hurling himself onto the tracks at "Tenway Junction" (*PM* II 191), Trollope's name for the junction at Willesden, the intersection (crosscurrents) of several local rail lines with the trunk lines from Euston to the North and connections to St. Pancras and Broad Street. His life of aggressive social and financial circulation ends at a regulated intersection of circulatory traffic in goods and humans, a Trollopian interest from his days employed at the GPO. The arriviste's life ends when he arrives too early at Tenway.

Once defined as a professional enterprise, retail politics, the cultivation of public opinion, creates a proliferation of *agents* and *managers*, as would the expansion of an estate, successful enterprise in the city, or a large corporation. Scruby and Grimes of *Can You Forgive Her?* are joined by the ironmonger protective of Palliser interests, Sprugeon, in *The Prime Minister* and Molescroft and Ruddles, electoral agents of Phineas Finn, when he is selected by the Liberals to run for the colliery country "rotten borough" of Tankerville in *Phineas Redux*. Divisions are present even among these teams. Although Molescroft is both a strong "Liberal and a Churchman," Ruddles is a dissenter who nonetheless advises his candidate to "take up the Church question" even though it "did not spring from his own convictions" (*PR* I 88). The good agent is able to forget himself in the pragmatic interests of his candidate (for a fee) and is hence either ideologically empty or "transparent" to all events, junctions and crosswinds of which he must take the measure,[36] restricting any sincerity of belief. This may account for the sketchiness, a near invisibility, with which electoral agents are drawn by Trollope: oil to wheels.

During the campaign for the Tankerville constituency, Phineas Finn is initially defeated by his opponent, Browborough, only to be informed by one of the electoral agents that his opponent had selectively paid 2 shillings/10 a vote in the Fallgate area. Though both parties had pledged no payment for votes at the urging of a reform watchdog, an Electoral Commission, there is evidence of voter fraud. This new regulatory institution with its mandate to sweep away corruption would indicate the recognized need for national regulation of local practices in which favorable opinion at the ballot box has a price, directly payable to electors.[37] The commission restores victory to Finn who, though urged during the campaign to pay to play (under the table) by Ruddles, is shocked to discover that his agent has the effrontery to "take credit" (*PM* I 117) for both the victory and the moral high ground, just as did Towers in *The Warden*. At the end of a congratulatory party held in his honor by the Liberals of Tankerville following his installment as the legitimate MP after the intercession of the Electoral Commission, Finn, to his great surprise, is "informed that as so much had been done for him, it was hoped that he would now open his pockets on behalf of the charities of the town" (*PM* I

118). A very thin legal line separates gross bribery from a "donation" (a gift) requested by influential electors *post facto*. As with the necklace in *The Eustace Diamonds*, the status in law of an asset or contribution once in circulation may differ from its nominal value, due to changes in the accompanying context or intention, often in dispute or dimly understood. Ruddles has been accurate in his assessment of the social practices and needs of the Tankerville constituency, only perhaps slightly premature regarding the due date of what is owed.

If people in Barsetshire desirous of political participation in the Palliser orbit begin to conduct themselves as if public opinion formation has an operational dynamic like that of capital markets, then the vocabulary of "trust," "credit," "discreet contributions" and public opinion transactions should have certain shared features:

1) a mechanical efficiency in adjusting to and incorporating new information that may render its players relatively passive, as in faith-based belief
2) A tendency to commodify emotional relationships by pricing reputations or ideas as interests and dividing these interests into short- and long-term duration
3) A need for agents and middlemen to act as negociants in supplying local information and lubricating contacts between candidates and opinion shapers
4) Imagines politics as a market with a price of entry necessitating sponsors
5) A resemblance between politics and the commercial world as market driven, with lowered barriers between them

"In-vestment" stems from the Latin "investare": related etymologically to "being clothed" (Fr. *vetêments*), as in the various "investment ceremonies" in which power was identified with donning the robes of office during a formal *investiture* ceremony, the donning of "long sleeves." The ceremonial assumption of the (external) mantle of power is made identical with an oath or speech act. During these ceremonies the "outside" (assumption of the mantle of power) is made identical with the "inside," upon some oath or enactment. *Credo* (belief) is often negotiable with variably denominated *credits*.

***

What is remarkable is an enhanced demand for support from the upper echelons of society by the relatively impecunious who wish to launch entry (as an IPO?) to this public opinion market. Silent partners, like Alice Vavasor, almost voluntarily become financial sponsors or are tempted to do so, before the candidate has a cause, an electoral issue to advance or has embraced a party line. Madame Goesler will become a dual sponsor of Phineas Finn, contributing the funds necessary to relieve him of the need to earn from writing for the editorially hypocritical *People's Banner* in the absence of a law degree. Her unconditional support eventually extends to the hiring of a private detective in Europe to redeem him from the criminal charge of murder, even though she has no knowledge of British parliamentary politics beyond power shared by parties which proffer different ideologies, often insincerely held. She must *imagine* what occurred on the night of the crime in order to offer an alternative opinion, whose truth is then confirmed by facts.

The Duchess of Omnium's (formerly Lady Glencora M'Cluskie, with a fortune of her own) interest in reform upon her husband, Plantagenet Palliser's election/appointment as prime minister, however, belongs to a different order of *agency* in the play of the public opinion market. Recognizing her husband's political liabilities, insofar as he is "not gregarious or communicative" (*PM* I 249), she attempts to rebrand him once he has become the prime minister in the hopes of maintaining Liberal predominance in a coalition government. This is an altogether different game plan than that followed by nobility with a half century of service in various positions in the government. His wife advises the new prime minister to "now prepare for the *coming of the people*" (*PM* I 167, ital. added) which he would separate into political and social:

'Popularity is the staff on which alone Ministers can lean in this country with security.'
'Political but not social popularity.'
'You know as well as I do that the two go together.'

(PM I 105)

To this end, Lady Glencora in celebration of her husband's power opens the well-named family property, Gatherum Castle, to highly placed and influential colleagues of her husband. The more symphonic body, carefully and harmoniously constituted to work together, is reserved for the equally well-named Matching where the upper classes can feel comfortable in their own skin, not open to the cacophonous vulgarity of *publicité*. The market is, even in the names of the two estates, segmented in the interests of preserving nuanced differences in the life of the privileged, not unlike that represented in the alternative hunting venues in Scotland in *The Duke's Children*.

Uncontrolled *exposure* to the public is appalling to Glencora's husband, the prime minister, as he views the decorated tents, loud music and a public trampling the grounds of his ancestral family estate. The courting of public opinion has rendered his garden another "hotel-of-the-world," a business expense of his wife's marketing his exposure to the press. Whereas social status had previously accorded a modicum of civilized control, the appeal to mass public opinion, suggested by a more liberal wife, is imagined as the loss of sovereign control to a socially intrusive market dedicated to opinion-shaping.

The expansive guest list is a cacophonous blend of the high and the low. Some use the occasion to seek the prime minister's support, by repetitioning a forgotten connection, like Major Pountney, asked to leave the premises as a consequence of his aggressive self-promotion. Quintus Slide more successfully offers free publicity in the *People's Banner* as a quid pro quo for an invitation, for which there is a tacit promise of the paper's endorsement; sociality is exchanged for political support. Editor Slide is offering favorable coverage of a social event in return for access that might extend beyond both to an *at large*. Noisy festivities now become part of a *public record* over which the host has the possibility of shaping public opinion:

But it must be the case that the *country at large* should interest itself in your festivities and should demand accounts of the gala doings of your ducal palace. Your grace will probably agree with me that these records could be better given by one empowered by yourself to give them.

(PM I 164, ital. added)

The heretofore radical and disruptive press is offering its services as a *spinmeister* controlling the image of a new government in exchange for access. Quintus Slide's success in gaining entrance to the festivities is followed up by his paper's editorial condemnation of Sir Orlando Drought, the Conservatives' representative in the coalition. A "people's paper," like the oligarchy that runs the country, aligns its "society" page and the pages dedicated to politics into a mutually beneficial marketing opportunity. Although the parties may have changed, politics remains a socioeconomic investment.

Political spin, however, like all marketing games, may have a short shelf life. The ostensibly radical *People's Banner* will turn sharply against the Liberals (and its former columnist, Phineas Finn) over the latter's moral indecency in allegedly alienating the affections of his old friend, Laura, from her mentally unstable husband and MP from Scotland, following an altercation. The courtship of public opinion is as risky as any other courtship. Momentum can change abruptly when other opportunities arise.

The sociologist Richard Sennett, in his *The Fall of Public Man*, locates the beginning of this blatant courtship of public opinion, at least on the continent, in the various revolutions of 1848, particularly in France, where liberal leaders like Alphonse Lamartine stressed their *credibility* as people as opposed to their *ability* as leaders.[38] This of course created a market in journalistic images and accounts of public men on holiday, often in increasingly international resorts like Honfleur. A soft humanity of political, intellectual or religious leaders was more easily marketed to the public than were relatively complex policy questions, which—as in Trollope—take a long time to elucidate for public interest and investment. Hence, an unstable exchange market in carefully constructed images, here managed by Slide, is on offer.

If the papers use politicians to gain access to heretofore private time and space, politicians also cultivate papers to cast dirt upon imaginary sexual or political rivals, creating a mutual dependency between political and social popularity. The *People's Banner* seems a forerunner of today's tabloid press, part of a "sleazocracy" in which the press inflates and deflates reputations by narrowing a line that previously separated the protected private lives (and estates) of an oligarchy from the nation's affairs *at large*. There is a quantum increase in both demand *for* and supply *of* organs of public opinion, just as Slope had achieved earlier in *Barchester Towers*. Reading habits must be adjusted to keep up with the increasing volume of information which comes to have a commodity value dependent on enhanced circulation, "rags" of the less literate lower classes:

> The Duke unfortunately also saw the "People's Banner." In his old, happy days, two papers a day, one in the morning and the other before dinner, sufficed to tell him all he wanted to know. Now he felt it *almost necessary to read every rag that was published*.

(PM I 359, ital. added)

The Balkanization of the press in the *Parliamentary Novels* accompanies an increasing polari-zation of other cultural options, as we have seen in the growth of *excess*: resorts for those genuinely interested in the hunt and others interested in modern amenities and sociality in the Highlands. The proliferation of recreational venues and ideological organs creates a fatigue of choice, not unlike that narrated in the ill-fated department store described later in *The Struggles of Brown, Jones, and Robinson* with its overflowing shelves. What is less clear is whether this excess of organs and advertising is a *response to*, a *cause of* or merely a *correlation with* the increasingly blurred lines of what had previously demarcated effective monopolies.

Among the other intrusively excessive guests is none other than Ferdinand Lopez campaigning for and receiving Lady Glencora's tentative offer of support (without her husband's knowledge) for the vacant family-controlled seat looming at Silverbridge. She recognizes, as did the Rev. Slope in *Barchester Towers*, that with the passage of the old order, democratic participation-as-speculation should be encouraged and is willing, like other restless, well-off women in Trollope, to lend her support to new political blood. In the mind of the prime minister's wife, the worldly Lopez represents an avant-garde that fills an absence—the *decadence* of an older order, to which she reluctantly belongs. In advance of the "limousine liberals" of our own time, she offers him the help of an ironmonger near Silverbridge to assist in seeing which way the crosscurrents of public opinion are blowing. It is to be noted that for Lady Glencora, the political market-open-ing gesture in Lopez's behalf is accompanied by a lament for the passing of a heretofore closed political market that she uses as an enabling excuse:

> All the good times are going [...] there is no reason that I know why you should not stand as well as anyone else.
>
> *(PM I 269)*

Her husband is shocked upon learning of his wife's advocacy for a candidate whose past beliefs and social affiliations are unknown, condemns her "wild impulses" and "imprac-ticability" (*PM* I 161), a common complaint against the liberal imagination. A suppressed romantic will within a boring, arranged marriage finds its outlet in a political dalliance with a stranger. The flirtation with new blood in Lopez' candidacy will be inherited by her eldest son and future patriarch, with an American commoner. A Liberal political operative in attendance, Rattler, a recurrent presence in the *Palliser Novels* as a press sec-retary, recognizes that Lady Glencora is using the public access to gain popularity at the same time that public opinion is using easy access to her for unforeseeable ends:

> "She ought to remember that people *make use* of coming here," said Rattler. She was of course the Duchess. "It's not like a private house. And whatever influence outsiders get by coming, so much she loses."
>
> *(PM I 99, ital. added)*

Party whips, accustomed to counting, here tally an incipient zero-sum game: influence obtained by outsiders is a loss of distanced personal prestige for those who grant access.

The political role of certain women in Trollope's *Palliser Novels* conforms to a consistent historical profile, unique in Victorian fiction. Lady Laura Kennedy (née

Standish), Alice Vavasor, Madame Goesler and Lady Glencora (the Duchess of Omnium and wife of a prime minister) have all had some previous socially or financially risky romantic involvement only to be restrained by familial or social pressures to a more accommodative marriage to maintain social or class status quo. Madame Goesler is the widow of a rich European banker, their relationship the subject of much speculation and little knowledge. She leads a lavish life of her own in an adopted London to whose social market she quickly adapts. The unsatisfactory or unsustainable antecedent relationships of these women lead to a larger interest in the public good or goods and how they are redistributed by Liberal candidates to whom they are initially drawn.

Unlike Lizzie Eustace, they have or can draw on private resources to support favored causes or social underdogs, a less openly admitted adjunct to the liberal imagination, as was the advocacy of open markets and free trade. If public opinion is a potentially confining disease, they seem to have acquired some immunity by previous emotionally injurious contact with Trollope's "Tenth Muse," the public opinion that partially censured them for having a past. Whereas men seem bound to their political beliefs as another form of property they have inherited, these women find an outlet by sponsoring unconventional candidates with sympathetic causes in a more open political market or at least one with a lower sociohistorical threshold of entry. They have all sustained emotional loss but retain confidence in the possibilities of redemption without the compromise of conviction so evident among the patrician politicians in their orbit. Once having been burned by the pressure for social accommodation in their affectionate lives, they all have an admirable steadfastness like that of the Duchess of Omnium, "her courage being too high for falsehood" (*PM* I 301). Lady Kennedy is described as one who "would like to have had around her ardent spirits who would have talked of 'the cause'" (*CYFH* I 111), which we never encounter among the MPs who talk only of tactics and strategies in the *Parliamentary Novels*. Lady Kennedy's differs from the singularly "ardent" nature of George Eliot's Dorothea Brooke in her plans for clean habitation for cottagers in *Middlemarch*, insofar as she has defined ideological causes across a range of interests, not merely singular projects.

***

One could identify with Ferdinand Lopez speculating with borrowed money upon various nineteenth-century economic bubbles like guano, Chilean copper or a seat as an MP, metaphorically made equivalent objects of open market speculation. Or we could identify with Melmotte of *The Way We Live Now* with his (excessive?) two classes of shares in the phantom, too expansive (perhaps even in nomination), *South Central and Pacific Mexican Railway*, one of which can be openly traded and the other, restricted. There is an ambiguous appeal of risk-taking in Trollope's work: publicly condoned and condemned by those with wealth founded upon land. Although the strategies of playing these various markets vary, depending on individual will and the economic and social dynamics specific to a unique market, we must be careful not to read the various venues for risk-taking by relatively impecunious newcomers as some radical or even subversive shift in values. For Trollope rather suggests that attempting to control risks even while assuming them was an unacknowledged social practice of the privileged.

The sporting games of the endowed classes in Trollope appear as both highly formal and requiring abundant investments of capital, inherited or earned. As with electoral politics, a class of managers, game keepers, grooms and assorted hangers-on, like the unsavory Major Tifto of *The Duke's Children*, who lames a horse in which he owns a share to collect a bet on another horse at the track (hedging his bets), proliferates. Some risky games, however, already seem anachronistic, as if they merely defined a formerly admirable etiquette of their participants, a kind of personal or cultural *rite de passage*. The recreational racing of expensively purchased and maintained horses over natural obstructions by well-outfitted riders might be a familiar example. A duel, replete with seconds and chosen weapons that is not a duel, given the pre-agreement to fire over the head of an opponent; or the cultivation of gorses for the breeding of foxes with salaried "masters" of the hunt all appear as luxuries, yet, simultaneously the glue of honor and social cohesion. Even if the Duke of Omnium has no real interest in the foxhunt, he nonetheless subsidizes their care and breeding on his private land, as well as granting the easements (not accorded poachers and only reluctantly to the public at Gatherum Castle) for the ceremonial trespass for cultivated game within his inherited property.

These socially defining activities carry personal and financial risks (as do all games and sports), but the illusion is maintained that the risks are controllable, partially because of the cultural and financial monopoly power of those who participate in them. There are financial and social barriers to entry and participation by the masses, without sponsors. Yet, card games at various clubs are increasingly being engaged in *on credit*. Long-term I.O.U. "chits" rather than money are being increasingly exchanged at the end of an evening of cards. If a burgeoning local press played with members of an Establishment, endorsing and then withholding endorsement for policy, by the time of *The Way We Live Now*, people have learned how to play the press in the interests of enhanced celebrity and access to the public.

The Way We Live Now opens when Lady Carbury, disappointed with the excessive gambling and general debauchery of her spendthrift son, attempts to supplement a diminished income by tapping the then mass market in historical romances. She offers a gossipy and derivative book on historically scandalous behavior by royals, *The Criminal Queens*, by manipulating advanced reviews. She achieves this by strategic critical hedging in an exchange market: the offer to review potential reviewers' books to three different editors, each representing competing fashions or factions as preparation for the launch of her own career. As a fledgling writer, as with fledging politicians, Lady Carbury must decide on a party to support, even in the absence of shared values, policy or ideology, which demands that she hedge her bets. She believes that one can gain market acceptance of her work by praising the work of potential reviewers of her future work.[39] The launch of her own product is to be preceded by praising the work of decision-makers, a "framing" public narrative:

> The once most essential obstacle to the chance of success in all this was probably Lady Carbury's conviction that her end was to be obtained not by producing good books, but by inducing people to *say* that her books were good.

> (WWLN *I 17, ital. added*)

Her "inveigling of editors and critics" (*WWLN*I 21) deploys a number of strategies familiar to writers and critics, alike, of playing one potential investor-critic off against another
to accelerate public opinion to take sides. She holds prepublication parties to which all
three journal editors are invited, teasing them with excerpts of her forthcoming work.
Perhaps most familiar to Trollope's modern readers is the ease with which she uses a
devastating early review of *The Criminal Queens* by an excessively academic reviewer in
the *Evening Pulpit* (whose very name would suggest the extent to which dubious organs
of public opinion have become a substitute clergy) to cultivate a more popular, less historically knowledgeable, general reader. She in effect buys into a cultural asset, initially
depressed by a bad review, realizing, as many authors have since discovered, that bad
publicity is better than critical indifference for self-promotion. Be it shallow historical
fiction, "made-up" marriages or fictional railroad projects, people are conditioned to
look to the "attractiveness of [...] a prospectus in the eyes of the outside world of *spec*ula-
tors" (*WWLN*I 83, ital. added). We can (strategically) buy on bad news as well as good,
given the nonexistent relationship between past and future performance.

Once a competitive market develops, be it Scottish hunting resorts, newspapers
or literary magazines—as with public opinion formation, generally—it becomes segmented so as to appeal to a division of tastes which it may have had a hand in creating.
There are three potential outlets for the appraisal and promotion of Lady Carbury's
popular literary production, intended for the vulgar, general reader. The intellectually heavy *Literary Chronicle* is edited by a professor of literature. The lightweight, bel-
letristic *Morning Breakfast Table* is edited by Mr. Broune, willing to exchange a kiss or
two for a favorable review. The most notoriously discriminating, the aforementioned
Evening Pulpit, is edited by Mr. Alf who pretends to some rigorous objectivity in judging
manuscripts that is part of the hypocrisy of a supposed neutral marketplace of ideas,
not unlike that advanced by Tom Towers of the *Jupiter*. Alf "directs" the judgment of a
supposedly anonymous outside reader, while he dedicates himself to a candidacy as an
MP under the Liberal banner. Nowhere else in British fiction before George Gissing is
there a comparable analysis of deputized judgment and publicity made to appear value-
neutral and objective. Editors use another narrative to shadow the submitted narrative,
framing it to appeal to a specific public, while distancing themselves from both the
author's narrative and the conditioning editorial narrative.

The *management* of the public opinion market initially involved granting wider access
to those in a position to shape it in the interests of a more democratically inclusive
society, for the likes of Lady Glencora. But this informational tolerance may also invite
"fake news," "spam" and other instances of what is now called "white noise." Lacking
knowledge of how public opinion is contextually generated or foregrounded by the situationality of the generators and intermediate producers, the increasingly free market in
informational organs no more *necessarily* hastens public democratic participation (save as
easily deceived consumers) than does any free market in goods and services.

Trollope sees this investment in public opinion formation as analogous to other
forms of risk in an unacknowledged *rentier* culture. Risk becomes another commodity
to be priced in to the delivery and promotion of any commodity from medical advice
to political participation. At least logically, then, there should be some transference of

strategies between and among the different markets, depending upon the acquisition of management skills. Lady Carbury, despairing of her Baronet son's indebtedness from gambling at his club, and considerable self-knowledge of her own tactics with editors, correctly sees no difference between what occurs at his club and what occurs in city financial institutions. Better that her son might learn from Melmotte's knowledge of financial speculation than the card sharks at this club.

> Of course, Mr. Melmotte could not like gambling at a club, however much he might approve
> of it in the City. Why with such a preceptor to help him, should not Felix learn to do his
> gambling on the Exchange or among the brokers or in the purlieu's of the Bank?
>
> (WWLN *I 112–13*)

Trollope is surely suggesting through Lady Carbury's question, if the mastery of financial markets can be taught to recreational gamblers in a market that might offer the insurance of some regulation rather than boozy card games at clubs. Melmotte would become a preceptor of gambling on stock futures, commodifying the Imaginary: a job description entirely applicable to impoverished authors, like Lady Carbury.

This would constitute an admission that playing the market is a discipline to be passed on to ne'er-do-well sons who have suffered losses in other markets, much as Phineas Finn believes that a year's course as an MP could teach him politics.[40] Of course, the attentive reader will recall that Melmotte's imaginary railroad venture in *The Way We Live Now* goes into liquidation at about the same time as does the Beargarden Club when the paid manager suddenly disappears with the assets and IOUs of the members, including those of Lady Carbury's son Felix.

Given such highly leveraged *positions* among those in habitual political, social or economic debt, we might ask what activity might represent the possibility of redistributing the speculative impulse to collective public benefit? The American Marxist critic, Fredric Jameson, has claimed that those who believe "the proposition that the market is in human nature" cannot be allowed to stand unchallenged.[41] Believing that the political struggle is really over the legitimacy of the concept, he sees such advocacy of free markets as a deceptive disguise for a prejudicial resistance to both collectivization and government interference with extreme market fluctuations.

Be it the liquidation of Robarts's household effects to resolve indebtedness in *Framley Parsonage*, the fluctuating prices of auctioned tickets for social occasions by those knowledgeable of Melmotte's impending bankruptcy in *The Way We Live Now* or the breakup of Lady Eustace necklace at the conclusion of *The Eustace Diamonds*, the auction or a market mechanism like it appears to have advantages for the seller in a poor bargaining position. In fact, so-called Auction Theory is a relatively new branch of applied economics dealing with how people act at auctions or simulated auctions while researching the properties of those markets according to specific auction designs, that is, "independence" would be reached when every bidder knows everything to know about the item and also has all information about other bidders' knowledge.[42]

The auction mechanism can thus be considered as one form of market creation. Auctions can be used to finance projects in the larger public interest (municipal bonds for sewer improvements) or for the reprivatization of heretofore public goods in the interest of efficiencies (the management of prisons). Alternatively, auctions can be used to appraise and evaluate demand before withdrawing the object of speculation as a way of teasing/testing which way consumer winds are blowing. The mechanism seems analogous to one feature of public opinion formation: semi-regulated gambling (in the sense that there is usually an entry fee) on the information possessed by other bidders as well as each bidder's toleration for risk, varying heuristically with other market forces.

Near the conclusion of *Can You Forgive Her?* Palliser resigns as chancellor of the exchequer, despite the future prime minister's reputation as a very successful "manager of the nation's purse strings," thereby potentially enabling higher positions. His temporary retreat from political life has been precipitated by a marital spat with his headstrong wife, Glencora, who had more romantic dreams at a younger age. During this short break from political life, along with an old familiar friend, Alice Vavasor, the couple journey across Europe on holiday, presumably to forget both Alice's former lover, the "scapegrace" (*CYFH* II 297) Burgo Fitzgerald, and the official purse strings of the country. Plantagenet Palliser and his party arrive in Switzerland, initially hoping to put themselves "beyond the reach of the German gaming-tables" (*CYFH* II 294). The former chancellor of the exchequer, apprised of privileged information given his former position, is of the opinion that "German finance was connected to gaming tables" (*CYFH* II 366), which nonetheless arouses his interest as an advanced form of revenue collection and redistribution, as it must have Trollope while a civil servant at the post office. He correctly surmises that the public purse on the continent may be partially filled by a levy on state-regulated *speculation* which it promotes as a financial interest. Gaming and speculation have become a sponsored market, administered for the public good in Germany, with the proceeds of gaming redistributed to public coffers, just as public lotteries now support art museums in some countries.

A detour from their well-planned itinerary brings them to "Baden" (Baden-Baden), which historically combined the features of the therapeutic spa with a luxurious casino. Frequented by an international set—croupiers from a variety of nationalities; curious, yet anonymous spectators, and seriously compulsive gamblers, and politicians—are all attracted to the temptations of "playing the market," at a government-controlled concession.[43] During their visit Lady Glencora discovers that she is pregnant—the metaphoric jackpot to her husband who wishes for nothing so much as a male heir. Perhaps just in time to solidify their difficult marriage, for his wife's old lover, Burgo Fitzgerald, is at the tables now venturing his last capital, having learned of his former friends' travel plans. He cannot "take anything off the table," reaffirming a romantic recklessness that has made him so attractive to women. He loses all he has won and then some, rendering him unable to pay either the casino or his lodging bill.

But the wealthy, future Duke of Omnium and prime minister, now on holiday in one of those political and chronological interregnums in Trollope, notes his expectant wife's panic at seeing her destitute former lover, Fitzgerald, lose all while stalking a former lover. He displays the generosity and condescension consistent with his class, by paying his former rival's massive gambling debts at the card table. The generous gesture brings the future prime minister and his wife, Lady Glencora, closer together. Her noble husband benevolently redeems excessive risk-takers by symbolically gifting a former rival for his wife's affections. It is a curiously indeterminate gesture in Trollope's narrative, open to different interpretations as to the imposed obligations (or not) of the bankrupt recipient of a future prime minister's largesse. As was the case with the diamond necklace in *The Eustace Diamonds*, the mixed motives of the (donation/loan/consolation prize?) generate different opinions as to the ulterior motives of the redemptive gesture in a world that has become a gaming table.

While a spectator alongside the gaming table, the future prime minister who can afford to be generous to the double loser (of Lady Glencora's affections, if not her memory, and his own money) notices that certain players, in contradistinction to Burgo Fitzgerald's irresponsible risk-taking, initially *hedge* their bets. Experienced gamers tactically work to reduce the chances of excessive loss by the *diversification of risk*:

> Many were very particular in this respect, placing their ventures on the lines, so as to share the fortunes of two compartments, or sometimes of four; or they divided their coins, taking three or four numbers.
>
> *(CYFH II 365)*

The strategy appeals to a cautious prime minister, "who knew the excitement of a near division upon the estimates" (*CYFH* II 363) when votes were called in Parliament. His mealy-mouthed political career has been defined by investing on *margin*.

A straddling of positions or assumption of multiple positions on various ideological gaming tables by both Trollope's omniscient narrator and those who play for public approval in Parliament, no less than for Rev. Slope's on religious doctrine, becomes institutionalized. These are soft borders, on the lines that define policy. Politically, this has the effect of *yielding* to an institutionalization of public opinion formation under the *managed* democracy of an ostensibly neutral administrative power: a regulative government bureaucracy dedicated to redistribution.

Notes

1 Johan Huizinga, *Homo Ludens: A Study of the Play Element in Modern Culture* (Boston: Beacon Press, 1971 rpt.); Roger Caillois, *Man, Play and Games* (Champaign/Urbana: Univ. of Illinois Press, 2001 rpt); C.L. Barber, *Shakespeare's Festive Comedy: A Study of Dramatic Form and Its Relation to Social Custom* Princeton: Princeton Univ. Press, 2011 rpt.).
2 See Mark C. Taylor, *Confidence Games: Money and Markets in a World Without Redemption* (Chicago and London: Univ. of Chicago Press, 2004), especially Chapter 3, "Figuring Capital" for a remarkable discussion on how the speculation in capital markets becomes a substitute for traditional forms of spiritual redemption.
3 Sheldon Wolin, *Politics and Vision* (London: Allen and Unwin, 1961), p.280.
4 Alan Ryan, *The Making of Modern Liberalism* (Princeton and Oxford: Princeton Univ. Press, 2012), p. 250.
5 John von Neumann and Oskar Morgenstern, *Theory of Games and Economic Behavior* (Princeton: Princeton Univ. Press, 1944), albeit the foundational study of "game theory" was later extended by Jimmie Savage (1954) and Johann Pfanzigi (1967) to include subjective possibilities in the light of newer information which had the effect of accommodating inference.
6 Benoit Mandelbrot, *Fractals and Scaling in Finance, Discontinuity, Concentration, Risk* (New York: Springer, 1997), p. 27.

7 If public participation in unimpeded political life were imagined as a plaza, always open to
   speculation, then there would be no need (because impossible) for Habermas's suspension of
   private interests in the more presumably productive interests of a dedicated, unitary discursive space. See the original work of neo-revisionists Lynn Hunt, *Politics, Culture, and Class in
   the French Revolution* (Berkeley and Los Angeles: Univ. of California Press, 1984) and Mona
   Ouzof, "Public Opinion at the End of the Old Regime," *Journal of Modern History* lx (1988),
   supplement S1–S21, the latter of whom finds a confusion between the adherence to a unitary
   notion of public opinion (among the Jacobins) and the need to enforce laws or traditions that
   would be no different under more liberal regimes.

8 See "Introducing the New Materialisms," ed. Diana Coole and Samantha Frost in *New
   Materialism: Ontology, Agency, and Politics* (Durham and London: Duke Univ. Press, 2010), pp.
   9–12. The so-called new materialists collected by the editors criticize the over-determination
   of Marx's materialism in favor of an emphasis on *how* things and ideas are *made* and how they
   respond to their *making*. Hence, the texture of the response becomes part of the fabric of the
   material, a collaborative phenomenology.

9 The late Paul de Man in *Allegories of Reading* (New Haven and London: Yale Univ. Press,
   1979) suggested that literary criticism in its quest to establish itself as a genre (with stable
   identifying characteristics) strategically overlooks the changes and *aporias* that deconstruct
   or otherwise modify "fixed" readings to tell another evolving story. The established church
   of the *Barsetshire Chronicles*, trained in allegorical readings of sacred texts, suddenly finds itself
   subjected to the perpetual rereading of public opinion, a new Higher Criticism.

10 John Halperin, *Trollope and Politics* (Basingstoke: Macmillan, 1977), p. 22, is among those
   critics who dwell upon Trollope's misogyny based on his comments regarding American
   feminists after a trip to North America. Trollope's admiration *of* and willingness to associate
   socially *with* George Eliot and John Henry Lewes as a couple suggests a more nuanced openness to alternative lifestyles and some resistance to public opinion in Victorian England.

11 Paul F. Camenish, "Gift and Gratitude in Ethics," *The Journal of Religious Ethics* 9, no. 1
   (spring, 1981), p. 2.

12 Jacques Derrida, *Given Time I: Counterfeit Money*, trans. Pegy Kamuf (Chicago: Univ. of
   Chicago Press, 1992), p. 7.

13 Georg Simmel, "The Adventure," trans. David Kettler, in *Georg Simmel 1858–1918*, ed. Kurt
   H. Wolf (Columbus, OH: Ohio State Univ. Press 1959), pp. 243–258, in a remarkable essay
   argues that what constitutes all genuine adventure in life as well as literature is risk-taking coupled with play, both detached from traditional historical time schemes. Gambling
   is potentially timeless and the return to immersion in lived life seems a boring retreat into
   convention.

14 Michael Sadleir, *Trollope: A Commentary* (London: Longmans, 1927), p. 367n.

15 Richard Mullen, *Anthony Trollope: A Victorian in His World* (London: Duckworth, 1990), p. 532.

16 Walter Bagehot, *Lombard Street: A Description of the Money Market* (London: John Murray, 1879).
   Reprinted with an introduction by Hartley Withers (London: William Clower & Sons, 1924),
   pp. 32–38 and p. 46.

17 Karl Marx, *Grundrisse: Foundations of the Critique of Political Economy (Rough Draft)*, trans. Martin
   Nicolaus (Harmondsworth: Penguin, 1973), p. 141. Marx's early work is filled with allusions
   to the capacity of paper money to constantly reconfigure itself while remaining groundless
   making of it, a transparency.

18 The absorptive, yet generative quality of public opinion which gives it some resemblance to
   "shadowy presences," is the subject of Michael Warner, *Publics and Counterpublics* (New York:
   Zone Books, 2002). For Warner, the absorptive quality of public opinion would extend to
   the creation of a "counterpublic"—a subversive avant-garde—which it might then struggle
   to hegemonize, disguised as the accommodation to an imaginary of its own creation. The
   relation between public and counterpublic would be like that between a host and a parasite:
   mutual dependency.

19 Theodore Levitt in *Marketing Myopia* (Cambridge, Mass.: Harvard Business Press, 2008 rpt.)
   advanced the notion that businesses often do not realize what business they are actually *in*
   until it is too late. Although his example was the passenger railroad industry in the United
   States, the argument seems very applicable to changes in marketing in the medical profession. That doctors are really in the opinion business rather than purveyors of often dubious

remedies would represent a commercial paradigm shift, as would news organs in setting agendas rather than reporting events.

20 The *domestication of the hunt* could be a metaphor for a number of deforming social activities in Trollope, a man who loved the authentic pastime. With the assistance of artificial breeding, gamekeepers, beaters and steel-barreled breech-loaded rifles, the hunt drew social amateurs, like Dorian Gray in Wilde's *The Picture of Dorian Gray*, rather than disciplined devotees.

21 See the work of a relatively neglected member of the Frankfurt School, Alfred Sohn-Rethel, *Intellectual and Manual Labor* (London: Verso, 1978), pp. 26–27 who argues that "the abstractness of an action" cannot be noted when it happens because the consciousness of its agents is taken up with their business and "with the empirical appearance of things which pertain to their use."

22 Pierre Bourdieu, "The Production of Belief: Contribution to an Economy of Symbolic Goods," in *The Field of Cultural Production* (New York: Columbia Univ. Press, 1993), pp. 74–111. In Bourdieu's prescient analysis of the art market, the associated agents, dealers and curators often go to great lengths to deny involvement in the commercial world in a gesture which is neither a real negation nor a simple dissimulation, but a strategy designed to make them scapegoats. Value becomes thereby only a *credit* with agents who have connections.

23 Raymond Fisman and Edward Miguel, *Economic Gangsters: Corruption, Violence, and the Poverty of Nations* (Princeton: Princeton Univ. Press, 2010), create a dichotomy between unseen corruption (a 10 percent handling fee for people wishing to start a new business in Indonesia) and the visible corruption requested by low-paid customs agents at airports. They make no distinction between "redistributed proceeds" and corruption which finds its ways into individual pockets and is never redistributed. Commentary often labels as corruption what may be democratic (redistributional) values.

24 George Soros, "The Capitalist Threat," *The Atlantic Monthly* (February, 1997), pp. 45–58.

25 Morris Fiorina, Samuel Adams, and Jeremy Pope, *The Myth of a Polarized America*. (New York: Longmans, 2004), argue that those with the loudest voices (the amplitude of public opinion) command attention in the media. Most along the ideological margins wait to see (or imagine that they see) more immediate rewards that have little to do with ideology: "what have you done for me *lately*?" becomes the mantra.

26 Paul Starr, *The Creation of the Media: The Political Origin of Mass Communication* (New York: Basic Books, 2004), sees an historical tendency toward the consolidation of the carriers of public opinion, despite various subsidies designed to favor a hybrid system as the best guarantee against hegemonizing forces: local control with national regulation. This is happening in Trollope's novels with the establishment of various commissions and as we shall see in Chapter 4, an expansive quasi-regulatory bureaucracy.

27 The noted economist, Robert Skidelsky, *Money and Government: The Past and Future of Economics* (New Haven and London: Yale Univ. Press, 2019), argues persuasively that the inertia of government responses to financial crises in the west is largely due to a residual belief that markets tend toward equilibrium if left alone. In fact, it is for Skidelsky, the perception of some lapse from stability that invites uninformed speculation which may exaggerate the instability, in effect enticing further participation by people like Trollope's Rev. Slope or Lopez.

28 John Stuart Mill, *On Liberty*, ed. Gertrude Himmelfarb (Harmondsworth: Penguin, 1985), p. 9, ital. added. Mill's description of the "masses" who obtain their information "secondhand" (and hence resistant to verification) would seem to reflect an elitist bias, as if gossip were a monopoly of a certain class of denizens. Yet, Mill's advocacy of unimpeded speech in *On Liberty* would not at all prevent the circulation of "secondhand" information, a kind of necessary, albeit distracting, "static" of deliberative democracy.

29 Helen Rosenblatt, *The Lost History of Liberalism: From Ancient Greece to the Twenty-First Century* (Princeton and London: Princeton Univ. Press, 2018), though not referencing the contribution of various eighteenth-century "benevolence movements" to the morally sympathetic condescension of Liberals like Palliser, does note that John Locke never used the word "liberal," which had become perhaps too closely aligned in the British imagination with the threats to civic peace represented by the French Revolution and Reign of Terror which ensued.

30 One's social beliefs would have previously been entirely predictable, given the values inculcated by family history and traditional party identification, as Trollope makes clear in *The Prime Minister*. The concept of a flexible ideological "position" on an issue gives it a curious

resemblance to positions taken in a commercial market in their temporality and vulnerability to liquidation on short notice. If hedging risk is *always-already* present as a self-adjusting systemic strategy, then social equality would not be a necessary precondition for the formation of a "public sphere," as Nancy Fraser, in defense of Habermas, has argued. See Nancy Fraser, "Re-thinking the Public Sphere: A Contribution to the Critique of Actually Existing Democracy," in *The Phantom Public Sphere*, ed. Bruce Robbins (Minneapolis: Univ. of Minnesota Press, 1993), pp. 109–142.

31 The embankment of the Thames between Westminster and Blackfriars Bridge was initially discussed in 1860 and undertaken in 1864. Any London reader would have known that Pimlico lies in the opposite direction, where there was no embanking until much later. Hence Vavasor's prospective electoral project seems simultaneously imaginative and in advance of its time (in the sense that it offers a new kind of public space).

32 Vavasor's proposed urban renewal political platform to which his fiancée stakes him seems to echo the transformation of Paris in the early years of the Second Empire. It would combine commercial business, flood control and spaces dedicated to performance and public debate— a new kind of "public square," avoiding some of the defects that drew Walter Benjamin's critique of the form as a space for flaneurs. See Walter Benjamin, *The Arcades Project*, trans. Howard Eiland and Kevin McLaughlin (Cambridge, MA: Harvard Univ. Press, 2002), pp. 48–51.

33 Anthony Trollope, *North America* I (London: Chapman and Hall, 1862), 379.

34 John Stuart Mill, *On Liberty*, p. 99.

35 The *habitus* for Bourdieu is a system of "structured" structures predisposed to functioning as structuring structures. These are unacknowledged principles which generate and organize practices and representations that can be adapted after the fact, as it were, to their outcomes without a mastery of the operations needed to achieve those ends. If the concept is applied to public opinion formation, the practices, agents and consumers of public opinion would have to operate homologously. That is not always the case in public opinion formation. See Pierre, Bourdieu, *The Logic of Practice*, trans. Richard Nice (Stanford, CA: Stanford Univ. Press, 1990), p. 53.

36 One critic who does discuss a "transparency" of ideology in Trollope is J. Hillis Miller, "Ideology in *Marian Fay*," in *Others* (Princeton and London: Princeton Univ. Press, 2001), p. 91. For the perceptive Miller, although the reader sees through its falsehoods, ideology in the novel nonetheless has a generative value which deconstructs any specific ideology, consistent with my attribution of a generative role to public opinion formation.

37 The direct payment to a prospective voter for his support was prohibited by law, but the varieties of indirect remuneration or "payments in kind" were countless and included the payment of tabs at pubs. Courtesy to those of (usually) a lower social status than the candidate for office was an expectation. The confusion of social *noblesse oblige* with bribery resisted effective policing by candidates as well as voters. Trollope's insistence on "no bribery, no treating" (A 273) during his candidacy for the Beverley constituency was greeted with little enthusiasm, obviously.

38 Richard Sennett, *The Fall of Public Man* (Harmondsworth: Penguin, 2003). What Sennett imagines as the fall of public man (somewhat nostalgically) is the moment when the (perhaps nonexistent) ideological component of a service vocation or inherited title was converted to a need to seek publicity that could show the human (softer) side of a political leader, often on holiday, engaged in common pursuits. He would, contra Sennett, become only a different kind of public man—at the disposal of the public.

39 Many years ago, there was gossip, hopefully apocryphal, of a critical book dedicated to the sworn enemy of the author in the hopes that having been so "dedicated," no journal would ever send the dedicatee the book for review (oral conversation with the late Professor Tony Tanner, September 1995, regarding the genre of "dedications"). The "dedication" became not a gift, but part of an exchange system that could be invested defensively. Lady Carbury is certainly thinking along similar lines as she requisitions review copies as a mode of playing the market in order to prevent negative reviews of her own books by her own favorable commentary on those of enemies.

40 Those denied (or in the case of the second of Plantagenet Palliser's sons, sent down after an attempt at formal education) have another chance at educating themselves in

markets—either financial or political. Playing the market among those less endowed, however, is doubly risky. Lacking social resources of their own (Burgo Fitzgerald, George Vavasor, Phineas Finn and Melmotte), all come to be perceived as too ambitious. Speculative political or financial ambition becomes an Imaginary placeholder for those without a social or historical place.

41 Fredric Jameson, *Postmodernism or the Cultural Logic of Late Capitalism* (Durham: Duke Univ. Press, 1991), p. 263.

42 See Paul R. Milgrow and Robert J. Weber, "A Theory of Auctions and Competitive Bidding," *Econometrica* 50 (1982), pp. 1089–1122. For his fascinating work on different kinds of auction formats, the behavior elicited by each format and calculations of equilibrium, Milgrow was a corecipient of the 2020 Nobel Prize in Economics.

43 Baden-Baden (now a UNESCO heritage site) during Trollope's time fashionably combined spa treatments that allegedly purged wealthy guests, including Queen Victoria, of physiological impurities at the same time that it purged them of money. Palliser is intrigued by the redistribution of part of the profits from gaming by the German government to the public in the form of pensions and social welfare. This early instance of social collectivity was enabled with odds and payouts calculated in advance. Trollope (and Plantagenet Palliser's) interest in the scheme is obviously an extension of the redistribution of commercial rents to flood control in *Can You Forgive Her?*

Chapter Four

THE "MANAGEMENT" OF PUBLIC OPINION IN TROLLOPE'S BUREAUCRACIES

The man who can manage the purse-strings of the country can manage anything.

(*CYFH* I 236, ital. added)

The words spoken by the Duke of St. Bungay, an elder Liberal Party patriarch, an endorsement of the candidacy of Plantagenet Palliser as a future chancellor of the exchequer, suggests that efficient *economic management*, like the maintenance of land or reputation, is a respected, if vaguely defined, skill. The discipline required by material management has potentially wider applications to policy. But his endorsement is no different from that of Scruby, the electoral agent (later, upwardly mobile as a clerk for Attorney Chaffanbrass in *Phineas Redux*), who urges *tight management* upon his client, George Vavasor, even while conceding that his candidate's advertising has been consigned to an agent with largely absentee supervision. Proper management involves delegation of authority, apparently, though the deputized are often invisible.

Although thought of as a thinly-veiled portrait of a younger Trollope's experience while at the General Post Office, *The Three Clerks* (1857) is much richer insofar as it portrays a *politics* (as the distribution of power) within government agencies charged with the regulation and maintenance of public services. The plot is driven initially by two young clerks, Harry Norman and Alaric Tudor, his close friend, apprenticed to Weights and Measures, and a third, cousin to Alaric, Charley Tudor, consigned to a less dignified branch, Internal Navigation (or "Navvies"). The class system is pervasive, even in institutions dedicating to servicing the public at large. There, Tudor enjoys a somewhat louche after-hours sociality with an assortment of barmaids and dance hall companions. In another of Trollope's interregnums, there are at least three possible (albeit conflicting) avenues to membership in the civil service. Political access to the governing class, enabling future bureaucrats to "hang on round the outer corners of the State's temple" (*TTC* 81), would appear to have a number of competing avenues. Friendship *with* or descent *from* nobility; a newly instituted system of rigorous examination by committee to determine entry and staged promotion; and finally—and most idealistically—knowledge acquired by direct experience would all qualify. Yet, a retired seaman on pension at half-pay, the crusty Captain Cuttwater represents the hopelessness of experience ever qualifying one for a position at, say, Admiralty, that might usefully make room for his vast knowledge of seafaring. Trollope treats Cuttwater's voice as a kind of aging (and often sleepily inebriated) chorus, a public asking for more expertise from its civil service which restricts its reform efforts to requiring a qualifying examination.

The civil service *traffics* in the circulation of public opinion insofar as it both generates regulation and is a unitary object of widely differential public critiques:

> Its enemies are numerous enough. We meet them in the columns of every newspaper. We hear their sarcasms in every railway carriage. They publish pamphlets. They utter their bitter denunciations in street-corners and open market-places. They are loud and wrathful in season and out of season. They are of all classes; the great landed magnate rails against the Civil Service; the independent member of Parliament who doesn't, perhaps, get all that he wants, talks of the miserable creatures of a miserable Government; the prosperous tradesman sneers at the government official as a dishonest, stupid drone; and even the young lady who fails to receive her book of beauty.
>
> *(TTC 308)*

The fact that a more representative bureaucracy is informed by generalized omnidirectional criticism suggests either a shared echo chamber or rare symphonic harmony of those invested in public opinion formation. Formerly a receptacle of those enjoying elite patronage, the bureaucracy under slow reform has become a different kind of institution. In the absence of other prospects, "the Civil Service is a kind of hospital, in which the parents of sickly sons seek for employment for their puny offspring" (*TTC* 309). One might add to this combination of external critique and therapeutic refuge, as Trollope himself does, a subject for novelists. For one of *The Three Clerks*, Charley Tudor seeks to become an author by writing a romance at whose heart is a love-struck member of the Episcopal Audit Board who must continually request grudgingly granted leave to maintain a courtship which, if successful, might offer a channel for escape. Presentationally, as Trollope's narrator suggests, "the number [of its enemies] must be reckoned apparently the whole British public" (*TTC* 308), that is, all it touches. The civil service has become an eleemosynary institution providing maintenance and employment to "men who might have found it difficult to obtain maintenance elsewhere" (*TTC* 516). Trollope makes clear, however, that government service also offers a prospective second life from an insurance policy on the first, given the stability of employment.

Trollope sites the timing of planted ambition among young members of the civil service very soon after initial appointment. Alaric Tudor's rapid ascent up the career ladder, initially at Weights and Measures, is boosted both by success over his best friend, Harry Norman, one desk over, in a competitive exam for promotion, but equally an encounter with a sponsor. The eleventh son of Lord Gaberlunzie and peer of the realm, the Hon. Undecimus Scott, redefines happiness as escape from the small pickings of the bureaucracy:

> If you are contented with your two or three hundred a year in the Weights and Measures, God forbid that I should tempt you to higher thoughts—only in that case I have mistaken my man.
>
> *(TTC 92)*

Scott's logic that Tudor "must be a mere clerk if you cannot do better than a mere clerk" (*TTC* 92) would denigrate the civil service as a warehouse for the *mere* who can do no more, as he offers his future coconspirator a sideline. To go outside the lines, to borrow a Trollope metaphor, is a necessity for parleying the life of the clerk into something better than mere success at examination over his friend, Harry Norman. Undecimus Scott has initiated his casual protégé to redefine the civil service as a preparatory rung for expanded financial prospects. These bureaucracies are institutional presences to escape *from*, as did Trollope himself, who combined the lives of civil servant and popular author.

This supplementary life in one sense is already potentially present in the dual structure of the civil service consisting as it does of both permanent staff and those adjuncts, elected members of Parliament, who may or may not survive shifts in political winds:

> The Civil Service [...] consists of those who go out as well as those who do not; and as those who are permanent, are entirely under the control of those who are not permanent, the two cannot be spoken of justly, unless they be spoken of together.
>
> *(TTC 310)*

Those electorally "turned out" attempt to get back "in" by maintaining their contacts within the corps, so in one sense, they are never completely beyond the loop of political preferment. Therefore, he must attempt to remain *exposed* to public opinion, obeying the cynical Undecimus Scott's rule: "an obscure man has nothing to sell" (*TTC* 261). For Scott, the civil service is a home for those with bankrupt self-esteem and minimal ambition.

This potential for a second life in Alaric Tudor's case encompasses two father figures. Undecimus Scott, the economic patron, who offers advice on supplementing his meager salary by an investment in the same Devon tin mines which Alaric is charged with inspecting. By loaning him money with which to speculate on margin, Undy Scott, known for his "financial sharpness, his talent for *public matters* or his aptitude for the higher branches of the Civil Service" (*TTC*, 170, *ital. added*) are all part of the same package in which he might tutor an initially reluctant disciple. On the other hand, Tudor's political patron, Sir Gregory Hardlines, is seconded from Weights and Measures to become a civil service commissioner, eventually appointing his adopted disciple to a succession of increasingly important positions. Although enjoying a reputation as a strong believer in absurdly difficult examinations (including a viva) for candidates for the civil service, Sir Gregory would not go so far as to hypocritically ban patronage completely: "the question of patronage might for the present remain untouched" (*TTC* 306). He hedges his bets.

Trollope seems to be suggesting that success in the new hell of civil service examinations and the financial success of an investment that supplements a stable civil service salary, contrary to exemplifying a hard-working self-starter, are something else altogether. The state bureaucracy, no matter what the stated qualifications for membership and promotion, is another institution replete with *sponsors* who guide their favorites in return for loyalty. Thus, the state bureaucracy functions as a kind of all-male family with its share of successes and ne'er-do-wells who return to rented quarters at night, usually headed by widows with an excess of dependent daughters (as in the Woodward family at Surbiton), pushing their eligible offspring upon stable members of the civil service. The successful junior bureaucrat, in contradistinction to the orphan of the Victorian novel, has an excess of fathers (as *patron*age) in the civil service. Trollope is surely criticizing an assortment of weights on the scales by which merit is measured and evaluated in the bureaucracy.

Two or three features of the bureaucracy are noteworthy. Firstly, we see very little productive work done in its enclaves. *Both the bureaucracy and its members share a conveyance system—they are in this sense what they do—passing careers and folders forward.* There is endless copying and filing of reports by deadlines, and an abundance of organizational indexing, resembling the keeping of accounts. Charley Tudor's presence at Navvies consists of carrying on "with the Kennett and Avon lock entries" (*TTC* 187). Alaric Tudor's partner in the inspection of the Devon tin mine is frightened to actually descend into the darkness of the pits with the miners after urging haste upon a bored and hungover Alaric Tudor. Whenever Mr. Neverbend, his companion on the assigned inspection of the Wheal Mary Jane tin mine, receives Tudor's opinion as to what should be included in their report, he demurs in favor of subjecting all proposals to a wait-and-see. Neverbend counters any strong opinions so as not to be caught out, resulting in an assessment to be filed away, a problem for later:

> There were points which were as clear as daylight, but Tudor could not declare them to be so, as by doing so, he would be sure to elicit a different opinion from Mr. Neverbend.
> "I am not quite clear on that point, Mr. Tudor," he would say.
>
> *(TTC 86)*

Nothing is ever made clear, but held in perpetual *durance* and the result, familiar to readers of Trollope, is another empty document, suggesting institutional indecision, even as Neverbend affects staying up all night, the characteristic dutifulness of the corps, to work on a report that hedges its recommendations. There is a curious combination of bureaucratic inertia coupled with the expenditure of massive amounts of time and the urging of useless haste upon colleagues. The same combination appears in Scott's urging haste upon Tudor's purchase and quick disposal of shares in the mine to reap short-term profits. The reader learns only incidentally that the tin mines are being depleted of their lode and will soon be as unproductive as Weights and Measures or Forests and Mines within the bureaucracy.

Unlike the selectively obsequious Butterwell of *The Small House at Allington*, who divides his life between that of a public clerk and a lavish private villa that came with the wife, Trollope suggests that Alaric Tudor is initially bound to the beliefs of his political patron, Sir Gregory Hardlines, to believe that membership in the state bureaucracy precluded all private interests. The civil service, to Sir Gregory, is already a *calling*, almost like a priesthood in terms of its chosen dedicatees:

> They should look on none of their energies as applicable to private purposes, regard none of their hours as their own. They were *devoted* in a particular way to the Civil Service, and

they should feel that such was their *lot in life*. They should know that their intellects were a *sacred pledge* entrusted to them for the good of the service, and should use them accordingly. This should be their highest ambition.

(*TTC 119, ital. added*)

His motivational talks to his charges in the bureaucracy are quite opposite the spirit of Undecimus Scott, whose influence in the bureaucracy depends on which party is in power. Ever the political cynic, the Scotsman believes that you take what you can when you can in a perpetually unstable political and financial marketplace where nimbleness should be valued over an inescapable *lot* in life—that of the clerk. Tudor's two fathers may share, respectively, a new England, speculating on the future with debt instruments and an older England with a belief in institutional commitment and an increasingly fictional belief in a meritocracy determined by rigid examination.

Initially, Tudor has a well-defined moral conscience, realizing an ethical errancy were he to buy shares in a mine using inside information inaccessible to the general public. Before accepting the loan to buy shares in the mine from Undy Scott, Tudor, the ambitious civil servant, had rebuked the initial proffer: "I should not think of buying mining shares, and more especially these, while I am engaged as I now am" (*TTC* 92), as an inspector. His official duty initially trumps private gain, only to be later trumped by the prospect of personal gain at small risk. Knowing Trollope's reluctance to embrace universal qualifying exams for entrance *to* and promotion *within* the civil service (see below), the reader is left to speculate on an intellectual offering in the form of a rhetorical question. Does success on competitive examinations, enjoyed by Tudor, create an overly ambitious class that betrays the public to which it supposedly dedicates itself? Is the betrayal of the public trust for private gain (on margin) allegorized in his betrayal of his best friend, Harry Norman, by alienating the affections of Norman's beloved whom Tudor spirits away into a marriage while both friends are intermittently living under the same roof? Is an emergent state-sponsored competition pitting a Tudor against a Norman simultaneously foundational (in British history) and destructive of a shared mission for which the bureaucracy is a synecdoche?

The civil service salary, albeit beyond that of the working classes, never seems quite sufficient for a secure family life in Trollope. Dedicated to *management* as a career, they seem helpless at managing their limited financial resources. In an age increasingly requiring a civil service examination for entry, an expanding bureaucratic corps is being populated by clever men from less socially privileged backgrounds. Confined to their desks, a better life can be obtained only by marrying it or earning it through conflicts of interest with the attendant risk of being discovered or touted as overly ambitious. Both routes to escaping the minimally remunerated life of the civil bureaucracy involve high levels of speculation which might include a financially secure marriage that in *The Three Clerks* proves as confining as Weights and Measures in the bureaucracy.

The third of *The Three Clerks*, Charley Tudor of Internal Navigation, with his high level of consumption at dubious entertainment venues, is forced to speculate in equally dubious financial instruments from the usurer, M'Ruen. Intriguingly, his turn to the moneylender to finance a lifestyle has a dynamic that parodies that of the civil bureaucracy in certain ways. M'Ruen's refrain is always the same "be punctual" (*TTC* 185) even as he rolls over due dates for repayment, a familiar pressure of prompt time-keeping on apprentices to the civil service. As the privileged classes, like Undecimus Scott, quickly learn that their good name can be monetized by well-timed speculative investments, so the lower orders transcribe the knowledge more literally:

> There was something delightful in the feeling that he could make money of his name in this way, as great bankers do of theirs, by putting it at the bottom of a scrap of paper. He experienced a sort of pride too in achieving a respectable *position in the race of ruin* which he was running.
>
> (TTC *183, ital. added*)

The circular dependencies of deficit financing are mimed when the impecunious Charley Tudor must pay for his creditor's lunch with cash he has just borrowed at an outrageous rate of interest. He reminds his creditor, M'Ruen, to bring along his certifying stamps, reenacting a transactional ritual that valorizes bureaucratic endorsement of reports at Internal Navigation. State bureaucracies and moneylenders share forms of *bond*age.

Hence, a more nuanced reading might suggest that the double-life characteristic of membership in the state bureaucracy in an attempt to enrich a straightened lifestyle is rather a continuation of the regulated routine at the desk. Signing a promissory note on which cash is advanced on a temporality is a mid-career move in Trollope's allegory of the bureaucratic life to a final evolution as a hack writer, obedient to a prescribed editorial format. Charley Tudor breaks the monotony of Internal Navigation by writing cheap romances to a deadline and a prescribed formula, initially for the *Daily Delight*:

> The editor says that we must always have a slap at some of the iniquities of the times. He gave me three or four to choose from; there was the adulteration of food, and the want of education for the poor, and street music, and the miscellaneous sale of poisons.
>
> (TTC *200*)

Like the civil service, Charley's themes are initially socially interested (chosen by the number from a kit as with amateur painters) but gradually shifting to potboiler romances for young women, and finally, to a legitimate genre rather than propaganda.

The apprentice author progresses to begin his major work on "Crinoline and Macassar," with a plot driven by a typically prolonged romance between the fashionable Lady Crinoline and a starchily repressed Macassar Jones, a clerk at the Episcopal Audit Board, evaluating church finances for the state while trying to get leave to pay call on an aging, well-heeled damsel. Macassar has been left an inheritance by an aunt, but only on condition that he marry before age 26 and father a son within a year. The long Victorian engagement is under pressure of a financial deadline, met when Lady Crinoline assents to marriage, the shy Macassar gets really busy and a male heir is born seconds before midnight, one year after the marriage. Under the circumstances, Macassar efficiently monetizes his name with a male heir in the nick of time.

Gradually, Charley Tudor masters another bureaucracy, climbing the career ladder from the author of didactic propaganda, to light periodical entertainments, to the narratively framed, semiautobiographical "Portrait of the Artist as a Young Bureaucrat," successfully married and "keeping to time." Negotiating with editors and publishers, Charley Tudor becomes a popular author writing freely about what is closest to him, the bureaucracy having become his creative writing course. Like his Charley Tudor, Trollope never fully abandoned the politics of state bureaucracies: how it manages institutional loyalties within which alumnae carve out an arena of self-determination that deconstructs as it thematically absorbs that life.

Near the conclusion of *The Three Clerks* Charlie's employer, Internal Navigation, as a representative part of the bureaucracy, withers away like Marx's capitalist state. In this case, it vanishes by absorption within another entity after an internal hearing during which younger, reformist blood is rejected. The fatal blow, however, is struck by the popular press; in this case, *The Times*, exposing the dead wood induced by a double life of overlapping bureaucracies:

> Now, we all know that if anything is ever done in any way towards improvement in these days, the public press does it.
>
> *(TTC 515)*

***

In Trollope's novels where underachieving sons and sexually restless or ideologically venturesome daughters (the two often appear in congress) can become the bane of their parents' lives, the *managed* life has its attractions. Lady Glencora mentions to a friend that she would be more at ease with her husband, Plantagenet Palliser, if he came and told her that he had lost a hundred thousand pounds at the gaming table, but that he could never do that, committed as he is to managed calculation:

> He'd make a *calculation* that the chances were nine to seven against him, and then the speculation would seem to him to be madness.
>
> *(CYFH II 290, ital. added)*

She realizes that her marriage, the result of a timely extraction from a relationship with Burgo Fitzgerald, "had been a matter of sagacious bargaining" (*DC* 90), another management skill.

She is contrasting her own ease with reckless speculation—as do so many horsemen on dangerous mounts throughout Trollope's novels—with what Walter Benjamin has termed the *coziness* of bourgeois comfort,[1] shared with the *stickiness* of the bureaucracy. In Benjamin's analysis, this arises at mid-century and is equated with a lassitude of the imagination. Not forced to concern themselves directly with "the forces of production," there comes into existence a notion of the institutionally guided life where things are in their proper place until they no longer are.

Symbolically, the *managed life* would seek to set boundaries which define the sovereignty of a discipline and disciplined sovereignty. It would restrict the new spaces of unbridled speculation by regulating those occasions of excessive outreach to unknown participants and practices. Bureaucratic management would seek to control the admission of an increasingly intrusive press and the subversion of manipulative political novices like Lopez and Melmotte of unknown background and unknown or volatile resources through restricted portals. One antecedent from which the managed life is surely descendant might be the various late eighteenth- and early nineteenth-century "societies" created in an attempt to *manage* the inputs of new knowledge or techniques by forming socio-professional "clubs." Roy Porter has convincingly noted (as regards the scientific and medical professions) that these organizations regarded themselves as a self-disciplined, quasi-regulatory elite charged (by whom?) with self-governance against the demands of a gullible public sphere, eager to view demonstrations condemned as *performances*.[2]

An imaginary "Republic of Letters," defended by politically aligned (and hence, editorially or ideologically qualified) journals like *Blackwood's Magazine* and the *Quarterly Review*, were initially institutional and hence, ideological filters on enhanced access. Women poets like Felicia Hemans were regarded as amateur, "idle chatterers," as opposed to serious, "committed novelists," as we saw in Chapter 1. The Old and New Watercolour Societies performed similar regulative function among water color artists by managing access to its ranks, thereby providing qualifying standards, editorial prerogative, *managerial guidance* and contacts with sympathetic dealers and publishers,[3] who often sought to control output by sponsoring subscriptions.

The defense against easy, fickle genres extends into the political realm. Mildmay, the prime minister on the occasion of Phineas Finn's election as an MP, believes that "nothing was wrong in the country, but the over-dominant spirit of *speculative* commerce" (*PF* I 352, ital. added), to which effective management would provide restraint. The public seems to be divided between those who take risks and those who fear rampant speculation and would endorse the regulation of administered management. Public opinion formation combines both: it is highly speculative, yet simultaneously censorious—though both are potentially determining.

Trollope, as a self-described "advanced, but still conservative Liberal" (*A* 262), would obviously concur with Finn's early mentor, Mildmay, a self-described "old-world Liberal," that

> the coach must be allowed to run down the hill. Indeed, unless the coach goes on running, no journey will be made. But let us have a drag on both the hind wheels.
>
> *(PF I 333)*

The words are so close to those in Trollope's *Autobiography*—wherein he speaks of the needs of "drags and boldfasts" on the "wheels of the [speeding] coach" (*A* 264)—that the modes of managed restraint must be assumed to have held a continual interest.[4] The brakes on the wheels of the speeding coach (an image of progress) would provide a measure of safety for both unexpected passengers and those outside, in the potential path of the vehicle, bound as shared, albeit on occasion, dissenting interests.

Professional guidance of our most creative, progressive and speculative impulses, which threaten historical values and domestic bliss, is a recurrent theme in both the

Barsetshire Chronicles and the *Palliser Novels*. A disciplined regulation certainly pervaded Trollope's own compositional modus vivendi, with a set number of words to be written at a set time each day even while working full-time at another occupation. Excessively disciplined production can also produce surpluses for author as well as civil servant:

> I quite admit that I crowded my wares into the *market* too quickly, because the reading world could not want such a quantity of matter from the hand of one author in so short a space of time.
>
> *(A 156, ital. added)*

He confesses a need for incremental management in politics, finance, manuscripts or engagement *with* or *by* public opinion combined with some lack of confidence that free markets exist in some *natural* balance until disrupted. A disciplined, nimble response to *excess* is highly valued in his politics, art and life.[5]

The enunciation of this theme may also suggest a division between (liberal) *creativity* and (conservative) *management* which mirrors a familiar late eighteenth-century attempt to bridge a gap between *enthusiasm* and *reason*. Coleridge's distinction between on the one hand, the primary and secondary *Imagination*(s) and on the other, *Fancy*, a logical faculty and mechanical ability to *use* devices, outlined in the *Biographia Literaria*,[6] would be one formal expression of the need for discipline to unify. George Robinson, a partner of the ill-fated Magenta Emporium in Bishopsgate in Trollope's underrated, *The Struggles of Brown, Jones, and Robinson*—an early haberdashery-cum-department store—is informed by his intended that he lacks the hardness necessary to manage his financial affairs as opposed to his incredible (for its time) creativity in advertising its wares. Management is *hard*; creativity, *soft* and unstable:

> "George," said she, in a confidential whisper, before the evening was over, "if you don't *manage* about the cash now, and have it all your own way, you must be soft." Under the influence of *gratified* love, he promised her that he would *manage* it.
>
> *(SBJR 118, ital. added)*

Max Weber's work initially advanced the notion that modern, largely autocratically creative patrimonial administrations were transformed into rational bureaucracies in mid-nineteenth century.[7] For Weber, the major advantage of the bureaucracy was in fact the calculability of its results which simultaneously rendered it incapable of dealing with intermediate particularities of individual choices. Hence it was a form assumed by the real or imagined need for *managed control*. The change had its origins in the French Revolution which perhaps paradoxically established a bureaucratic state that surpassed the absolutism of the Bourbon Monarchy in scale and penetration of local practices under Napoleon.

For Weber, Bismarck's creation of a powerful centralized bureaucracy and the first modern welfare state came at the cost of charismatic political leadership. Without a vibrant public politics, there was no way to develop a future generation of political leaders, as the bureaucracy slowly became self-perpetuating. Although distinct realms of collective activity—given that the charismatic politician *embodied* public opinion—Weber felt that both politics and bureaucracy were necessary to the modern state, albeit often at odds.[8] The recovery of Weber's lost charisma motivates the emotional and financial investments of Trollope's restless women, initially drawn to the extroverted.

Jürgen Osterhammel argues that the rate of growth of a genuinely rational state bureaucracy can be only approximately documented by calculating the increase in government employment compared with the increase in the birth rate. If such criteria be accepted, the largest increases in mid-nineteenth century occurred in Britain and France, often in support of colonial administration. The largest share, apart from the army and the police, worked in railroads, the post office and the customs service.[9] Enhanced opportunities for employment at set, incremental wages, less subject to the economic fluctuations endured by those outside the landowning classes, provided one form of regulated, predictable stability.

When governments incurred debts—as all governments do—there was an understandable reluctance to depend on individual financiers (as previously throughout Europe on wealthy princes or as the Confederate States of America by marketing bonds denominated in cotton). Britain rather uniquely in the 1860s began to introduce scheduled debt management, over and above specific ad hoc measures in support of various enterprises regarded to be in the public interest. Public borrowing to cover deficits became a normal instrument of financial *planning*, just as imperfectly dedicated public spokesmen (like Slope) do for the obligations of church and government. With the institutionalization of public borrowing, investors came to have a stake in the financial health of the state and privileges of the church, its putative partner, providing a measure of possible restraint or regulated austerity.

Although probably not yet thought of as a redistributive state (insofar as revenue was not used to alter the stratification of society), how the state bureaucracy manages its money does enter public opinion.[10] Contemporaneously, the civil service, perhaps protectively, came to rest upon an ethos of *public service* at public cost, as Trollope understood from his experience rationalizing postal deliveries in Ireland. In order to avoid corruption, there were provisions for civil service salaries to be paid out of public funds and those in its service were regarded as being, if not apolitical, then somehow beyond politics.[11] Officials were allegedly appointed on the basis of competence, though as we see in *The Small House at Allington*, the means of measuring competence was often contested, in transition between tests, experience or class entitlement.

As elsewhere in Trollope, as illustrated by the Rev. Slope of *Barchester Towers*, Johnny Eames of *The Small House at Allington* or Phineas Finn of the *Palliser Novels*, the subordinate bureaucrat of clergy or state strives for the highest position so that the actual work is subordinated to the attainment or *necessary maintenance* of personal status within a *system*. The bureaucracy, to whom a membership feigns or actually is, in compliance, increasingly appears as a vast *network* of personal contacts, informants and strategic collaborations: a *field* of organized *activity*. Here too, of course, the individual member is often tested, prior to admission or as he rises through its ranks, even unto his culinary habits and social associates, as well as his knowledge. Although state and clerical bureaucracies assuredly impact public opinion formation, these bureaucracies retain only a distantiated presence, at least initially, to the elective political realm, which it regards as simultaneously separable and inseparable. It both *serves* and *regulates* the public in the interests of (presumably) nonideological *planning*, as civil rather than private servants. Its ostensible political neutrality, as we shall see, is occasionally crucial to its own self-maintenance: a defensive posture and reluctance to be identified, not unlike that of Tom Towers of the *Jupiter*, to affect a faceless anonymity.

Relationships of informal mutual dependency within the civil service gradually supplant relationships defined by the division of labor or divisions of social class. The government bureaucracy, like public opinion, potentially caters to all and is therefore always potentially present to consciousness, as it comes to penetrate corporate as well as private interactions through regulatory agency. As a long-term member of the state bureaucracy, including a stint as what would now be termed a "policy analyst" (surveyor) in the West Country and Ireland, for the General Post Office, Trollope was well placed to narrate the evasions and engagements of an increasingly "administrative state" vis-à-vis the *public*. Uniquely among British novelists, he is interested in *distributive questions*: learning costs, psychological costs and compliance costs to an increasingly critical culture at large.[12] Like public opinion, the various bureaucracies both regulate and are constituted *by* an anonymous, and occasionally ir-responsible, in the sense of incompletely communicative or illegible, vox populi.

The civil bureaucracy is well represented by the experience of Johnny Eames of *The Small House at Allington*—assuredly a link between the *Barsetshire Chronicles* and the *Palliser Novels*, insofar as Trollope initiates a debate over the institutional regulation of narrative. The bureaucracy, be it elected or appointed, is partially charged with regulating what would be defined as a public sphere from a quasi-monopoly position. In the plots of Trollope's novels, the public sphere makes its presence felt, at least initially, as an inclusive spatial presence that must respond *to*, while also penetrating (presumably for purposes of regulation) spaces previously set aside, dedicated to less transparent interests. As its actions affect the nobility, it comes to be seen as socially pervasive and invasive, resembling public opinion.

As a result of the phenomenal growth in population and commerce, the General Post Office that provided the occupational background for Trollope's life for 33 years had begun extraordinary expansion, which by 1839, covered two acres of what had once been an insalubrious section of London at St. Martin's-le-Grand with up to 1,000 employees housed in a massive edifice whose portico was lined with granite columns. Public opinion had forced the architect, in opposition to his initial plan, to make the building part of a public thoroughfare to replace the old streets covered over by the new building.[13] The expansion of public spaces as a feature of the topography of urban areas—an issue for which there had been no constituency for George Vavasor's candidacy in *Can You Forgive Her?*—accompanies the intrusion of public opinion and its representatives into what had been thought of as private enclaves: house parties of the nobility, Houses of Parliament, gentlemen's clubs and marriage itself.

Public paths thereby came to spatially intersect the relatively inaccessible working spaces of increasingly bureaucratic institutions, symbolically duplicating the penetration of a public press into working life narrated in the *Barsetshire Chronicles*. As the evening mail left the premises, constables would shout "stand back" or "clear way" so as to make a pathway *through* the public for the commencement of a journey for private narratives and protected commercial shipments from the GPO. Although drawn from and supposedly serving the public on "Her Majesty's Service," the postal bureaucracy, even from the time of Trollope's initial appointment as a junior clerk, was negotiating "administrative passages" with the public.

The General Post Office was simultaneously a bureaucratic institution, and a distributive conveyance system for private discourse, commercial goods and an employment placeholder for those lacking other *prospects* and *vistas*, marking intersections or fields of occasionally conflictual activities and interests. Junctions seem understandably to hold a special interest for Trollope, as with the busy rail intersection at the fictional "Tenway Junction" where Lopez of *The Prime Minister*, at the end of his financial tether, commits suicide by throwing himself upon "convergent rails" from "every quadrant" (*PM* II 191). He is claimed by the communicative grid of a distributional network.

A potential obstruction to the multiple social roles of the post office appeared in 1837 in the person of Rowland Hill who advocated sweeping efficiencies in the management of the postal service. While the cost of communication had traditionally been borne by the recipient (depending on how far a letter or parcel had traveled, and hence subject to arbitrary inflation and intermittent detours by the carrier), peers and MPs did not pay, their signature in effect being a frank. In effect, this provided free postage/ passage for seven million letters a year. Further distortions arose from highly variable postage fees (for those who bore the costs) which had no relationship whatsoever to distances traveled.

The actual press of Trollope's day assumed a role in both shaping public opinion not unlike that of his fictional press, the *Jupiter* and the *People's Banner*. Contemporaneously, Rowland Hill was appointed in an attempt to internally reshape staff morale. His internal organ, *The Post Office Circular*, contained humorous sketches by a young cartoonist named William Makepeace Thackeray, generally advocating reform of the GPO. A local advocacy internal to the bureaucracy, and hence potentially subversive of its conventions, was now challenging established bureaucratic convention from below. Eventually, as often happens with innovators for better and worse, Hill was "kicked upstairs" through an administrative secondment: a "consultant" to the exchequer where he successfully introduced the uniform penny post, even while advocating a reduction in postal workers' salaries which Trollope strenuously resisted. Uniform fees for government services were introduced only shortly before Trollope's innovative Dr. Thorne was adjusting his fees for *private opinion* to include the distances traveled to render that opinion to a patient: early logistic fees. Home delivery is now consolidated with medication and opinion, an amalgamated monetization. While in the private sector, the resistance to be overcome is part of the cost of the service, in the public sector, a combination of monopoly and duty creates a relatively uniform cost, once the previously privileged have to pay their fair share,[14] an effect of redistribution.

Like clerics called to the service of the Lord in the *Barsetshire Chronicles*, the state bureaucracy (and increasingly a political class that resembles it) is subject to the obedient discipline of a comparable body *in service*. If not exactly sharing Barsetshire Close with its churches, chapels, parsonages, collateral eleemosynary missions and legal consultants, those attached to the civil service in *The Small House at Allington* do in fact dwell in *close* proximity in crowded desks at the Internal Revenue (Income Tax) office where Johnny Eames assumes his initial appointment. What we might term "bureaucratic proxemics," an alternative tribal spatiality, is partially attributable to the fact that different commissioners and secretaries are arbitrarily shifted between branches, thus serving simultaneously to integrate them into a unified, dutiful body and to prevent the singular assertion of uncontested power within the ranks by tenure.

Even before the physical altercation between Johnny Eames and Adolphus Crosbie, the reader learns that Eames's superior, the huffing and puffing Sir Raffle Buffle, has been transferred from the General Committee Office (a generic branch of every civil service office, if ever there was one!) where he had formerly supervised Crosbie, to the Income Tax office where Eames will be one of his charges. In their official capacities, everyone seems to have some knowledge *of* or shared experience *with* other parts of the bureaucracy, because of the relative, even mechanical ease of transfer.

This is an understood operational quid pro quo, as Sir Raffle Buffle establishes his relationship with the apprentice, Johnny Eames: "That's right! Stick to that and I'll stick to you" (*SHA* 308). This mutual back-scratching is of course a *managed* exchange system which posits a (vulcanized) shared interest. But in Trollope, the assumed sharing of interests extends, even when off duty, for, as in *The Three Clerks*, junior members of the civil service inhabit the same quarters—a necessity given their steady, but meager incomes—in the Burton Crescent boarding house of Mrs. Roper: a guardian as potential informer. The after-hours life of these bureaucrats, like those of *The Three Clerks*, forms a significant subplot of *The Small House at Allington*.

The enforced collegiality and absence of free time enhances the fiction of strong institutional identification, a feigned commitment, as would be expected. New recruits undergo an apprenticeship, invariably finding themselves occupying the same desk with another man to whom he found himself ignominiously bound, "as dogs must feel when they are coupled" (*SHA* 506). Members of the civil service bureaucracy, once purged of ideological bias, form a cohesive administrative family such that an attack by the press upon one member is read as an attack on the institution. When Johnny Eames is identified as a civil servant in the press after his retaliatory attack upon Adolphus Crosbie in defense of a wronged damsel, it is read as an assault upon the reputation of the whole corps of bureaucrats. Private behavior cannot be separated from public response. As the bureaucratic family is enlarged, so does the *Jupiter*'s coverage. Noticeable only to the attentive, serial reader, Towers's paper has changed its name from the *Jupiter* to the *Daily Jupiter* between *The Warden* and *The Small House at Allington*, perhaps suggesting an enhanced frequency of circulation and hence enhanced penetration, in the interests of influencing public opinion over a shortened news delivery cycle.

Given the shared background of the parties involved, and the *Daily Jupiter*'s long-standing editorial support of Sir Buffle's less autocratic successor, Mr. Optimist, as head of the General Committee Office early on in a bureaucratic rotation, it might be expected that the paper would seek to scapegoat Johnny Eames as Buffle's protégé. The history of one's charges and associations shadows him to a new posting. The newspaper in Trollope, although it may change an editorial advocacy, always seems to have a long memory, enabling confusion as to its ulterior motive: advancing its own financial interests with increased circulation, illuminating inconsistencies in policy between regimes or as a guardian of civic duty. But Trollope also intimates that the voice of the press, in this case, the now *Daily Jupiter*, with a more active civic presence, may also be motivated by revenge.[15]

Hence, the confusion between the administration of a public discourse and an antecedent, private grievance, impacts newspapers as well as private citizens like Johnny Eames and Adolphus Crosbie. A shaper of public opinion seems to act, like a singular person, with a memory of past imagined affronts. The bureaucracy, though going to great lengths to establish its independence from political life, is nonetheless answerable to public opinion. Sir Raffle Buffle must straddle ideological fences, as a *buff*er between a supposedly political civil service and the politics of self-appointed guardians of public opinion in competition with other organs by putting his "chips" on the margins of this raffle, as it were.[16] Eames, accused of alleged assault, has unwittingly allowed a private dispute, enlarged by press coverage, to impact an agency of public life and must answer to a bureaucratic supervisor. If public opinion is an abstraction, it has the power of making the concept of a *private* life and *private* acts a similar abstraction insofar as they become of universal interest: part of public opinion.

Though the bureaucracy might strive to shape public opinion in terms of its efficiencies of service, its existence is partially defined as existence (and exposure) to public opinion. Sir Raffle Buffle does his best to preempt any publicity regarding the incident by following a real or imaginary manual. He advises poor Johnny Eames that he may be subject to reputational double jeopardy, much as was the equally impecunious Rev. Crawley in *The Last Chronicle of Barset*:

> And are you aware, sir [...] that it would become a question with the Commissioners of the Board whether you could be retained in the service of this department if you were *publicly* punished by a police magistrate for such a disgraceful outrage as that?
>
> *(SHA 397, ital. added)*

Public opinion has become a rival bureaucracy, challenging the institutionalized concept. Though not specifically establishing an official position vis-à-vis Eames's assault upon a fellow member of the civil service as is the wont of "neutral" bureaucracies, Sir Raffle Buffle devotes considerable energy to *position* himself at the margins within a field of competing interests, just as did Trollope ideologically and his amanuensis, Plantagenet Palliser, did while visiting the gaming tables at Baden. To be a member of the bureaucracy is to be always held accountable by the public, even placed in double jeopardy, for highly individuated grievances, as was the Rev. Crawley in *The Last Chronicle of Barset*, for acts unrelated to professional duties in a way that the wayward heirs of the landed oligarchy seldom are. Private grievances and public life are increasingly continuous, even in the (initially) private, social club, whose membership initially determined by class or political affiliation, provided a disappearing refuge against the penetrations of public opinion.

If the civil service is structured as a horizontal network of relationships accumulated over time across a number of presumably separable administrative firewalls, its senior members are also related to an unacknowledged administrative oligarchy. This cohort has a habit of recommending second (or successive) sons with diminished future prospects to a new bureaucratic family for adoptive supervision, another genre of nineteenth-century apprenticeship that mimes the traditional family. Sir Raffle Buffle, incorporating familiarity and stern warning (as do traditional fathers), is quick to remind Johnny Eames of his long friendship with Eames's patron/guarantor. After acknowledging the patronage of Lord De Guest, the novice bureaucrat, Eames, is informed by his supervisor of the parallel history of a vertical network antecedent to his patrons' intervention, so crucial to Eames's initial appointment. Class familiarity trumps geographic dislocation:

> "Ah, well, I've known the earl for many years—for many years, and intimately at one time. Perhaps you may have heard him mention my name?"
> "Yes, I have, Sir Raffle."
> We were intimate once, but those things go off, you know. He's been the country mouse and I've been the town mouse. Ha, ha, ha! You may tell him that I say so.

(SHA 510)

The bureaucracy, an agent of public opinion formation or its defense as well as a receptacle of directed grievances, is thus supported vertically by an enforced ad hoc operational loyalty among ranked members of the dedicated *corps*. But it is supported horizontally as well, through historical connections assumed almost unconsciously, with selected members of the landed oligarchy who may have drifted into political appointment. Connections and contacts have to be personally renewed or fall idly resistant to enforcement. There is an assumed discursive connection through historical association: intimacies persist over time even in the absence of recent contact or shared ideological space as an inherited identification. Adverse *publicité*, however, must be managed, for it threatens both the vertical and horizontal axes of quasi-intimate relationships by interrupting the social *corps* with another body, public opinion—which the bureaucracy is charged with regulating. It becomes thereby vulnerable to a perpetual interpretational network with no antecedent vertical or horizontal connections.

As the Tax (Inland Revenue) Office is often in negotiation with the merchant class as well as the nobility (for estate taxes), the civil bureaucracy, like the public press in Trollope, seems to penetrate diverse corners of what Sir Raffle Buffle terms "publicly shared interests," that now pretend to transcend social class, as he informs Johnny Eames in denying a request for leave early on in Eames's tenure as private secretary. Although Trollope was initially appointed in November 1834 as a junior clerk in the Secretary's Office at St. Martin's-le-Grand under Sir Francis Feeling, the premises had a dual function: a center of postal administration, but also a staff college for training future administrators of the General Post Office. An apprentice/tutorial system, like that which binds Phineas Finn to Mildmay, persists within a functioning government institution. Not unlike Parliament itself in the *Palliser Novels*, then, a noninstitutionalized (and partially informal) attendance (as in the Fr. a*ttendre*) was internal to both the bureaucracy and to parliamentary politics, to which Phineas Finn and Lopez wish to apprentice themselves as students. Hence, internally, this bureaucratic site of the then impoverished Trollope's initial probationary tenure adhered to a similar system, traditionally deployed among the working classes learning a trade or service, even as the supervisory personnel sought to maintain contact with an increasingly detached nobility. The hybrid nature of bureaucratic power in Trollope lends it, as we shall see, a resemblance to the operational strategies of the House of Commons both strategically, in its uncomfortable personal and ideological proximities, and in its relationship to public opinion formation.

Sir Raffle Buffle is initially privately dismissive of Eames's bureaucratic skills, as he says to himself, "He'll never do [...] has no go in him [...] wonder why the earl has taken him by the hand in that way" (*SHA* 558). But, of course too much reformist zeal would be a threat to the organizational structure of bureaucracy. Civil servants are natural incrementalists with no incentive to launch genuine reform which might threaten the institutional prerogative of a permanent class of *fonctionnaires*. Trollope's "drag on both the hind wheels" is a systemic feature of most bureaucracies. His supervisor fears that Eames, despite his derivative familiarity with an Old Boy network, may not be assimilable into the bureaucracy, due to a lack of *acceptable* ambition. So as to protect himself should the long-standing social connections become unstuck, Sir Raffle Buffle decides upon a politically strategic use for his new charge in the Income Tax Office: the granting of an unusual early leave so that Eames might more usefully serve as a "back-channel" communication between the section head and his new charge's sponsor-cum-patron. This of course is the site of a strategic confusion between state-sponsored and private superiors. Like the press, the bureaucracy must *stay in touch*, banking contacts for later draw. Eames thus initially becomes a bearer, not of information or goods and services, but the maintenance of historically shared interests among his superiors.

Messengers and agents are crucial to the bureaucracy, electoral politics and *management* of all "estates" in Trollope's work, insofar as they enable both deniability and the cover of temporal coincidence which is personal deniability under the rubric of a shared (even if temporarily forgotten) interest:

> Tell him, will you, how very glad I shall be to *renew* our old intimacy. I should think nothing of running down to him for a day or two in the dull time of the year—say in September or October. It's rather a coincidence *our both being interested about you*, isn't it?
>
> (SHA *557, ital. added*)

One crucial defining quality of institutions responsible for the administrative management of public opinion is simultaneously, both the *absorptive* capacity and selective resistance of the bureaucracy. It not only assimilates the financially neglected second sons of nobility, whose oldest sons were typically consuming the familial seed corn, but does the same with incipient ideological dissent and puts them in close quarters. Adolphus Crosbie is appointed to his position at Whitehall—"before Lady De Courcy's influential relation had [...] even time to write a note upon the subject" (*SHA* 301), suggesting the a priori recognition of his standing. As with Winston Churchill's infamous (albeit possibly apocryphal) letter of recommendation for a colleague—"this candidate needs no letter of recommendation from me"—Trollope intimates the ambiguity of influence. Trollope obtained his own post, thanks to the similar personal intercession of Sir Francis Feeling. Whether one is promoted "because he knew more about his work" (*SHA* 391), as is Crosbie, or simply by virtue of a reciprocated act of favoritism to an old friend, as is Eames, the civil service does appear remarkably inclusive of administrative, intellectual and accumulated social skills including influence. These are represented as associations, often obscuring the distinctions between them which often defined social stratification in nineteenth-century British life.[17] The danger occurs when the elite comes to be regarded as part of a *meritocracy*, an oxymoron giving rise to accusation of hypocrisy, which Trollope is marvelous at exposing.

No wonder, given the extensive network of contacts across a small sliver of the population that Sir Raffle Buffle feels, given Eames's lack of hustle, that "a *bargain* was being made with him" (*SHA* 512, ital. added), a metaphor more appropriate to markets. In wishing to have his regards given to Lord de Guest, Eames's sponsor, Sir Raffle Buffle, informs his new charge that his patron is "one of our most thoroughly independent noblemen" (*SHA* 557). Although we see no indication of that bureaucratically vaunted ideological independence in the novel, Sir Buffle calls attention to an institutional goal: maintaining the illusion of an independent bureaucracy, a nominally unaligned (and undecided) corp. The bureaucracy is reluctant to grant independence of spirit to its own civil servants, the better to function as a self-maintaining machine along the edges of negotiations with nobility while maintaining general public services.

This exchange system is enabled when a gift or investment is vulnerable to redemption on short notice. At the lower levels, this summons may remind one of how he obtained his positions and where his loyalties lie among patrons and creditors in the network. The bureaucracy hence serves as both an organizational and an informational tool within an *a-filiative* community of interests, miming that of the nuclear family, though positioning itself as a neutral agency, not unlike omniscient narrators. Although it is a commonplace of political thought to think of the bureaucracy's vast network of informants and contacts as maintaining relationships of dependence that are substitutes for relationship objectively (and materially) defined by divisions of labor and social class, Trollope goes to great pains to suggest that government bureaucracies are really political fulcrums, not unlike other agents of public opinion formation. These agencies adapt by alternatively pressuring, consolidating and subsidizing rather than merely mirroring, social divisions.[18] Like railroads and ports, the bureaucracy knits the country together as an informational storage, employment and conveyance system. It resembles public opinion insofar as it replies (directly or indirectly) to complaints and manages the distribution of responses, mediating between institutions, the application of law and the people.

For both the clerical bureaucracy in the *Barsetshire Chronicles* and later, the secular bureaucracy in the *Palliser Novels*, life operates *pragmatically*, entirely consistent with the French term for a bureaucrat: *fonctionnaire*. This pragmatic flexibility nonetheless differs in one crucial aspect from that of public opinion: *it seldom extends to perceived or actual disloyalty*, entirely separable from ideals. Few are true for long to ideals, not unlike members of Parliament. This is a feature of its everyday life marvelously expressed by Trollope's narrator as he describes the opportunistic Butterwell of Crosbie's office who "knew that he was not very clever, but he also knew how to *use* those who were clever" *(SHA* 382, ital. added), which could as well apply to the Rev Slope's negotiations with the *Jupiter* and vice versa. Administrative skills involve self-protective management of those who are intelligent, "use-value." But they must also know when not to make use of them so as to store *credit* for later use.

Trollope illuminates the ease of confusion in the bureaucratic and political realms through the questioning of independently minded women. Although Lady Glencora, like Alice Vavasor, detests Bott, the Liberal whip, as among a number of gossiping "buzzing flies" surrounding her husband (*CYFH* II 181), the tabbed future chancellor of the exchequer reminds his wife of the man's utility, just as George Vavasor does with Alice's query about a friendship with an untrustworthy colleague. There is an element of the involuntary or obligatory, dedicated to a larger public good, in an involuntary association.

Butterwell, if not the oily fount his name would suggest, is a source of political lubri-cation like that enacted by other agents in the business of "wiring deals," like Slope and Slide. Along with his civil service colleague, Fiasco, he devises an investment strategy with which to *manage* an independent future in competition with that advanced by the protocols of the underpaid bureaucracy. Fiasco, like Butterwell, had "begun his life striving to be honest" but "now regarded all around him as dishonest" (*SHA* 302). This is a response compatible with the shock of a previously idealistic, but cynical *Phineas Finn, as he watches the Tory opposition abruptly abandon long-held positions* against the dises-tablishment of the Irish Church, in order to topple a Liberal government in *The Prime Minister*. Cynicism among bureaucrats assumes two distinct, but related, forms of mini-mizing risk, as do those with parliamentary ambition. Butterwell marries extremely well; his bride is accompanied by a Putney villa which comes first, "his duty to the public afterwards" (*SHA* 302). Like Charley Tudor of *The Three Clerks*, he has a second life, suggesting that redundancy is perhaps built-in to bureaucracies.

If temporal and spatial dutifulness is one self-definition of a bureaucracy supposedly perpetually "on public service" even when ostensibly off duty, the attempt of Butterwell to carve out a private life beyond the reach of supervisors and cohorts is understandable. When, however, the two lives cross, the life of the bureaucracy is impacted, perhaps disproportionately, as Johnny Eames discovers after the encounter with Crosbie on a station platform over a very private matter, becomes public knowledge. Hence, mem-bers of the state bureaucracy often acquire ideological ventriloquy in order to provide a cover for an alternative, occasionally hidden life that is compatible.

In terms of ideology, Butterwell, possessing the skill of symphonically adjusting his tone of voice and ideology to separable addressees, just as do Slope and Editor Towers, "believed in many things" (*SHA* 302), as do all who successfully adjust their touch to that of the public in Trollope. Yet, he nonetheless remains anchored in his emotional investment "in the material comforts of the villa above all" even as he utters the con-stant reminder to himself in dealing with the public, the censoring mantra, "Tact, Tact, Tact" (*SHA* 302), a self-imposed drag on speeding conversational wheels. What is now termed "message discipline"—but from another perspective might be perceived as an obsequious flexibility—enables him to melt (like butter) into potentially antagonistic mouths otherwise prone to criticism. The *acquired taste* of oily tact trumps any possibility of ideological temptation.

Self-censorship, another variety of managerial control, is one manifestation of the internalization of service personnel, crucial to the face it presents to the public. As with public opinion formation and perhaps to financial market investors, there are abundant pressures, neither fully articulated nor capable of being quantitatively mapped, toward operational equilibrium. This is not to say that reputations formed by public opinion and valuations of commodities do not have their ups and downs despite hedging and trimming along the margins of tact. But it is to say, to borrow from the nautical nomenclature of the "crosswinds" of public opinion in Dicey, that ideological tacking and trimming may assist in maintaining a career course: "steady as she goes."

This habitual reminder of the need for both discursive and ideational discipline in effect would replace innovation with a policy of pragmatic self-protection in the interests of maintaining a fragile institutional harmony. This is achieved in Butterwell's case by lightly laughing at any colleague's attempts at humor. He wishes to go along to get along, in symphonic harmony with those both above and below, much as did the mild-mannered Rev. Harding of *The Warden*, with this admittedly self-interested endorsement of cooperative sympathy with the plight of pensioners who are made to think that they want more. The expansive bureaucracy, at least, symbolically, is a choir, representing an imaginary or forced harmony when more traditional forms of identification are threatened or disappearing: a disciplined corps drawn from the people.[19]

Noteworthy in the attitudes of Fiasco and Butterwell is confusion between *tactical* behavior *toward* the bureaucracy enabling transcendent interests and the *strategic* need (dictated from above) to remain a collaborative corps. Michael Hardt and Antonio Negri have argued that the formula should be reversed: *strategy* should go to the mass of employees (who have more knowledge about how to remain nimble) and *tactics* to supervisory personnel who would be called in the event of emergency.[20] Even as they denounce the corruption of an insignificant game they are playing, both men—and Eames as well—continue to play by the rules, seeking within the rules only a flexibility to supplement their status with private gain. In their posture toward a public institution, the civil bureaucracy differs little from politicians in the ensuing *Parliamentary Novels*. Strong beliefs are eschewed with the realization that public support is gained only by appearing to transcend the need for it rather than directly addressing it and earning his party's contempt, as did the wealthy populist, Turnbull.

The pressure on such a totalizing, absorptive capacity of the bureaucracy, not unlike that of mass opinion, is surely illustrated in Mr. Optimist's address to his charges after assuming his (even linguistically) vaguely defined position as first commissioner of the General Committee. Opinions are welcome (though a royal "we" define what is important), but duty regulates internal discipline:

> We shall always be glad to have your opinion on any subject of importance that may come before us; and as regards the internal discipline of the office, we feel that we may leave it safely in your hands.
>
> *(SHA 308)*

Supervisory personnel will decide what is important enough to consider, while leaving internal discipline to be internally deliberated: managed laissez-faire. But *apartheid* decision-making is abandoned when an external event impacts the reputation of the bureaucracies. The strategic amnesia of bureaucracies is intimated when the first commissioner seems to forget what he had said in the immediate preamble to new recruits: "I am quite sure that you will perform [...] with equal credit to yourself, satisfaction to the department, and advantage to the public" (*SHA* 308).

The unitary alignment of accumulated *credit* to such diverse interests—individual, civil service and general public—is a fictional loyalty, as is the behavior of civil servants struggling to individually increase their salary with an assortment of extracurricular supplements, a practice the struggling Phineas Finn will emulate. The openness to new ideas and opinions in a free market for opinion is a myth, as the social beliefs of Plantagenet Palliser will suggest. Any bureaucratic agency may substitute its own interests for those of individual members while appearing to serve the public and its staff. This peculiar *amnesia*, both in practice and rhetorically, shared by bureaucracy, politicians and agents of public opinion formation illuminates a larger contradiction between a theoretically open and receptive, yet administratively and practically closed, decision-making apparatus. Trollope, as we shall later see, deploys this strategic *amnesia* within his own narrative technique, illuminating the prejudices of his characters through a self-contradictory forgetfulness of what they had previously said, but the attentive reader remembers.

Trollope's self-described political positioning along a line that straddled the Liberal/Conservative divide is reflected in *An Autobiography*:

> During the whole of my work in the Post-office it was my principle always to obey authority in everything, instantly; but never to allow my mouth to be closed as to the expression of my opinion. They who had the ordering of me very often did not know the work as I knew it—could not tell, as I could, what would be the effect of this or that change.
>
> *(A 123)*

Trollope, always the pragmatist, is interested in future effects, how ideas are invested. The presumably joint dedication of the state bureaucracy and Parliament to mediating competing interests is compromised because the bureaucracy and Parliament too are unacknowledged, but carefully managed self-interests, often in conflict with traditional knowledge: as accumulation. Adjustment of knowledge to practical effect, for Trollope trumps bureaucratic order, though order warrants obedience to *form* and the *formal*.

***

A digression into Trollope's own practices might be in order here. Although a historical account of the foxhunt as a social practice verging on the institutional seems not at all relevant, Trollope was an aficionado of the hunt throughout his life:

> I have written on very many subjects, and on most of them with pleasure; but on no subject with such delights as that on hunting. I have dragged it into many novels, into too many, no

doubt, but I have always felt my life deprived of a legitimate joy when the nature of the tale has not allowed me a *hunting chapter*. Perhaps that which gave me the greatest delight was the description of a run on a horse *accidentally taken from another sportsman*.

(A 58, ital. added)

On at least one occasion, Trollope conceded that his affection was not subject to rational analysis (*A* 155), especially given the higher expense of horses, on his return to England from Ireland. Yet the pursuit seems applicable to even the casual reader of the galloping rivalry between suitors in *Can You Forgive Her?* which occupies four chapters, including serious injury and lengthy recovery to one of the participants. The extended discussions between the disinterested Plantagenet Palliser and his various estate managers in the cultivation of the gorse for foxes in *The Prime Minister*, and the discussion of the granting of easements across his land for the hunt, initially seem a narrative diversion. The courtship of Phineas Finn and Madame Goesler on a tedious hunt with the balky, borrowed mount, *Dandello*, occupies plural chapters in *Phineas Redux*.

Yet at another level, the hunt combines competition, regulated access to terrain, a supervisor (the Master of the Hunt) who supposedly formally "invites" participants, even though they may have paid a subscription, and various factotums including two or three whippers-in to assist reconnaissance (much like Bott does in Parliament). The bureaucracy of the hunt also includes grooms and second horsemen who ride relief horses for the master, the master's staff and leading followers as well as the lowly earth stoppers who are charged with closing up all the fox dens or holes. Each rank is severally identified with subtle distinctions in the "kit," or uniform, including cap and buttons. Thus, even metaphorically, in his discussion of social and institutional access of the lower classes, Trollope invokes the imagery of the hunt as it seeks easement across barriers:

> The gates of the one class should be open to the other; but neither to the one class nor to the other, can good be done by declaring that there are no gates, no barriers, no difference.
>
> *(A 37)*

Access to the nimble fox requires dedicated cultivation and regulation across boundaries.

As with Sir Raffle Buffle's ministerial department, the hunt combines internal competition, formal rules (with "no go" areas), mounts often loaned or obtained on credit or by trials, the cultivation and maintenance of an artificial market in foxes or other fleeting interests by those of means, and a certain threshold income level or "recommended nomination" for active participants. In short, the foxhunt, like political parties, appears as a proto-bureaucracy or social club, whose acceptance Trollope courted, ultimately extending his (invited) membership to include the Garrick Club, the Arts Club and the Cosmopolitan Club. In his *An Autobiography*, he readily concedes that books are preferable to cards at clubs, but the choice has become narrower as he admits that he can "seldom read with pleasure for over three hours a day," though longing to ride to the hunt for longer stretches:

> As I write this, I am aware that hunting must soon be abandoned. After sixty it is given but to few men to ride straight across the country, and I cannot bring myself to adopt any other mode of riding.
>
> *(A 143)*

The bureaucracy circulates government, corporate goods, sociality, services and power in terms of its collective reach, but it also simultaneously circulates the *prestige* of its individual members and itself, prone to easy confusion.[21] As it becomes a consultative adjunct to everyday life, the bureaucracy exhibits the familiar signs and syntax of specu- lative materiality. At the same time as its incipient materialization, its membership will be gradually extended to include even those lacking prestigious antecedents or contacts to serve as "referees," especially with the spread of civil service examinations. The fear of the loss of prestige is one reason why it must be circulated, or, failing this, to seek out acceptable alternative models of prestige. To imagine the bureaucracy as totally corrupt, as do Butterwell and Fiasco, is in one sense to position a bureaucratic self as simultaneously *above* it and *within* it, an enviable position that in microcosm, reflects the curious status of the larger bureaucracy itself vis-à-vis public opinion formation. One is above the masses, but riding to a quasi-exclusive *call* and hence like other investments and positions, open to *being called* at unexpected times, even though much of the work seems unproductive or redundant.

The *Barsetshire Novels* chronologically straddle the extended debate on the recom- mendations of the Northcote-Trevelyan Report on the Civil Service (1853), not widely implemented until the early 1860s, which urged promotion on the grounds of merit, determined by examination. By the mid-1860s, this eventually led to the requirement of a civil service qualifying examination for new recruits. Trollope adamantly opposed such merit promotions and appointment, in favor of the historical tradition of promo- tions based only upon seniority.[22] For Trollope, experience (seniority) became a form of knowledge, less open to measured evaluation than successful "swatting."

The "certain amount of cramming" (*A* 34) that enhanced the possibility of success in set exams was, for Trollope, no substitute for other kinds of slowly accumulated wis- dom that enabled efficient responses to unforeseeable situations and issues, rather than the irrelevant petty questions asked on exams in *The Three Clerks*. His comments per- haps contain a veiled critique of the idea that a "genuine" (insofar as exam-determined) *meritocracy* was possible or desirable, given the exclusion of large parts of the population unschooled in the procedural skills and deferences demanded.[23] If the experience of examination narrated in *The Three Clerks* be typical, candidates were really examined on what they did *not* know: how a candidate "might compute the distance from London Bridge to the nearest portion of Jupiter's disc at 12 o'clock on the first of April" (*TTC* 120). How to know was valued over knowledge, experience or application.

In a patronage system of admission, an inductee into the civil service could challenge seniority by accumulating enough power in the second life outside the service to chal- lenge authority. Alaric Tudor attempts to stand for Parliament while retaining his posi- tion in the civil service, diluting the authority of his mentor, Hardlines. Alternatively, if we identify Trollope's position with that of the omniscient narrator of *The Three Clerks*, a dedicated civil service academy would be a preferable qualification:

> Let provision be made for the instruction of government clerks, and rewards set apart for their encouragement, as is now done for all the other professions.
>
> (TTC *320*)

The reform of bureaucratic management *for* the civil service might include institutes and think tanks for a *corps bureaucratique* to match the *corps diplomatique*, in an attempt to professionalize public service by improving morale. What intrigues is Trollope's attempt to criticize any single way of determining *meritocracy*, opting instead for a holistic management of entry to the civil service. The result would be a diversity more like that constituting the British public, resembling that advocated now by elite universities in the UK and the United States—at increased costs of training.

***

If there are (newly) diverse ways of becoming part of the bureaucracy—symbolized in the antagonism between Adolphus Crosbie and poor Johnny Eames with their different routes to participation—the absorptive, consensus-inducing activity extends to differential enunciations between *creativity* and *management*. There is an incompletely articulated modus operandi in terms of the procedures for generating new ideas. Whenever a new first commissioner is appointed, inducing fear in the resident staff, justifiably anxious about new procedures and innovative disruptions to routine or policy, the permanent staff invariably engages in an act of ideological dissimulation.

As with public opinion formation, the individual contribution to the final product is dispersed, much as it is in tradition, subsumed under a kind of managed *branding* for which a supervisor must lend final approval:

> As for 'old Opt', there would be, they say, no difficulty about him. Only tell him such and such a decision was his own, and he would be sure to believe the teller.
>
> *(SHA 308)*

In an instance of inverse plagiarism, subordinate innovators give undeserved credit to preserve the myth of a creative senior echelon. If power can be dissolved within the abstraction of generalized public opinion, agents of public opinion can self-protectively retrocede phantom power to those singularly authorized or entitled to hold it, though they may no longer be directly involved. As with public opinion, one can never trace an original source, enabling either deniability or anonymous *mismanagement* as an excuse, which has the effect of disbursing responsibility as "system failure" rather than an individual lapse, to be corrected by heightened protocols of enhanced management. The bureaucracy can arbitrarily extend, but also deny, credit for innovations in order to *maintain* itself, as a fictionally consensual, yet selective, establishment. As with organs of public opinion formation, the attribution, denial and redistribution of *authorial credit* may determine public acceptance.

The bureaucracy, as well as its component members, positions itself as nonideological, a neutral transactive channel between the government and the people. This stylized objective, but in reality, managed neutrality, is what allows it to be trusted in an ever-expanding custodial/agential role. Any insufficiencies or dereliction can be addressed by the need for reorganization or a change in *management* or procedural adjustments by which the civil bureaucracy retains a feigned independence from questions of *policy*. Once it becomes involved in making policy in other than an advisory capacity, the bureaucracy would lose its neutral protective posture, and with it, institutional integrity. Only if it is vulnerable to periodic reorganization or staff reshuffling, can it remain dutifully watchful. Yet, this mandated, watchful, albeit anonymous collective guardianship, like that of organs of public opinion in the *Barsetshire Chronicles*, is precisely what renders it immune to easy representation in an age of incipient representative democracy.[24]

Of course, the sine qua non of the Victorian public servant (as with household servants) was duty, a compound of loyalty and punctuality: always on call and ready to be of service. Unlike the landed nobility in Jane Austen with a surplus of leisure, but like the organs of public opinion formation, the state bureaucracy has an invisibly inattentive attentiveness not unlike the 24/7 news cycle in our own time. A new kind of servant, Johnny Eames, is informed early on of the requirement of "obsequious attendance" (*SHA* 507). The well-managed bureaucracy must always appear to be under duress, even though the sacrifice is totally symbolic, designed for public consumption, thereby confusing "service," "duty" and real "work" with their disguises:

> You must give up all dinner engagements, for *though there is not much to do*, he'll *never let you go*. I don't think anybody ever asks him out to dinner, for he likes being here till seven. And you'll have to write *all manner of lies* about big people.
>
> *(SHA 507, ital. added)*

Trollope's narrative raises the question—unique among Victorian novelists—of what is known to political scientists as "regulatory capture." This situation occurs when a presumptive watchdog, the bureaucracy, bends to the wishes of the parties it is charged with supervising. There is the intimation that this may occur after normal hours, as a form of surveillance, not unlike that of the watchdogs of public opinion, insufficiently *open* to self-regulation or assigned hours of operation.

How people are compelled or obligated to "stay in" or "carry on" in the absence of real work is of course characteristic of all bureaucracies. But Towers's *Jupiter*, albeit not part of the traditional bureaucracy, nonetheless has assumed an institutional management skill typical of bureaucracies, be they clerical or parliamentary. After its initial and direct involvement in the campaign questioning Harding's *entitlement* to an emolument, the paper disguises its role by making the whole issue an object of speculation. It pretends passively not to know with certainty, thereby opening its pages to future contributions, which it strategically invites in order to *keep the issue* before the public, as a preliminary map for further participation:

> Whether it be that the diminished income does not offer him sufficient temptation to resume his old place, or that he has in the meantime assumed other clerical duties, we do not know. We *are*, however, *informed* that he has refused the offer, and that the situation has been accepted by Mr. Quiverful, the vicar of Puddingdale.
>
> *(BT II 184–85, ital. added)*

Speculation is followed by a rhetorical question which is then amended by an informant, with presumably additional certainty. The effect is that of setting up an adventure story, diagraming alternative outcomes and playing out some of the scenarios without forcing the reader to invest too much in the unforeseeable outcome. It is a rhetorical technique by which the public's suspenseful interest (and hence its expectations) might be continuously managed,[25] thanks to the fiction of continuous open access.

The evolution of an information society with close ties to both the bureaucracy and the general public in the nineteenth-century British novel is of course present in Inspector Bucket of Dickens's *Bleak House* with his contacts across all the social classes in the interests of detection. In *Modeste Mignon*, the fifth of the *Scènes de la vie privée* in *La Comédie Humaine* (1844), Balzac addresses the attempt to remain unknown in the midst of a civilization which takes note of everything through the tentacles of an expanding bureaucracy: scheduled arrival and departure times for public transport, of a post office which counts every letter and stamps it twice and of the dimensions of houses on surveyors' broadsheets. The reader sees its effects on private life in both Dickens and Balzac, but the operational politics internal to bureaucracies remains a mystery—a mystery Trollope singularly explores. A bureaucratic rhythm enables unassigned informants, the convenience of predictability and the potential of internal and external surveillance to become consumer commodities in a supposedly service economy.

This absence of real work (unless the maintenance of influence is a form of work) extends to other upper-level administrative activities in Trollope's oeuvre, as we learn early on with an appraisal of the activities of the preeminent foundational member of the Liberal Party, the Duke of St. Bungay, recurrently present as a stand-in for achievement:

> Regarded as a strong rock of support to the Liberal cause, and yet nobody ever knew what he did, nor was there much record of what he said. The offices which he held, or had held, were those to which no very arduous duties were attached. [...] He never grew hot or cold on a cause.
>
> *(CYFH I 251)*

Careful not to leave a track record by which he might be held accountable, the Duke of St. Bungay's support is symbolic only, leaving the heavy lifting of real rocks to party stalwarts, a clear sign that the patriarchs of both church (Bishop Proudie) and state (the duke himself) have distanced themselves from the nuts and bolts of their respective institutions in favor of a neutral ecumenism or its political equivalent. Leaving no record behind them, they lend moral support only by social standing, leaving—and in that sense creating—a "field" that appears open, but is managed from behind.

Not yet at the individually terrifying level of Kafka's bureaucratic network with the perpetual dissimulations of vague "General Committees" for those brought before it, Trollope's nonetheless seems to hold employees of the bureaucracy in the same kind of *durance* as was the Rev. Harding of *The Warden* or the Rev. Crawley of *The Last Chronicle of Barsetshire*. They are simultaneously held and free, by a divided jurisdiction that reflects larger ideological divisions: lives unwittingly devoted to the unforeseeable "impending." In the process, thinking becomes merely a continuous reevaluation of circumstances. After initially denying Eames's request for a premature leave, Sir Raffle Buffle arbitrarily changes his mind, granting the desired leave with a reinforced assumption: "*Of course*, you'll be careful to leave everything straight behind you" (*SHA* 558, ital. added). The "of course" constitutes a number of features shared by bureaucracy and political alliances: a strategic amnesia, necessitating mechanical reminders; inordinate attention dedicated to mechanical alignment and self-maintenance; the importance of administrative redundancy and finally, the imaginary totalization ("everything") as the deictic of vague work.

One *work* of the bureaucracy is that of managing chance, one representation of the volatility attendant upon public opinion formation in Trollope. Although punctuality and attendance are demanded (a calling bell or a facsimile thereof being often deployed by Sir Raffle Buffle, the sargeant-at-arms at Westminster, as previously by patriarchs at the head of table) and vacation leave only grudgingly granted, the activity is characterized by Trollope as "manufacturing" (*SHA* 301), as if the bureaucracy was some materially productive process, hence in alliance with the working classes. Or, alternatively, energy is spent "indexing" letters in order to assure that enquiries from other agencies ("A" for Admiralty) can be easily located. Identifying, locating, correctly using and *properly* maintaining channels for onward transmission are thus not only part of the selective process for appointment to the bureaucracy, but also constitute in large part, its curious work: getting it done by keeping it moving.

***

Although former British prime minister Sir John Major, a dedicated reader of Trollope's "burly, clumsy" and on occasion "snoozy" novels, regards *The Small House at Allington* as an "interloper" in the *Barsetshire Chronicle*, he may well have overlooked its position as a connective fulcrum to the *Parliamentary Novels*.[26] What they share is another kind of *vacancy* or vacuity with which both series commence: a chronic boredom to those who live a life dedicated to the demands of obedience to a higher order on the one hand or perpetual response mode on the other. Nothing can be originated, without being perceived as subversive of the order. The Rev. Obadiah Slope, who explains the "wheels within wheels" which forecloses any explanation of clerical politics to an interlocutor in *Barchester Towers*, shares with the Johnny Eames of *The Small House at Allington* an enforced passivity before an organizational order. Life being always-already decided for me, so they may explain to themselves, I am needed only to apply oil to preexistent machinery. To identify one as a mere "cog in a wheel" has an historical legacy, after all, combining boredom, irresponsibility, the presence of others and self-defense within a highly mechanized system.

Paradoxically, the *situationality* of institutional agency might also serve as a self-conscious recognition of a certain kind of automated belonging. To be part of a regulated institutional order is to confirm my lack of uniqueness and the freedom to choose otherwise. As Trollope remarks in describing the post office bureaucracy while under the supervision of the reviled Rowland Hill and his brother:

> To the two brothers, the servants of the Post-office—men numerous enough to have formed an army in the old days—were so many *machines* who could be counted on for their exact work, without deviation, as wheels may be counted on which are going always at the same pace and always by the same power.
>
> (A *121, ital. added*)

Once one confirms an obedient membership within a larger order, he becomes part of a self-protective anonymous mass—like public opinion—not tied to class identification or ideological position, both of which are potentially disjunctive. This mechanical boredom is not the *acedia* of the Middle Ages (punished one suspects only because it grounded so many other sins), nor is it among the modern boredoms catalogued by Lars Svendsen in his perceptive, *A Philosophy of Boredom*, with its emphasis upon experiential ennui,[27] but a boredom attendant upon *repetitive belonging*. The boredom of bureaucratic and political life (and of the sighs of women associated with its members in Trollope) is rather that of a life cut off from past and future in favor of a present that fills the entire time horizon: others may go, but I *must be* here, even after there is no longer a transactional *here*, here.

Martin Heidegger had an enduring interest in boredom, unrelated either to medieval sin or Simmel's contraceptive to the *nervosité* of modern life enunciated in the 1903 essay, "The Metropolis and Modern Life."[28] Boredom, for Heidegger, is both repressive and potentially conducive to a curious freedom, if reimagined under the rubric of *Dasein* which gives it a resemblance to the hybrid quality of public opinion. In *The Fundamental Concepts of Metaphysics*, a distinction is advanced between three different kinds of boredom.[29] The first (*Gelangweilwerden von etwas*) is merely situational boredom like that of Johnny Eames at his desk or a passenger delayed for five hours at an airport: the boredom of too much time on one's hands from which escape is impossible. As soon as the situation changes, the boredom ends. The second type is to bore oneself *with* something (*Sichlangweilenbeietwas*). Boredom would have an identifiable cause: the recognition that I have wasted my time in voluntary attendance at a quasi-obligatory party (social or political) that proved unenjoyable, given other choices, a frequent social postmortem after Trollope's parties.

Only a third type of boredom (*es isteinemlangweilen*) in which the recognition that my whole being has become indifferent and bothersome in its *lack of being* would enable a radical transformation. The individual is brought into a naked encounter with the unmanageable world (a synecdoche of public opinion) in a wearisome situation. In Trollope the encounter is often represented in the repetitive "buzz" of public opinion which holds Plantagenet Palliser, as it did Rev. Harding and Crawley, in limbo as he learns of the gossip that accompanies his wife's too close dancing with a former suitor, Burgo Fitzgerald. The "buzzing flies" (*CYFH* II 181), as narrated in Trollope's text (because plural), is gossip raised to a collective key which cannot be read save as an interference, from which I must restore my freedom; otherwise it dooms me to the imprisonment of the repetition. Once reflected upon, Palliser sees the "new" information about his wife's past, as a reminder of what he knows, but has repressed and from which he is now free:

> He looked at Burgo, and some thought of the young man's former hopes flashed across his mind,—some remembrance, too, of a caution that had been whispered to him.
>
> *(CYFH II 96)*

The management of public opinion is complicated insofar as it is simultaneously remembered and forgotten until it intermittently returns as gossip thought to have been laid to rest by the book of marriage. History is not an heirloom to be preserved and passed on, but a reminder of something one already knew or should have known.

This strategic amnesia, once recognized, is crucial to any hope of liberation from the boredom that characterizes bureaucratic, political and on occasion, marital life in Trollope. The obsequious Butterwell of *The Small House at Allington*, when apprised of new information or directives to the Income Tax Office, admits "that one knows a thing of that kind and yet doesn't know it" (*SHA* 302), so as to ensure the fluid deniability that preserves harmony, not unlike that of the future prime minister, Plantagenet Palliser, regarding his wife's past social indiscretions. The selective loss of individual memory (and knowledge of the sources of the information), as we have seen, also characterizes organs of public opinion.

An institutional indifference (to historically privileging, centripetal marriages or political alliances of equivalent convenience) must be recognized as part of *me* rather than external. It is this internalized or perhaps unconscious directive from which I must liberate myself—*as if from a mechanical system* (wheels within wheels) in which I am enmeshed. The recognition that the bureaucracy is indeed a system suggests that it is rational, stable, possesses intentional design and is in some sense self-sustaining, yet sufficiently open to enhanced operational efficiencies.

Palliser's son, Lord Silverbridge, achieves this by converting from his family's historical Liberal Party to the Conservatives, to his father's dismay, in *The Duke's Children*. His decision marks a change insofar as he acts upon an earlier realization of the equally novice Phineas Finn: "those in direct service of the government were absolved from the necessity of free-thinking" as a consequence of a "system of parliamentary *management*" (*PF* II 47, ital. added) of which he was previously unfamiliar. But in order to become free from the lack of freedom represented by the boredom of assumed ties to the Liberals and Lady Mabel Grex, the boredom is suddenly seen as not entirely systemic, but affected by my choices. Those situations arise when one is beyond any system which can be acquired as a discipline, usually as a result of public exposure: a displacement from the illusion of privatized space.

In the *Parliamentary Novels* the future prime minister's encounter with Fitzgerald at a gaming table far from the familiar regulation of domestic social and political life and the time spent in jail by Phineas Finn, unjustly accused of Bonteen's murder, both qualify as potentially liberating occasions from the loading of time that characterizes the first two types of Heidegger's boredom. Once so liberated by an incapacitating exposure to what the world thinks, Palliser learns that he will have an heir (and hence a future time) from a wife, the gossip of whose renewal of a previous relationship had occasioned his unexpected resignation. Phineas Finn, bored and hence resigned both *from* and *to* a political life that has never met his expectations, similarly recognizes that Madame Goesler's sponsorship of his now diminished political ambitions was an investment in him and his impulses rather than any ideology which she has never quite comprehended anyway. The time (Palliser's temporary resignation from politics for a European holiday) and space (of Finn's incarceration for Bonteen's murder) are crucial to the realized benefits of the third type of boredom, the space to become what one *is*: biologically, through the conception of a descendant son, or in Finn's case, politically, by a recognition that financial support can both enable and occlude love. Donations can be differentially denominated.

What obstructs recognition of the possibilities advanced in Heidegger's third category of boredom in the *Parliamentary Novels* is obviously the concept of a somewhat mechanical, even manufactured, *career*, forgotten only with difficulty and recognizable only after a temporal interval. The nobility never needed a political career, having been already made for them by descent or social prestige. Plantagenet Palliser has the luxury of being a genuine public *servant*, needing no remuneration. But, for the arrivistes to bureaucratic appointment or election to Parliament after the democratizing spirit of Reform Bills, like Johnny Eames or Phineas Finn, the lockstep progress on a defined, temporally incremental career ladder is crucial to self-definition and earned income. But it also produces the ennui appropriate to achieving one's *career grade*. As with all who labor to accumulate the curriculum vitae, Phineas Finn strives for the next level, even as he remains bored with petty committee work: contracts for potted peas for the armed forces or (in the case of Plantagenet Palliser) decimal currency deliberations:

> He had taken up politics with the express desire of getting his foot upon a rung of the ladder of promotion.
>
> *(PF II 44)*

Once denied the next rung and having learned of the marriages of two noble-born women whom he considered eligible, Violet Effingham and Lady Laura Standish, Phineas Finn seems detached from boring work. Trollope's text, however, makes clear that there is a "big subject" (*PF* II 129) in the Colonial Office to which he has been assigned: notably, whether or not the government should finance a transcontinental railway from the Canadian Northwest to Halifax with attendant oversight. A combination of political ambition and relative poverty obscures his ability to distinguish between minor and major issues in the national interest as opposed to one's own private interests. Melmotte of *The Way We Live Now* attempts to create a rival railroad south of the Canadian border with private financing to compete with the publicly financed northern project. Speculative private investment rushes in to fill a space vacated by bureaucratic delays in achieving bureaucratic (public) consensus.

Once having redeemed Alice Vavasor's lost financial investment in her previously quasi-affianced George Vavasor's political career, John Grey, a man previously defined by material comforts, moral sensitivity and elegantly restrained tastes, feels that the way to her heart is through political engagement: she is the Victorian equivalent of "radical chic." He rather too suddenly professes to having "new views" (*CYFH* II 381), although Trollope makes clear that the phrase involves not ideology, but the choice of a career rather late in the game as he confesses to Plantagenet Palliser: "I have not begun *it* so young" (*CYFH* II 417, ital. added). Political investment in public opinion enables an affluent class of single men to catch up with a fashion chosen by intelligent women in Trollope: active political work or sponsorship of it. In the absence of sincere belief, opinion or ideology, like George Vavasor whom he replaces, John Grey is in need of, if not belief, at least a theme. Feigning a shared ideological interest becomes an alternative way to a woman (or man's) heart, a charismatic pathway. Hence ideology becomes merely transactional, as intimated in the later work of Max Weber.[30]

Becoming a member of Parliament involves no dedication, but is merely another career move, not unlike that which defines Trollope's bureaucracies as John Grey reveals in an unguarded moment to a future prime minister and object of Trollope's admitted respect in the *Autobiography*: "I don't believe it all as you do. To you the British House of Commons is everything" (*CYFH* II 417). His is a *managed* insincerity, like that of Trollope's bureaucrats, for which political interest is a cover: a bangle (like a diamond necklace) with which to attract an acceptably privileged wife. Public opinion attracts other new entries into a market, like Towers and Lopez, but with enhanced resources accumulated on speculation or credit. A future partner has to be seen to have a public interest, to have been engaged with the formation of public opinion, rather than merely appraised by it.

This cynicism extends to others who "play at having a Church, though there is not sufficient faith to submit to the control of the Church" (*WWLN* I 178). If there is neither faith in the church, nor fast ideological positions for politicians, nor a consistent *ideological line* for organs of public opinion like the *Jupiter*, nor enough work within the bureaucracy, but only a rough road map for *attendance*, then the "hollowing-out" of substance in favor of management is a result. Ideological infidelity comes to be compared with the mere inference of the Church of England to a Catholic priest's words or to Lady Carbury's indifference to thematic content of her novel in favor of prolonged negotiations with reluctant publishers to raise rivalry and hence inflate demand:

> "I don't know that it is worse than a belief which is no belief," said the priest with energy,—"than a creed which sits so easily on a man that he does not even know what it contains, and never asks himself as he repeats it, whether it be to him credible or incredible."
>
> (WWLN *I 178–79*)

***

If it is the chance takers (and by implication, the insufficiently resourced gamblers) who alter any system by identifying gaps that compromise its points of over-determination, Obadiah Slope, Tom Towers, John Bold, Phineas Finn, Burgo Fitzgerald, Ferdinand Lopez, Alice Vavasor, Lady Glencora, Lady Eustace and Lady Laura Standish locate these gaps of over-determination, in the accepted values and practices of their respective culture(s). In the case of the women, the initial potential choices of partners seem overdetermined by either family or the conditions attached to their wealth, often held in some kind of escrow. Hence, they must find a way to creatively innovate with the opportunities afforded by the system as does Alice Vavasor with her investment in George Vavasor's political future or later John Grey's attempt to parley a love interest into an only lukewarm political interest as a candidate for Parliament. This is not a conversion to genuine political agency or ideological cause, but rather the vague longing to escape a life devoid of horizons, as do the bureaucrats in *The Three Clerks*. Lady Mabel Grex, abandoned to the life of the spinster within a faux-Gothic pile after Lord Silverbridge puts an end to an understood marital arrangement in *The Duke's Children*, would be one representation of this confinement. Her father had been one of the "chance takers"—an

inveterate gambler—leaving his bored daughter with an empty title, diminished financial resources, a house in need of repair and the need for management.

There rather exists a system of choices on a consumer grid in which each must differentiate "actions" from "engagements," the confusion of which is the cause of both Laura
Standish and Alice Vavasor's distress: they (or their family) have backed the wrong
horse. The individual must determine how to negotiate the opportunities afforded.
Playing with the cards one has been dealt or flipping a coin to decide whether to mail a
letter to a former object of desire (Burgo Fitzgerald) is one way of representing "playing"
the game as a perpetual gamble.[31] Obviously both an overdetermined management that
defines a predestined life and the introduction of "chance" by gambling are at opposite
ends of the spectrum, yet exhibiting a parasitical mutual dependency.

Culture then comes to be perceived not merely as a set of inherited values and practices, but as a distributor, providing *symbolic balances*—contrasts of compatibility and
compromises, all more or less temporary. This is the kind of analysis that is carried
out in other markets insofar as *bureaucratic management* must be more or less continuous, just as it is in the public opinion market. One example might be the analysis by
the Duke of St. Bungay pondering whom to endorse for chancellor of the exchequer:
Finespun, who possesses tactical "philosophical induction" or Plantagenet Palliser, in
possession of strategic political "instincts" (*CYFH* II 12–13). Tactics cannot always be
distinguished from strategy a priori, but only in practice in Trollope's political novels, as
in de Certeau. This opens the way to a market-managing model, insofar as *tactics* would
have no locus (unlike inductive logic), but must, like nimble public opinion, adjust situationally in the interests of arriving at a mutually agreeable settlement.

Wondering at the injustice of regular parliamentarians receiving no remuneration whereas cabinet membership to which he aspires is compensated work, Finn is
reminded of the fiduciary resistance posed by the nation's overly reluctant subscribers to
the idea of paid representation. Barrington Erle, a Liberal Party operative—read *manager*—reminds Finn of the difference in status which necessitates his moonlighting as a
journalist to make ends meet. A distinction is made between underpaid work dedicated
to ideology-formation and overpaid *management*:

> The country gets quite as much service as it pays for and perhaps a little more. The clerks in
> the offices work for the country. And the Ministers work too, if they've got anything to *man-
> age*. There is plenty of work done;—but of work done in Parliament, the less said, the better.
>
> *(PF 126)*

The state of boredom in which Finn finds himself, both during his first speech and later
when his fellow MPs are inattentive at best, is significant. Erle's explanation opens an
ideological, and as it turns out, conflictual space of public management. Although only
the cabinet is paid for its work, they assume the titular responsibility of the public servant, but with diluted loyalty to the constituency they allegedly represent as they do what
Erle regards as the nation's real work. Work is made separable from representation, to
which the existence of a faux-representative nobility had previously testified. Trollope
believed that "to serve one's country without pay is the grandest work that a man can

do" (*A* 262), though he wrote that from the vantage of someone, like Butterwell in *The Small House at Allington*, who had an independent income from both his novels and a modest superannuation from retirement when he entered the political arena as a candidate for Beverley. The irony is obvious: one becomes a genuine public servant only when he does not need the *work*.

Hence delocalization is being subtly subsidized, perhaps doubly so, given that some of the placeholding members of Parliament from Rotten Boroughs had never visited, much less been resident, in the locales they only virtually represent. Trollope himself would have known this from his disillusioning run for the Beverley constituency as a Liberal. Candidates are subsidized by the party, whereas *administrative* and *managerial* positions are paid by the state, from the public purse. A presumably representative MP actually would inhabit (en-*durance*) a kind of "holding area" for his own ambition with narrow openings for a selected few for the remunerated cabinet: the political correlate of what in Scottish topology is known as a "lough." These landlocked bodies of water with a narrow opening to the wider sea comprise an allegorically denominated topography in Trollope in the variously isolated fictional constituencies in which Phineas Finn or his rivals stand: *Lough*shane, to *Lough*ton (a second victory), to *Lough*linter.

Two kinds of political agency are thus in effect placed into an implicitly antagonistic relationship as addressing two different publics: the cabinet having a duty to the larger realm, even a political empire, and the MP, representing a smaller, local public as an unpaid, quasi-volunteer, selected by the political party as a placeholder-cum-manager. He is in need of some income supplement (often as a solicitor or barrister), given that "democratic representation" is not paid work, but only given the lip service accorded duty (a priori obedience). The management of the political market proceeds then, as did the market in hunting lodges, by segmentation. While future MPs struggle in the boring backwaters and loughs of the local, the real work of empire is done out of public view, where, for example, decisions are made about whether or not to finance canals in Canada which might facilitate the shipment of grain to Britain.[32] Would a loan be repaid; would the project offend the United States, just reunited after a divisive civil war; would a new status as a "Dominion" (another "durance" between colonialism and independence) be an acceptable bureaucratic status? These crucial questions remain less exposed to the vagaries of public opinion and are *managed* so out of sight, that they have a shelf life of only a sentence or two in Trollope's *Parliamentary Novels*.

Hence, on the one hand, the MP would represent, in many cases only nominally, the interests of the entire constituency at the same time that those selectively promoted (on the basis of loyalty) to cabinet membership have no legal (in the sense of constitutional) authorization, but exist officially solely for the higher purpose of the "work of the country and the Queens's comfort." The irony lies in the fact that the cabinet is thus in some sense a fiction that exists at the discretion of the Crown and is hence equally temporary. Hence, genuine public opinion—were it to speak in its own name—might conceivably have a grievance that its voice is not directly *heard* on the major issues, lying beneath (or above) two other imaginary representations.

Barrington Erle believes in fact that "thinking is not possible that any vote be given on a great question" (*PF* I 15) in Parliament, thereby endorsing political instincts and incremental management (even of the vote itself; hence the need for party whips). What happens at Westminster, for Erle, is a kind of "Punch and Judy" show, performatively engaging the public, not unlike say, Oxford Union debates today, the kind of "play" for which de Certeau (and Trollope) provide a rationale. Populists like Turnbull are marvelous entertainers with an audience that so exceeds the walls of Westminster as to create a too well-attended public disturbance contrasting with institutional boredom on the inside. Boredom may thus be a defense against the intrusive, noisy enthusiasm of both an underrepresented but increasingly vociferous public and those who would politically appeal to them by an excess of rhetorical skills, both regarded as empty.

In *The Duke's Children*, Turnbull's Tory counterpart, Sir Timothy Beeswax, is the subject of a conversation between Lord Silverbridge, a newly elected MP, and his father, Plantagenet Palliser, now promoted to the House of Lords and hence forever unable to return to the Lower House. A *"fluent* speaker [...] possessed of a great many words" (*DC* 200, ital. added), the Conservative Party leader even in name (like Slope, Slide and Butterwell) is ideologically malleable, melting and "tacking" when heated, to the flow of opinion to his party's advantage. Although less happy to either defend or suggest legislation, Beeswax, like Turnbull performatively, "simulates anger" while behaving so that "every detail should be troublesome to his opponents" to such an extent that they found themselves "checkmated" (*DC* 201) on the board *game* of public opinion:

> It was to these purposes that he [Beeswax] conceived that a great Statesman should devote himself! Parliamentary *management*! That, in his mind, was under this Constitution of ours the one act essential for Government.
>
> (DC *202, ital. added)*

Simulated outrage becomes a transactional tool of (imaginary) popular representation.

Management, however, now has a rhetorical component, insofar as it is the default value of simulated hope. In contradistinction to love (which desires a "soul mate") or fear (which acknowledges a superior), Sir Timothy offers only hope in his speeches, "which refers itself to benefits to come" (*DC* 165). Hence, even political rhetoric, insofar as it references future redemption, is speculative, borrowing both from the upper-class penchant for gambling (track, casino or political candidate) or alternative ventures in the city, like those promoted by Melmotte, in the interests of imaginary returns upon a nonexistent railroad. Beeswax had "invented a pseudo-patriotic *conjuring* phraseology which no one understood but which many admired" (*DC* 165) as a result of his training as an attorney. Like many who seek to influence public opinion, he has learned that glib rhetoric *attracts* public interest. An empty bureaucratese can be a summoning tongue.

Trollope's narrator obviously distinguishes, however, between two philosophies of *administrative management*—those of Plantagenet Palliser and Beeswax. He distrusts Beeswax's oral glibness whose only purpose is influencing public opinion:

> It is,—as style is to the writer,—not the wares which he has to take to *market*, but the vehicle in which they may be carried. Of what avail to you is it to have filled granaries with corn,

if you cannot get your corn to the consumer? Now Sir Timothy was a great vehicle, but he had not much corn to send.

(DC 201)

The Conservative leader has mastery of empty rhetorical carriage (no restraints on the wheels) not unlike the Trollope who reminisces that he may have dumped too much production in too short a space upon the reading public. Beeswax is rather managing the fiction of a product in the absence of *work*, the exaggerations of which Trollope will enlarge in both *The Way We Live Now* and, for comic effect, in *The Struggles of Brown, Jones, and Robinson*. Logistics of delivery come to rival the logistics of public opinion formation, sharing a frequent insufficiency of content.

George Gissing's unsuccessful hack, Henry Ryecroft, ironically blamed Trollope for the revelation of this "secret economy" of mass production made public in *An Autobiography*, for the devaluation of Trollope's reputation:

> It would be a satisfaction to think that the "great big stupid" [public] was really somewhere and in its secret economy, offended by that revelation of mechanical methods which made the autobiography either a disgusting or amusing book to those who read it intelligently.[33]

Gissing, through Ryecroft, blames Trollope, not entirely in jest, for revealing (and thereby cheapening) the novelist's work as a "secret economy," like a bureaucracy, generating reams of paper. As his narratives allegedly devalues the work of the clerical and political bureaucracies of Victorian England by examining the operational mechanisms by which they are maintained, so the argument goes, Trollope's confession as to how many words were produced each day over what time span is a revelation of trade secrets like those on display *within* his novels. One may believe that the public is deficient in intelligence, but public opinion quickly responds to the intimations of deception, just as it does to Melmotte's larceny in *The Way We Live Now*. If public opinion is an unacknowledged character in Trollope's novels, it may be entirely just that a marked decline in sales occurred after the revelations of *An Autobiography*, as it does with the values of shares in the *South Central and Mexican Railway*. We play with the "Tenth Muse," but as public opinion, she also plays with us. The "great big stupid" is not so stupid after all in its response to the market which, Ryecroft argues, must be better managed (deleting the instruction manual) in order to preserve the value of fiction.

As every reader of Trollope's *Parliamentary Novels* knows, Palliser's son will temporarily break his father's heart and family tradition by shifting allegiances to become a Conservative Party member in a previously safe Liberal seat at Silverbridge in *The Duke's Children*. The privileging of administrative management (of image and ideology) segments the political market just as for Ryecroft, it segments the publishing market. But given the slow convergence of politics to the work of administratively managing public opinion in both the *Barsetshire Chronicles* and the *Parliamentary Novels*, the turn of events should come as no surprise. As Chaffanbrass had complained of the compromised splitting of differences (in order to avoid the segmenting of a market between guilt and innocence in judicial judgments) by weak-kneed judges in *Phineas Redux*, so in Trollope's last of the *Parliamentary Novels, The Duke's Children*, a politician changes labels in such a way as to reveal the real values of his heritage.

If historical political allegiances and loyalties are so easily abandoned across an indeterminable boundary, some are sure to lament the loss of an era when ideological differences had not yet entered a negotiable marketplace, a presumptive political golden age when "Juno and Venus never kissed" (*CYFH* II 12) as opposed to these times when anyone can kiss anyone in "the absence of good, honest hatred among them" (*CYFH* II 13). Another side effect of an administrative rationality is the repression of ideological differences in the interests of feigned consensual unanimity that binds them to the people. In *Phineas Redux*, a minor character attempts to deconstruct all allegiances of the nobility by suggesting that the privileged never have firm ideological loyalty anyway:

> These Pallisers have always been running with the hares and riding with the hounds. They are great aristocrats, and yet are always going in for the *people*.
>
> *(PR I 126, ital. added)*

Some skeptical individuals know that "the people" exist for aristocrats much as do their estates—an interest to be managed through an (often) absentee presence.

***

If *tradition* is partially reproduced as social *identification*, then subtle changes in the spaces of association and social evaluation should be revelatory. Dickens's novels, with the possible exception of the didacticism of *Hard Times* with its antagonistic models of industrial production (Coketown) and play (Sleary's Circus), concentrate upon individual characters and the choices that shape or determine them, enabling comic exaggerations. They are invariably memorable, as a result of a distinctive grammar: a clicking noise in the throat of Magwitch, Mr. Dick's kite, or a Podsnappian wave of the hand that fixes them in our memory forever. Trollope's characters, however, lack sufficient autonomy to be fully comic, rather addressing and responding *to* the varying moral worth of a culture's social *arrangements* and how they are continuously reevaluated by a volatile public opinion.[34] They exist as perpetually attentive antennae, producing an alternative notion of the comic. Public opinion forgets whom it speaks *for*. Hence, individually defined "character" is less memorable in Trollope, their defining "tics" and "clicks" lacking. Madame Neroni, like Miss Havisham of *Great Expectations*, is physically paralyzed and bears the wounds of abandonment. Yet, like the public opinion which she manipulates, Madame Neroni is not at all frozen in time but quite nimble in response, coming alive at unpredictable occasions in response to the public's response to her.

Throughout the *Parliamentary Novels* the Liberal Party conducts its social life and policy caucuses either at private homes or at the appropriately named *Reform Club*, accessible only to members. As with the press (pre-*Jupiter*) which had previously been identified with sponsoring ideologically shared political parties, so both the Conservatives and the Liberals had their own after-hours redoubts. But, in *Phineas Redux*, some MPs have come to frequent the politically unaffiliated *Universe Club*, where on a fateful evening

Phineas Finn is confronted by the operative/agent, Bonteen. He vociferously complains of Finn's abandonment of the party line on the question of the disestablishment of the Irish Church, an issue later legislatively amalgamated with the larger question of home rule for his native Ireland. Because of Finn's dissent and the ensuing loss of a majority, Bonteen is not appointed to the cabinet, but instead assigned to the Ministry of Trade, another unpaid position, hence enhancing personal debt, given his wife's high consumption among wealthy friends like Lizzie Eustace.

"Unlike other clubs" (*PR* I 308) the *Universe Club* keeps disciplined hours, open "only one hour before and one hour after midnight" (PR I 308) in a small building. Although its members have mixed interests, they are associatively bound by inherited or earned entitlement:

> A member of the Cabinet, a great poet, an exceedingly able editor, two earls, two members of the Royal Academy, the president of a learned society, a celebrated professor, and it was expected that Royalty might come in at any moment, speak a few benign words, and blow a few clouds of smoke.
>
> *(PR II 53)*

Yet Trollope suggests that dutiful service, like that expected of a mixed bureaucracy and mixed obligatory sociality, is no longer invariably sufficient to secure the administrative golden apple when one's obsequious service is perceived as undisguised ambition. Highly nuanced judgments are arrived at, yet they remain tenuous, in contradistinction to David Miller's assertion that "Trollope's characters always display mixed motives."[35] They rather never quite identify with certainty to whom they are speaking nor who is speaking *through* them in the disguise of ambition. Bonteen is but one more resentful, indebted political *agent*,

> useful, dull, unscrupulous politicians, well-accustomed to Parliament, acquainted with the bye-paths and back-doors of official life,—and therefore certain of employment when the Liberals came to power.
>
> *(PR I 311)*

Like Bott, Bonteen has practical, tactical knowledge of how administrative management works. Yet, on this occasion where he officially *needs to be*, Bonteen is simultaneously exposed to assault upon leaving the premises. Unable to adjust to a new bypath of sociopolitical life after being bypassed for an expected Cabinet position, Trollope's plot commits him to a Darwinian fate. The consummate insider familiar with the hidden doors and pathways to the political house, he suddenly finds that the locks and paths have been changed, leaving him displaced.

Plantagenet Palliser, despite his dull dedication to service and relative absence of new ideas in the interests of maintaining a majority, is sincere in defense of his mildly held beliefs. Like most of us, he is a mixture of tolerance and prejudice, but is perhaps most sincere in his desire to separate private from public life. This is a separation difficult to maintain in the face of the continual intrusions that public opinion and its organs threaten. For Palliser, in the choices of private associations one is free to discriminate, yet on public service tolerance and equality of access rule. On public service, one surrenders private choice, as was the case with the ballot (and just perhaps the Liberal opposition to the secret ballot). He instructs his son of the differences:

> In the former, you choose your own associates and are responsible for your choice. In the latter you are concerned with others for the good of the State; and though even for the State's sake, you would not willingly be allied with those whom you think dishonest, the outward manners and fashions of life need create no barriers. I should not turn up my nose at the House of Commons because some constituency might send them an illiterate shoemaker; but I might probably find the illiterate shoemaker an unprofitable companion for my private hours.
>
> *(DC 204)*

The new Duke of Omnium believes in equality of representation, but not in demands for social integration, despite the increased assimilation of the less advantaged into branches of the government bureaucracy. He embraces the less educated and uninformed when sent to Parliament (as fictionally "representative" of the people) in the same way that he admits more newspapers to his morning reading, but resents being obligated to as*sociate*.

Yet the future prime minister can modify his prejudices and beliefs, adjusting to new information and new institutions where access is mixed. When his son, Lord Silverbridge, contemplates his candidacy under the Conservative banner, betraying his family's long-controlled Liberal seat, the disappointing news to his father is delivered at the *Beargarden Club*. Palliser is shocked to discover this is a curiously mixed venue, a gentlemen's club open at all times to nonmembers and hence, even more universal in its clientele than the *Universe Club*. The private domains of what were formerly party enclaves are being diluted. As at the garden party at his castle penetrated by the press, access to the Beargarden seems relatively uncontrolled and unregulated. The occasion foregrounds Silverbridge's preparation for informing his father of his relationship with an untitled American, Ms. Boncassen, who dances with anyone, an embrace of "the public" that must initially appear as, like the *Beargarden Club*, too receptive:

> "We don't care about that at all. Anybody can take in anybody."
>
> "Does not that make it promiscuous?"
>
> "Well;—no; I don't know that it does. It seems to go on very well. I dare say there are some cads there sometimes But I don't know where one doesn't meet cads There are plenty in the House of Commons."
>
> *(DC 204)*

Unrestricted openness to the public, and derivatively to public opinion, appears as promiscuity (and hence a contract betrayed), not unlike his wife's perceived flirtations with an old lover, Burgo Fitzgerald, or a political rally/picnic organized by his wife. Despite his reservations, the Duke of Omnium and future prime minister concedes that the soup at the "open membership" *Beargarden* "was better than what he received at home" (*DC* 205). The *Beargarden* is simultaneously, like Marie Goesler, both promiscuously open (in the sense that she has had a rumored assortment of prior relationships) and yet tasteful. His son, sensing his father's possible discomfort, however, wisely advises "avoiding the *publicity* of the smoking-room" where the patriarch might encounter a mix of nobility, toff, and riffraff like Tifto, a turf gambler. The public should be absorbed in small portions so as to slowly immunize an elite against sudden exposure.

Heretofore privately affiliated clubs are now evolving into a new, more open venue, in the same way that the former *Jupiter* progressively morphs into the *Daily Jupiter* and finally, the *New Jupiter* by the time we reach the last of the *Palliser Novels*. These are obviously new social and discursive spaces, continually under revision as "new and improved." The reader must have a good memory to notice their evolution through numerous volumes, but unlike the Book of the Peerage, shaping public opinion and access much as do new international resorts like Killancodlem. One way of defining this newly evolving space might be an intrusive cosmopolitanism that is the ultimate threat to established institutions, to which the heir, Lord Silverbridge, appears to dedicate himself.

His temporary conversion to the Conservatives, despite his contempt for its leader, Beeswax, shares his father's ambivalence when the latter consented to join a very provisional coalition government. Silverbridge, when queried by his father at the *Beargarden*, is strong in his defense of private interests as opposed to the symphonic and more national interests which was the backbone of Liberal thought. To his father's Benthamite belief that "the greatest benefit to the greatest number was the object to which political studies should tend," thereby appealing to "wider interests" (*DC* 57), Lord Silverbridge, like Slope in *Barchester Towers*, replies that his responsibility is essentially defensively protective with respect to class interest, but socially open:

> His own and his class. The people will look after *themselves*, and *we* must look after ourselves. We are so few and they are so many, that we shall have quite enough to do.
>
> (DC 57, ital. added)

Though not as unruly as a "mob," the public are a "many" which create the "work" of defensive self-maintenance: the nomenclature of bureaucracies.

The state as a distributor of benefits to the population at large is perhaps anticipated by the metaphor of *management*, an argument not lost on the former chancellor of the exchequer. His son, in opposition to his father's preference, would open the gates socially to admit all people to the *Beargarden*, but would restrict mass public opinion in political participation. Their party affiliation would appear to be in opposition, but their actions in everyday life are remarkably aligned in defense of "us," be it social or political. This suggests, as Trollope did in *An Autobiography*, that party labels are relatively meaningless (as are so many labels in Trollope), given that most identify with the historical affiliation of the family rather than sincere ideological conviction. Hence Lord Silverbridge's break with his father could be read as merely a form of re-branding in an attempt at historical independence, as if the Conservatives were now "new." The Silverbridge constituency similarly votes for "family" rather than party, in electing him; the rebellion against family values will assume another form later in literally, the family's last stand in *The Duke's Children*.

Less calculable than the greatest good for the greatest number and less definable than private, class interests and their *property*, the management of public opinion (*propriety*) is the repressed activity in which so many of Trollope's characters seem to be fighting a rearguard action. Silverbridge's ostensible partner-trainer in horseflesh, Major Tifto, lames their jointly owned entry, a horse appropriately named "Prime Minister" (given the handicaps under which his father, like previous prime ministers, has worked in the *Parliamentary Novels*) in order to collect a wager upon a rival "hidden" partner in crime. Like bureaucrats, politicians and lovers, the tout manages or hedges his investment. Public opinion is mixed as to whether the disqualifying injury inflicted upon "Prime Minister" occurred naturally or was a "plant" (*DC* 352), though Trollope's narrator suggests that "general opinion" (*DC* 355), a synecdoche for the majority, tilted toward belief in criminal intent, giving the narrative velocity:

> The story was about England, about all Europe. It had travelled to America and the Indies, to Australia and the Chinese cities before two hours were over. It was so *all-pervading* a matter that down to tradesmen's daughters and the boys at the free-school, the town was divided.
>
> *(DC 352, ital. added)*

The Liberal, Plantagenet Palliser, now Duke of Omnium upon the death of his elderly uncle, covers his newly Conservative son's enormous gambling loss (70,000 pounds) consequent upon the incident, only in defense of the family's good name. Such is assuredly a private interest but also, given the knowledge of public opinion, increasingly of public interest as well. But the patriarch is also contributing to his son's new party affiliation, thereby operating along the margins; "hedging," consistent with his interest at the Baden gaming tables.

Though the swindle is a near certainty, any dependency by the son on unregulated city moneylenders (suspected of being Jewish) would enhance the family disgrace, as the circulation of discounted credit notes would in tandem circulate as gossip, thereby devaluing reputation. Although Palliser will attempt to manage both, balancing the "purse strings of the nation"—the Liberal Party will attempt to reduce the budget of the Royal Navy in the *Parliamentary Novels*—is different from protecting the family from the deleterious effects of bad publicity. But, apparently, the management of parliamentary majorities and the defensive management of family reputation are similarly dependent upon loyal agents, but given the family reputation, not unrelated. A family retainer and financial adviser, Mr. Moreton, advocates "wise discretion" (*DC* 360), Butterwell's "tact" writ larger, compatible with his belief that "the boy must be *made* to settle himself in life" (*DC* 352), by shared administrative guidance.

Being *settled* in one's life requires managed labor: something to be invested in and *made material*. Settlement outside of court in Trollope has the advantage of avoiding unsettled and unsettling publicity while exercising the benevolent condescension of a patriarchy to bring about its synonym, closure. Effective management is keeping transgressions out of the papers and beyond the range of city moneylenders—distributive vehicles—who similarly spread information with paper. The dissemination and efficient delivery of private communication had defined Trollope's career during his work for the post office in especially Ireland and the West Country to such an extent that he had come to regard his "mission" as "angelic" (*A* 82).[36] But there are less benign devils to be *managed*.

***

If risk-taking in the form of gambling, institutionally sanctioned shams (like Melmotte's railroad) or unsecured investments in the political potential of a future speculative marital partner are all speculative activities crying out for the hedges provided by sophisticated management, then the reader is left to wonder how *management* might be combined with romantic creativity without incurring the subversive speculation of public opinion. Neither the boredom of the settled, *managed* career ladder (in a bureaucracy or a family-arranged "bureaucratic marriage") nor the loss of reputation or money in dubious practices and investments would strike the balance between the disciplined novel machine and the creativity that Trollope's career represents.

Once a financial, marital, bureaucratic, political (or probably any other) problem is defined as amenable to management, the solution to the problematic often requires both long-term thinking and a dedicated flowchart of designated duties and responsibilities. Problems of *management* appear as systemic, requiring a plurality of hands to solve. Hence its ease of delegation to agential, supplementary figures like Scruby, Bott, Bonteen and Moreton—the retained who live our lives for us—and on occasion live too much of it. Everyone is "so connected with the acts of his agents as to be himself within the reach of the law" (*PR* I 284), though nonetheless using them for an increasingly ineffective immunity, as with organs of public opinion. Some of Trollope's women in the *Palliser Novels*, however, seem to avoid needing the confession of the "mismanaged life" embraced by Alice Vavasor in *Can You Forgive Her?* after her campaign contribution is squandered by her *dual partner*, George Vavasor.

Lady Laura Standish, though attracted to Phineas Finn, accedes to the wishes of her family to marry landed wealth in the form of the austere Calvinist, Kennedy of Loughlinter, with his rigid church attendance, rather than an impoverished Irish Catholic. She distinguishes between a love *for* and admiration *of* the Irish Catholic's rather undefined, but generally liberal, ideological posture in her conversation with Violet Effingham, another woman to whom Finn was romantically attached, in explaining her wish to a rival. Restless upper-class women, apparently need the embrace of an ideological *cause*, often aligned and confused with other embraces:

> It isn't a matter of love at all. It's a womanly *enthusiasm* for *the cause* one has taken up.
>
> *(PR I 103, ital. added)*

Violet Effingham's management skills are similarly dedicated to controlling her husband Lord Chiltern's aggressive behavior, including a history of staged duels, gambling and excessive drinking. She *manages* by rechanneling his life into the controlled responsibility of master of the foxhunt, a form of discipline that involves social engagement and accepted rule enforcement, not unlike the bureaucracy. Lady Laura Standish "had wanted to meddle in *high* politics" (*PF* I 209) and grand projects, yet finds herself totally bored with responding from a set format to the correspondence of her husband's constituents, finding it "all form and verbiage and pretense at business" (*PF* I 210): her share as secretary in a bureaucratic-political marriage.

Effective management involves neither "meddling" nor Slope's early career of "dabbling," but an alternative lightness, equally necessary, but less intrusive. She is a literal amanuensis, who works at avoiding work (one definition of what it is to be a member of the privileged class), as do MPs and bureaucrats. Yet, like Tom Towers of the *Jupiter*, she has too much time on her hands and suffers the boredom typical of the bureaucracy in its dedication to managing various *correspondences*, political and epistolary.

Suffering from frequent headaches consistent with the symptomatology of boredom, Lady Laura finds only temporary relief during a visit from the prime minister's private secretary in discussion over the chances of the new Reform Bill. This is an expansive discourse from which her participation is socially embargoed. Forbidden by her jealous husband from renewing a relationship with Phineas Finn, as Dorothea Brooke was forbidden (by the terms of a will) from renewing a relationship with Will Ladislaw, she confesses to Violet Effingham, another friend of Phineas Finn, of the restraint upon women: "women cannot be *useful* as can men" (*PF* I 210, ital. added), suggesting that utility is gendered. In this remarkable assertion, Lady Laura suggests that even her *managerial* usefulness is circumscribed as an involuntary dedication to dictation and *copying* as opposed to representing (as would a genuine political agent)—an intriguing distinction in forms of representation. These endowed women resist participation in a "shadow bureaucracy" which attracts men desirous of the security of administration.

Yet one female character in the *Parliamentary Novels* manages to combine intense friendship, political usefulness and general public admiration (save from women jealous of her skills), while avoiding the condition of the sociopolitical secretary. Madame Goesler is an administrative manager who preserves autonomy without sacrificing sociality. She is the ultimately successful *manager,* to which her assimilation into society (despite a questionable marital life and her allegedly Jewish background prior to her move to London) lends abundant testimony. Like Phineas Finn, Ferdinand Lopez and Melmotte, she is a cosmopolitan interloper in London society whose biography is replete with interstices, given frequent absences to manage—with obvious success—her business affairs in Europe. Madame Marie (Max) Goesler is rumored to have been widowed by "a German Jew living in England in the employ of Viennese bankers" and, succeeding his death, a friendship with "an Austrian Count, to whom she is rumored to allow ever so much a year to stay away from her" but in fact "*nobody* [...] knows anything" (*PF* II 31, ital. added). With an inconsistently readable past she accepts a volatile presence in a community's narrative, while graciously lubricating it with very sociable dinner parties. Though alien she is assimilated.

With dark complexion and an abundance of curls, Madame Goesler is indifferent to the company of other women whom she finds boring. Her dress is equally difficult to read, preserving a stylistic autonomy: "unlike in form for any other purpose than that of maintaining its general peculiarity of character" (*PF* II 25–26), a peculiarity entirely

in keeping with her suspected Jewish physiognomy. An aggressive participant in political debate, she becomes a magnet of public opinion while sharing with bureaucracies a
"great ingenuity in *management*" (*PF* II 42, ital. added). The social milieu highly evaluates her skills, hosting dinner parties to which she invites a carefully planned mixture
of nobility and politicians, even as she is subject to periodic reassessment and speculation. Without intimate knowledge of the culture, she arranges seating, as is the case
with Trollope's state bureaucracies, in accordance with her intimation of conversational
compatibility. In an environment where everyone seems related *to* or fully knowledgeable *of* the lines of descent, income and peripheral family of everyone else, she reevalu-
ates as she goes along.[37] Madame Goesler expresses sincere, albeit radical political ideas
with which her guests are aghast, partially to mock "mealy-mouthed" British reserve
with ironic wit:

> Politically I should want to out-Turnbull Mr. Turnbull, to vote for everything that could be
> voted for,—ballot, manhood suffrage, womanhood suffrage, unlimited rights of striking,
> tenant right, education of everybody, annual parliaments, and the abolition of at least the
> bench of bishops.
>
> *(PF II 27)*

Her stated views are a kind of ideological mid-nineteenth-century Radical Department
Store, like the material one, "Brown, Jones and Robinson," in an earlier novel set before
Phineas Finn. Programmatic ideals are aligned on the same shelf as inclusively branded
interests, with no discrimination between them. She covers over previously separable
(and defining) issues and interests in such a way as to generate abundant opinions at her
dinner parties as a facilitator of mass participation.

According to the perceptive Madame Goesler, politicians resign their positions
over indiscernible and irrelevant differences of opinion, finding that "public virtue
cannot swallow some little detail" (*PF* II 140), resulting in petty, polarized bitter-
ness over an unimportant offense that is then publicized. People are defined by their
hatreds. When her guests commence a socially disruptive disagreement at table,
Madame Goesler jokes that henceforth she will refrain from having two politicians at
any future formal dinner at her Park Lane residence. This suggests a desire to manage
the adversarial views of her guests so as to insure adhesive sociality, one role of the
bureaucracy in public life.

As an assimilated alien—like the public opinion that appraises other of Trollope's
arrivistes—she easily admits to an imperfect understanding of an unfamiliar system,
as a ploy to stimulate conversation. Though feigning ignorance, she understands how
aggressivity (feigned or real) is rewarded as a signal of bureaucratic loyalty.

> As far as I can understand the way of things in your Government, the aspirants to office
> succeed by chiefly making themselves uncommonly unpleasant to those who are in power.
> If a man hit hard enough he is sure to be taken to the Elysium of the Treasury bench,—not
> that he may hit others, but that he may cease to hit those who are there.
>
> *(PF II 28)*

The mysterious Madame Goesler astutely sees the Treasury Bench not as a goal for the ambitious (as would Phineas Finn), but as a holding pen where critics of financial policy might be defanged until housebroken by political expediency. Though believing the English to be "so stiff and heavy," she "would not have cared to succeed elsewhere than among the English," and "gradually, the thing was done" (*PF* II 136), a nuanced acceptance of cultural frailties and ultimate assimilation. She alternatively praises and criticizes her British guests and their system of representative government, establishing a reputation as a balanced observer of a local life foreign to her experience, much as did Frances Trollope while in America. Even "suspicious people could not put their fingers on anything wrong" (*PF* II 136), as if Madame Goesler had escaped the threat of devaluation at the hands of a public opinion that afflict the reputations of even privileged natives. If informed political critique and social management were not enough, she has acquired a more than superficial knowledge of the culture represented in the ballads of Sir Walter Scott with which she entertains Phineas Finn, to his surprise. Little wonder, given her social skills and cultural knowledge, that other women in the *Parliamentary Novels* should confuse criticism with cattish envy, complaining of the "pushing, dangerous, scheming creature" with supposedly "Medean tricks" (*PR* II 225) to maintain her youthfulness.

    She might most usefully be thought of, perhaps, as the "split" that defines mystified subjects as sites of misrecognition—what Althusser calls an imaginary relation to the real conditions of social production—but also of a distancing of the self that makes possible criticism as a mode of recognition, the recognition of a possible misrecognition, in which I find myself, albeit circuitously.[38] Her cynicism of institutional reform combined with a belief in individual intervention resembles most closely perhaps Sir Isaiah Berlin's appraisal of Herzen's thought; given Madame Goesler's Central European origins, not as farfetched as it might seem. She distrusts any ideologically conditioned utopian ideal which ignores material desires and status insofar as that would merely substitute one narrative for another,[39] eliminating autonomous choice:

> The truth is, Mr. Finn, that let one boast of one's independence,—and I do very often boast of mine to *myself*,—one is inclined to do more for a Duke of Omnium, than for a Mr. Jones.
> *(PR I 148, ital. added)*

Yet, the remarkable Madame Goesler can pay a partner to stay away and decline a financially generous marriage proposal from the aged, wealthy patriarch, the Duke of Omnium (Plantagenet Palliser's uncle). After a three-year friendship as companion and nursemaid in his dotage, she declines his marriage proposal which would come with an Italian villa. During their association, her closest friend, Lady Glendora, turns sharply against Madame Goesler, as a potential threat to a family legacy if she were to deprive Lady Glencora's offspring of their legacy by having a child by her husband's uncle. Once Madame Goesler rejects marriage to nobility, all of her friendships are magically restored—suggesting that she knows the limits of assimilation and how to manage public opinion by timely restraining marital ambition. Happy to live within an indeterminate relationship with British nobility outside of marriage, her superior management skills combine the roles of servant and master (of his desire). Like public servants, her skills require both "tacking" and tact.

If read allegorically, she has the skills of selective engagement *with* and detachment *from* public opinion, much as do state bureaucracies. Her relationship with Phineas Finn reflects similar skills at negotiation. Unlike other women in Trollope, Madame Goesler, a unique figure in nineteenth-century British fiction, continually strives to elide what she wants for her adopted country and what she wants for herself. Having escaped the censure of public opinion over a life shadowed by a cloudy past, Madame Goesler marries the impoverished Phineas Finn in another international marriage like that of the future Duke of Silverbridge with an American. But the marriage in *Phineas Redux* occurs only after she proffers a "gift" that escapes an exchange economy, in contrast to the political donation Alice Vavasor makes to her cousin, George, as a deposit on their future in *Can You Forgive Her?* Finn, however, although lacking support from his fellow Liberals in Westminster, declines her generosity, announcing his plans to return to his native Ireland as yet another unlicensed, indebted lawyer (like Trollope's own father), abandoning political life.

In response to her queries about his future upon returning to his native Ireland, having abandoned the moral and economic expense of politics, he responds that "in a barrister's way that may be brought to me," he will do "anything honest" (*PF* II 315). Madame Goesler reminds him that insofar as it too is enmeshed in public opinion (as is politics), the practice of law at the margins is no different from "going in" for the people:

> You will stand up for all the blackguards, and try to make out that thieves did not steal?
>
> *(PF II 317)*

Near the end of *Phineas Redux*, in a chapter ironically entitled "Madame Goesler's Legacy," the remarkable woman deconstructs her temporary "possession of the duke's legacy" (*PR* II 322), 25,000 pounds left her in the Duke of Omnium's will by, in effect, "passing it on" as her own legacy. She becomes a bureaucratic conduit for potential redistribution of excess to the less privileged. In deeding the money to the duke's niece, Adelaide Palliser, the victim of a patrilineal culture whose genuine love for a (relatively) impecunious Gerard Maule, she carefully ascertains, Madame Goesler converts a "legacy" to a "gift," by delegating foundational authority. Her generosity enables what we might term, a *facilitated* love marriage, combining romance and a secure line of credit, becoming thereby a radical figure of redistributed wealth, not unlike the bureaucracy of Inland Revenue. She strategically *manages* public opinion by redistributing a bequest from a wealthy lover to the less advantaged enabling a genuine love marriage; by supporting like-minded ideological causes in Phineas Finn's political career; and, avoiding rivalry with the native nobility. She also functions as a model of effective state surveillance in her information regarding a criminal who has fled to another country. Her foil is the assimilated "ci-devant Jew" (*ED* 427), the popular Rev. Emilius, who flees to the Prague of which she has considerable local knowledge. Madame Goesler functions like a one-person bureaucracy, combining research, local knowledge, an absence in presence and a presence in absence and a justly redistributive bias.

Yet, after Finn's acquittal of murder, Marie Goesler is flexible enough to understand his withdrawal from politics altogether on the grounds that his reinstatement to the Colonial Office (though offered by the new Liberal Head, Gresham) would be read by public opinion as either compensation for his pain (while under detention for murder) or a guilt-gift in consideration of his Irish origins, rather than any endorsement of his consistently held ideas. Martyrdom places him in a false position vis-à-vis his ideas: a charitable vote from the remorseful. How a character anticipates and responds to imagined public opinion, rather than erecting protective barriers in defense of reputation or fleeing from it altogether, is one index of an increasingly open society and its discontents.

***

In *The Eustace Diamonds*, the scheming Lizzie Eustace, also a widow, reports from Carlisle that her contested jewels (indeterminate as to legacy or gift) have been stolen, even though she has in fact concealed them only to have them stolen afterward from her Hertford Street abode in London. The police are unable to determine whether there were (1) two robberies (one of which failed); (2) one robbery with the other concealed so as to retain possession of the jewels under cover or (3) no robberies at all, but only alternative strategies of concealment for the purpose of managing the retention of possession in the face of legal requests for their return. Bunfit and Gager, the two detectives entrusted by Scotland Yard with the investigation of the case, have rival theories to account for the disappearance of the contested asset. Precursors of Holmes and Watson, the pair compete with speculative public opinion in the construction of a master narrative to account for the crime. Gager warns his partner, Bunfit, to avoid "*running away with ideas, just as if you was [sic] one of the public*" (*ED* 427, ital. added).

The need to *manage* speculation by professional sleuths is posed against the *runaway* (unmanaged) theories of the press, even as the press is praised as a legitimate competitor of the police. The criticism of the press directed toward police incompetence in solving the "theft" of the Eustace Diamonds is tempered by a belief that organs of public opinion formation enhance competition. The press and the police in competition create market efficiencies: both are implicated in surveillance. Trollope narrates the competitive market in a trope repeated throughout his novels and *An Autobiography*, managing the speeding coach:

> Two or three of the leading newspapers had first hinted at and then openly condemned the incompetence and slowness of the police. Such censure, as we all know, is very common, and in nine cases out of ten it is unjust. They who write it probably know little of the circumstances;—and, in speaking of a failure here and a failure there, make no reference to the numerous successes. […] It is the same in regard to all public matters,—army matters, navy matters, poor-law matters, and post office matters. Day after day, and almost every day, one meets censure which is felt to be unjust;—but the general result of all this injustice is *increased efficiency*. The coach does go the faster because of the whip in the coachman's hand, though the horses driven may never have deserved the thong.

(ED 369)

Regulation by emergent bureaucracies and emergent organs of public opinion makes them simultaneously *partners* and *rivals* with a presumptive interest in efficiency.

The intrusion of bureaucratic management *of* and surveillance *into* familiar practices appears as a new dispensation, a more democratic contractual, which binds society as an imaginary collective. It is necessary because the binding of men to their word and historically mandated contracts has been challenged by open markets. An aging aristocrat, Lady Fawn, is pained upon being told that the "theory of life and *system* on which social matters should be *managed*" (*ED* 449, ital. added) had changed:

> Under the new order of things promises from gentlemen were not to be looked upon as binding, that love was to go for nothing, that girls were to be made contented by being told that when one lover was lost another could be found.
>
> *(ED 449)*

Bureaucratic management must be sufficiently nimble to be familiar with regulatory changes in an open market which it has had a hand in facilitating. Chapter XLVII of *The Eustace Diamonds*, entitled "The Eye of the Public," posits a collective with a singular organ, supplementing ear and voice. Open markets create excesses: of keys, diamonds, copies, unattached women and eventually, organs and platforms of public opinion creation.

A bureaucracy dedicated to management shares a number of features with the public opinion it both serves and regulates, as if there were an osmosis that creates a mutual dependency. Neither has a singularly permanent, locatable home, but seems to be embedded in everyday life as an omnipotency. Both government bureaucracy and public opinion appear as a composite, a maze, but in referentiality, singular. Both have a regulatory function, but that function can become (almost imperceptibly) monopolistic or even tyrannical in operation, stifling innovation and dissent. And, finally, both public opinion and state bureaucracies have an anonymous impersonality that enforces a deniability of personal responsibility in favor of the systemic. Both assume the power of the *contractually* inescapable, against which both its membership and those under its regulatory spell seek to carve out some arena of personal sovereignty.

Notes

1 Walter Benjamin, *The Arcades Project*, p. 342. Unlike the landed nobility who live off of rents, the bourgeois for Benjamin never have to think about how the forces of production impact their lives and live in "veiling fabric" of false comfort.

2 Roy Porter, "Science, Provincial Culture, and Public Opinion in Enlightenment England," *British Journal for Eighteenth-Century Studies* 3 (1980), pp. 20–46, argues that there was a conflict between various "scientific societies" (which remained closed to the public). After Humphrey Davy's rather theatrical chemistry demonstrations, open to the public, fears of public anarchy as a response of the uneducated arose.

3 Although seldom conceded, the attempt to create a restrictive "society"—at least among literary critics—may be one way of describing F. R. Leavis's definition of a novelistic "Great Tradition." Defined by exclusion and inclusion (as were British journals and clubs of the nineteenth century), his "moral canon" is quite vague.

4 Although Trollope's oft-repeated description of his "advanced Liberal-Conservative" ideology has been condemned as "mealy-mouthed," his belief that only education could continue the reduction in social inequalities (*A* 265), as opposed to other forms of government redistribution or upper-class protectionism, would align him quite closely with intellectual liberals around the *Westminster Review*. This may explain his enormous respect for a favored social critic, George Henry Lewes.

5 Perhaps the most notorious example of Trollope's readjustment of strongly held principle is his violation of a prejudice against serial publication on the grounds that those who engaged in the practice (i.e., Dickens) were inhibited in making the ending match the beginning because of insufficient planning. Ever the believer in bureaucratic planning and advance surveying, Trollope nonetheless admitted to "thinking it fit to break my own rule" (*A* 127) by submitting a serialized novel to the new *Cornhill Magazine* which later became *The Small House at Allington*.

6 Samuel Taylor Coleridge, *Biographia Literaria, or Biographical Sketches of My Literary Life and Opinions*, ed. Nigel Leask (London: J.M. Dent, 1997), see especially chapter xiii.

7 Max Weber, *Economy and Society: An Outline of Interpretive Sociology* [1922], ed. Guenther Ross and Claus Wittich, Vol. II (Berkeley and Los Angeles: Univ. of California Press, 1978), p. 1403.

8 Ibid., pp. 1381, 1404–1405.

9 Jürgen Osterhammel, *The Transformation of the World: A Global History of the Nineteenth Century*, trans. Patrick Camiller (Princeton: Princeton Univ. Press, 2014), pp. 206–212.

10 Most government revenue in the mid-nineteenth century was collected by customs excises, taxes levied on derivatives of agricultural products (beer and hops), as suggested by parliamentary debates over the Corn Laws in Trollope, or relatively small "legacy taxes" on inheritance. Revenue was hence heavily tilted toward consumption and therefore disproportionately collected from those less well-off, like the patrons of pubs. Recently, however, one notably forgotten effort at genuine redistribution in the period between 1834 and 1838 has been identified: the effective "bailout" of relatively wealthy British Caribbean slave owners after the abolition of slavery by paying compensation to those who could provide written proof of ownership and value. As slaveholders were not an impoverished class, they collectively received compensation (in today's monetary value) of an amount which rivals the bank "recapitalization" of the period 2008–11. David Olusoga, "The Price of Freedom," Episode 2 of 2: *Britain's Forgotten Slave Owners*. BBC 2: 22 July 2015.

11 See the excellent survey/comparison on the expansion of nineteenth-century bureaucracies by G.E. Aylmer, "Bureaucracy," in *The Cambridge Modern History*, Vol. 13: *Companion Volume*, ed. Peter Burke (Cambridge: Cambridge Univ. Press, 1979), pp. 164–200.

12 Only recently have these considerations (opportunity costs and benefits of the bureaucracy) entered academic discourse. See Pamela Hurd and Daniel Moynihan, *Administrative Burden: Policymaking by Other Means* (New York: Russell Sage Foundation, 2018).

13 Mullen, p. 83. In Trollope's novels, the impingement of a "public" upon institutions previously regarded as either sacrosanct (like Parliament now open to debt collectors) or institutional anonymities (like the GPO) is a subject surely open to further study.

14 Ibid., pp. 84–86.

15 Michael Ignatieff, *Fire and Ashes: Success and Failure in Politics* (Cambridge, MA and London, Harvard Univ. Press, 2013) in recounting his experience as the leader of Canada's Liberal Party, argues that in politics, explanation always comes too late. Revenge against an adversary, insofar as it mobilizes public opinion, occupies the position of absent or postponed explanation: personalization displaces explanation.

16 Naming (and nicknaming) being a kind of "branding" in all of Trollope, one wonders whether the excessively managerial Sir Raffle Buffle is an "adaptation" of Sir Stamford *Raffles*, the highly regarded governor general of the Federation of Malaysian States during Queen Victoria's reign. Both baffling and a buffer, he is nominatively a representation of a strategy of the Foreign Office in a Southeast Asian to act as a buffer between the competing interests of the French (Indochina) and the Dutch (Indonesia).

17 The role of the nineteenth-century British bureaucracy in unifying, if not disparate classes, at least enunciating some shared class interests and diluting conflict is a relatively neglected subject. It may have served a role comparable to that of the racial integration of the U.S. armed forces during World War II under President Truman.

18 A sophisticated critique of this idea is offered in Claude Lefort, *Elements d'une Critique de la bureaucratie* (Geneva: Droz, 1971), pp. 288–314, who argues that bureaucracies only have the power reflected in those appointed to compose it and hence is another anonymous agent of feigned distantiation.

19 Nicolas Poulantzas, *Political Power and Social Classes* (London: New Left Books, 1973), pp. 139–140, suggests, in opposition to Althusser, that the bureaucracy must appear almost without author or authority in order to create the illusion that "we" are all one family. An "administrative family" built into the system and drawn from it would be only symbolically responsible while perfecting myriad modes of response: an intriguing model which lends it a relationship to public opinion formation as opposed to the aggression of interpellation.

20 Michael Hardt and Antonio Negri, *Assembly* (Oxford and New York: Oxford Univ. Press, 2017), advance the idea that the practice of the "people" need not adhere to a party line, since such supervisory discipline impedes local information including the need for adjustments to public opinion flow, regarded as (locally) situational.

21 A similar argument, an application of the work of Bourdieu, has recently been advanced to explain the divided professional response when various cultural prizes are publicly announced, in James F. English, *The Economy of Prestige: Prizes, Awards, and the Circulation of Cultural Value* (Cambridge and London: Harvard Univ. Press, 2005).

22 See Anthony Trollope, "The Civil Service" in *Fortnightly Review* II (October, 1865). Despite his opposition to tests for admission to the civil service in the United Kingdom, Trollope hedged a bit during his travels to the colonies. In testimony before the New South Wales Parliamentary Committee on the Civil Service, he recommended the adoption of a competitive examination for the Australian Civil Service. Given the absence of powerful patriarchal families in Australia, perhaps Trollope felt that there would be no threat to historically descendant interests. See "The Civil Service as a Profession," in the *Four Lectures* that comprise the so-called Parrish MS in the Princeton University Library. I thank the curatorial staff of the Princeton University Library for a facsimile of those essays.

23 Trollope's position on the issue seems remarkably prescient given the recent critique on the defects of "meritocratic testing" at elite universities in the United States, given the disparities in preparatory education between the classes. See Michael Sandel, *The Tyranny of Merit: What Became of the Common Good* (New York: Farrar, Strauss, and Giroux, 1920).

24 A number of restrictions are often placed upon the members of government agencies in order to preserve neutrality and inhibit the possibility of a separate political power base. Restrictions on political contributions (the Hatch Act in the United States), control on intimacies with locals for foreign service personnel in the colonies and frequent rotations and secondments (Trollope's posting to Ireland as a deputy surveyor) are among the means by which bureaucracies might purge themselves of private interests or internal criticism. In nineteenth-century England, employees of the postal bureaucracy were not allowed to vote (*A* 122) for an MP, a restriction strongly opposed by Trollope on the grounds that public service should never disenfranchise.

25 Christy Wampole, "What is the Future of Speculative Journalism?", *The New York Times International Edition* (26 January 2018), p. 9.

26 John Major, "Burley, Clumsy, But One of Our Literary Greats ... My Friend for Sixty Years, Anthony Trollope," (Daily) *Mail Online* (11 April 2015).

27 Lars Svendsen, *A Philosophy of Boredom* (London: Reaktion, 2005), pp. 18–48, suggests that boredom is a defense against the multiplication of the "particularities" which impinge on modern, especially urban existence. His boredom is often the result of informational excess.

28 Georg Simmel, "The Metropolis in Mental Life," in *Simmel on Culture*, ed. David Frisbee and Mike Featherstone (London: Sage, 1997). Boredom, for Simmel, is essentially a mask of impassivity defending against the unorganizable plethora of sensory impulses impinging on modern life, lacking the capacity for liberation.

29 Martin Heidegger, *Fundamental Concepts of Metaphysics, World, Finitude, Solitude*, trans. William McNeill and Nicholas Walker (Bloomington: Indiana Univ. Press, 1995), pp. 136–149.

30 Max Weber, *Charisma and Disenchantment: The Vocation Lectures*, ed. and with an introduction by Paul Reiter and Chad Wellmon and trans. from the German by Damion Searls (New York: New York Review of Books Press, 2019). In the second of these lectures, Weber seems to imply that people hold to their beliefs with such an irrational passion that conflicts of value

resist resolution. By contrast Trollope's bureaucrats and politicians are almost too flexible, their beliefs are always in service of something else.

31 Michel de Certau, *The Philosophy of Everyday Life* (Los Angeles and Berkeley: Univ. of California Press, 1984), xvii and pp. 34–37.

32 In 1865 (during the distraction of the American Civil War), the deliberations over the financing of a Canadian Transcontinental Railway as an investment and policy issue, given the fragile nature of the resolution of that domestic conflict, would seem a larger issue than potted pea contracts or Palliser's interests in decimal currency. Is Trollope suggesting that larger issues entail such risks that the politically ambitious avoid them in favor of the management of the more incremental issues (in order to appear as administratively managerial) as a career move?

33 George Gissing, *The Private Papers of Henry Rycroft* (London: Phoenix House, 1993), p. 166.

34 James R. Kincaid, *The Novels of Anthony Trollope* (Oxford: The Clarendon Press, 1977), similarly sees Trollope's comedy as mildly subversive of systemic assumptions rather than defining character.

35 D.A. Miller, "Secret Subject, Open Secrets" in *The Novel and the Police* (Berkley and Los Angles: Univ. of Clifornia Press, 1988), p. 124.

36 Kate Thomas, *Postal Pleasures: Sex, Scandal, and Victorian Letters* (Oxford: Oxford Univ. Press, 2012), p. 81, argues that Trollope's delight in "facilitating deliveries" may have been compensation for the stagnant structures of his youth narrated in *An Autobiography*.

37 Mieke Bal, "De-Disciplining the Eye," *Critical Inquiry* 16 (1990), pp. 506–532, and in other formats as well, argues that metaphoric readings are archaeological insofar as they attempt to find a foundational ground (ancestry, antecedents, family "connections," education) which we read *through* a surface representation *for*. In metonymic readings, by contrast, nothing lies beneath or behind. The eye must be re-disciplined to appraise systemic disruptors: hence the difficulty in "reading" the likes of Madame Goesler, Lopez and Melmotte. One form assumed by the failure to re-discipline the eye is to ascribe to all of unknown origin an unconfirmable Jewishness, the conversion of metaphor to metonymy which occurs with the absence of knowledge of antecedents.

38 Louis Althusser, "Ideology and Ideological State Apparatuses," *Essays in Ideology* (London: Verso, 1984), pp. 18–24, suggests that this misrecognition of the self *in* the act of interpretation is crucial to interpretation. Madame Goesler, astute in her analysis of mid-nineteenth-century British politics, misrecognizes herself as more than a liberal supporter of Phineas Finn: a possible lover. She would resemble the curious arriviste of *Hard Times*, the upper-class, previously expatriate drifter, Harthouse, who though, "playing" with the provincial culture of Coketown, discovers that he *really* loves Louisa Gradgrind rather than "seeing" her merely as an object of easy seduction away from an unhappily "arranged" marriage with Bounderby.

39 Isaiah Berlin, "Herzen in his Memoirs," in *Against the Grain: Essays in the History of Ideas*, ed. with a bibliography by Henry Hardy (London: Hogarth Press, 1979), pp. 208–211.

Chapter Five

THE SUGAR

He was coming almost as full of politics, almost as devoted to sugar, as Mr. Palliser himself.
(*CYFH* II 413, ital. added)

The ease with which both men and women develop an *appetite* for politics—as did Trollope himself—transforms how we think of public opinion and its component suppliers. A porously defined public comes to sit at previously exclusive or at least potentially monopolized metaphoric tables (with indifferent guardians), be it catering to ambition, enhanced social intercourse or reciprocal affection. This taste initially appears as "neo-Liberal," perhaps akin to Trollope's self-identification insofar as it is potentially more socially inclusive. The attraction of favorable public opinion is a relatively universal taste across all classes and political parties.

Adam Kotsko has argued that neoliberalism is a form of political theology, albeit often exemplifying *predatory inclusion*. In both the theological and political novels of Trollope there is an emphasis on freedom and open markets, though not necessarily as an expression of choice or human creativity and dignity. Such open access by the public is rather an apparatus for reducing responsibility in favor of shared blameworthiness.[1] Systemic failures are so dissolved as to be granular and individually unidentifiable, as the duke's eldest son, Lord Silverbridge, does under the duress of a public sympathetic with the foibles of the less advantaged, like Major Tifto in *The Duke's Children*. The dream of an inclusive discursive "commons" might be a preamble to Lawyer Chaffanbrass's judges in *Phineas Redux*, habitually handing down compromised verdicts by splitting the middle and dissolving differences, the better to avoid offending sensibilities.

This waiver of sovereignty (as firm judgment) yields to a general sugarcoating—a strategic neutralization of blame—which universally attracts while disguising what lies beneath. One might think of it as an *adulteration* of the sovereignty of private judgment by pressures of an imaginary collective voice. The negotiation of the loss of these sovereignties which had previously defined ideological, social and even narrative identity recalls Adorno's "constellation" with its pressures to "think about nonthinking."[2] Surely, this is one definition of public opinion, rhetorically touched upon by Trollope: "it should be a matter bound by *our opinion* rather than your *own*" (*DC* 171, ital. added) or perhaps more succinctly as a part of a negative dialectic "a thing not to be thought of which must be thought of" (*DC* 172).

Although there is no evidence of Trollope's familiarity with Kant, the provisional judgments narrated in his novels come to resemble certain implications in the philosopher's work on aesthetic judgments. When we dwell in a world of commonly held cultural assumptions and presumptions, we share a range of judgments. This ought or ought not to be done because it is against the law, embodies a conflict of interest (as in *The Three Clerks*) or is against church doctrine. All are what Kant termed "determinative judgments." But there is clearly another kind of judgment that is neither non-determinative nor rule bound. These judgments are generated not by knowledge, law or belief, but by reflective thinking and fall into the category of aesthetic judgments: for example, Goya's *Desastres* are more significant than the *Tauromaquia* as a contribution to modern perspective. My judgment, though initially subjective, engages the opinion of someone else,[3] an opinion to which I attempt to woo him. We hope to have the courage of our convictions, even when our deepest convictions are challenged by putting ourselves in the *position* of everyone else. Consequently, we may modulate our vaunted independence of thought, one definition of sovereignty. In Trollope's work this process is narrated as coming into a second life which, perhaps not coincidentally, mirrors the "coming into one's own" when an heir (to whatever) reaches the age of his majority, as does Lord Silverbridge, to his father's dismay.

John Gray in *Can You Forgive Her?* had previously been apolitical, secure in a gentleman's life, until, (relatively) radicalized by desire for a woman, he becomes a substitute for George Vavasor's volatile marital and political ambitions that come to be displaced *onto* him. Gray's self-sufficient emptiness, subject to further *dissolution*, along with a love interest, subsidizes his shallow embrace (via an anonymous financial contribution) as a "thoroughfare" to her heart. Entrance into the hurly-burly of public opinion (as a political candidate) *opens* him to the possibility of sharing his heart, previously dedicated only to the (determinative) maintenance of a squire's lifestyle.

The taste for the approval of public opinion as the touch of the "Tenth Muse" is often mixed with other, often disguised, private interests—reestablishment of a faith threatened by internationalism, a love interest or financial opportunity. The restoration of individual sovereignty (as self-determination) is difficult given the shared appeal to the variable appraisals of public opinion involved in such transactions which have the effect of demanding (often unmeasurable) responses.[4] Slope can no more interpret the imagined, whispered calls of Madame Neroni than he could the vagaries of public opinion, vacating both enterprises in tandem. In a parodic reversal of the threatened dismemberment (of body or reputation) of women who resisted advances in Greek myth, Madame Neroni is already effectively dismembered. A defeated Slope opts to return to a more material Olympus by pledging his troth to a sweet ending: the daughter of a Baker Street sugar refiner into which his affections are dissolved. If marriage to *sugar* (as in Tate and Lyle) is both the tempting, universal taste for politics and the default position of those who abruptly retire from politics like the Rev. Slope in marriage or Trollope's omniscient narrator catering to a public with self-confessed "sugary" deserts at the conclusion of his novels, then it might represent both our attachments and the need to wean ourselves from them, simultaneously. Sugars, as a derivative, easily form compounds with other substances, its presence vulnerable to disguise and even artificial confection, much like public opinion. Once refined, the initial source of a particular sugar—beets, cane or corn—is difficult to determine. And some humans metabolize sugar with difficulty, compelled to refrain from consumption for their own well-being. Its quickly induced "highs" and "lows" constitute a threat to balanced regulation.

The philosopher, Kwame Anthony Appiah, has argued that though many of our attachments and obligations are to patrons, party members or lovers, those with whom we *share* possibilities of reciprocity in activity, for which we search, are often undervalued.[5] Public opinion might then, like other emergent rather than determinative materialisms, resemble immature or emergent bodies, searching for shareable "likes" on emergent thoroughfares of exchange.[6] Hence, public opinion can be ignored as the noisy gossip of the disenfranchised or it can call for assistance to those needing physical or ideological support (embodiment), or even combining both at the same time, as does the crippled Madame Neroni in *Barchester Towers*, both victim and agent of gossip. For public opinion initially lacks a substantive legitimacy, unlike land or inherited wealth, or the "train" of legal record or historic precedent (deeds): a narrative that is inseparable from a vanishing ephemerality. It is *there*, but only intermittently registrable, except as highly adaptable, dissolvable as both instigator and component of tentative reciprocities.

Public opinion cannot permanently represent itself to itself, except in the forms of polls or surveys to which Trollope dedicated his civil service energies in Ireland and the West Country. This resistance to easy formalism(s), unless measured as a spot in time, gives public opinion some immunity against the representational models it alleges to advance. It does not represent a consistent interest or a consistent identity, but rather exists as a *seasoning* or *sensibility* to another comestible. Sugar seems part of an edible infrastructure insofar as we never consume it directly from the sugar bowl, but as a facilitator that binds or adulterates other flavors, whetting the appetite for more.

Similarly, public opinion lacks some features common to the traditional subject of philosophical discourse. It often thrives on an appeal to sympathetic consumers who exhibit unthinking behavior, which might be described as the hydraulics of being easily (and often, mechanically) moved without justifiable explanation, especially at first exposure when the perception of its presence is often disruptive. The subject would only arise as a particular response or openness to critique, some temporal sensitivity to the inexplicable "call" of another: hence, curiously resembling Levinas's intriguing "religiosity of the self."[7] A hitherto autarchic subject is deconstructed, absorbed or dissolved—like sugar—into the constitution of political plurality to which, having been awakened, it adheres, but often only as a vague aftertaste. In response it becomes a sentient being. Possessed by external or internalized "voices," as with much religious belief, those in the sway of public opinion can easily become conspiracy buffs, dedicated to a largely invisible reality less accessible to secular rationality.

Yet, a residual question might remain: What happens to the traditional subject and where does it *go* in this pressure of response to public opinion? The public's maintenance of open options, the alteration of resolve and *dissolve* (or abandonment) depending on verifiability and adjustment to new information, and the ability to bond with other elements collectively contribute to the representation of public opinion as an alternating *energy* or *pressure*, a *force*, instantiating itself frequently as a false subjectivity.[8] Sugar may metaphorically represent this false subjectivity: empty calories that are nonetheless a facilitator in stimulating appetite. One is moved, but never realizes quite why or how. Invisibly sponsored, increasingly cheap as an "open-access" enhancer and invisibly omnipotent, public opinion has some of the reflective qualities, forcing those it touches to exist in *response mode*.

Questioned about her affectionate, yet undefined, relationship with the infirm, wealthy elder Duke of Omnium, the strong-willed Madame Goesler imagines herself to have become will-less. She questions any restoration of sovereignty, swallowed as it is by public opinion which has openly criticized an extralegal relationship, the "handicapped subjectivity" of love:

> I have wondered at it myself sometimes,—that I should have become as it were *engulfed* in this new life, almost *without a will of my own*. And when he dies, *how shall I return to the other life?*
>
> *(PR I 151, ital. added)*

Although confining her to a purgatorial social status, her caring friendship is also a *consciousness* that *moves on* if not metabolized, carrying those exposed to it in its wake. The operative metaphors for those caught up in public opinion are tilted toward force fields, measured in terms of quantum social effects.

Although *The Struggles of Brown, Jones, and Robinson* is seemingly a thematic (though not a chronological) outlier to both the *Barchester Novels* and the *Parliamentary Novels* in critical opinion, its elaboration of reciprocal pressures both *by* and *upon* public opinion seems a logical development of Trollope's interests. On opening day of a new department store domiciled in Magenta House, a huge poster appears on each window of the emporium, announcing an indiscriminate pressure on an establishment:

POSTPONED TILL ELEVEN
Immense *Pressure* of Goods in the Back Premises

> *(SBJR 43, ital. added)*

Eager customers "are half across the street," blocking another of Trollope's thoroughfares as they constitute public pressure. Crushed against large glass windows, calculated by the proprietors so as to maintain desire in *strategic durance*, the *lumpenproletariat* resembles the piles of unsorted merchandise in the back as a mass to be picked through. As with Towers's *Jupiter*, traditional *gatekeepers* are intentionally challenged by circulating informational pollution. This systemic multiplier effect, with loitering doubling as a conveyer of information, has been described by Mark Zuckerberg, the founder of *Facebook*, as "scaling," which eventually entails "dark patterns" of sharing "likes" to continue to get people to log in.[9] This is a literal crush against *transparency*, not too distant from Trollope's own strategy of maintaining the forced presence, novel-to-novel, of the same family members in continuous circulation.

As Trollope confessed to the manipulation of mass retail markets on numerous occasions in *An Autobiography*, so posters, people and goods, crowded against each other, are effectively dissolved as an interpenetrating expansion of "stock." Like public opinion, both "stocks" are simultaneously excessive and lacking easy identification, insofar as, like sugar, it both constitutes and creates pressures to consume:

There were two other chief matters to which it was now necessary that the Firm should attend, the first and primary being the *stock of advertisements* which should be issued; and the other, or secondary, being the *stock of goods* which should be obtained to answer the expectations raised by those advertisements.

(SBJR *34, ital. added*)

Similarly, Melmotte's railroad consists entirely of advertisements for future rolling stock disguised as questionable stock certificates. Trollope's spaces, as opposed to Dickens's vaults and hidden duplicates of wills, are almost too open: occasions for allied *display* so as to draw investor/believers to a different kind of emptiness, opposite the recovery of hidden secrets.

Like the "mass," "mob" or "buzzing flies" often imagined by its detractors as the disruptive potential of appeals to public opinion, Trollope's stock of consumers in *The Struggles of Brown, Jones, and Robinson* are an aggregate (of desire) whose individual subjectivities are obscured in group consumption. They are part of a curious dialectic noted by Walter Benjamin in his unfinished masterpiece on new forms of retailing that evolved contemporaneously with the re-spatialization of Paris. The crowd of anonymous shoppers is attracted to novelty as a stimulus to demand at the same time that the ever same is manifested in mass production on show.[10] They are motivated, like investors in Melmotte's imaginary railroad, by FOMO, the celebrated "fear of missing out." When considered as a consuming mass, the public is stripped not only of individual subjectivities, but also of any notion of dedication to a project as would be the case, were they in service of some class-based ideology as was say, the crowds drawn to hear the Radical, Turnbull, in *Phineas Finn* and equally resistant to easy police control. Consumerism reduces ideology as part of a dialectic, but preserves it as a vestige—a label—crucial to marketing. Faces pressed against the plate glass windows of the Magenta House department store, intermittently controlled by the law, are surely a trope of a public opinion itself—drawn to the illusions of transparency.

One wonders if this reciprocity between heaps of goods and ideas for sale (a plaza) and crowds enticed to view them are part of an alternative critical space which Nicholas Spencer has identified as crucial to the history of nineteenth-century American fiction.[11] This admittedly rhetorical conjecture would imply a space within Trollope's oeuvre where rhetorical questions might be posed in such a way as to stimulate debate by a presumptive audience constituting a competing *stock* to be convinced even as they are potentially future participants. This obviously involves a particular kind of question posed with an urgency even while in *durance* (like readers of novels), perpetually open to critical debate. Trollope's exploration of this imaginary space is really not so distant from John Stuart Mill's attempt to identify a form of public discourse that would eventually draw everyone, save those who would threaten the existence of such a space by screaming "fire" in a theater when there was none: an early version of terrorism as an ultimate test of mass consumerism.

Of course, the opening of this rhetorical space, as with other market-opening strategies, may necessitate the *bracketing* of more familiar literary as well as traditional ideological subjects, strategies, grammar and topology. The dominant role of, say, character in defining a plot or defining others through his actions might be suspended in favor of a critical space in which characters, author, reader and institutional agencies attempt to mutually explore (1) where their increasingly collective interests intersect and (2) how the public (including the reader) responds to the shifting intersections and partitions of judgments, both threatening and defining individual sovereignty. Vastly different from the privatized *hortus conclusus*, George Eliot's praise of Trollope emphasized the *public* nature of his metaphoric spaces where meditational health is a side benefit:

> The books are [...] like pleasant *public gardens* where people go for amusement & whether they think of it or not, get health as well.[12]

Her remarks on Trollope's re-spatializations were reciprocated in his admiration for George Eliot's work. Trollope appeared in public with her despite public censorship as a consequence of her open relationship with a legally married critic, George Henry Lewes, whose liberal opinions Trollope equally admired.[13]

Trollope, during one of his visits to North America, though objecting to certain features of rampantly individualistic democracy, was impressed by communitarian spaces in the states. He commented upon the abundance of public squares and meeting halls where public opinion shared among all classes had free play, as opposed to the British tendency to dedicate private gardens to meditation or controlled entertainment.[14] Some of these American *agoras* would of course, particularly in upstate New York, have been under quasi-religious sponsorship and practice like the communal settlement of the Oneida Community, combining political debate, religious fellowship and commercial entrepreneurship.

These public spaces, albeit not identical to the contested rhetorical space of criticism, are similarly resistant to easy formalism. Although earlier in his career, Jürgen Habermas had argued for the suspension of private belief in the creation of a public sphere, he has more recently allowed a space for private belief in its creation. He would achieve this by partitioning the market, much as does Trollope. There is for Habermas an unregulated wild public sphere of *publicité* (occupied by celebrities and politicians) and a second, defined as an arena of "*reasoned* communicational exchange,"[15] as if they were separable. He concedes, as would Trollope, that religion can give a voice to the second type, to those marginalized in society (like the pensioners at Hiram's Hospital in *The Warden*), the "vulnerable forms of common life," and thus have a place in opinion and will-formation. Habermas's only requirement for such participation is that religion must renounce its claim to a *monopoly* on interpretation, agree to a separation of church from state and most importantly, agree to a translation of religious ideas into a secular language "that is a publicly intelligible language,"[16] and therefore crucial to public opinion formation. But its tendency to monopolization would be enhanced if translated.

Writ large, Trollope's achievement might be read as an exploration of the forms assumed by this perpetually emergent monopoly no matter how the market is divided. A more inclusive, secular faith from another perspective, however, could be imagined by the faithful as having been stripped of the exclusive magic crucial to the wild, charismatic arena of the church and activities like, say foxhunting—a near-irrational religion of a certain class, as Trollope freely admitted, at mid-century. Once translated into a more accessible (rational) regime, religion might lose its *charm*, even etymologically, the private appeal of enchanting voices at prayer, overtaken by the competitive *chant* of public opinion, as occurs in *The Vicar of Bullhampton* when a noisy dissenting chapel is erected adjacent to an Establishment vicarage. In a colloquium with (then) Cardinal Ratzinger, Habermas seemed to endorse the presence of the "church" as a normative value for the inevitable volatility of unregulated public opinion, remarkably close to Trollope's drags on the wheels of the metaphoric stagecoach.[17]

Habermas's demand for translation of the charismatic into secularity would be a next of kin to a religion frozen into secular allegory advanced by G. H. Lewes, George Eliot's companion.[18] Habermas would suggest some sugarcoating of the more aggressively divisive rhetoric and practices of traditional religious faiths, in favor of an ecumenism, as a price for absorption into negotiable public opinion. The semiotics appropriate to this opening of narrative space as well as strategically unstructured, open retail emporiums—as we shall see later in this chapter—involves a specialized grammar, replete with subjunctive voice, conditional clauses, multiple productive agents, speculative conjectures and reductions to a symbolic fluidity. Assertions are easily modified in parataxis by ensuing clauses, transparent to each other, all serving to subsidize consensual public participation, while dissolving the charismatic sovereignty of the untranslatable. It resembles the hedging qualifications common to parliamentary debates, calculated to *draw con*sent and easy absorption into general practices rather than steadfast commitment. This grammar, like Brown's insistence on "a great quantity of [...] plate glass" (*BJR* 32), is crucial to the creation of competition for obstructed access.

At the same time, however, this characteristic verbal and visual syntax typifies what so many people find objectionable about political utterance: the exaggerated qualifications that prevent a speaker from ever being held *accountable* on the basis of abstract principle. A curious pragmatics seems to be at work in Trollope's narratives. Positions are to be advanced while opening the physical or ideological postures to other speculatively incremental translations or investments less open to traditional symbols. This separation of liberalism from the utopian seems, retrospectively, to owe something to the then MP John Stuart Mill's assertion in an otherwise unmemorable (save perhaps to the Irishman, Phineas Finn) address to Parliament in 1868 regarding Irish tenant rights: that no single rule could be applicable in all cases, when the knowledge of local circumstances is absent.[19] Because public opinion often misreads or exaggerates, Mill and Habermas's bias toward the *translation* of the local for more easy general absorption, intrigues. If characters in Trollope often err in their attempts to read public opinion, as did Slope, public opinion also misreads—as a strategic errancy—character.

In Trollope's work, public opinion is compatible with liberalism only when it embraces and expands incremental knowledge. Under this rubric it becomes a *system*, implying that its components (production, processing, delivery, security, application, retail consumption) all work *in conjunction* ("wheels within wheels"). A malfunction in any component compromises operational efficiencies and general toleration. Like sugar biologically, how public opinion is metabolized or precipitated is crucial. To "cater" to the public by sweetening the pot of social access, as does Lady Glencora at Matching or paying for votes by settling a bar tab, is to whet taste for a confection, rather than using public opinion to modulate, supplement or revise my own beliefs: the perversion of genuine reflection on my individual sovereignty to merely placating insatiable taste. To (only superficially) "go in for the people"—as opposed to genuinely representing them—is to have one's voice (or merchandise) become conflatable with the fickle vox populi, only to suddenly discover that the individual voice of sincerity is not recoverable.

Given the temptations of easy access induced by unimpeded transparent entry, public opinion as an apparently discursive commons becomes an arena of contestation and control, not unlike land. It can be broken up as parcels for "re-contextualization" with an alternative purpose hidden from original investors or guardians. Public opinion can be put to unforeseeable future applications or itself become an object of further speculation, as it devolves into a commodity capable of being banked, shared or spent.

If one subtext of the *Parliamentary Novels* is the political education of Phineas Finn, then a conversation with one of his tutors, Monk, an impecunious Liberal cabinet minister, is instructive. Owing his position to popular appeal with the less advantaged public, he confesses his mistake while accompanying Phineas Finn home to Ireland:

> You have no cause for regret, but it is not so with me. If there be any man unfitted by his previous career for office, it is he who has become, or endeavoured to become, a popular politician—an exponent, if I may say so, of *public opinion*. As far as I can see, office is offered to them with one view only—that of clipping their wings.
> And of needing their help.
> It is the same thing.
>
> *(PF II 251–52)*

Like sugar, public opinion is both needed (as an additive to stimulate ambitious appetite), but also prey to unexplained and unpredictably sudden withdrawal. Utilitarianism being utilitarianism, to have only transactional utility is to be vulnerable to unanticipated shifts in opinion. The metabolism of one's relationship to the public calls for regulation.

At an early private social excursion with his patroness and eventual wife, Madame Goesler, Phineas Finn rides an unaccustomed mount at the hunt, the balky Dandolo, borrowed (leased) from a friend. Finn is warned that the animal "pulls" when approached by a "crowd" (*PR* I 141) and meets with near disaster by either repressing or forgetting the warning. The rider in advance "cannot discount your trouble at any percentage," the vague knowledge coming to exist as a persistent "weight on your mind" (*PR* I 141), but insufficiently processed until too late. The incident could be read as an allegory of the weight of public opinion on a political career that has been leased, with a new leaseholder/partner: the sponsorship of the affluent Madame Goesler.

These warnings, in whatever field, appear as something dimly remembered after the fact, a small bump on the learning curve. Given the patient, measured condescension and forbearance of the nobility, public opinion presents a *guerilla discourse* or inharmonious cluster of voices, not easily regulated into singularities. Even though Rev. Slope of *Barchester Towers* had criticized the "meretricious charms of melody" in favor of "divid[ing] the word" (*BT* I 51), he too is drawn to Madame Neroni's unfinished whispers which have some features of ventriloquy, insofar as she is skilled at projection. The plural voice threatens to displace the singular Word. In the six *Parliamentary Novels*, public opinion speaks in a voice inclusive of the contrapuntal, resistance or even silence, and hence has an enormous range in scale and volume, able to disguise, reject or *absorb* the small and amplified voices of individuals or to appear as a voice of various modulations.

Melmotte of *The Way We Live Now* imagines himself to be possessed by a cacophony of voices (a counter-charisma) prior to the suicide marking the end of an equally imaginary enterprise, his railroad. The scrip (stock certificates) for his imaginary *South Central Pacific and Mexican Railroad*, distributed at no initial cost to investing partners, should be redeemable or recoverable, but instead exist only as advertising posters with which to draw other investors into a vast Ponzi scheme. The value has already been dissolved for those latecomers at the bottom of a symbolic glass pyramid of buyers *entrained* from as far away as San Francisco by Melmotte, Cohenlupe, Longestaffe, and for a while, the suspicious Paul Montague. Investment, both financial and marital, is becoming international, an abandonment of the local and hence the commercial correlate of Bishop Proudie's ecumenical outreach in *Barchester Towers* which ultimately abandons the Rev. Slope. A cosmopolitan draw, like Magenta House with its large windows that draw a public's attention, stimulates general desire by appealing to a wide range of tastes (like sugar) while threatening niche markets and nuanced tastes.

This might partially explain why public opinion formation has been metaphorically compared with exaggerated, collectively eroticized energies which may be politically or economically unproductive, not unlike *sugar*. What we are addressing is a peculiar emptiness at the foundation of a discourse allegedly *open* to the public whose value vanishes upon successive exposures at the hands of some public. Insurgent opinion banks can accept grievances and bundle them (as do moneylenders, financial markets and social media platforms) from an assortment of entirely unrelated inputs, only to *retail* them at strategic intervals as social or discursive capital, as newspaper editors do in Trollope.

Resentments may be part of the bundle, an assemblage of fickle carriers. When Augustus Melmotte attempts to convert his social and dubious financial assets to political assets, there is a counterintuitive attraction of the poor to his candidacy as an MP for Westminster in the first vote to be taken after the approval of the private ballot in Trollope's fictional time scheme. The newly enfranchised could care less about issues, contradicting the advice of Scruby in *Can You Forgive Her?* as well as traditional markers of party allegiance. Melmotte's affiliation is hollowed out in Trollope's narrative as merely a "*so-called* Conservative cause" (*WWLN* II 126, ital. added), even as he fights allegations and investigations of financial fraud. All "causes" are vulnerable to being *called* (in some double sense) as provisional—held to account. Despite the fact that "his own party is ashamed of him" (*WWLN* II 129), Melmotte easily secures the working-class vote traditionally accorded Liberal candidates. The swing of the working-class vote to Conservatives is a shock to punters speculating on the election, but perhaps less so in the twenty-first century in both America and Europe: the politics of resentment toward historically insincere caterers who sweeten the pork barrel with sugar at election time.

His Liberal opponent, Alf, the editor of the well-named *Pulpit*, is suspected, albeit not ascertained, of being Jewish (Aleph?), so that the electoral contest pits two relative arrivistes surrounded by speculation regarding their ethnic origins. Even though he controls an organ of public opinion, Alf takes the high road in his campaign, declining to condemn Melmotte for his fraudulent financial schemes, increasingly public knowledge:

> We know not how such an opinion *forms itself* [...] but it seems to have been formed. As nothing as yet is really known, or can be known, we express no opinion of our own upon that matter.
>
> *(WWLN II 133, ital. added)*

Alf refuses to take any firm position, because public opinion has in effect done it for him. His early version of "no comment" would imply that Alf need not "go negative," since the *negative is already there* in the speculative nature of opinion. An excess of the negative while Melmotte is held *sub judice* by judicial courts and the court of public opinion would run the risk of overkill, eliciting public sympathy and hence, electoral victory for his opponent. The tarrying of the negative can be overplayed.

Even as traditional Conservative allies shun him because of rumors of his fraudulent finances and possible future indictment, Melmotte taps into an incipient populism that is counterintuitive, as suggested by the American social critic, Thomas Franks.[20] He has the sympathy of public opinion which conceives of him as a victim and hence, singled out, separated from the people. Assimilation works in curious ways:

> It was supposed that the working classes were in favour of Melmotte partly for their love of a man who spends a great deal of money, partly from the belief that he was being *ill-used*— partly, no doubt, from the *occult sympathy* which is felt for crime, when the crime committed is injurious to the upper classes. Masses of men will almost feel that a certain amount of injustice ought to be inflicted on their better, *so as to make things even*.
>
> *(WWLN II 128, ital. added)*

Melmotte's theft comes to be imagined in public opinion as justly redistributive, and hence amenable to an equally redistributive public opinion that usually conspires to bring the privileged down to its own level. At the margins, public opinion operates to restore equilibrium imagined as justice by the excluded, in fact or in their own imagination. Father Barham is a perfect example of the wide populist tent of public opinion sheltering Melmotte's candidacy. A Catholic priest in an impoverished diocese, he contributes to Melmotte's candidacy out of the belief that the suspected Jew might successfully be converted, and under obligation to contribute to impoverished charities like the Curates' Aid Society (*WWLN* II 50–52). His counterintuitive advocacy is entirely self-interested. Even the dissenting clergy are now playing a futures market in the hopes of material benefit, and hence allied with the clerics in the *Barsetshire Chronicles*: one indication that the Establishment (like the ecumenist, Dr. Proudie with his outreach) is no different from minorities. Rich and poor alike are drawn to Melmotte's candidacy in the interests of a materiality indistinguishable from faith: "credit, being the belief of other people in a thing that does not exist" (*SBJR* 9).

Melmotte's appeal to those not normally sympathetic to the candidacy of ostenta-
tious wealth is enhanced when the market in public opinion expands its range to include
what are now termed *derivatives*. All classes (not merely Lopez or relatively aged young
women in search of marital opportunities) are mistaking intangible future returns for
a material commodity while in reality buying in to volatile public reception on *credit*—
which is then "priced-in" (bundled) to fluctuating valuation. *Occult sympathies* are often
open to analysis only after the fact.

The most radical instance of this bundling of derivatives with resentments occurs at
the *Beargarden Club* in *The Way We Live Now*. The regular members who gamble into the
wee hours of the morning—a collection of young toffs including Dolly Longestaffe, Sir
Felix Carbury and Miles Grendall—rack up large "carried over" losses and gains from
smoky card games, on occasion conducted with marked decks. Cheating, in Trollope,
is never the domain of a specific class. The redemption of any promissory note, the
financial equivalent of the long Victorian marital promise, is forever postponed under
the assumption that *trust* potentially keeps "settlement" in *durance*. A ledger of gains and
losses is held as promissory notes (chits) by the club manager, Herr Vossner. Trusted
to keep the ledger as well as manage the finances of the club, he abruptly disappears
with IOUs and the cash receivables in a parody of the vanishing fractional shares of
Melmotte's railroad.

Dolly Longestaffe suggests that club members subscribe to theft (thereby becoming
investors) in a venue dedicated to gambling and theft. They would be a priori directly
investing in theft as common shareholders rather than an unknown derivative:

> What we ought to do [...] is to get some fellow like Vossner and make him tell us how much
> he wants to steal above his regular pay. Then we could subscribe that among us.
>
> *(WWLN II 430)*

His proposal, which would give a cooperative "stake" in theft to any newly appointed
manager, recalls (to the attentive reader of Trollope) the comparison of the country's
choice of a prime minister to the "cook for a club" (*CYFH* II 234) in one of the earlier
Parliamentary Novels. Theft would become one more regulatory cost of doing business.
Under Longestaffe's scheme, it would be incorporated (*dissolved*) as a share of managerial salary and *subscribed to* by purchasers, not unlike hedge funds with high management fees built (but dissolved) into the price. Appetite is presumed to be a constant;
how to best regulate the exposure to it becomes the strategic question. The model has a
measure of resemblance to the Limited Liability Corporation, in regulating individual
responsibility.

Subscription to contractual theft is not logically different from those who ped-
dle unverified information to the *Jupiter*, given that the original supplier/donor could
not with assurance recover or reprivatize an unsecured investment with certainty.
Longestaffe's imaginative scheme is ultimately rejected by his fellow member, Lufton,
on the grounds that the amount of potential theft in the initial contract could take no
possible account of future "cupidity" (*WWLN* II 430) which varies over time. Though
the appetite for theft always has a future, inflation cannot be easily priced in, given

expansion or the standard deviation into the derivative of a derivative. What all the gamblers are looking for, as are all who invest in any derivative, is future *predictability* and *stability*. There is a desire to know all the *facts*, not unlike their noble parents' wishes that they marry well, and hence familiarly—in the case of the Earl of Silverbridge, the aging, lady-in-waiting, Lady Mabel Grex, daughter of an inveterate gambler.

Gambling has been a persistent theme in Trollope, be it in political ventures (Alice Vavasor); trust (or not) in blackmailing electoral agents; more respectably, the fathers of Lizzie Eustace and poor Mabel Grex who gamble away the family inheritance; or in gaming tables at Baden-Baden. Finally, in *The Way We Live Now*, gambling evolves into a more general culture of *spectra*lity, a concept combining speculation with the insubstantive or ephemeral. What had appeared substantive can be liquidated, or dissolved on short notice, with proceeds disappearing in transactional costs. The resort to facilitators like Attorney Squercum (the culture is gradually being "lawyered up"), results in Dolly Longestaffe's success, alone among investors in Melmotte's venture, is successful in reclaiming his original investment before the imaginary railroad is wound up. "Ripeness" may be all, but best before all, since proceeds may be used up in a genuine liquidation (fiscal entropy) in which all the sugar is dissolved in supposedly resolutional (bureaucratic) proceeds.

Karl Popper long ago advocated a necessary relationship between the testing so crucial to scientific advancement, free markets and the sifting of the choices that define public opinion formation, and hence open politics.[21] Open societies alone in Popper's scheme give *space* to create new options and opportunities in the interests of resolving dissolved or disguised problematic issues, given that no social determination of scientific issues is ever possible. The (unstated) corollary would be that no special qualities of the mind assume rationality; only an alternately *corrosive* and *enhancing* "give and take" of criticism (not far from "supply and demand") creates (one kind of) community, open to second opinions. Political knowledge would accrue, for Popper, only through the continuous possibility of falsification, which errant public opinion provides in *excess*. The (potentially) negative is never potential, but always a component of free discursive markets, and must be (or has been) absorbed within any resolution. But negations of engagements or total estrangements from promissory notes or the family-designated portfolio (Alice Vavasor, Lady Glendora, Lady Mabel Grex, Marie Melmotte) are a consistent feature of Trollope's novels. These *negations* are of course *there*, as Mildmay—aging passive tutor to the political novice, Phineas Finn—or the now intermittently attendant Rev. Harding, illustrates with an insufficiently committed presence after their fall.

There are no guarantees that a free market in either consumer goods or political choices results in the highest quality goods, genuinely dedicated managers of clubs or uncontaminated political representatives. Nor, as an emergent China has demonstrated in the early twenty-first century, do open markets (feeding speculation) necessarily hasten political transparency. But the illusion of an open market does whet speculative appetite in the sense, if not the fact, of unregulated access, often confused with democracy.

The status of public opinion and the organs and procedures dedicated to its care and feeding are open to debate, another familiar form of *testing* in a market newly opening to unforeseeable competition. The occasions of *testing*, at the hands of public opinion being obscured, we never quite know when or where we are being *tested*. The next election, the next response, the next review in the press, the next legal opinion or the next speech in Parliament carries excessive weight at ever narrower margins, given fluctuating evaluations, while suitors and participants wait. There is a checking of responses, results and "standings," the markings and responses of lives and ideologies lived in incremental response to the waves of real or imaginary evaluations. Lives lived in the tyranny of temporality, prey to public opinion, are opposite to those shaped by historically descendant class consciousness.

Even though Trollope obviously embraced rapid publication in incremental bursts, later in life he conceded that the error of *plentitude*—appealing to the crowd—can create another tyranny, earlier recognized by John Stuart Mill:

> But such a principle becomes a tyrant if it cannot be superceded upon occasion. If the reason be "tanti," the principle for the occasion should for the occasion be placed in *abeyance*.
> (A 127, ital. added)

Experience creates *inputs* different from that of exams for civil service positions. This may explain why Trollope was hesitant to embrace only exams as qualification in the nuanced discussion of the rivalry between Johnny Eames and Adolphus Crosbie in *The Small House at Allington*. The earners of highly favorable public opinion had passed a different kind of rigorous test, which maintained a hybrid, an "inherited meritocracy."

There is no easy way of distinguishing a *public good* from a *common good* either in the nineteenth century with its massive investments in infrastructure and empire or in the twenty-first century with its epidemic of "privatization." There is one question, however, that might partially clarify the difference when we consider public opinion formation. Does this particular resource require *management* (as so many managers and "fixers" would perform in the *Barsetshire Chronicles* and the *Parliamentary Novels*) as a social mandate or is it a genuine expression of social mutuality and collaborative interest and engagement? Neoliberalism, perhaps a modern descendant of Trollope's hyphenated "Advanced Liberal-Conservative" ideology in behalf of the (nineteenth-century) Liberal Party, has recently redefined the public sector. It now apparently refers not to citizens providing their own resources for collective benefit, but to institutions of government provisioning which claim to improve collective goods, now referred to as *public goods*.

Trollope's *public* is a vague, constantly evolving notion, perhaps not sufficiently recognized by those unable to differentiate common goods from common-pool resources (CPRs). CPRs like public opinion are open-access regimes with no predetermined system of management, like unrestricted social networks. No rights or values exist for governing them. In a collective, that is, *commons*, by contrast, people negotiate their own agreements—functional and cultural—to manage shared resources, as at certain dedicated spaces at the *Beargarden Club* or Houses of Parliament.

Resources we use in common are initially identified as public goods, then on occasion "deregulated" and auctioned off to the private sphere for reproduction and redistribution on the grounds of greater efficiency: a good description of Towers's modus operandi in the *Jupiter*, but also to reprivatization of what had been thought of as a public, commonly held resource. The public no longer signifies a community's authority to manage its resources in response to its own demands, but rather some transcendent authority to which we surrender control of the resources (even for information, being a resource) which then repackages our demands for resale *to us*.[22]

Deregulation in a subtle way acknowledges a residual, albeit often unacknowledged, potential dilution (structural reciprocity?) built into any notion of a *public*. Because public opinion shares a dual status—it is both a *commons* and a CPR—it has both foundational features (where people negotiate their own restricted access). The lands of Plantagenet Palliser to which he grants easement to hunters (controlled access and hence *transparency*) during the foxhunting season would be an instance of inherited property held in trust, not unlike information leaked to the *Jupiter*. Is access being "held" for the public in the interests of a (perhaps condescending) benevolence by certain organs displacing a patriarchy?

For once monetized or otherwise privatized, public opinion has a tendency to become a consumer good, even a need, especially at election time or in organs of public opinion. As the cost of what had been heretofore imagined as a public good rises for both producers and consumers, it is increasingly pressured by various forms of privatization. Competitive cost control against a monopoly defined by exclusion, unless somehow incorporated, brought in from the margins, is entirely consistent with Habermas's late thought.[23] And conversely, as rampant private initiatives threaten state, church or familial monopolies (like land and its income), open markets in information and selection, like the secret ballot, are vulnerable to repression by historical interests.

Trollope's figurative "Tenth Muse" seems to straddle a line between the interests of the commonweal and the distribution of information and opinions for private use or redistributed commercial interests, just as has historically, the British GPO, partially privatized recently. The possibility of alternative, unforeseeable delivery systems and competing distributional exchanges compete with monopolies, by offering larger windows to access, open to mass participation.[24] When Lady Carbury calculates the value of a "sweet," an embrace from Mr. Broune, in exchange for a favorable embrace of her manuscript, she is collating two forms of submission. Her prospective British historical novel on neglected queens, later fulfilled by Ford Madox Ford in his underrated *The Fifth Queen*, is exchanged for a promissory note which may or may not be redeemed in a vague future's market. Futures are incorporated into pricing, as a cost to be recovered (or not) later. *Submission* and *acceptance* are spectral secret sharers.

***

What we are addressing is no less than what Žižek has termed the "tarrying of the negative."[25] "Tarrying" is a marvelous concept for various forms of dalliance which might imply calculated delay, *durance* and postponed resolution: a fore-play, tempting gesture or Initial Public Offering which accompanies a counterintuitive activity not easily accessible to quick or easy representation (hence the need for the symbolic). It would also comprise various forms of *gaming* and *hedging* as with Slope's courtship of Madame Neroni in *Barchester Towers*. It might represent the "undecided," those "playing-while-not-playing" or managing deniability, along the spectral margins.

In Žižek's model what drives personal, ideological and often ethnic antagonism is a collectively driven denial of our own enjoyment: our unacknowledged playmate is our adversary. This would be a lovely description of a number of playmates in Trollope's clerical and political novels who become something more: Madame Neroni, Alice Vavasor, Lady Glencora, Madame Goesler, even Marie Melmotte who retains money in her own name, refusing to be a lender of last resort to her legally questionable "father."[26] They are all masters of dalliance, holding suitors and parents in suspension. The adherents to any ideology are often unaware of the underside—which Trollope imagines as a repressed truth—of social reality. Any ideology seeks to disenfranchise some group as a condition of its own self-definition. The methodology of the attempted exclusion encapsulates, even as it maintains, the vulnerabilities of the society in the very gestures of exclusion.

The social reality in Trollope is that clerical and political life, in the wake of intermittent pressures for reform, has *already* become so sufficiently speculative as to enlist new organs of public opinion formation and new plazas of exposure by which conflict was not merely illuminated, but created. The Rev. Slope's intercourse with the *Jupiter* or the vox populi at Gatherum Castle, which Lady Glendora organizes to promote her husband's candidacy, both speak to the need for public *presentation* in the service of ambition, unnecessary when dominant orders or families were in complete control. Trollope's own ill-fated candidacy as an MP, during which he was encouraged to buy votes with an assortment of transactional currencies, reveals that politics has become a speculative enterprise which blurs the distinction between gambling, investment, simple exchange, a gift and outright deception. Trollope's candidacy for the Beverley seat in Parliament, according to *An Autobiography*, was scorned by a historical Liberal supporter who "turned up his nose at me when I told him there should be no bribery, no treating, not even a pot of beer on one side" (*A* 273). These are all *transactional sweeteners* absorbed into a functioning system capable of so easily metabolizing them as to leave few traces of their presence. Resistant to easy reading after absorption, they exist as either temptation or a slight aftertaste.

Public opinion in Trollope's time, as now, can be in error, fabricated or redirected for financial or political use, plagiarized as a counterfeit or illegally subsidized; hence, potentially destructive or constructive of reputation. It can also be corrective of monopolies or create the illusion of enhanced democratic participation (as it does among the senile Hiram's Hospital pensioners in *The Warden*). Although its various organs are grounded in a belief in *transparency* and *enhanced access of the masses* as conducive to liberalizing a closed social order, in practice the result may be *shadowy* in the sense of both *excess* and *confused insufficiency*. Begging to disagree, pardoning an intrusion, nodding in agreement, reminding of what was previously agreed upon and offering another view are all nuanced ways of saying, "look to me," for nuanced amendment. Public opinion can disguise narcissism in rhetorical trappings.

Genuine *transparency*, though promised by open access without censor or filter, is impossible because all narratives are vulnerable to perpetual renegotiation and recontextualization with unforeseeable *negociants* (often under concealed sponsorship) of indeterminate motives, just as are the waylaid checks (in *The Last Chronicle of Barset*) or various *circulating* political or marital promissory notes.[27] Unlike courts and judges which must attempt to reconcile legal, personal and empirical narratives (even if they have to reconcile or restructure competing narratives so as to make them consistent with the law), public opinion narratively dissolves all within all for individual belief-formation. The occasions of the precipitation of some consensus cannot be foretold.

The possibility of speculative loss is a threat to monopolies equivalent to unforesee-able digressions of plot in novels for which the reader has been inadequately prepared. Public opinion formation is both creative and destructive, perhaps a social next of kin to the theories advanced by respondents to Darwin, contemporaneous with Trollope's "major phase." Like most adventures (including Trollope's numerous foxhunts in life as well as narrative), it is both sustaining of community participation, on occasion danger-ous to the participants, and raises such moral concern, as to periodically demand regu-lation.[28] It is a potential monopoly disguised as enhanced participation.

***

In Trollope, it is the figure of the often inconclusively defined, imperfectly assimilated or conditionally accepted Jew, whose presence in his fiction has become a critical cot-tage industry in our age of identity politics.[29] Although public opinion of Jews is replete with a history of discrimination, it cannot be indiscriminately discriminatory because the Jew lacks the transparency to be identified with certainty in Trollope's novels. As a metabolic system, how does public opinion come to tolerate an unfamiliar taste, given that the culture also prides itself on an unthinking, generous civility? Therefore, when lacking easy visibility, ethnicity can be interrogated only up to a point.[30]

Partially because of an emergent "cosmopolitanism" which will become the focus of much garden variety anti-Semitism between 1865 and 1945 throughout Europe, the Jew becomes a figure of an unwelcome internationalism, precisely because he is attached to images of a rootless diaspora, as deracinated as "money words" (*Gerede*), attached by Heidegger to gossip, a first cousin to public opinion. In the *Grundrisse*, though address-ing economic flows, Marx was surely addressing other forms of social circulation: the disclosures of public opinion, monetary instruments or the flows of unsettled Jews in nineteenth-century Britain:

> *Circulation* is the movement in which general alienation appears as general appropriation. Though the whole of this involvement may well appear as a social process, and though the individual elements of this movement originate from the conscious will and particular purposes of individuals, nevertheless the *totality of the process* appears as an objective relation-ship arising spontaneously; a relationship which results from the interaction of conscious individuals, but which is neither part of their consciousness nor as a whole subsumed under them. The conditions give rise to an alien social power standing above them. Because *cir-culation* is a totality of the social process. It is also the first form in which not only the social relation appears as something independent of individuals as, say a coin or exchange value, but the whole of the social movement itself.[31]

Like public opinion, Jews seem to circulate as a borderless currency, threatening more permanent, staked values. Here again, both are defined in/by *general acceptance*.

In *Framley Parsonage*, Lady Lufton and her ne'er-do-well son and inveterate gambler, Lord Lufton, enjoy a transactional relationship with her protégé and nominee as Vicar, Mark Robarts, at the young age of 26. She has supported young Robarts's appointment to the "living" at Framley with the assent of the "Gatherum set," as well as Mrs. Proudie, the Duke of Omnium and Harold Martin, the MP, in an arrangement which Trollope's narrator refers to as an "appanage" (*FP* 418): a *grant* of land or its attendant emoluments from a sovereign power (Crown or state). A marriage to the impecunious Lucy Robarts would dilute Lord Lufton's mortgaged social appanage.

Lady Lufton distances herself from shame by explaining that she is only dabbling, deciding it a "good thing to have land on *the market sometimes*" (*FP* 170, ital. added) as long as the clientele is restricted. In testing the market, she would exclude access by a cosmopolitan investor/speculator in history, a cutter of cloth, not timber:

"Why yes. I don't exactly want to see a *Jew* tailor, *investing* his earnings at Lufton," said the lord.
"Heaven forbid!" said the widow.

(FP 170, ital. added)

There is always resistance to totally open markets, even by those compelled to monetize assets previously regarded as fixed and immune to speculation in order to tempt the return of a prodigal son with the liquidated proceeds. The open circulation of land, diamonds and counterfeit stock certificates—and the public opinion accompanying knowledge of these circulating assets—is metaphorically associated with Jewish middlemen and negociants, even as the landed classes are already parceling away its value at cards and horses.

Simultaneously, Sowerby (indirectly) and Lord Lufton (directly) approach Vicar Robarts, sponsored by Lady Lufton, for a loan made in the form of a signed *acceptance* vulnerable to being renegotiated outside the regular banking system with which the upper classes had a cozy relationship. Allegorically, the church is now lending to the indebted nobility in return for its continued patronage of Robarts's clerical sinecure: an accommodation of mutual benefit. The young Robarts, like Bishop Grantly, a modernizing cleric who "would not be known as a denouncer of dancing and card tables, of theatres, or novel-reading [...] would take the world around him as he found it" (*FP* 108), including his own life of excessively high consumption at the parsonage. Sowerby's renegotiated notes under Robarts's endorsement become thereby a derivative investment. Informed by the local, friendly family banker, Forrest, that the acceptance would seldom be presented for immediate redemption at his distinguished bank, the status of the note is "depend[ent] partly on how you *manage* with Sowerby and partly on the hands it gets into" (*FP* 163, ital. added), a status like that of (circulating) public opinion which tracks it. A financial acceptance hence resembles public opinion, increasingly dependent on unpredictable outcomes of timing, *placement*, circulation and an assumed, but by no means assured, discretion in conversation.

An alternative market exists in which debts are negotiated and discounted after passing through a variety of hands with different demands and maturity dates for redemption or continuance by anonymous, discounting negociants. The refusal of the formerly easy concession of time and overdrafts falls upon the hands of the initial guarantor, Mark Robarts.[32] The threat of civil suits for recovery of Lufton's debt, combined with *Jupiter* editorials criticizing the lifestyle of the Establishment, subsidizes harassment at the hands of public opinion. The stereophonic crosswinds carry a whiff of anti-Semitism in the unregulated circulation of wandering people and notes:

> "To grand jury, and special jury, and common jury, and Old *Jewry*, if you like," said Sowerby. "The truth is, Lufton, you lost money, and as there was some delay in repaying it, you have been harassed."
>
> *(FP 243, ital. added)*

There is now an assortment of "juries" (moneylenders, the press, lawyers, the public) threatening to leak circulating information about a class previously in control of their sociality. The loss of money is a coefficient of the loss of narrative control.

The *tenured* classes face, as a collective antagonist, the scrutiny of the law as their promissory notes (initially directed to each other) enter general as opposed to protected circulation. To get into the hands of city moneylenders—a euphuism for Jewish brokers—is to be exposed to a vox populi who circulate information with discounted promissory instruments. Gentlemen, in one version of a community, trust each other without looking too closely to verify as do tenants of Plantagenet Palliser in *The Prime Minister* who so trust a landlord as never to demand a lease. But increasingly, speculation on instruments of *trust* is read as a violation of *trust*, imagined to exist beyond the *law* or *moneylenders*. Christians should not look too closely at the letter of the law (an Old Testament Regime) or deeds unless one is a clergyman trained to parse documents, drawing an ironic comment directed toward Vicar Robarts: "any man but a parson would be too good a *Christian* for such an intense scrutiny" (*FP* 166, ital. added). Imaginary or real Jewish moneylenders demanding the promissory Word rather than the abiding Spirit of transactions share an unchristian interest. Vicar Robarts, at the commencement of his career forced into youthful misjudgment, has implicated Establishment patrons in Old Testament justice.

Those who advance credit to insecure or unreliable debtors are under threat of premature financial (equated with oral) liquidation, by hands which can no longer be played close to the chest. A community's opinion formation speculates on the holders of *unknown acceptances, rejections of acceptances* or the application of *a higher discount rate* which might indicate the loss of easy credit. Public opinion exposes knowledge and financial need previously held in close confidence. Information, like other credit claims, is disbursed across self-organizing, open-sourced networks. The conditions of *acceptance* and its resistances might be the perfect metaphor by which to link public opinion, Trollope's Jews and new instruments of speculation in a time of high consumption.

The oxymoron of emancipatory assimilation had been sought by the British Jewish community, intermittently supported (though never becoming law) by various Reform Acts, through the first half of the nineteenth century. Gradually admitted to the bar and other professions, full citizenship and the right to sit in Parliament were ultimately granted in 1858, contemporaneous with Trollope's initial popularity. Jews gradually become reluctant participants in half-full standing of public opinion formation, open to both amended critique and democratic participation. Mr. Hart, another Jewish tailor and surprise candidate for the Baslehurst constituency in *Rachel Ray*, is the object of Mrs. Ray's initial contempt, only later to induce a grudging acceptance of his campaign oratory. He possesses a certain "volubility" of speech as opposed to public expectation of stereotyped "slushy Jewish utterances" (*RR* 121) by which members of the Baslehurst Christian community had thought he might disgrace himself. Distinctly articulated glibness is given inflated valuation by the gentry, a group reluctant to endorse a class which holds neither land nor often, historically traceable antecedents, one of which would be a proper accent, rather than the cacophony of "slush" and "buzzing," the impolite vernacular of public opinion.

Joseph Emilius (aka Yosef Mealyus), a name recovered after fleeing England and charged with both murder and bigamy during a life in Prague, is similarly initially socially accepted as a consequence of his glib oratorical skills. The talent enables a smooth conversion to Christianity which resembles both the Radical Whig, Turnbull, of *Phineas Finn*, "so intent upon his speech that it may be doubted whether he heard [...] interruption" (*PF* I 164) and the Conservative Sir Timothy Beeswax in possession of a "pseudo-patriotic *conjuring* phraseology" which, "when not known to be conjuring, is very effective" (*DC* I 165–66). Emilius is both loved and scorned, like public opinion. Through his extraordinary evangelical rhetorical skills, equated with a sugary tongue, Emilius "had moved,—if not in fashionable circles,—at any rate so *near* to fashion as to be brought within the reach of Lady Eustace's charms" (*PR* II 38–39, ital. added).

Trollope's narrator, however, creates a small, generative opening between a cloudy past history and populist rhetorical appeal: between self-identification and public *supposition*. Ideologically and politically tactical conversions being epidemic in Trollope, the question, "is he or isn't he?" or—given his apparent conversion—"what is he?", is a logical subject of the reader's speculation:

> Mr. Emilius, though not an Englishman by birth,—*and, as was supposed*, a Bohemian Jew in the early days of his career,—had obtained some reputation as a preacher in London.
>
> (*PR II 38, ital. added*)

The "Jewish question" is initiated as a speculative, passive supposition lacking attribution and hence an object of potential investment for readers of Trollope's novel as well as those drawn to his rhetorical skills. Emilius's reputation is that of a hyphenated, successfully assimilated figure in a community's highly fallible suppositions, enabled by the initial sugarcoating which covers past sins. The preacher's background cannot be determined with certainty, having passed through at least one conversion. He can say anything he wants, just like public opinion in practice.

In *The Way We Live Now* Trollope is both cognizant of the problem, of stable identification and colored by the cloud (in the public mind) over what a Jew or a Liberal or a Conservative precisely *is*, given the shallowness of genuine conviction and indeterminacy of identification, until called to account by the public. Politicians and Jews share the desire of assimilation, to "go with the *flow*" not of Marx's alienated circulation, but a stabilizing, favorable public opinion. Melmotte's past is so vague (given that he is never seen practicing the faith) that the origins of the man and his money remain obscured in tandem. A meek Madame Melmotte is not Marie's mother, "nor in the eyes of the law, could Marie claim Melmotte as a father" with "*various accounts* […] given of his […] birth, parentage and early history" (*WWLN* II 449, ital. added) after Melmotte's death at his own hand. She is an inversion of the nineteenth-century orphan of dubious birth but, exceptionally, with her own money, which she refuses to lend to her father.

Trollope's omniscient narrator throws Melmotte's putative faith upon which we have judged his behavior throughout the novel into doubt at the hands of an equally speculative appraisal which raises the specter of a "coiner," a counterfeiter. General opinion is here a circulating derivative of a single, apparently authorless "memoir":

> *General opinion* seemed to be that his father had been a noted coiner in New York,—an Irishman of the name of Melmody,—and in one memoir, the *probability* of the descent was argued from Melmotte's skill in forgery.
>
> (WWLN *II 449, ital. added*)

Of course, Irish ancestry, an archetypal Jew interested in money, and rumors of Prussian banking affiliations would not be mutually exclusive in the public imagination. Given an associatively loose, assembled packaging of public opinion speculators on the origins of the unlanded cosmopolitan, Melmotte, Trollope's reader too becomes an incompletely informed investor in the inconsistent narratives which swirl about him. Be it printed deed, stamped specie or in a community's oral discourse, what creates social identity has become so various and contested as to produce a virtual bank of indeterminable, because resemblant, products: counterfeit narratives, counterfeit money, a counterfeit child, counterfeit deeds to property and, for all we know, counterfeit ethnic identification. Melmotte cannot be consistently *read*, a symptomatic illiteracy of public opinion.

Stereotypical names that have the supposed sound of the Jew about them awaken a coded response, even as the actual ethno-religious affiliation is being interrogated in Trollope's novels. Contrary to being a transparent member of an ethnic group, men with allegorically coded names like Breghert and Cribal, the "city moneylender," along with the preacher, Emilius, do not fully conform to the identity which general opinion ascribes to them. Trollope suggests that our stereotypes betray our prejudices both by not conforming to the categories that define them and by an easy re-branding, counterfeiting or speech lessons that sugarcoat prejudices, easing reluctant social assimilation.

Now, in competition given the compulsive need of the gentry for discretion, the moneylenders compete by impossibly (like gossips) giving an "assur[ance] of absolute secrecy" (*DC* II 359). Their services in aggressive competition with the discretion of friendly family bankers come to include assumed verbal insurance against disclosure. The debtor now pays a higher interest rate, for a financial "nondisclosure" clause: a premium to keep information out of public opinion: negation demands a price.

For Trollope, like no other British author of the nineteenth century, there are no true stories, only indeterminate facts woven by a general public into a persistent search for narrative securitization. The dedicated and presumably Jewish attorney, Squercum, differs from his rival, the gentlemanly, soporific lawyer Bideawhile, who, as his name suggests, like Forrest, the family banker (with land as a security), is rather casual about the enforcement of due dates. Squercum's aggressive pursuit of his client's interests rouses suspicion that is quickly attributed to his race, much as was the case with Lopez in *The Prime Minister*. In an unusual singular proprietorship law practice accentuating his socio-commercial isolation, Squercum is the victim of a prejudicial public narrative by rivals who use the flow of rumor to impede his ambition:

> He seldom or ever came to his office on a Saturday, and many among his enemies said that
> he was a Jew. What evil will not a rival say to stop the *flow* of grist to the mill of the hated
> one?
>
> (WWLN *II 71, ital. added*)

Competitive rivals assert Squercum's Jewishness, yet because he keeps horses and often rides on Saturdays in Essex, he apparently is less faithful in keeping the Sabbath. Trollope's omniscient narrator reflects this persistent indetermination in the appraisals of public opinion, not invariably efficient at separating fruit from chaff. A shared habit of the British gentry (riding) can erase, disguise or sweeten social assimilation and both commercial acceptance and professional resentment.

One must digress here to note that "Jewish exposure" in Trollope does not elicit the inversion of so-called hate speech that Cherian George has noted among members of a dominant religion (in certain political environments) so as to create the illusion of an offense against the Establishment.[33] There is no pretense to victimage in the interests of personal gain among the gentry, and no calls for action against a minority that might incite violence. The more subtle pressures are rather those common to public opinion formation. Is he or is he not Jewish and if he is Jewish, is his Jewishness sufficiently disguised as to pass the test of social acceptance and assimilation? Possible confirmation, how the "truth" is to be embodied, socially transacted and conditionally negotiated (with securitization against surplus "acceptances") are crucial to Trollope's narrative.[34]

The corpulent widower, Brehgert, partner of a successful trading firm on Lombard Street, is a suitor of Georgiana Longestaffe, a late-term marital candidate. Lady Monogram, the girl's social chaperone, asserts a knowledge she proceeds to discount:

> *Absolutely a Jew*;—not a Jew that had been, as to whom there might possibly be a doubt,
> whether he or his father or his grandfather had been the last Jew of his family, but a Jew
> that *was*.
>
> (WWLN *II 92, ital. added*)

Although using a variety of past and past perfect tenses, Lady Monogram has no knowledge of Breghert's religious practice *now* (as in *The Way We Live Now*), recasting an assumed certainty into one more speculation. Yet, even in the homonym he bears as a nominative, Breghert conforms to one stereotypical attribute of the Jew in elite public opinion: vulnerable to aggressive verbal inflation. "Absolutely" seems, in this context, an affirmation, yet quickly revealed to be under qualification as too insistent, calling itself into question. The concept "Jew" is rhetorically and perhaps biologically "grand-fathered in," whether or not the person is observant, converted or never identified with it, as when we use the phrase "must be" as both an affirmation and, simultaneously, an interrogative in search of an elusive consensus.

Trollope's rhetorical technique is to initially suggest certainty—everyone knows that he is really a Jew—and then to qualify certitude in the collective imagination, as merely rhetorically established—hence perpetually under pressure of reestablish-ment (like Mealyus), thereby *risking* itself in the very repetitive confirmation for which it searches. Political construction occurs only through the rough equivalence of a plurality of demands. As a consequence, these particularities are also split: through their equiv-alence, they do not remain themselves, but pretend to universality. The discourse of public opinion, as Judith Butler has suggested, "works through" its effective movement in the present.[35] It becomes dependent for its *maintenance* on the contemporary instance, an *is* disguised as a *was* to lend it an unconvincing historical authority. The narrator's *control* is really part of a renewable wager that is systemic, in the process compromising direct responsibility in favor of unpredictably enhanced environmental or social inputs to which timely response is crucial if the narrator is to remain in control.[36]

Given that "Jewishness" is capaciously applied to so many professional endeavors by characters of both Sephardic and Central European origins in Trollope—con-verted dissenting ministers (Mealyus), attorneys (Squercum), speculators in commodi-ties (Lopez), newspaper editors (Alf), highly placed representatives of Lombard Street trading houses (Breghert), politicians of competing parties (Lopez and Melmotte) and honorary members of the nobility (Lady Goldscheimer's rich husband)—the concept itself becomes an umbrella term. Unlike members of the British Establishment, the reader never encounters them in clannish association or observant postures with other members of the ethno-religious tribe. Social groups are *fractal* insofar as they can always be divided into subsets or, like sugar, lumped together. As "Black" exists on a wide spectrum of pigmentation and geographic origin (African, Afro-Caribbean, Indian subcontinent, indigenous people of the South Pacific), so Trollope's "Jew" exists on a wide *spectrum* of attribution, beliefs, presentation, geographic range and actual behavior.

Trollope's nuanced treatment posits an interruption or breakdown in the process of representation, as the hegemonic group comes to correspond to one model of the *floating signifier* with a simultaneous excess and deficiency of signification. It relies on supposedly unique properties of "Jew" and empties the stereotypical properties (of the excluded/ oppressed) at the same time. As the oppressed loses a determinate specificity, the pos-sibility of *equivalence* arises, as it seeks, if not the political access of Lopez, Melmotte or Breghert, at least access to social life and marriage (another model of equivalence). Again, Laclau's argument seems persuasive: any universality is not dependent on some underlying essence or unconditioned principle because it has no content of its own. It rather functions as a placeholder for "the transient articulation of equivalential demands," that is, an exchange economy under continuous reevaluation and specula-tion,[37] in response to liquidation or recapitalization. Any positive content would inevi-tably betray itself as inadequate to the task of universalization. Public opinion negates some aspect of the particularity of each singular component which, like the process of symbolization, allows for different kinds of investments at differential entry points.[38] The chain of equivalence must remain *open*; otherwise, some "fullness of the community," complete democratic participation, would seem to have been already achieved.

Because it is based on distinction, difference specifies an essence that is then stored as knowledge. François Jullien in a number of formats has suggested the concept of an *écart* which would establish a distance and maintain some tension between the entities it separates, in this case a presumptive ambitious Jew and an established gentry losing its foundational status.[39] There is a *betweenness* that philosophies of Being (ontology) are inadequate to map, without collapsing differences in the interest of universals or its antipode, differed *différence*. More interested in how a culture *lives* with alterities and the strategies of negotiating the limits of our living in specific communities, Jullien is concerned with how alterities continually forge accommodation and dissolution which he refers to by the French notion of a *ressource* (a means). Public opinion is imaginable as a continuous remapping of the spaces created and abandoned by social circulation.

Response to imperfect assimilation or outright exclusion, elaborate disguises of the unassimilated (the counterfeit) and the desire of prejudiced people to hedge their prejudices cannot be distinguished in every instance. A socially conscious Lady Monogram goes to great pains to show that she harbors no religious prejudice in rejecting the request of her more than eager, aging ward, to invite the eligible and ostensibly Jewish widower, Mr. Breghert, to dinner, even as she embraces a conditional restriction on complete assimilation. She offers a "covering" compromise—a "Third Way"—to her social ward. He is assimilable as long as his ethnicity is dissolved, like sugar, within a collective mass of the upper classes at gathering:

> If you like Mr. Breghert to come here on a Tuesday evening, when the rooms are full, you can ask him, but as for having him to dinner, I-won't-do-it.
>
> *(WWLN II 91)*

Once granulated into an anonymity, the Jew is assimilable, but in singular, sovereign presence resists easy digestive tolerance.

A similar fear of public (or public opinion's) intrusion upon privacy is expressed by Plantagenet Palliser when he objects to Lady Glencora's support of the suspected (but never ascertained) internationalized Sephardic Jew, Lopez, in *The Prime Minister*. Inviting him to the public garden party at Gatherum, a political exposure organized in behalf of advancing her husband's electoral prospects, is tolerated, as consistent with the wide tent of Liberal ideology.[40] Social acceptance of the ambitious Lopez as part of a large public gathering is encouraged as social outreach, but encouraging Lopez's upstart candidacy to the safe, traditional "family seat" draws Plantagenet Palliser's condemnation, even though Lopez would carry the Liberal banner. In these novels, Breghert, Squercum and Lopez are simultaneously welcome, unwelcome and of indeterminate subjectivity given some opacity in determination of identity. They exist as a vaguely identifiable effect, insufficiently assimilable. These instances include imaginary responses to the responses of public opinion, a kind of *partitioned response*.

The importance of well-defined and identifiable historical lineage (and hence access to the socially privileged) is interrupted by the aggressive Jew, whose history as well as beliefs seem narratively entailed or unknowable. Yet, ironically, the subaltern can be assimilated, or washed of social stain by money or rank, enabling a provisional social acceptance and another kind of invisibility: the negation of any particularity. The respected Lady Goldscheimer has married a Jew, but her husband has been partially sanitized and socially accepted, even though he is known with certainty to attend a synagogue, in Trollope's narrative. Lady Goldscheimer is granted a symbolic "mulligan" by public opinion as is her socially ambitious husband, because he married a lady of the realm. Gold, even nominatively, trumps prejudicial dirt as sweetness contributes to the acceptance of an excess of the savory at tea time. The reader is told that the husband is "believed to" have continued the practice of his faith, an indeterminacy. Once dissolved into social acceptance, his commitment to his ostensible faith is simply no longer of importance, one way or another, to public opinion.

In the later novel, *Nina Balatka*, significantly set in Prague (where Madame Goesler and Mealyus had previous undefined investments in property), the impoverished heroine from whence the novel takes its title is forbidden to marry the Jew, Anton Trendelssohn, the descendant of a Swedish banking family with whose father the now bankrupt father, Balatka, had once been a partner. When the dwelling inhabited by her family is threatened with foreclosure, the young Trendelssohn allows the Balatka family to remain indefinitely, as if in compensation for his father's bitter transgressions. He is a *haut bourgeois* Jewish banker with forgiveness (a combination of money changer at the Temple and New Testament charity) which enables, as with Lady Goldscheimer, a varnishing of identifying racial blemishes to overcome the "split" into an agglomerate. The Jewish rival for his hand, Rebecca Loth, sacrifices her own love to rescue Nina from imminent suicide from the Karls-brucke Bridge. The assimilated Jew, in contradistinction to the self-interested moneylender and bogus antiques dealer, Benjamin, of *The Eustace Diamonds*, is institutionally sanitized as a benevolent commercial banker. Trendelssohn is totally lacking in charisma, like the Pallisers and their political associates of the privileged classes in Trollope's *Parliamentary Novels*—one characteristic of successful assimilation.

Shared boredom (toleration of the minimally sufferable on social occasions or in Parliament) can be one index to successful assimilation: they are simply no longer of interest to public opinion; *they* have become "one of us." From one perspective, boredom is one sensibility of a class with the luxury of benevolence as a consequence of "loaded" historical time (unlike the new category of hourly wage earners who internalize a rigid accounting of time). Although this boredom is a collective condition afflicting groups of parliamentarians, clerics and the gentry in Trollope as well as some readers if we are to believe Sir John Major, it perhaps represents the opposite of the crowds pressed against the large windows of Magenta House in *The Struggles of Brown, Jones, and Robinson*. It is not the desire of the other's desire, to borrow from Anna Karenina, but its opposite, a satiation. This real or affected enfeebled power of attention characterizes social acceptance and is energized only as long as the alterity must be resisted or controlled. The Jew no longer stands out, with no (particular) voice of his own: *absorbed*. One index of successful social assimilation would be the absence of the need to affirm identity by aggressive self-promotion. One might wash oneself from stereotypes, in favor of unobtrusively, even inattentively, working *invisibly*, to remove oneself from public exposure by say, *pretending* to work on a parliamentary committee dedicated to the letting of contracts for the supply of potted peas.[41] Trollope ironically enough, initially published *Nina Balatka* anonymously in *Blackwood's Magazine* (July 1866) as he also did with *Linda Tressel*. The author (like other *author*ities) can become anonymous, as does Robinson, the narrator of *The Struggles of Brown, Jones, and Robinson*, similarly absorbed within a variety of editorial emulsions that come to constitute his attempt to monetize the failure of the enterprise with a popular book intended for mass consumption which replaces the failed enterprise.

If Jewish assimilation or segregation is so inconclusive or indeterminable as to open identity to social speculation, then "Jew" is no longer an *identity*. It becomes akin to a *sensibility* which no longer corresponds to anything fixed: a vulnerability to an assortment of intermittently present muses. It could be potentially applied to anyone who does not know who they are or even to anyone who speculatively evaluates them. A corollary could also be adduced. In contradistinction to Robert Putnam's argument that *social capital* differs from other forms of capital accumulation and investment, it could be argued that they are not so easily distinguishable.[42] Citizens invest in both social and financial capital with the hope of some guarantee of *acceptance* with mitigated risk.

One wonders if the vague sensibility represented as *Jewish* (as in *coldish*) might pose the same problematic as does the question of canonicity in literary history interrogated by John Guillory in his *Cultural Capital: The Problem of Literary Canon Formation*. He suggests that there is much more to the idea of canonicity than mere social identification, insofar as value may be intrinsic or extrinsic—or neither. Canon formation may not be a repository of cultural value at all, since the qualifications for inclusion or exclusion change almost as frequently as fashion and surely as contingently. They may include—depending on the period—genre, formal experimentation consistent with conceptions of modernity, an approved "flowery" literary language or the inclusion of ethnic or ideologically neglected works. Canonicity is not a property of the work itself, but of the conditions of its transmission and response and its relation to other works in a collection of works. Inclusion, exclusion or manipulation of the canon "market" is partially determined by the critical investments of insiders as well as outsiders.[43]

Similarly, public opinion can cleanse as well as throw dirt, but obscuring and dissolving particularities are often undifferentiated. It can grant a variety of provisional *acceptances* or forgiveness and forbearance as well as socially exile its victims (as it does the converted but unassimilated Mealyus). It can detach itself from its institutional organs and representatives as a free-floating force partially created by them, while at the same time attempting to restrict these organs as untrustworthy. Simultaneously capable of censoring and liberating, Trollope's "Tenth Muse" can be concentrated in its attentions so as to scapegoat the unsuspecting (like Warden Harding) or, alternatively, provide a wider realm of social judgment than the law, and even render a pyrrhic victory to its victim: accusatory and potentially redemptive at the same time.

It can consolidate voice, yet free the solitary voice, given its absence of determinate *content*. The vox populi can scapegoat the innocent; define the conditions of social assimilation; reveal indeterminacies in our judgments, opinions and evaluations as potentially "fake news" or misidentification—even as, on occasion, it misidentifies itself. But it can also create an uncontrollable, stateless informational *diaspora* that can never quite be held responsible for content, but exists as a mysterious *platform* for a culture's supposed content. No wonder that the Jew (and the operations of the post office as well as other bureaucracies) saturates Trollope's interests: scattered effects which can be absorbed within the system or *go astray*, or be indeterminately trapped within an aspirational system, like Lopez.

Messrs. Harter and Benjamin, who initially loan Lady Eustace money with which to marry an infirm, noble youth and the Eustace (family) jewels accompanying the marriage, share a speculative investment. The pawn brokers, as it turns out, can be buyers of valuable goods, sellers, loaners on credit, dealers or (through subsidiary fences) re-claimers, like other "trolls." They occupy not city premises as with other moneylenders in Trollope, but a posh shop on Bond Street, no less. This is surely a sign of a latent indeterminacy in the provenance of the wares, a mixture of low and high quality on offer at the same premises, another instance of a "varnishing" which achieves a rough equivalence among a varied *provenance* of customer. Risk is shared with customers at relatively high transaction costs. Benjamin is speculatively identified as Jewish late in the novel when a biased witness to his attempt to "call" the collateralized necklace as a repayment for the loan which enabled her marriage, "imitated the *Jew's* manner so well that he made Lizzie shudder" (*ED* 378), as if "manner" was always determinative. Throughout the novel the jewels have been either hidden or otherwise sequestered from legal and financial claims by the clever Lady Eustace as a protected asset, inseparable from her body and yet, at novel's end, sovereignty has been lost.

Upon news reports of the theft of the jewels in a train robbery, Lord Fawn, a potential mercenary suitor of Lady Eustace, believes, in accordance with all known information, that "the property has been stolen [...] and *dissipated*" (*ED* 504, ital. added), initially by unknown hands while the owner was aboard a train. Given the absence of the contested asset, there is speculation that the necklace could have been "broken up"—a strategic loss of singular sovereignty—so as to realize greater material gain with anonymity. An analogy is made between the jewels and "Umpty Dumpty" (*ED* 430), never to be reconstituted *as is*—a lovely metaphor for a different kind of diaspora inhabited by jewels, public opinion and Jews: one representation of the loss of determinate identity. As with the jewels, large estates of church, nobility and Crown lands adjacent to infrastructure, "improvements" are all under recurrent threat of partition prior to being sold off or sold out in both the *Barsetshire* and *Parliamentary Novels*. So, as it turns out, are politicians. At the conclusion of the novel, another *unsettled settlement*, a narrative trace, of the infamous diamonds is suggestive, but never ascertained:

> The diamonds had been traced first to Hamburg, and then to Vienna;—and it was *to be* proved that they were now adorning the bosom of a certain enormously rich Russian princess. From the grasp of the Russian princess it was found impossible to rescue them.
>
> (ED *588, ital. added*)

As with public opinion, once dissipated (like the excessive borrowing of ne'er-do-well, wastrel sons of the rich) either by being broken up or as a consequence of having passed among various hands, the status within the narrative is obscured: "to be" could mean either "already known" or "not yet known." The necklace can no longer be identified with certainty, given an infinite number of presentational disguises, conversions, an uncertain ontology and contested accompanying historical narratives. Trollope's Jews and their place in public opinion are also often similarly *dissipated*.

Applied to narrative re-contextualization, the same purpose could be detected in Towers's editorials for the *Jupiter*. Stolen jewels, counterfeit deeds, repackaged, worn-out ideas on the floor of Parliament, incompletely assimilated Jews—all require negocians to ease the transition to assimilation. Like other agents, they are part of an informational network to be tapped, and can easily turn freelancers, as do diamonds remounted into other contextualizations (settings). The redemption of the lost jewels *in their original form* is increasingly difficult, a thematic connection with the church in the *Barsetshire Chronicles*, drawn to the public opinion market, as were both Bishop Proudie and his nemesis, Slope, rather than the redemption of souls. Once they have been re-contextualized, spiritual and material integrity (as sovereignty) may be compromised.

***

If the point-of-view technique of the early twentieth-century British novel illustrates how events are radically privatized by those it affects, Trollope's technique is perhaps its notional antipode. Banked investments in realities can turn sour, unrealizable or otherwise dissipated or liquidated, to borrow from economic parlance. As we respond to public opinion—voices beyond those of individual speakers or the omniscient narrator who *author*izes these voices—there is a general dissolution of *all within all*. Nothing can be predicted if each voice belongs both to itself and a collective, from which the post-facto recovery of individual sovereignty is difficult: one definition of narrative *competition*. What had previously defined the self-control of characters and narrator (a mutual investment in sovereignty), seems merely instances of the temporarily *proprietary*, under threat of dissolution along with other holdings of gentry and nobility. Anyone, any material possession or any ideology can be washed, dissolved, partitioned, reconstituted with "gold-plating" or artificially fabricated as sugar, a pleasing effect that compromises authorial sovereignty by Trollope at the end of his novels. No legal body or literature can inhibit this *perpetual contingency*.

Quentin Meillassoux in *After Finitude: An Essay on the Necessity of Contingency* is perhaps unique among contemporary philosopher-critics who address the potential of unknowability with applications in Trollope. For Meillassoux, *contingency* expresses the thought that all of our laws and conventions remain indifferent as to whether an event occurs or not. This indifference is not to be confused with mere *chance*. We can describe logical principles inherent in every thinkable proposition, but cannot deduce their absolute truth. We can no longer claim that contradiction is entirely impossible, for the only thing that is really given to us is the fact that we cannot *think* anything self-contradictory.

Absolute idealism and strong correlationism each share the same indefensible starting point in Meillassoux's scheme, albeit drawing opposite conclusions. The absolute is experientially or deductively thinkable (for correlationists) or equally unthinkable (for idealists), surrendering before the unknowable. For him, "facticity" forces us to confront the *possibility* for that which is wholly other to the world, but yet invests the world: in short, a possibility which is invariably hypothetical.[44] The subject (in our case, public opinion) is transcendent only insofar as it is perpetually positioned—if not actually residing—in the world, of which we can only discover some finite, fleeting representation, as it does for its contributor/investors.

If we can demonstrate the absolute necessity of everything's nonnecessity, it would be possible to demonstrate the contingency of everything, designated by Meillassoux as "factiality," a term he uses to imply the unbounded nature of our intersection with the world. What can be said in logical discourse, does not imply that we are bound by it. There are regimes of meaning that remain incommensurable with rational meaning (based on facts) because they have no relationship to the facts of the world, as is often the case with both "idle gossip" and public opinion. Unable to distinguish between necessity and contingency,[45] only a *speculative materialism* (rather than a determining materialism or the increasingly compromised fideism of the *Barsetshire Chronicles*) aptly describes our lived lives. "Truthiness" might be an appropriate conceptual synonym. Public opinion is an amalgam of rational logic and irrational discourse packaged as a quasi-rhetorical summons to indeterminate recipients.

One alternative to the dilemma is simply to surrender altogether to the unknowable, given the vagaries and indeterminacies of public opinion. The politically ascendant (of convertible ideologies) Lord Silverbridge, when confronted with whether or not to press charges against Major Tifto, a former manager/trainer of his horse, for his role in laming an animal, demurs. Unwilling to press charges, the heir to the Palliser fortune in *The Duke's Children* declines judging, preferring to have society rather than courts pass judgment. Although the laming of the horse has reputationally and financially cost him dearly, the future heir accepts Tifto's exculpatory confession, "I wanted to 'edge [*sic*], I only wanted to 'edge [*sic*]" being "a man of small means" (*DC* 395). Hedging has become a democratizing practice, shared by the poor and the well-off, a useful tool in moderating the volatility of speculative materialism which defines all markets, social reputation and ideology—as does Lady Monogram with her situationally contingent social acceptance of an alleged Jew. They live along the hedgerows, the margins, as do foxes in Trollope's topography. The risk is that in a world of such quickly shifting *weights* and *crosswinds*, a totalizing indifference to signification—a *weightlessness* (one incarnation of transparency and boredom)—is a logical effect. The alleged offense is surmised and asserted in public opinion, but "nothing had in truth been discovered" (*DC* 391) nor can it be, given the dispersal of the untraceable proceeds.

The legal case, thought to be dropped, nonetheless exists as a continuance. Major Tifto, after voluntarily resigning his membership in the Beargarden Club—as we have seen the arena par excellence of theft, cheating at cards and speculation—"becomes an annual pensioner, living on the allowance made him in some obscure corner of South Wales" (*DC* 597). He is exiled from an already threatened social life at the hands of public opinion, like Mrs. Norris and her charge confined (while supported) by Sir Thomas Bertram to a Caribbean sugar colony in Jane Austen's *Mansfield Park*. Major Tifto remains untouched by the law, subsidized by a pension from his defrauded patron. Insurance against the speculation of public opinion is a cost born by the privileged. Silverbridge's father's warning—gentlemen avoid the law—is imaginatively assimilated: a *domestic colony*, maintained as a circuitous fine exacted by public opinion rather than the law.

To pun on the French (in which *solution* and *dissolution* are synonyms), the problem is solved by dissolving, making it go away, in a privately reprivatized space less visible to public opinion and the law. Ironically, it is a disposition which Trollope seems to share with Edmund Burke's in *Reflections on the Revolution in France* (1790) where manners (and discretionary benevolence) exalt or debase by giving form and color to our lives, whereas the law (and presumably the mass law of public opinion) touches us only intermittently. In the absence of ascertainable intention, the gentry are increasingly happy with the moral equivalent of laissez-faire coupled with a tacit acknowledgment of disguised fiduciary responsibility. During a hearing, Silverbridge abstains from all judgment with the words, "I will have nothing more to do with the matter [...] one way or another" (*DC* 395): an equivalent hedging, a *backing away from determined judgment and conviction*. Silverbridge's attempt at apolitical evasion seems of a piece with his acquiescence to the words of Mr. Sprugeon, a Conservative Party stalwart, as he contemplates breaking with his family's Liberal tradition: "the borough is anxious to sink politics altogether for the moment" (*DC* 111): a political posture.

The threat to go to law to enforce private choice against family wishes suggests an alternative guide, overturned by Ms. Boncassen's demurral until she consolidates public opinion regarding the disruption. This probing of social consensus by a fiancée takes time, another form assumed by dalliance and postponements, in order to test public opinion for a wider social approval in the light of a father's determined opposition. Equally determined to marry a woman made available by open international markets, despite his family's opposition, yet without going to law, the prodigal son (in both marital choice and in his reconversion to the Liberals after his "Conservative Phase") opens ideology to material exchange. Having recanted his departure from familial ideology, Silverbridge seeks permission to marry the woman of his choice as a "bargaining chip" to reclaim his political heritage as a (strategically lapsed) Liberal. Having embraced an inherited "politics of convenience," not demanding ideological conviction, the future Duke of Silverbridge abandons what had been a marriage of convenience arranged by his family by exchanging it for an *ideology of convenience*. One can rebel against a family-endorsed marriage to Lady Grex or to an inherited family ideology, but not both at the same time.

Ideology, too, has become transactional, a mere tool to win a grudging father's consent to an extraterritorial marriage in exchange for a return to increasingly compromised or content-less family political "values," now indistinguishable from those of the Tory opposition. How can the emptiness of a transactional conviction be narratively represented? Accepted on both sides, *material speculation* tends toward equilibrium (one version of the civilized British Compromise): finding the agreeable price in exchange.

His eventual marriage to Ms. Boncassen, the daughter of a Boston scholar, with her peculiar New England cacophonous "wonk," is preceded by her own conditions for *acceptance*. She initially returns the Lord Silverbridge's engagement ring, holding him in a three-month *durance* by wisely asking her beau to first (1) seek the opinions of those around him before he consents and (2) to teach her how to be assimilated into noble society. Ms. Boncassen has neither experience nor knowledge, recognizing that it is difficult to "learn how to be a duchess" (*DC* 326). Mediating between the vulnerably innocent American celebrated in the "International Theme" of Henry James or her sisters eager to escape the intense competition of an American marital market in favor of the security of a title, she attempts to manage her acceptance by potentially hostile public opinion.[46] Public opinion has become a risk factor (a contagion?) against which one needs insurance. Similarly, Marie Melmotte goes west (reversing the flow of the American title-hunters eastward to an exchange system). She chooses a prenuptially insured marriage to an American speculator after her father's disgrace. Insecurity spawns the need for institutional hedges against the risk of international marriage.

Ms. Boncassen wisely cautions her future husband to take precautions against the judgments of his marital choice by taking the public pulse in the form of a poll which has become a feature of political canvassing in Trollope's political novels:

> Go to your friends and ask them. Ask that Lady Mabele—and your father;—ask that Lady Cantrip. *And above all, ask yourself.*
>
> (DC *326, ital. added*)

The altar of public opinion—a shared, plural social "show round" of dissolved particularities in the interests of a blessed acceptance—is an acknowledged rival to other sacred altars. Ms. Boncassen recognizes the need for an "oiled," "sugarcoated" assimilation of the foreigner that is acquired, not inherited, for a successful domestic assimilation, perhaps in contradistinction from Wallis Simpson or Meghan Markle.

A fiancée's request that her future husband seek the approval of a wider public opinion in advance may suggest a further evolution in the paradigm shift enunciated by the historical sociologist, Eva Illouz. She argues that romantic love displaced religion insofar as it promised a version of individual sovereignty, invented a series of ideological oppositions (selfishness and selflessness, public and private), while simultaneously uniting oppositions (giving/receiving). Yet it is the act of consumption that controls secular love, as transcendence does for religion.[47] What we are addressing (in its British vernacular) is an *accommodation*, the search for a community's *acceptance* with harmonious resonance in the debits and credits: what is believed to be owed to some Other and what is inextricable from individual sovereignty. Even etymologically, *accommodation and commodification* seem related agents of transformation.

Public opinion indeed becomes both a welcome and alienable commodity by the last of the 12-volume epic that comprises both the *Barsetshire Chronicles* and the *Parliamentary Novels*. Yet, its always conditional acknowledgment surely constitutes a potential crisis in *representation* which would fluctuate. If in public opinion, "all can be one" and "one can be the voice of all," then whom it ostensibly represents is increasingly indeterminate and open to another kind of speculation. Lord Silverbridge trades marital innovation (and the risk of "new blood") for the return to the increasingly empty Liberal Party ideology given the likes of Mildmay and Plantagenet Palliser, in the hopes to strike a balance mediating between rebellion (in his choice of marital partner) and obedience to a party now indistinguishable ideologically from its opposition.[48] An exchange system displaces the last vestiges of ideological conviction or theological belief into unanticipated negotiations with intermediaries who lubricate the transition from private intention to social or, as we shall see, commercial acceptance. No one completely controls his own story.

***

If professed belief or familial ties can become so negotiable as to have a life of its own, then this *transparency* should be internalized, present as a rhetorical and stylistic feature of Trollope's texts. The life of Trollope's characters, when exposed to public opinion, is often that of losing sovereign control of a narrative in which they have invested. Paul Montague in *The Way We Live Now*, apprised of his fiancée's violent reputation, is forced to describe this loss of control of narrative:

> He was then forced to *exculpate himself*, to confess rather than tell his own story,—and to admit facts which wore the air of having been concealed.
>
> (TWWLN *II 320, ital. added*)

If we never quite narratively belong to ourselves when facing the seemingly omniscient *critique* of potentially revelatory public opinion, then loss of sovereignty should extend to Trollope's own omniscient narrator. Even omniscience, a fraudulent transcendence, could never stand outside public opinion—because there could be no "outside" which would render it merely another formalism—but rather yields to it as part of a dialectic, a *material* dimension, within an immaterial transparency. This is represented as a loss of self-possession or authorial sovereignty, the threat of which has been there from the outset as a potential dilution. This dilution impacts people, ancestral diamonds, previously sacred timber, promissory notes, letters to and from the *Jupiter*.

In Stanley Fish's paradigm, the unbounded flow of free speech and unrestricted access (*pace* Editor Towers) can be woven into alternative narratives that may disguise their speculative nature by pretending to offer enhanced rational choice.[49] Transparency (advocated by the press, public opinion, liberal democracy and lowered cost of access to information) would become instrumental in the production of the very inequalities it presumes to remedy through open access and the proliferation of monopolizing features that the gospel of openness had promised to remove. Transparency of access produces the opacity of public speculation: "Whose news?" If there is so much of what was once relatively inaccessible that its truth value remains elusive given its vulnerability to easy re-contextualization or even guided reconstitution from unacknowledged or invisible mediators, this emptiness should be represented in Trollope's texts. The solubility of the speculative might be one representation: an acknowledgment of a self-conscious, continuous fabrication.

Sugar and "sugarcoating" are appropriate metaphors in Trollope for an assortment of faux materialisms that obscure differences and prejudices. Empty calories from an easily re-constituted refined import might well represent what has become of faith, ideology and even a crystalline necklace of brilliants in the case of the Eustace Diamonds. That thought to have a solidly universal and hence potentially transcendent appeal is broken into easily consumable fragments or comes to have only a self-consciously decorative function, as metabolizable *particulates* that can be infinitely rearranged. At the novel's conclusion, Trollope's omniscient narrator goes all "squishy," dissolving himself by conceding that "the end of a novel must be made up of *sweetmeats and sugar plums*" (*BT* II 256, ital. added), airy confections of narrative dessert to satisfy and placate the demands of (a readerly) public opinion. After catering to the circulation of public opinion, his omniscient narrator runs right up against it as a more omniscient omniscience.

Trollope's metaphor has a particular chronological as well as thematic resonance. Until the late eighteenth century when sugar manufacture became highly mechanized, as some would argue along with public opinion and Trollope's novels, the consumption of "free" or "added sugar" was very low, largely confined to lactose in dairy products and fructose in fruit or honey. The advent of cheap, plentiful sources of sweetness progressively led to today's daily average consumption of 19 teaspoonfuls of added sugar in yogurt, salad dressing and breakfast cereals. Whether or how we should regulate the consumption of artificially confected public opinion, as with sugar consumption, is obviously of enduring interest.

If the prospect of gain in appeal is the basis of production, then the appetite it induces and embodies functions as a double-edged sword. It simultaneously mimes the freedom to cut through designated monopolies of historical or legal power, while establishing itself as a competing monopoly. A universality (of admittedly disruptive and unpredictable energy) that has no content of its own—like the fiction of an omniscient narrator—reflects an inertness in discourse that might invoke the presence of ideology. If *spectacle* is capital accumulated until it becomes a concentrated image, as Guy Debord has argued,[50] then public opinion might be its antipode: a dissolution that mimics ideology. In the words of the wise Monk to a disappointed Phineas Finn,

> —think is too high a word; as a rule, men don't think. But it [debate] makes them believe there is something in it.
>
> *(PF II 341)*

If public opinion is a peripheral particularity which expands the market for a subject, it resembles sugar insofar as it can be a supplement, an additive to whet the taste for a comestible, or a deceptive disguise. The self-conscious surrender of Trollope's *persona* to the variously composite sugars of public opinion suggests a shared *deputization* within an exchange system. Contrary to Alexandre Kojève's assertion that "*authority* is the possibility of an agent acting on others without these 'patient' other's reacting against it despite being able to do so,"[51] the authority of public opinion in Trollope's novels often lies in both the way it disguises its presence and responds to the absence or presence of response.

In *Framley Parsonage*, the "high-bred, courteous giants" in power insincerely assure the masses that "they preferred the *dignified sweets* of retirement" (*FP* 281, ital. added) as part of the calculated yielding up of authority rather than being held accountable for some malfeasance. Sugary desert is the consolation prize for those "caught out" by the demands of public opinion to dissolve oneself rather quickly and move on. The threat of resignation, the dissolution to empty presence, mobilizes the heretofore indifferent masses to support power. The "voice of the people" (*FP* 281) is drawn to a disguising dissolution.

Perhaps the best illustration of this metaphoric representation of the dissolution of ideation at the hands of public opinion into empty calories is to be found in Trollope's narrator's curious intercession in the penultimate chapter of *Phineas Finn*, marking the occasion of his party's defeat, entitled "*P.P.C.*" (*PF* II 336). Our Irish protagonist will be forced to return home, his ambition temporarily thwarted by the loss of a Liberal majority. The curious chapter title is the abbreviation of the French "*pour prendre congé*," literally, "to take one's leave." The phrase is typically used after consuming the dessert at meal time to accompany one's imminent departure. Trollope's rhetorically self-conscious political, social and narrative retreats upon the presentation of the *sweet* are related. No matter the presentational table, public opinion has its registers of materiality, but it is perhaps better described as a consciousness that moves on.

This loss of sovereign control shared by characters and omniscient narrator in Trollope's novels extends remarkably among nineteenth-century novelists, even to self-conscious representations of any singularly particulate authorship, given variously unacknowledged agents in production. In *The Struggles of Brown, Jones, and Robinson*, the partner in charge of advertising (with early temporary success) for the ill-fated Magenta House wishes to publish his post-bankruptcy memoirs of the venture, a more original genre in the nineteenth century than is the case now, with the popularity of collapsed financial institutions between 2008 and 2012 by those with a presumably insider's perspective. In the framing "Preface" to his *Memoirs* (enfolded within the text we read) written after the collapse, Robinson, attempting to capitalize on bankruptcy (as Trollope's father never could), is advised by his publishers that an anonymous coauthor/ghost writer is to be employed:

> It was arranged then that one of Smith and Elders's young men should look through the manuscript and make any few alterations which *the taste of the public might require*. It might be that the sonorous, and if I might so express myself, magniloquent phraseology in which I was accustomed to invite the attention of the gentry to our last importations, was not suited for the purposes of light literature.
>
> (SBJR *6, ital. added*)

The author has as much difficulty recovering his authentic self in the highly edited published version of the history of the short-lived venture as do individuals searching for themselves in public opinion formation or—for that matter—public opinion formation can identify authentic Jewishness when confronting their socially assimilated presence.

Assuming (unfashionably) that Heidegger's notion of *authenticity* has relevance, this fall into publicness, the threatened loss of domestic home, commercial bankruptcy and authorial sovereignty, is potentially redemptive:

When in falling, we flee into the "at home" of *publicness*, we flee *in the face of*

the "not-at-home," that is, we flee in the face of the uncanniness which lies in Dasein—in Dasein as thrown Being-in-the World, which has been delivered over to itself in its being.[52]

Although reluctantly accepting intercession at the editorial hands of some anonymous "young man," who thereby becomes a silent shareholder in another joint-stock enterprise, Robinson nonetheless hopelessly attempts to retain his lost (imaginary) authorial sovereignty. His treasured "necklace" is effectively broken up, dissolved, in order to realize value by publishers who enter the narrative as Smith & Elder. As in political life in the *Parliamentary Novels*, an assortment of anonymous handlers, managers, rewriters and negociants shapes the narratives of public life. Robinson's surrender to this unsigned share in the production is reinscribed within it:

I have now expressed what editorially few words I wished to say on my own bottom. As to what has been done by the young man who has been employed to look over these memoirs and put them into shape, it is not for me to speak. It may be that I think they [the Memoirs] have read more *natural-like* had no other cook had a finger in the pie. The facts, however, are facts still. These have not been of public opinion.

(SBJR 11, ital. added)

The "sugary" pie is a concession to the diluted productive presence of many hands in the need to appeal to a wider public opinion now seen as a derivative confection of facts.

If the *trace* is the appearance of nearness of something distantiated into inaccessibility as a singularity, then it would be the opposite of Benjamin's *aura*: the appearance of a distance no matter how close the thing is, given that it cannot be mechanically reproduced.[53] As the object is brought closer (a desire of the masses), it loses its auratic cult value which is displaced onto market value, for Walter Benjamin. Does public opinion formation occupy a contested space between them? The "Tenth Muse" of public opinion shares features of both the *auratic* and the *trace*. It appears (auratically) distant no matter how close the thing is that calls it forth at the same time that it touches us no matter how remote it is or how remotely historical its intercessions have been. Trollope's confected endings, designed to palliate the appetites of public opinion in sympathetic harmony with characters who do the same, operate at the interface between real time and novelistic time. Public opinion seems like a conversation that existed before our presence that will continue after our death.

In his early *The Theory of the Novel*, Georg Lukács argued that only when the novel depicted the unfolding of lives in *real time* can life impose its own form rather than having an external form imposed upon it,[54] as does say, the sadly abandoned Lady Mabel Grex in her decrepit castle or the equally abandoned Duke of Omnium by Madame Goesler. The Hungarian critic's embrace of the lost (but recoverable) orality of the epic is the dream of a collective sharing, but not unrelated to a deinstitutionalized homelessness of public opinion that is both immanent and transcendent in the novels of Anthony Trollope.[55] Is public opinion one version of this lost orality held in suspension (like sugar) within the near-epic mastery of the *Barsetshire Chronicles* and the *Parliamentary Novels*, yet also a force outside the novel *to which it yields*? Like his Robinson of *The Struggles of Brown, Jones, and Robinson*, Trollope's narrator self-consciously *affects* an inability to tell his own sovereign story.

The loss of this totalizing orality occurred, for Lukács, through historical changes where objective institutions become merely conventional, as an "external nature," mechanized. The life of public opinion would be squeezed or repressed, the energized velocity of its circulation channeled into objective platforms in the interests of control.

***

For Ernesto Laclau, democracy becomes possible only if the exclusionary limit of any belief system (theological or political) be thought of as an empty signifier, an equivalent perhaps of empty calories:

> The universal has *no necessary body and no necessary content*; different groups, instead, compete *between themselves to temporarily* give to their particularisms a function of universal representation. Society generates a whole vocabulary of empty signifiers whose temporary signifieds are the result of a political competition.[56]

There is an undisguised pessimism in this displacement of content by empty signifiers that ground speculative materialism and political competition for which the empty calories of sugar are a synecdoche. What makes Trollope's yielding to a public that prefers "sweetmeats and sugar plums" so prescient is that, like public opinion, its status as *cause*, *effect* or *correlation* cannot be easily distinguished. In such a realm what public opinion actually represents would be indistinguishable from failed representation. Unidentified agents in the composition of any narrative designed to appeal to public opinion, renders it as authorially anonymous and insincere as public opinion itself. This is a radical *leveraging* of the subject (as often the case with other derivatives).

It is precisely this inadequacy that enables it to serve as a placeholder/generator (like oil and sugar) for the articulation of (often unrelated) equivalential demands. A rough equivalence, subject to persistent revision and renegotiation, is sought among heterogeneous particularities. The traditional way of doing politics—mass movements, ideological commitment, political parties with a defined agenda, religious and political ideals—has been replaced by a universally attractive, but often monopolizing and harmful taste capable of self-dissolving into invisibility or transparency. By the time we recognize its deleterious effects on the body politic, it already constitutes it, impeding traditional forms of regulation.

Perhaps this constitutes a "return of the repressed." For, in Hobbes's *Leviathan*, a foundational text of British jurisprudence, the surrender of individual voices in favor of the collectivity represented in the voice of the Sovereign in return for state protection was crucial to the contract that created a genuine commonwealth.[57] Is the politics of public opinion a record of the way in which particulate subjects, repressed into intermittent invisibility, come alive in an ephemerality that comes to constitute a field?

These previously unacknowledged fields manifest themselves as vehicular particularities which interact in apparent randomness. Sociality in Trollope's work (like spatiality and time in the work of the physicist Carlo Rovelli) consists of the web of interactions and responses to interactions, rather than meticulous character determination.[58] Detailed descriptions of landscape, household furnishing, distinctive apparel or even distinguishing physical characteristics are sparse. Even the plots seem recycled, calling attention to the continuous circulation of opinions and characters rather than the exaggeration of traits that make a presence unforgettable in Dickens's novels.

Like reputation, necklaces and singularly authored, revelatory narratives, once adulterated in alternative productions by increasingly anonymous hands to conform to imagined public demand or pressure, subjects more nearly come to resemble *circulating events*, than objects, not unlike literary criticism itself. Public opinion converts all not to a *thing*, but to a continuously mutually distributional *event* which can both awaken and threaten an aspect of the self previously unacknowledged, like a letter entrusted to the collective, bureaucratic mouth of Trollope's post office. Initiating circulation with an apparently closed format, opening is both transgressive and enabling. Public opinion has as both premise and promise the social and political benevolence of participation in the unforeseeable. Like the ephemeral *kiss* or *touch* of the "Tenth Muse," it opens us (and it) to the vulnerabilities and possibilities always attendant upon emergent feelings and tastes, resistant to control.

Notes

1 Adam Kotsko, *Neoliberalism's Demons: On the Political Theology of Late Capital* (Palo Alto and London: Stanford Univ. Press, 2018), pp. 9–20, argues that the global competitiveness and self-branding allegedly promoted freedom in the form of freedom of access (to markets) or enhanced consumer choice is deficient. The marketplace is a poor model for human development, for access is as likely to ratify as it is to induce change.
2 Simon Jarvis, *Adorno: A Critical Introduction* (New York: Routledge, 1998), p. 105 in his analysis of Adorno's *Aesthetic Theory*. For Adorno, "identity sovereignty" must be eliminated in order for any dialectical procedure to be effective. The feeling that one has lost a sovereign self or belongs to some Other is common to the victims of public opinion, but also the profoundly faithful.
3 Immanuel Kant, *Critique of Judgment*, trans. and with an introduction by Werner S. Pluhar (Indianapolis, IN: Hackett, 1987), pp. 159–160.
4 In another context, Frances Ferguson has astutely argued that utilitarianism (a component of Mill's Liberalism) had the effect of removing the individual from the social conditions which previously defined a self (including class) and emphasized *action* which was to be judged by its social good ("the greatest good for the greatest number"). The body then became a *functioning machine*, more easily absorbed within the machinery of public opinion. See Frances Ferguson, *Pornography, The Theory: What Utilitarianism Did to Action* (Chicago and London: Univ. of Chicago Press, 2004).
5 Anthony Appiah, *The Ethics of Identity* (Princeton and London: Princeton Univ. Press, 2004), especially chapter 3.
6 In biochemistry, a tightly bound specific non-polypeptide unit is required for the biological function of some proteins. These compounds, known as "prosthetic groups," are bound

tightly to proteins (as are electoral agents and financial backers in Trollope) and reattached as a covalent bond, as opposed to substrates. They are conversationally referred to as facilitating or "helper molecules": another way of talking of the dissolving agential in another discipline.

7 Emmanuel Levinas, *Totality and Infinity: An Essay on Exteriority*, trans. Alphonso Lingis (Pittsburgh: Duquesne Univ. Press, 1969). Levinas regarded face-to-face communication (as opposed to the written which has already passed by the time we read it) as sacred. Public opinion formation, in contrast to Levinas's privileging of the expressive, would seem to be a composite. It is both verbal (word of mouth) and written, given the various mutual reproductions in Trollope in such a way as to leave no Other. Like church services in its combination of the oral and written word, it seems to share qualities of the pluralities of the call *of* and response *to* religious devotion.

8 The Japanese concept-word *sontaku* (忖度) marvelously represents the decision of a subordinate (without being directly ordered) to read "tea leaves," thereby anticipating and conforming to the wishes of a superior. He is unable to distinguish between his own will, informed anticipation or response to an unenunciated, but felt, pressure, granting him a qualified immunity in the event of blame. This invariably raises a question: "Whose sovereignty?"

9 Evan Osnos, "Ghost in the Machine: Can Mark Zuckerberg Fix Facebook Before It Breaks Democracy," *The New Yorker* (Sept. 17, 2018), pp. 32–47.

10 Walter Benjamin, *The Arcades Project*, p. 331. Although Benjamin discusses both the new establishments like department stores defined by glass-covered "passages" and windows and the flaneurs like Baudelaire drawn to the environment, he does not so far as I know address other features of the innovative large department store and its creation of a public. Prices were fixed as opposed to the prolonged individual negotiations and reciprocal "bargaining" and incentives to repeat customers at traditional municipal markets. The large emporiums advertised (with dedicated budgets) to the public "at large" especially during seasonal or so-called clearance sales. Like the independence of a provincial press from newspapers affiliated only with those who shared the same ideology, the emporiums within the arcades expanded the accessibility of general public consumers. Another new feature of the early department store was the sale of gift certificates that would separate the purchaser from the end consumer, allowing the latter a choice from a donor unfamiliar with the recipient's taste.

11 Nicholas Spencer, *After Utopia: The Rise of Critical Space in Twentieth Century American Fiction* (Lincoln: Univ. of Nebraska Press, 2006), see especially Chapters I and II.

12 George Eliot to Anthony Trollope, 23 October 1863. Parrish MS: AM 15542, ital. added. I wish to thank the Princeton University Library and its curatorial staff for a facsimile of this letter from an unpublished manuscript. George Eliot was of course no stranger to the spaces of public opinion formation, perhaps most notably in the "Finale" to *Middlemarch* where Dorothea's son, though inheriting Mr. Brooke's considerable estate, declines to represent Middlemarch in Parliament, "thinking that his opinions have less chance of being stifled if he remained out of doors." He declines institutional membership in favor of an "outdoors" presumably free of coercion and compromise under the pressure of real or imagined public opinion—in favor of natural crosscurrents.

13 Michael Sadleir, *Trollope: A Commentary* (London: Longmans, 1927), p. 367n.

14 Anthony Trollope, *North America* (London: Chapman and Hall, 1862), I, 379.

15 Jürgen Habermas, *Between Naturalism and Religion: Philosophical Essays*, trans. C. Cronin (Cambridge: Polity Press, 2008).

16 Ibid., pp. 111–113.

17 The debate on January 19, 2004, was organized by the Bavarian Catholic Academy, Munich. See Jürgen Habermas and Joseph Ratzinger, "Les Fondments prepolitiques de l'État democratique," trans. J.L. Schlegel, *Esprit* 306 (July 2004), pp. 5–28.

18 Trollope's profound admiration for Lewes as both a social and literary critic is best expressed in his *An Autobiography* (*A* 137).

19 John Stuart Mill, "Public and Parliamentary Speeches Part I" (November 1850–November 1868) in *The Collected Works of John Stuart Mill*, Vol. XXVIII, ed. John Robson and Bruce L. Kinzer (Toronto and London: Univ. of Toronto Press, 1988), p. 263 ff. In the same address, Mill used the word "dys-topia" to characterize the way in which liberal ideals may redound to produce its opposite when local "circumstances" are unknown or unaddressed.

20 Thomas Franks, *What's the Matter with Kansas: How Conservatives Won the Heart of America* (New York: Henry Holt, 2005).

21 Karl Popper, *The Open Society and Its Enemies* with a new introduction by Alan Ryan and an essay by E.H. Gombrich (Princeton: Princeton Univ. Press, 2013), especially Chapters 21–23. Perhaps in anticipation of the work of C. P. Snow in the attempt to bring two disciplines under one rubric, Popper advocated a regime of continuous testing of both political and scientific theorems in order to eliminate "confirmation bias." This would emphasize the role of the incremental rather than the predeterminations of ideology.

22 See James B. Quilligan, "Why Distinguish Common Goods From Public Goods?" in David Bollier and Silke Hefrich (eds.), *The Wealth of the Commons: A World Beyond Market and State* (Amherst, Mass.: Levellers Press, 2013 rpt.), pp. 284–291. Along with Quilligan, one wonders about the attempt to distinguish social capital from more traditional, easily denominated capital investments as advanced by Robert Putnam, *Our Kids: The American Dream in Crisis* (New York: Simon and Schuster, 2014).

23 The distinction between public goods and private goods was of course confused by the expanded notion of the duty of the Liberal Party to improve the plight of the relatively poor as a general idea, while simultaneously preserving residual private privilege. Duty was, ipso facto, a defining obligation of one class to those beneath it: hence assimilation would have seemed a threat to private dutifulness, always present in Plantagenet Palliser's tolerance of the underprivileged in every aspect of public, but not private, life. He would restrict them from personal or social access, but not political representation.

24 Targeted to a consumer with defined interests, new institutions have caused educators to ponder whether high costs at elite universities have, in effect, made it a consumer good available only to those with abundant resources (like the foxhunt or "friendly village bankers" in the early nineteenth century). This protective good is opposed to general public goods like clean water, air and in certain regimes health care, available at low cost to all, equally. See the discussion in William G. Bowen, *Higher Education in the Digital Age* (Princeton: Princeton Univ. Press, 2013). Similarly, Trollope had great faith in alternative models of education.

25 Slavov Žižek, *Tarrying With the Negative: Kant, Hegel, and the Critique of Ideology* (Durham: Duke Univ. Press, 1993), pp. 44–60.

26 Marie Melmotte's refusal to grant a loan to her bankrupt father (from money he has set aside for her) suggests the monstrous revenge of a marginal archetype of nineteenth-century fiction, the orphan figure. She escapes her stepfather's public disgrace to insist upon a prenuptial agreement as a condition for any prospective marriage with Hamilton Fisker, the American partner of the now defunct *South Pacific and Mexican Railway*. She proposes insurance, a third-party guarantor, outside the family. This represents a remarkable evolution from Alice Vavasor's uninsured loan for her cousin's political ambitions in *Can You Forgive Her?* to the institutionalization of *hedging* by third parties in emotional decisions like love (now a "good" to be insured). This suggests the institutionalization of hedging risks in international ventures once parents can no longer be quasi-guarantors as was the case with "arranged marriages."

27 Because raw data cannot distinguish between benign and malign uses to which it might be put, more data does not necessarily lead to *transparency*, only more re-arrangeable narratives which potentially enhance polarization on the one hand and the substitution of advertising for issues on the other. See the reservations of Lawrence Lessig, "Against Transparency: The Perils of Openness in Government," *The New Republic* (October 9, 2009), pp. 37–41, a now increasingly reluctant advocate of *transparency*.

28 Although the foxhunt had previously been banned in most of Europe by the mid-nineteenth century, it continued to have a devoted following in the UK (though regulated in Scotland). Finally banned in 2004, there has been recent talk of its re-instantiation with restrictions. Given the polarization of public opinion toward the practice of fox-hunting in the UK throughout history, one might wonder whether the practice occupies the same place in British life (as historically foundational) as gun ownership does in American history and literature. See Anthony Trollope, "On Hunting" in *British Sports and Pastimes* (London, 1868), rpt. of a collection of essays originally published in *St. Paul's Magazine* and Anthony Trollope, "Mr. Freeman and the Morality of Hunting," *Fortnightly Review* (December, 1869), p. 11.

29 See Bryan Cheyette, *An Overwhelming Question: Jewish Stereotyping in English Fiction and Society, 1875–1914*, unpub. PhD dissertation (Sheffield University, May 1986) pp. 34–73, especially p. 46, Ann Marlowe, "Why Anthony Trollope is the Most Jewish of the Great English Novelists," *Tablet Magazine*, April 24, 2015, and Ronald Berman, "Jews in the Nineteenth-Century Novel," *Journal of Aesthetic Education* 32, no. 2 (Summer, 1998), pp. 57–67.

30 Gotz Aly, *Europe Against the Jews: 1880–1945*, trans. by Jefferson Chase (New York: Metropolitan Books, 2020) persuasively argues that anti-Semitism throughout many European countries simultaneously might be explained by a Jewish realization that educational success and mastery of test-taking (learned from religious study of the *Talmud*) was suddenly more important than blood lines. See especially Chapter II, "Sluggish Hate Versus the Ambitious."

31 Karl Marx, *The Grundrisse: A Contribution to the Critique of Political Economy,* in Marx and Engels, *The Collected Works*, vol. 28 (Moscow: Progress Publishers, 1986), pp. 131–132.

32 The use of the name "Tozer" in the context of exposure to moneylenders is curious and may have been picked up while Trollope was resident in the West Country. A dissenting family involved in the wool trade, a large Tozer family moved to the Midlands, acquiring financial success in the manufacture of table cutlery at mid-century.

33 Cherian George, *Hate Spin: The Manufacture of Religious Offense and the Threat to Democracy* (Boston and London: MIT Press, 2016), addresses the practice of creating some imaginary offense in the name of a dominant religion so as to further marginalize minority faiths, for example, "we must resist all moves to remove Christmas trees in public spaces as an a front to Christian belief."

34 The *regulation* of social and institutional assimilation of Jews, rather than overt anti-Semitism in Trollope's novels, more closely resembles the findings of Fareed Zakaria regarding admissions to Harvard during the 1950s under the direction of then-president James Conant. Surprised by the increasing number of successful Jewish applicants with high scores on standardized tests, Conant devised four categories gleaned from the applications: "Definitely Jewish," "Probably Jewish," "Possibly Jewish" and "Unknown" with an unstated quota of 10 percent for all categories. So-called legacy admissions (relatives of alumnae) now comprise over 20 percent of the incoming freshman class at Harvard each year, an advantage for the endowment of a private institution seeking donations to maintain a self-sustaining "establishment" has a logic of sorts. Fareed Zakaria, "The Scandal of University Admissions," *GPS: The Global Public Square* (CNN, 24 February 2020). As among Trollope characters tentatively identified as Jewish, the indeterminacy harasses the judgment.

35 See the essay by Judith Butler, "Restaging the Universal," in *Contingency, Hegemony, Universality: Contemporary Dialogues on the Left,* ed. Judith Butler, Ernesto Laclau, and Slavoj Žižek (London: Verso, 2000), pp. 11–43.

36 Once seated next to a captain taking a rest-break on a long intercontinental flight, I made the mistake of asking him what it felt like to fly 278 passengers in a closed tube for 14 hours. His reply mocked my naivete: "I really don't fly the plane; the job is managing over a hundred variable information systems." Almost any error could be therefore potentially systemic rather than an individually ascribable (human) error. Trollope's narrators and characters are like an airplane and its crew and passengers insofar as everyone comes to simultaneously need and bleed information.

37 Laclau, *Emancipations*, op. cit., p. 57.

38 See my essay, "Symbolic Futures as *Investment*," *Symbolism* 20 (2020), pp. 33–50.

39 See François Jullien, *De l'écart a l'inouï: Un Chemin de Pensée* (Paris: Edition de L'Herne, 2019) In this dialogue with himself, Jullien advances the notion of this betweenness as a *ressource*, the space of exploration and exploitation that is singular, but never determinative. Cultural identity pretends to a self-definition that it never possesses. The *ressource* "s'explore et s'exploite; elle s'explore encore en s'explorant" (p. 37). Exploration and exploitation are in effect a mutually heuristic for all the parties.

40 With his comment, "the *liberaux* comprise every shade of public opinion," John Stuart Mill was perhaps suggesting that the Liberals had become merely a comforting label that accommodates and absorbs many particularities—like sugar, the Church of England or public opinion itself with which it enjoys an uneasy cohabitation in Trollope. Cited in David A. Bell, "The Many Lives of Liberalism," *New York Review of Books* XVI, i (2019) (January 17–February 6), 25.

41 Plantagenet Palliser's persistent presence through six novels, despite a less than bland personality devoid of charisma, seems to anticipate the posture (perhaps even ideologically as well) of Clement Attlee in the post–World War II years. Although his heart is in the right, nuanced place on many issues (neither extreme Left nor Right on social issues), an easy willingness to join impossible coalitions coupled with a lack of rhetorical skills gives Palliser a resemblance to the man of whom Churchill continuously poked fun. See the recent restorative biography by John Bew, *The Man Who Made Modern Britain* (Oxford: Oxford Univ. Press, 2017).

42 Robert Putnam, *Our Kids: The American Dream in Crisis* (New York: Simon and Schuster, 2104).

43 John Guillory, *Cultural Capital: The Problem of Literary Canon Formation* (Chicago: Univ. of Chicago Press, 1993), pp. 55–56.

44 Quentin Meillassoux, *After Finitude; An Essay on the Necessity of Contingency*, trans. Ray Brassier (London and New York: Continuum, 2008), pp. 28–50.

45 Ibid., p. 53. In Meillassoux's scheme, the absence of reason should not be thought as an obstruction to our knowing, but a property of the object, as with Mill. The capacity-to-be-other might be his definition of the Absolute: any transition inexplicable to education/induction, empirical testing or historical determination. Hence, speculative materialism, an intellectual gamble with contingent information, displaces reason as a stairway to transcendence.

46 Anne de Courcy, *The Husband Hunters: American Heiresses Who Married into the British Aristocracy* (New York: St. Martin's Press, 2018), would not apply to Ms. Boncassen. She is neither well-off nor a gold digger, but seems to have developed management skills in regard to public opinion and social acceptance. She appears especially unique among the title-hunting heiresses willing to buy into management of often distressed estates in a strange country with a rheumatic climate and unmanageable servants: Lady Mabel Grex's home.

47 Eva Illouz, *Consuming the Romantic Utopia: Love and the Cultural Contradictions of Capitalism* (Berkley: Univ. of California Press, 1997), pp. 29–30, p. 76.

48 Dani Rodnik, *Straight Talk on Trade: Ideas for a Sane World Economy* (Princeton: Princeton Univ. Press, 2017), argues that offers of access through free trade to previously politically isolated countries in return for vague promises of future political liberalization are merely setting forth distributional choices which can be revoked or suspended (sanctions, tariffs) at any time and hence only another input to future "pricing." His suspect, because always revocable, "internationalism" might be one representation assumed by public opinion against the forces of nationalistic (familial or party) preservation, the rivalry for which he (like Trollope) searches for an equilibrium.

49 Stanley Fish, "Transparency, Mother of Fake News," *New York Times International Edition* (7 May 2018), p. 12.

50 Guy Debord, *La Societé du Spectacle* (Paris: 1967), p. 24.

51 Alexandre Kojève, *The Notion of Authority (A Brief Presentation)*, trans. Hager Weslati (London: Verso, 2014), p. 8. Kojève's point is that real authority need do nothing in order to exert authority since the "patient" upon whom it acts most often chooses only to act in accordance with it (nonaction). He thus wonders whether authority is not a category but a condition emergent from an aborted conversation whose content is empty.

52 Martin Heidegger, *Being and Time*, trans. J. Macquarrie and E. Robinson (Oxford: Blackwell, 1962), p. 234.

53 Walter Benjamin, "The Work of Art in the Age of Mechanical Reproduction," in *Illuminations*, ed. Hannah Arendt and trans. by Harry Zohn (New York: Schocken Books, 1969), pp. 5–6.

54 Georg Lukács, *The Theory of the Novel*, trans. A. Bostock (London: Merlin, 1971), p. 46.

55 Ibid., p. 40, 60. The Hungarian advocate of the orality of classical epics obviously embraced the promise of a novel that might reestablish a relationship between the individual and the world uninhibited by the traditional bourgeois novel's externally informed form. The implied vocality of public opinion in Trollope, from this perspective, might be a precursor to the restoration of an implied collective "voice" that previously defined the epic.

56 Ernesto Laclau, *Emancipation(s)* (London and New York: Verso, 1966), p. 35.

57 Thomas Hobbes, *Leviathan*, ed. with an introduction by C.B. Macpherson (Harmondsworth: Penguin, 1982), I-15, pp. 216–217.

58 Carlo Rovelli, *The Order of Time*, trans. Erica Segre and Simon Carnell (London: Penguin, 2018), pp. 115–124, argues that *time* is emergent, rather than part of the elementary grammar of the world in the same way that other social units are. He compares this emergence

with a group of boys on a football field who choose sides before commencing the match. The "teams" emerge, though nonexistent previously. Hence any a priori measurement of time would be absurd, even though our daily lives depend on watches and clocks that measure time. Is public opinion—as a formation—similarly *emergent*, in which the modes of measurement become (later) somehow constitutive?

INDEX

Note: Page numbers in bold refer to figures. Page numbers followed by "n" refer to notes.

Society for the Diffusion of Public Knowledge 15

Sohn-Rethel, A.: *Intellectual and Manual Labor* 124n21

solidarity 13, 15

sontaku 213n8

Sophocles: *Antigone* 80n36

Soros, G. 102

South Central and Pacific Mexican Railway, The 98, 117

sovereignty 21, 40, 57, 177, 179, 202; authorial 203, 207, 210; charismatic 183; disciplined 133; identity 212n2; individual 178, 182, 184, 203, 206; of the law 71; loss of xii, 207; personal xii, 132; restoration of 180; temporal 29

spectrality culture of 185–87

speculative materialism 204

speech acts 12, 71, 92, 93, 113

Spencer, H.: law of the differentiation of organ function 10

Spencer, N. 181

Stephen, L. 8

Struggles of Brown, Jones, and Robinson, The (Trollope) xiv, 25, 81n45, 186, 201, 211; bureaucracy 135, 157; loss of sovereign control 209; Magenta House in 200; mass retail markets, manipulation of 180–81; play in 103, 116; transparency of goods offered 201

subscription to contractual theft 187–88

suspense-fulness 58

Svendsen, L.: *Philosophy of Boredom, A* 153

symbolic power 102

temporal power 102

sympathy 11, 16, 65, 69, 90; community 25; cooperative 145; lack of viii; public 70, 186; universal 5, 96

"tarrying of the negative" 190–91

Temple, Sir William: " On Popular Discontents" ix

temporal power 102

temporal variability 33

temporality ix, 29, 34, 53, 66, 68, 125n30, 132, 189

"Tenth Muse" of public opinion ix, 27, 29, 35, 45, 84, 117, 178, 190, 201, 210, 212

territoriality: extraterritoriality 41; institutional 13; of public opinion 66

Thackeray, W. M.: *Pendennis* 101

Thatcher, M. 374n39

Theatre About Glasgow 80n36

theological internationalism 15, 16, 42

Theory of the Novel, The (Lukács) 210–11

"Third Estate" 40

Thomas v. Bradbury, Agnew & Co. (1906) 81n44

Three Clerks, The (Trollope) 24; bureaucracy xiii, 127–33, 139, 144, 148, 156; criminal breach of trust in 72; law in public opinion 54–55

thrownness 52

Times, The 133

totalized (internal and external) care 5–6

trade of authorship 106, 194–203

Trafalgar Group 36n25

transcendence ix, 19, 33, 52, 58, 61, 98, 206, 207, 216n45

transparency 180, 207, 214n27; genuine 191; political 188

tribunal of public opinion 20

Trollope, A.: absence of detailed description 212; clergy 42; cynicism 14; familiarity with the postal service 14; on ideational wavering in clerical community 18; "Tenth Muse" of public opinion ix, 27, 29, 35, 45, 84, 117, 178, 190, 201, 210; works (*Autobiography, An* 77, 84–85, 109, 134–35, 146–48, 152, 156, 160, 171, 180–81; *Barchester Novels* 2, 40, 196; *Barchester Towers* xi, 1, 2, 4, 9, 13, 17, 23, 24, 27, 28, 53, 60, 62, 65, 67, 74, 76, 83–87, 90, 96, 106–7, 109, 115, 136, 150, 179, 184–85, 190; *Barsetshire Novels* viii, ix, 148, 202; *Barsetshire Towers* 42, 74; *Can You Forgive Her?* 35, 43, 81n44, 103–10, 117, 121, 126n43, 127, 137, 144, 147, 151, 153, 155–57, 161, 170, 178, 185, 187; *Doctor Thorne* 67, 81n45, 99–102; *Duke's Children, The* xiii, 43, 61, 90, 100–101, 107, 114, 118, 154, 156–57, 159–65, 177, 204–6; *Eustace Diamonds, The* 74–75, 89–96, 98, 99, 110, 113, 117, 120, 122, 170–72, 200; *Framley Parsonage* xii, 13, 24, 60–62, 65, 73, 104, 120, 193–94, 209; *Last Chronicle of Barset, The* xii, 20, 33, 40, 44, 66, 68–70, 73, 74, 88, 98, 140, 151, 191; *Nina Balatka* 200, 201; *Phineas Finn* xiii, 18, 62–65, 77, 79n18, 90, 105, 134, 144, 154, 155, 157–59, 167–70, 195, 209; *Phineas Redux* xiii, 18, 42, 68, 72–74, 90, 112, 127, 147, 160–62, 166, 169, 170, 177; play in 84–85, 109, 191; *Prime Minister, The* xiii, 90, 110–15, 124n30, 138, 147, 199–200; *Rachel Ray* 195; recycled plots 212; *Small House at Allington, The* xii, 42, 43, 70–71, 130, 136, 137, 139, 141–46, 149–52, 154, 157, 189; *Struggles of Brown, Jones, and Robinson, The* xiv, 25, 81n45103, 116, 135, 157, 180–81, 186, 200, 201, 209, 211; *Three Clerks, The* xiii, 24, 54–55, 72, 127–33, 139, 144, 148, 156; *Vicar of Bullhampton, The* 55–57; *Warden, The* x, xi, 1–2, 6, 14, 16, 17, 26–28, 35, 39, 42–44, 51, 60, 67, 74, 88, 90, 93, 96, 139, 145, 151, 155, 182, 191; *Way We*

www.ingramcontent.com/pod-product-compliance
Lightning Source LLC
Chambersburg PA
CBHW020238290326
41929CB00044B/254